T0311463

Inflation in China

Inflation plays a central role in macroeconomic and financial policy regulation, and its dynamic formation has gradually become a popular research topic in this field. This book comprehensively studies the dynamic mechanism of inflation in China from the perspective of New Keynesian economics.

By combining the dynamic trajectory of price changes since China's reform and opening-up under Deng Xiaoping as well as the underlying economic operating characteristics, the book deploys a multifaceted approach to understanding the mechanism of inflation dynamics. The author explores the microfoundations of inflation dynamics, and underlines their importance in the context of modern monetary policy. In particular, he builds upon the traditional New Keynesian Phillips curve to include factors of globalization and financialization within the inflation formation regime of modern China.

As the book explores the dynamic mechanism of China's inflation from different perspectives including inflation cycle theory, price index internal conduction, price index chain transmission, capital rotation, and industry inflation mechanisms, international readers will gain a full understanding of China's inflation, monetary policy, and economy.

Chengsi Zhang is Cheung Kong Distinguished Professor of Finance at the School of Finance, Renmin University of China, specializing in monetary policy, inflation mechanisms, and financial development. He has published articles in leading journals, including the *Journal of Money, Credit and Banking, International Journal of Central Banking*, and *Journal of International Money and Finance*, among many other academic journals.

China Perspectives

The *China Perspectives* series focuses on translating and publishing works by leading Chinese scholars, writing about both global topics and China-related themes. It covers Humanities and Social Sciences, Education, Media and Psychology, as well as many interdisciplinary themes.

This is the first time any of these books have been published in English for international readers. The series aims to put forward a Chinese perspective, give insights into cutting-edge academic thinking in China, and inspire researchers globally.

Titles in economics partly include:

Game Theory and Society
Weiying Zhang

China's Fiscal Policy
Theoretical and Situation Analysis
Gao Peiyong

Trade Openness and China's Economic Development
Miaojie Yu

Perceiving Truth and Ceasing Doubts
What Can We Learn from 40 Years of China's Reform and Opening-Up?
Cai Fang

Demographic Perspective of China's Economic Development
Cai Fang

Inflation in China
Microfoundations, Macroeconomic Dynamics, and Monetary Policy
Chengsi Zhang

For more information, please visit https://www.routledge.com/series/CPH

Inflation in China

Microfoundations, Macroeconomic
Dynamics, and Monetary Policy

Chengsi Zhang

Routledge
Taylor & Francis Group

LONDON AND NEW YORK

This book is published with financial support from the Chinese Fund for the Humanities and Social Sciences

First published in English 2021
by Routledge
2 Park Square, Milton Park, Abingdon, Oxon OX14 4RN

and by Routledge
605 Third Avenue, New York, NY 10017

First issued in paperback 2022

Routledge is an imprint of the Taylor & Francis Group, an informa business

© 2021 Chengsi Zhang

The right of Chengsi Zhang to be identified as author of this work has been asserted by him in accordance with sections 77 and 78 of the Copyright, Designs and Patents Act 1988.

All rights reserved. No part of this book may be reprinted or reproduced or utilised in any form or by any electronic, mechanical, or other means, now known or hereafter invented, including photocopying and recording, or in any information storage or retrieval system, without permission in writing from the publishers.

Trademark notice: Product or corporate names may be trademarks or registered trademarks, and are used only for identification and explanation without intent to infringe.

Publisher's Note
The publisher has gone to great lengths to ensure the quality of this reprint but points out that some imperfections in the original copies may be apparent.

English Version by permission of China Renmin University Press.

British Library Cataloguing-in-Publication Data
A catalogue record for this book is available from the British Library

Library of Congress Cataloging-in-Publication Data
A catalog record has been requested for this book

ISBN: 978-0-367-89882-3 (hbk)
ISBN: 978-0-367-53603-9 (pbk)
ISBN: 978-1-003-02168-1 (ebk)

DOI: 10.4324/9781003021681

Typeset in Times New Roman
by Deanta Global Publishing Services, Chennai, India

Contents

Figures

Tables

1 Introduction

Inflation is a core element related to the harmonious and sound development of the national economy and the effective implementation of monetary policy. It is also an important reference indicator for macroeconomic and financial policy regulation. Since there is some time lag in terms of the macroeconomic policy of all countries from its formulation and implementation to its impact on inflation, understanding the mechanism of inflation dynamic formation is of great significance to the timeliness and effectiveness of macroeconomic policy. As a result, the dynamic formation of inflation has gradually become an important research topic in the analysis of macro finance, especially modern monetary policy.

Although the inflation rate of all countries in the world has shown a steady declining tendency after the 1990s, the inertia or persistence of inflation is still strong. For example, it is shown in some studies that there is still strong persistence or inertia in terms of the inflation rates of the United States and most countries in Europe.[1] According to the studies on the persistence of China's inflation by Liu (2007) and Zhang (2008a), there is also strong persistence in China's inflation. By definition, inflation persistence refers to the time it takes for inflation to deviate from its equilibrium state after being hit by random disturbances. Therefore, the longer it takes, the more persistent the inflation is and the more obvious the lagging effect of monetary policy will be.

These dynamic characteristics of inflation rate have attracted many economists and experts of monetary policy to continuously update and improve their dynamic mechanism theory. Relevant theories have evolved from the early dynamic model based entirely on macroscopic perspectives (e.g. Gordon, 1982) to the dynamic mechanism of short-term inflation rates with a microfoundation of the modern New Keynesian school. The latest inflation dynamic mechanism theory is based on the staggered contract model of Taylor (1979, 1980) and Calvo (1983) and the quadratic price adjustment model of Rotemberg (1982), which describe the dynamic process between the current inflation rate and the rational expectations of inflation rates, and between historical inflation rates and real output gaps. Woodford (2003) elaborates and explains this classic theoretical framework.

In the past 20 years, many outstanding monetary policy experts in China have continuously studied and explored the importance of the dynamic mechanism of

China's inflation rate in current monetary policy analysis, including the important literature of Liu (1997a, 2007a), Yu (1999), Xie and Shen (1999), Hu (1999), Lu (2001), Fan (2002), Liu and Xie (2003), Zhang (2007a), Zhang (2010), and Yang (2011). The existing research is mainly based on the traditional macro-inflation dynamic model, but research on the dynamic mechanism theory of micro inflation in modern times is rarely seen. In addition, the research is seldom expanded by relating it to the realities of China's inflation dynamics.

At the same time, it is worth noting that after the 1980s, China's inflation seems to show similar dynamic trends to major Western countries. Namely, after high price fluctuations from the mid-to-late 1980s to the mid-to-late 1990s, it has shown a steady and low trend in a dozen years recently since 2000. However, since there is still strong persistence of inflation, the cost of inflation (or deflation) has not decreased significantly, and the monetary policy authorities are still very concerned about the trend of inflation. In this context, it is of great practical significance to portray the dynamic formation mechanism of China's inflation scientifically and accurately. At the same time, on the basis of the theory of inflation dynamic mechanism, the research methods of rational expansion, meticulous characterization, and scientific modeling are conducive to the improvement and development of relevant theories.

In view of this, this book attempts to comprehensively study the dynamic mechanism of inflation from the perspective of existing theories, combining the dynamic trajectory of price changes since China's reform and opening up and the economic operating characteristics hidden behind it to develop multiple logics to understand the mechanism of China's inflation dynamics. Next, we will sort out the theoretical framework of the macro-inflation dynamic mechanism based on microfoundation, clarify its importance in the framework of modern monetary policy analysis, and summarize the latest research on this theory, so as to provide a research basis for us to study the dynamic formation mechanism of China.

Reviewing the development of related academic research, we can find that the theoretical framework of the latest inflation dynamic mechanism gradually established its vital importance in the analysis of modern monetary policy after the publication of some far-reaching articles written by Roberts (1995), Clarida et al. (1999), and Gali and Gertler (1999). Classical works in modern macroeconomics and monetary economics (e.g. Walsh, 2003a; Thomas, 2006; Romer, 2006; Mishkin, 2007) emphasize the role of the inflation dynamics model in monetary policy analysis, highlighting its importance in macro theory and monetary policy analysis mechanisms. The monograph by Woodford (2003) demonstrates the core position of the dynamic mechanism of inflation in the transmission mechanism of modern monetary policy. Although Woodford's monograph is mainly based on mathematical language, and many of the proof processes feature bound thinking, we can still feel the author's preference for the theory of inflation dynamics if we read his book carefully, and this love comes from the author's deep understanding of the importance of the dynamic mechanism of inflation.

In fact, after Roberts (1995) proposed the concept of the New Keynesian Phillips curve based on micro-pricing for the first time, the academic community rekindled its enthusiasm for researching the dynamic mechanism of inflation. This can be confirmed from the fact that a series of important documents were published in the world's top academic journals after the mid-1990s.[2] Although the focuses and researching methods of these studies vary, a broad consensus is reached that the theory of inflation dynamics plays an indispensable role in the transmission framework of modern monetary policy.

This consensus complements the important research on the scientific analysis of modern monetary policy proposed by Clarida et al. (1999) The 50-page article published on QJE elevates the monetary policy analysis framework of the New Keynesian Phillips curve to a scientific monetary policy analysis for the first time, which marks the core status of the inflation dynamic mechanism model in the framework of modern monetary policy analysis. In essence, the scientific analysis method proposed by Clarida et al. (1999) is a modern monetary policy transmission mechanism based on the dynamic general equilibrium model, which embodies the cutting-edge research methods in modern macroeconomics. John Taylor (1999a), a well-known economist at Stanford University, elaborated on the close relationship between the inflation dynamic mechanism based on the dynamic general equilibrium model and macro-monetary policy analysis in a comprehensive and detailed manner and collected micro-level data such as prices and wages. He demonstrated with the application of rigorous econometric analysis that the inflation dynamic mechanism model with expected factors is most consistent with the actual data in explaining the dynamic relationship between monetary policy, economic growth, and inflation.

Because of this, the micro-based macro-inflation dynamic model has gradually become a core element in the transmission mechanism of modern monetary policy. In summary, this transmission mechanism is mainly manifested in three segments. The first segment is the central bank's monetary policy. For example, the central bank's adjustment of short-term interest rates impacts on the total output by affecting investment. This segment is based on the classical Euler equation after logarithmic linearization. If we use i_t to represent the nominal interest rate, then the actual interest rate r_t should be equal to the nominal interest rate minus the effect of inflation, i.e.

$$r_t = i_t - E_t \pi_{t+1} \tag{1.1}$$

So the first segment can be formulated as

$$y_t = -\alpha_r r_t + E_t y_{t+1} + \varepsilon_{yt}, \ \alpha_r > 0 \tag{1.2}$$

$E_t y_{t+1}$ represents the rational expectation of the total output gap, and ε_{yt} is used to capture the influence of random factors such as demand shocks on the total output gap y_t. Obviously, with other conditions being the same, the higher the actual interest rate is, the smaller the total output gap will be.

Although according to early macro theory the change in the total money supply will affect the aggregate demand, and the change in aggregate demand will further impact on the total output, the role of the monetary aggregate has gradually been weakened by the analysis of modern monetary policy. The main reason is that it has been proved in plenty of literature in recent years, especially the work of Clarida et al. (1999) which is of watershed significance, that using monetary aggregates as the central bank's monetary policy tools generates more volatility in the macro economy than using the policy of interest rate adjustment. In fact, the People's Bank of China has gradually revealed its tendency to use interest rates as a major monetary policy tool in the process of continuously improving its central bank functions. The central bank's increases and cuts of interest rates have become the weathervane for people to observe in order to understand the change of monetary policies.

Among the major developed countries in the world, especially the United States, the first aspects mentioned above have been fully demonstrated in the actual operation process. Of course, for China, although the People's Bank of China has gradually paid attention to the role of interest rate indicators as an intermediate target of monetary policy in recent years, the regulation of monetary aggregates has been an important measure for a long time. Therefore, when examining China's monetary policy and inflation interaction mechanism, the monetary aggregate indicator cannot be ignored. Chapters 4 and 8 of this book will explain this aspect in detail.

The second segment of the modern monetary policy transmission mechanism is achieved through the dynamic mechanism of inflation. In the first segment, changes in total output will affect the current inflation rate. For example, larger GDP gaps caused by the growth of real output will put upward pressure on the current inflation rate. At the same time, the second segment highlights the impact of people's expectations of future inflation rates on current inflation rates. Of course, the over-emphasis on the expectation of inflation rate and the neglect of inflation inertia (i.e. persistence) in the inflation dynamic mechanism is precisely a shortcoming of modern inflation dynamic mechanism theory, which will be explained further.

Finally, the third segment portrays the response of monetary policy tools to total output and inflation. Specifically, changes in total output and inflation rates in the first two segments have an impact on monetary policy makers, prompting the central bank to adjust its monetary policy tools (such as short-term interest rates), i.e.

$$i_t = \rho_\pi \pi_t + \rho_y y_t + \rho_i i_{t-1} + \varepsilon_{it} \tag{1.3}$$

ε_{it} stands for the variables of monetary policy shocks. The reason the lagging nominal interest appears on the right side of the equation is because of the existence of interest rate smoothing which is widely accepted (e.g. Rudebusch, 2002b). This segment is often referred to as the currency response equation. If interest rates are used as a monetary policy tool, then this reaction equation is known as the famous Taylor Rule, which is named after the important study of John Taylor in 1993 (Taylor, 1993). Since then, Taylor (1995, 1999b), Judd and Rudebusch (1998), and Clarida et al. (2000) have conducted further empirical research on the application of the Taylor Rule in monetary policy analysis. The basic conclusions are relatively consistent, that is, the Taylor Rule works well in reflecting the central bank's monetary policy response mechanism.

In this way, monetary policy acts upon total output, total output affects inflation, and inflation and changes in total output impact on the formulation and regulation of monetary policy, thus forming a dynamic transmission mechanism of monetary policy. Since the interest rate is the major monetary policy instrument in Western developed countries, the above-mentioned transmission mechanism weakens the function of monetary aggregates, so it is often referred to as the "currency-free" monetary policy transmission mechanism (e.g. McCallum, 2001).

Since the 1990s, the "currency-free" monetary policy analysis framework has gradually become the basis for studying the interactions between monetary policy, inflation, and economic growth. For example, based on this framework, McCallum and Nelson (1999) studied the effects of monetary policy and the US economic cycle. Boivin and Giannoni (2002) studied the stability of the transmission mechanism system of monetary policy. Rudbusch (2002a) analyzed the impact of the uncertainty of model and macro data on the implementation of nominal income target systems. Roberts (2006) and Stock and Watson (2002) compared the monetary policy shocks and the unobservable random disturbance factors in terms of their influence on the total output and the fluctuations of the inflation rate. Bernanke et al. (2005) further proposed using the "factor-augmented" vector regression model to analyze the effects of monetary policy.

All these significant studies emphasize that the dynamic mechanism of inflation is indispensable in the analysis of monetary policy. It is worth noting that Roberts (2006) and Stock and Watson (2002) applied similar model systems to study the same problem but the result was not exactly the same. One of the important reasons is that the two studies had different weight hypotheses for the predictive variables in the inflation dynamic model. This shows that the specific manifestation of the dynamic mechanism of inflation may significantly affect the analysis of the effects of monetary policy. Indeed, the studies by McCallum (1999), Ball (1999), and Svensson (1999) also show that the specific form of the inflation dynamics model plays a decisive role in the analysis of the effects of monetary policy. McCallum (1999) used the inflation dynamic model based on rational expectations to analyze the effect of the nominal-income-oriented monetary policy by taking advantage of the transmission mechanism of monetary policy we summarized earlier, finding that this monetary policy can ensure the steady growth of the macro economy. Therefore, McCallum (1999) believes that the Federal Reserve should use the nominal-income-oriented system as the goal of monetary policy. In contrast, the theoretical studies of Ball (1999) and Svensson (1999) found that if rational expectations have minimal effects on the dynamic model of inflation, then as long as the central bank adopts the nominal-income-oriented system as the goal of monetary policy, it is bound to cause violent fluctuations in the overall economy.

It can be seen that the manifestation of the inflation dynamic model plays a crucial role in the analysis mechanism of monetary policy. This is also one of the important reasons why researchers have expanded the studies on the traditional theory of the inflation dynamic mechanism based on the micro perspective in recent years. From the traditional point of view, the theory of the inflation dynamic mechanism mainly explains the dynamic decision mechanism of inflation from a macro perspective. The "the Phillips curve with expected inflation rate" represented by Phelps (1967) and Friedman (1968) can be seen as the prototype and theoretical basis of the traditional inflation dynamic mechanism. This theory was originally used to analyze the long-term and short-term relationships between inflation and unemployment, to emphasize the differences between the actual and the expected inflation rate as well as their relationships with unemployment levels. According to Okun's Law, there is an inverse relationship between the unemployment rate and the actual GDP gap (namely the difference between actual GDP and potential GDP).

Although Phelps and Friedman's inflation theory introduced dynamic mechanisms and was highly regarded by academics before the end of the 1970s, in the 1970s and early 1980s, due to the global oil crisis, the inflation of different countries seemed to be significantly affected by fluctuations in oil prices, so Gordon (1982), Ball, Mankiw, and Romer (1988), and Fuhrer (1995) proposed that, on the basis of traditional inflation dynamic theory, the impact of supply shocks on inflation should be taken into account explicitly. Gordon's (1982) modification to the inflation dynamic mechanism did not completely break out of the basic theoretical framework proposed by Phelps and Friedman in the early days. He just further considered the impact of supply shocks on the current inflation rate.

However, a series of far-reaching studies in the mid-to-late 1990s, especially by King and Watson (1994), Staiger et al. (1997), and Stock and Watson (1999), have shown that although supply shocks such as oil price fluctuations may have some impact on inflation, actually the impact is minimal, the functions of which in the short-term inflation dynamic mechanism can be ignored in most cases. At the same time, these economists also pointed out that due to the existence of certain time lags in the interaction of various variables in real economic life, the traditional theoretical model of the inflation dynamic mechanism should be defined in such a way that the current inflation rate is the linear function of the historic inflation rate and the GDP gap (or unemployment rate) in the lagging period. This model has been widely used in recent studies by Rudebusch and Svensson (1999), Stock and Watson (2003), and Rudbusch (2005).

Compared with the early theoretical models of Phelps and Friedman, the theoretical framework proposed by Stock and Watson (2003) has a richer dynamic mechanism, that is, there is also a dynamic trade-off relationship between inflation and real economic variables. This theory is often referred to as the "inflation dynamic mechanism of complete backsight behavior." However, these models are not derived from the microeconomic level. The establishment of dynamic relationships among variables also has relative arbitrariness. For example, the setting of the lag period in the polynomial of the lag operator does not have a strong economic theoretical basis.

What's more important is that these theoretical models that emphasize the backsight behavior assume, without exception, that the expected mechanism for the formation of inflation is adaptive, which is precisely the key to the well-known "Lucas Critique" (Lucas, 1976). Lucas (1976) pointed out that with the changes in economic policies, even in the short term, the formation mechanism of people's expectations of future inflation rate will not remain unchanged, and changes in the currency system will certainly be reflected in the mechanism of expected formation. Economics masters Kydland and Prescott (1977) also agreed with this view. However, the core assumption of adaptive expectations is that a fixed autoregressive process can fully capture the inflation rate expectations formation mechanism for all periods. Such assumptions are clearly contrary to the view proposed by Lucas in 1976, which was widely accepted by the academic community.

Therefore, in the mid-to-late 1990s, a new generation of the micro-based inflation dynamic mechanism theory emerged, represented by Roberts (1995) and Gali and Gertler (1999). This theoretical model can be derived from the micro company pricing mechanism, and is closely related to the general dynamic equilibrium theory. At the same time, it has a solid microfoundation and emphasizes the role of rational expectations in the dynamic mechanism of inflation, and builds a bridge between the micro and the macro. It also lays the theoretical foundation for the landmark modern monetary policy transmission mechanism proposed by Clarida et al. (1999). A more detailed model description of this theoretical content can be seen in Zhang (2010). At the same time, Chapter 14 of this book will also cover the details of the microfoundation model.

Although the existing research has covered long-term and continuous studies on the dynamic mechanism of inflation, the research perspectives are still limited to the traditional demand-side model. Even though recent studies have made significant progress in the micro-mechanism of theoretical models (such as Rudd and Whelan, 2006, 2007; Zhang et al., 2008, 2009), the micro-mechanism is still essentially about the pricing decision-making of enterprises, and there is no systematic study on the macro-level economic structure and the globalization process. More importantly, for China, the evolution of the dynamic path of inflation also contains a lot of typical facts with distinctive Chinese characteristics, such as structural changes before and after China's economic transformation, the coexistence of internal and external shocks, and the impact of industry surges and commodities financialization on the dynamic mechanism of inflation. Therefore, the extension of the theory of China's inflation dynamic mechanism based on existing theories is a significant problem that this book hopes to solve.

In Chapter 2 to Chapter 14 of this book, we carry out hierarchical and in-depth exploratory research on the dynamic formation mechanism of China's inflation from different perspectives such as inflation cycle theory, price index internal conduction, price index chain transmission, capital rotation, and the industry inflation mechanism, so as to understand the multiple logics of China's inflation dynamic formation mechanism. Finally, Chapter 15 of this book provides a summary of the differences and similarities of the multiple logics of inflation dynamics formation mechanisms.

Notes

1   Some influential economists, including Taylor (2000), Cogley and Sargent (2001), Stock (2001), Willis (2003), Kim et al. (2004), Levin and Piger (2004), Cecchetti and Debelle (2006), Pivetta and Reis (2007), Zhang, et al. (2008a) target their research on inflation in the USA, while some economists like Gadzinski and Orlandi (2004), Corvoisier and Mojon (2005), and O'Reilly and Whelan (2005) study inflation in Europe.

2   Such as Yun (1996), Fuhrer (1997), Goodfriend and King (1997), King and Wolman (1999), Estrella and Fuhrer (2002,2003), Jensen (2002), Walsh (2003b), Svensson and Woodford (2003,2004), Ireland (2004), McCallum Nelson (2004,2005), Gali et al. (2005), Svensson (2005), etc.

2 Dynamic evolution of inflation in China

2.1 Inflation evolution path: Inflation cycle

China began to initiate the reform and opening-up policy in 1978. Since then, the world economy has witnessed highlights and wonderful developments. The development of China's economy is without a doubt one of the most dazzling highlights on the world stage. This is not only because China has achieved economic development that attracts worldwide attention, but also because China has pioneered an unprecedented development model in the course of economic development. In this process, China has hit economic problems not experienced by other countries and regions in the world, and undergone a unique economic transformation model. Therefore, for both economists and policy makers, "the socialist economic development model with Chinese characteristics" is the most attractive research topic and policy choice.

During the four-decade Chinese economic development, the dynamic evolution path of inflation has been particularly eye-catching. During this period, China's inflation rate has experienced many ups and downs. Representative periods of high inflation include 1980 and 1985 in the early years of reform and opening-up, 1989 and 1994 in the mid-term, as well as 2001, 2004, 2008, and 2011 in the 21st century. From the perspective of the law of time, it seems that there is a local peak period of inflation every three to five years, but the specific value in each peak period varies greatly in most cases. This chapter reviews in detail the dynamic evolutionary path and cyclical changes of inflation in China since 1978, and compares the characteristics and causes of each cyclical change. This chapter encompasses a summary of the causes of China's previous periods of inflation from the traditional perspective, and highlights the periodic theory of the dynamic evolution of inflation, with a view to offering a broader perspective on the research on the dynamic mechanism of inflation.

In terms of content organization, the second section of this chapter draws on the concept of the business cycle to define the inflation cycle. According to the monthly time sequence data published by the National Bureau of Statistics of China from 1978 to 2014, the consumer price index (CPI) year-on-year growth rate is used as a measure indicator of the inflation rate. The cycles of China's inflation are divided, and the statistics on peaks, troughs, and the rise and fall periods in each cycle are clearly enumerated. After analyzing the statistical characteristics of the dynamic path of inflation, the third section of this chapter analyzes the background, dynamic characteristics, and causes of each inflation cycle from a dynamic perspective. The fourth section of this chapter is devoted to the outlook on the causes and predictions of inflation in China. Finally, the fifth section sums up and generalizes the core content of this chapter.

2.2 Divisions of China's inflation cycle and its features

As economic issues become increasingly prominent in China's development process, China's statistics on economic data have gradually improved and matured since the reform and opening-up. From 1978 onwards, China has amassed more than 30 years of statistics, which provide a favorable basis for analyzing relevant issues in China. Therefore, this section examines the cyclical change characteristics of the monthly CPI inflation rate[1] from 1978 to 2014 according to the data published by the National Bureau of Statistics in China Monthly Economic Indicators (CMEI). Based on the basic definition of the "low–high–low" cycle and the recommendations of Artis et al. (1995) on the characteristics of the division of the inflation cycle, a statistical description of the cycle of inflation since China's reform and opening-up is given. Artis et al. (1995) offered a few key documents for the study of inflation cycles.

As we know, there is a rich literature on the economic cycle or business cycle. Early classics include those by Mitchell (1927), Mitchell and Burns (1938), and Burns and Mitchell (1946). In the last 20 years, Hamilton (1989), Sichel (1994), Zarnowitz (1992), Stock and Watson (1999), Harding and Pagan (2002), Harvey et al. (2007), and Tommaso (2008) studied economic cycle issues, and gave further contributions. Classic economic cycle analysis describes the main characteristics of each operating stage of the cycle based on the speed of economic growth, the duration of different cycles, and turning points of economic expansion and contraction. Specifically, there is both a simple "expansion–contraction" two-stage model and a more detailed "recovery–expansion–contraction–recession" four-stage model. Wang and Ai (2010) hold that it is most reasonable to divide China's economic cycle into four stages: recovery, expansion, recession, and contraction. Figure 2.1 illustrates a four-stage division in a complete economic cycle.

Countries worldwide set great store by research on economic cycles. The American National Bureau of Economic Research (NBER) and the UK's Central Statistical Office (CSO) have published statistical indicators related to the officially calculated economic cycle. However, there is little literature on the study of the inflation cycle, and no country has yet announced an official inflation cycle.

Artis et al. (1995) conducted an in-depth study on the measurement methods for the division of the inflation cycle, and the state space measurement method is used to divide the inflation cycle in British history. At the same time, using the inflation time sequence for the simple division of cycles is proposed. In summary, these recommendations can be divided into the following aspects.

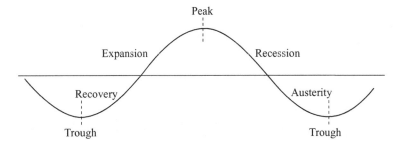

Figure 2.1 Division of the stages of economic cycle.

Firstly, inflation time sequence chart shows there will always be troughs after peaks.

Secondly, the interval spanning the rise or fall period must be at least nine months.

Thirdly, the inflection point of the cycle interval is defined as the extreme point between two adjacent intervals.

Fourthly, if the above three conditions are met in many points, the most recent is the inflection point of the cycle interval.

We adopted the above recommendations in dividing China's inflation cycle. Because the method of defining the inflation cycle according to the division criteria given by the time sequence diagram is straightforward, we did not use the state space analysis method in this chapter to identify the inflection point of the inflation cycle. Future research can be directed to this aspect. To this end, we first depicted the time sequence diagram of China's major inflation indicators and the year-on-year growth rate of CPI from 1978 to 2014 in Figure 2.1, where the vertical line indicates the peak period of each inflation period. It can clearly be seen from Figure 2.2 that according to the "low–high–low" complete cyclical change, the dynamic path of China's inflation from 1978 to 2014 can be divided into ten cycles. If we look at the dynamic trend of inflation levels, we can see that the peak periods of inflation in previous cycles occurred in 1980, 1983, 1985, 1989, 1994, 2001, 2004, 2008, 2011, and 2013.

In the existing research, some scholars did not divide the Chinese inflation cycle to such a detailed extent. For example, Yang (2006) divided the interval from 1978 to 1986 into two inflation cycles, one from 1978 to 1983 and the other from 1983 to 1986, while ignoring the periodic performance of temporary inflation in 1981–1983 as depicted in Figure 2.1. Similarly, related research in recent years (such as Gong and Lin, 2007) regarded the period of nearly ten years from 1997 to early 2007 as a period of low inflation in China (deflation period). So, the local peaks of inflation in 2001 and 2004 are not regarded as corresponding to an inflation cycle. However, according to the dynamic time sequence diagram of inflation as depicted in Figure 2.2, this research still defines these periods as the periodic change intervals of inflation.

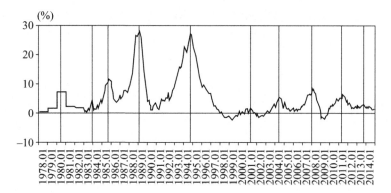

Figure 2.2 China CPI inflation rate: January 1978–December 2014. Note: multiple shaded vertical lines in the diagram indicate the peak period. Source: National Bureau of Statistics.

The cyclical changes in China's inflation since 1978 reflect not only changes in China's economic development, but also the dynamic changes in China's pricing mechanism during the economic restructuring. In the process of fluctuations in inflation, the background and causes of inflation each time deserve our analysis and thinking. We have noticed that most economists reach a certain consensus on the causes of inflations in China in the 20th century, and hold different views on the reasons for the high inflation in recent years. We will elaborate on related questions below.

According to the inflation time sequence performance shown in Figure 2.2, Table 2.1 summarizes the relevant statistical descriptions of China's inflation cycles from 1978 to 2014, including the start time corresponding to the cycle interval, the time span of the cycle, the time span in the rising period of the cycle, the time corresponding to the peak, the peak value, the trough value, and the average value and volatility of each cycle (volatility measured by standard deviation).

Some useful information can be obtained from the statistics reported in Table 2.1. For example, from 1978 to 2014, China's longest inflation cycle occurred in 1990–1999, about nine years (106 months); the shortest was 1982–1984, less than two years. The remaining six cycles typically span two to four years. Closer observation of the information in Table 2.1 reveals that before 2012, volatility in the inflation cycle seems to be in direct proportion to the average inflation level in the cycle. For example, the highest average inflation rate in the fourth inflation cycle (1986–1990) is 12.33%, and the corresponding volatility in this cycle is also the largest, or 8.76 as measured by standard deviation; on the contrary, the lowest average inflation rate in the sixth cycle (1999–2002) is 0.05% and the volatility in the corresponding cycle is also the lowest; information on the remaining cycles basically confirms the judgment that the inflation mean in the cycle is proportional to the inflation volatility. It is worth noting that in the

Table 2.1 Statistics of China's inflation cycle

	Cycle interval	Cycle span	Rising period span	Peak date	Peak value (%)	Trough value (%)	Mean in the cycle (%)	Volatility in the cycle (std.)
1	1978.01–1982.06	54 mo.	30 mo.	1980.06	7.5	2.0	3.02	2.50
2	1982.07–1984.01	19 mo.	17 mo.	1983.11	4.7	1.3	1.96	1.15
3	1984.02–1986.08	31 mo.	20 mo.	1985.09	11.9	3.9	6.16	3.46
4	1986.09–1990.07	47 mo.	30 mo.	1989.02	28.4	1.1	12.33	8.76
5	1990.08–1999.05	106 mo.	51 mo.	1994.10	27.7	-2.2	8.69	8.30
6	1999.06–2002.04	35 mo.	24 mo.	2001.05	1.7	-1.3	0.05	0.97
7	2002.05–2006.03	47 mo.	27 mo.	2004.07	5.3	0.8	1.70	1.78
8	2006.04–2009.07	40 mo.	23 mo.	2008.02	8.7	-1.9	3.35	3.14
9	2009.08–2012.07	36 mo.	23 mo.	2011.06	6.5	1.8	3.52	1.97
10	2012.08–2014.12	29 mo.	15 mo.	2013.10	3.2	1.4	2.26	0.50

recent inflation cycle, the data showed a medium inflation mean and low volatility, which may be a manifestation of the "new normal" in the current macroeconomic performance.

Moreover, it is not difficult to see from the cycle span and the rise period span in Table 2.1 that, except for the longest period from 1990 to 1999, the time span of the rising-inflation period in each cycle is longer than or even far longer than the time span of the declining period of inflation in the cycle. This discovery gives rise to an intriguing question: Why is the process of China's inflation rise slower than the decline period in most cases in the past 30 years? Does this mean that the macro policy by the central government is not implemented in a timely manner or the initial impetus is not enough when inflation appears? Or are there any other reasons? We further explore these issues in Chapter 3.

2.3 China's inflation cycle and its causes

According to the criteria for inflation cycle division in the second section, the time sequence path of China's inflation can be divided into ten major cycles from 1978 to 2014. In this section, the author will further introduce the background, causes, and characteristics of each inflation cycle that has occurred since the reform and opening-up, and explore the causes of cyclical changes in China's inflation.

2.3.1 1978–1982

2.3.1.1 Background

In December 1978, the Third Plenary Session of the 11th Central Committee of the Communist Party of China officially initiated China's reform and opening-up. The central government shifted its focus of efforts to economic development and decided to carry out economic reforms. Due to the imbalance in proportional relation in national economy caused by the long-term economic development in China, the Central Working Conference decided in April 1979 to adjust the national economy in three years and implement the policy, namely "adjustment, reform, rectification, and improvement."

The centerpiece of the policy is adjustment, mainly the adjustment of the proportional relationship of the national economy. At that time, the state required concentrated efforts in promoting agricultural development, speeding up the development of the textile industry, and accelerating the production and construction of the coal, oil, electricity, and transportation sectors. At the same time, the production scale of existing enterprises was adjusted according to the possible supply of fuel, power, and raw materials. The central government hoped to gradually promote the coordinated proportional relationship between agriculture and industry, light industry and heavy industry, fuel, power and raw materials industries, and processing industry through a host of adjustment strategies. Reform refers to the reform of an adverse economic management system, which does not yield economic benefits, such as "excessive concentration, constricting management, unified state control over income and expenditure, unified purchase and sale of materials, and unified system of foreign trade." The state hoped to stimulate the enthusiasm, initiative, and creativity of all departments, local governments, enterprises, and employees through the reform. Rectification refers to the rectification of existing enterprises, especially enterprise management. Improvement means improving the management level and scientific and technological competence of enterprises. The meeting determined that a general rotation training should be held for officials at the first level or above at enterprises through various forms, and literacy improvement and technical training should be held for employees.

The policy aims to eliminate the influence of long-standing misconceptions in economic work and put the entire national economy on the right track of healthy development. The proposal of this policy reflected an important turning point for the Party in guiding economic development.

In this context, the state initiated a slew of price reforms in 1979. For example, the government has increased the procurement price of 18 types of major agricultural products such as grain and cotton since 1979; of these, the grain procurement price increased by 30.5%, cotton 25%, and oil and oil plants by 38.7%. The government has also implemented a policy of higher prices for above-quota purchases for major agricultural products such as grain, cotton, and oil, and expanded the scope of purchases based on negotiated prices. However, while the procurement prices of agricultural products have been raised, the sales prices have not been adjusted accordingly, resulting in serious losses in production and sales of non-staple food related to agricultural products. In November 1979, the state raised the prices of eight kinds of non-staple foods such as livestock products, aquatic products, and vegetables, and gave urban residents a price subsidy of 5 yuan per person per month accordingly.

In April 1979, the government further increased the ex-factory prices of coal, iron ore, pig iron, steel ingots, billets and non-ferrous metals, cement, and so on in a planned manner. The increase in the prices of fuels and raw materials caused a hike in costs in the closely related downstream products and high value-added cigarettes and wines and others. In the early reform and opening-up, China's macroeconomic growth was also relatively robust. In 1978, the nominal GDP growth rate reached 13.85%. In 1979 and 1980, nominal GDP also saw a high growth rate of nearly 12%. At the same time, prices of commodities began to rise significantly. The annual CPI inflation rate rose from 0.7% in 1978 to 1.9% in 1979, while the inflation rate in 1980 soared to 7.5%. Since the state began to implement the austerity economic policies in 1981, the economic growth rate in 1981–1982 slowed down somewhat, and the CPI inflation rate began to fall. For the sake of comparison, Figure 2.3 indicates the annual data time sequence chart for China's annual CPI inflation rate and nominal GDP growth rate in 1978–2014.

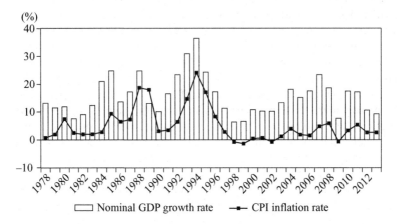

☐ Nominal GDP growth rate   ━■━ CPI inflation rate

Figure 2.3 China's annual CPI inflation rate and nominal GDP growth rate: 1978–2014.
Source: Calculated by the author based on data published by the National
Bureau of Statistics.

2.3.1.2 Causes and characteristics

The cyclical changes in inflation from 1978 to 1982 occurred in the early days
of reform and opening-up policy. The focus of the state's work shifted to socialist modernization. The fast macroeconomic growth, expanding scale of investment, rising fiscal expenditure, and so on led to a large fiscal deficit. The blind
expansion of imports caused a foreign trade deficit, and the foreign exchange
reserves were depleted rapidly. Therefore, in 1979 and 1980, obvious price
increase momentum occurred. Therefore, the economic leap forward in the
early days of reform and opening-up, the obvious overheated domestic investment, imbalanced proportions, and increased consumption expenditure, and the
rapid increase in government fiscal expenditure in the short term led to serious
fiscal deficits and other factors, which were finally exhibited as an increase in
inflationary pressures.

Of course, at the first signs of inflation, the state paid close attention to economic indicators as the economic reforms were just initiated. So, when inflation rose in 1980, the government had a quite timely response. In particular, the
State Council issued the "Circular on Strictly Controlling Commodity Prices and
Rectifying Bargaining" in December 1980, stating that inflation should be regulated. In this way, inflation was curbed through a host of measures such as cur-
tailing capital construction investment, monetary stringency, and price control.
According to the statistical information in Table 2.1, the first inflation cycle after
China's reform and opening-up occurred in 1978. By June 1982, a relatively com-
plete "low–high–low" cyclical change had basically formed.

Looking at the first inflation cycle,[2] it is not difficult to see that the inflation
cycle of 1978–1982 stemmed from the adjustment of national macroeconomic

policies and also ended with macroeconomic policy adjustment. The inflation cycle is characterized by a longer duration and by the fast results of inflation control.

2.3.2 1982–1984

2.3.2.1 Background

In the second section, it is mentioned that China's CPI inflation rate exhibited a brief cyclical change from 1982 to 1984. Existing research does not pay much attention to the inflation cycle of this period. This is not surprising, as the cyclical changes in inflation during this period can be viewed as a continuation of the first inflation cycle in some way. This is mainly because, although the State Council began to check inflation at the end of 1980 and inflation was initially controlled and fell back to 2.5% in 1982, inflation was not cured thoroughly at the time as the whole Party did not have a unified and deep understanding of economic form and economic development at the time. It is largely caused by a lack of knowledge about economic issues at the time. Therefore, although the state had the same understanding of economic reforms in the 1980s, there was a lack of consensus on the macro environment of reform. In particular, local governments and enterprises tended towards rapid development, while the mainstream "economic liberalism" in theoretical circles was fond of promoting reform through development and ignored the stable macroeconomic environment (Yang, 2006).

However, the success of the reforms in the early 1980s, the rapid economic development, and the initial prosperity greatly encouraged the reformists. "Disequilibrium theory" appeared in theoretical circles. Inflation was understood as the "disequilibrium" normalcy in the transition economy. It believed that a certain level of inflation helped economic growth and reform instead of having bad effects. It should be said that this view stands to reason to some extent. But this logic does not mean that the government did not need to take targeted measures to cope with inflation then and thereafter. In this view, the lack of timely macroeconomic policy control was one of the key reasons for short-term inflation at the end of 1983. Therefore, China experienced another short-term cyclical change in inflation from 1982 to 1984. Relevant content on the policy implications of China's inflation cycle is discussed in detail below.

2.3.2.2 Causes and characteristics

The main characteristic of the inflation cycle from 1982 to 1984 was that the time span was relatively short and the peak value was not high (nearly but less than 5%). That the cycle peaked at the end of 1983 is mainly due to the continuation of the reforms in 1980. Investment growth accelerated somewhat in 1982–1983. For example, in fixed assets investment, state-owned companies made capital construction investments of 59.4 billion yuan in 1983, an increase of 3.9 billion yuan over 1982, up by 6.9%.

Overall, China continued to implement the principle of "adjustment, reform, rectification, and improvement" and achieved certain goals in national economy development from 1982 to 1983. At the same time, while investment was accelerated, the total product of society in 1983 reached 1105.2 billion yuan, up 10% over the year 1982. The gross output value of industry and agriculture saw a year-on-year increase of 10.2%, while the national income increased by 9% compared to the year 1982. According to the bulletin of the National Bureau of Statistics in 1983, the market still showed signs of prosperity on the basis of production development.

The economic growth momentum was relatively robust in 1982–1983. Economic growth exhibited the acceleration of nominal GDP growth, and real GDP (namely the economic output after the deduction of price factor) saw rapid growth. According to the data released by the National Bureau of Statistics, China's real GDP growth rate in 1981 stood at only 5.2%, but it soared to 9.1% and 10.9% in 1982 and 1983 respectively. In less than two years, the growth rate nearly doubled. Figure 2.4 depicts the dynamic trend of China's real GDP growth rate and annual CPI inflation rate from 1978 to 2014.

Driven by economic growth, the CPI inflation rate rose to 4.7% in November 1983. There were still some problems in the development of the national economy. For example, the supply of energy and some raw materials was insufficient, transportation was still in short supply, and the economic output in the fields of production, construction, and circulation was not fundamentally improved. The state finance still had a deficit, and the retail prices of some commodities, especially vegetables, fruits, and aquatic products, increased significantly.

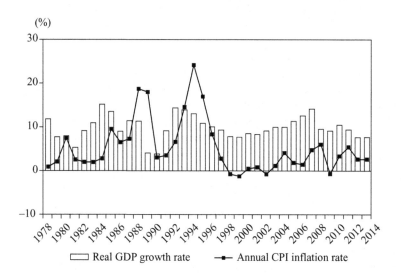

Figure 2.4 China's annual CPI inflation rate and real GDP growth rate: 1978–2014.
Source: Calculated by the author based on data published by the National Bureau of Statistics.

2.3.3   1984–1986

2.3.3.1   Background

The inflation cycle from 1984 to 1986 is a representative cycle of the period after China's reform and opening-up. The background to this inflation cycle is mainly the price reform, which eventually led to inflation peaking in September 1985. In September 1983, the 12th National Congress of the Communist Party of China officially determined the strategic goals and strategic steps for the gross output value of industry and agriculture to quadruple by the end of the 20th century. In September 1984, the Third Plenary Session of the 12th CPC Central Committee further stated the reform goal of the socialist commodity economy. At that time (1984), the real GDP growth rate reached 15.2%, while the nominal GDP growth rate was up to 20%. In 1985, the economy maintained rapid growth. Therefore, in this process, the commodity price level began to rise significantly. The CPI inflation rate jumped from 2.7% in 1984 to 9.3% in 1985.

2.3.3.2   Causes and characteristics

This inflation cycle is the first inflation cycle in which the peak value of the CPI inflation rate was higher than 10% after the reform and opening-up. During this period, the peak value and the trough value were large, and volatility was also obvious (see Table 2.1). There are two reasons for this formation of inflation: The excessive scale of fixed assets investment leading to excessive social demand, and the growth rate of income from wages and salaries exceeding the increase in labor productivity.

Moreover, the rapid expansion of infrastructure scale, social consumption demand, and the issue of monetary credit led to an overheated economy in 1986. For example, judging from the growth rate of domestic credit growth and money supply (including M0, M1, and M2 in circulation) in 1978–2007 as depicted in Figure 2.5, the credit growth rate rose from 13% in 1983 to 31% in 1984 and maintained this growth rate in 1985. Money supply also experienced a sharp increase in 1984, in which M0 and M1 reached local peaks in 1984 and M2 soared to local highs in 1985.

While the scale of credit expanded and the money supply accelerated, domestic scholars reached a broad consensus on inflation in 1984–1986. They believe it was mainly driven by costs, namely price reform. Indeed, the government increased the procurement price of 18 types of major agricultural products such as grain, cotton, and oils and oil plants and the ex-factory prices of industrial products such as coal, iron ore, pig iron, steel ingots, billets, non-ferrous metals, and cement. Prices rose one after another and salaries rose likewise. In this context, credit and money supply naturally saw rapid growth.

In addition, the rise in domestic commodity prices forced the devaluation of the renminbi, which led to the increase in prices of imported goods, thus promoting domestic inflation in a cost-driven manner. As an example, Figure 2.6 depicts the dynamic trend of the renminbi-to-US dollar exchange rate (direct quotation method)

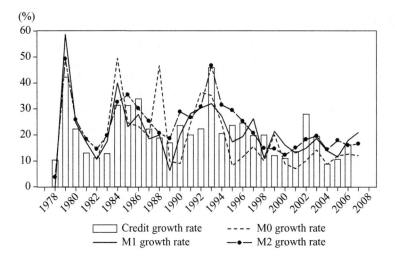

Figure 2.5 China's annual credit growth rate and money supply growth rate: 1978–2007.
Source: calculated by the author based on the data from IFS.

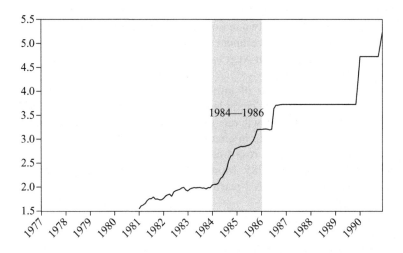

Figure 2.6 RMB to US dollar exchange rate: January 1981–December 1990.
Source: Federal Reserve St. Louis Branch.

from 1978 to 1990. It can be clearly seen the renminbi depreciation relative to the currency of major trading country the US dollar from 1984 to 1986: From January 1984 to January 1986, the renminbi depreciated by nearly 60% against the US dollar.

To curb inflation, the State Council issued a host of macro-control measures from November 1984 to October 1985 to rein in the scale of investment in fixed assets, tighten commodity price management and supervision, and conduct comprehensive credit checks. Following a series of measures, the CPI inflation rate began to fall at the beginning of 1986, from 7.4% in March to 5.4% in April, and then further to below 4% in August 1986.

On the whole, the inflation that occurred in 1984–1986 was mainly reflected in the excessive scale of investment in fixed assets, which led to excessive social demand. The growth rate of income from salaries exceeded the growth of labor productivity, which led to cost increases. In the wake of expanding infrastructure scale, social consumption demand, and money and credit supply, the economy overheated and inflation intensified.

2.3.4 1986–1990

2.3.4.1 Background

The high inflation that occurred in 1985 was not completely cured. Due to a lack of macroeconomic regulation and control, fiscal deficits and income inflation were aggravated. Deep-seated problems accumulated over the years in economic operations became increasingly prominent, such as imbalances in the economic structure, the expansion of investment scale, and the continued expansion of consumption. The CPI inflation rate began to rise again in the second half of 1986 after a brief downward adjustment in July–October 1986. By 1987, China's real GDP growth rate reached 11.6%.

The CPI rose by 19.2% year-on-year in July 1988. From August 1988 to June 1989, the CPI inflation rate hit record highs, reaching the highest level of 28.4% in February 1989 since the reform and opening-up. From 1989, China began to implement strict credit austerity policies. However, due to the prevailing inflation expectations in the market and the inertia of inflation, inflation was not checked until July 1990. The inflation inertia mentioned here means the time required for inflation to return to its static level after being impacted by random factors. The longer it takes, the greater the inertia (Zhang, 2008b). The issues of China's inflationary inertia characteristics are elaborated in Chapter 3.

2.3.4.2 Causes and characteristics

Although the price system adjustment in 1985 triggered inflation, the country still prepared for comprehensive price reforms thereafter. At this time, the price increase occurred in the initial stage of the transition from a planned economy to a market economy. It is worth mentioning that on August 19, 1988, the news of the price increase broadcast by China National Radio promoted society's expectation of inflation to a certain extent. It became the trigger for the biggest wave of panic buying since the founding of New China.

According to analysis by Yang (2006) of China's inflation in the 1980s, the rise in commodity prices and panic buying sparked serious social problems. The first is that panic buying spread far and wide, almost sweeping major cities and some rural areas nationwide. It involved upwards of 500 types of goods in 50 categories. The second is blindness. Regardless of the variety, quality, and price of goods, many defective shopworn products in many shopping malls were purchased by consumers, resulting in a huge increase in the total volume of retail sales. The third is the run on banks following the panic buying. The run at the time was not only for demand deposits, but also for premature time deposits.

Looking back at this inflation in the mid-to-late 1980s, Wei (2007) believed that it was a time when China had just initiated the market-oriented reforms and the results of rural reforms had begun to emerge. At the same time, as the market system was not yet established in the early days of reform and opening-up, the macroeconomic regulation at that time lacked foresight. A general consensus on the reasons for inflation during this period is that after the temporary cooling of China's economy following regulation in 1985, the leadership did not take a firm enough line on inflation, leading to unstable macro-control policies and overheated economic development. Inflation rebounded immediately after a brief downward adjustment. It is worth noting that the inflationary expectations that prevailed at the time were also the crucial driving force of high inflation in 1986–1990. Besides, since the reform and opening-up, China had been implementing deficit fiscal policies to stimulate the economy, while monetary policy always lacked the necessary independence and effectiveness. Monetary policy follows fiscal policy. At that time, the money supply growth rate and domestic credit growth rate approached 30%, playing a role in fueling the high inflation.

Of course, the country recognized the hazards of excessive inflation in the wake of this round of inflation. From the second half of 1988, the state strictly controlled the scale of bank credit, raised deposit and loan interest rates twice, implemented a value preservation subsidy method for fixed savings deposits for residents, stabilized the scale of savings deposits, curbed the momentum of consumption expansion, and strictly checked the expansion of the credit scale. At the same time, the state strictly controlled and disposed of fixed-asset investment projects, and compressed the scale of infrastructure construction. A total of 44.2 billion yuan of investment in fixed assets was compressed nationwide. After rectification, inflation was gradually curbed. By January 1990, the CPI inflation rate fell below 5%.

2.3.5   1990–1999

2.3.5.1 Background

At the end of 1980 when the state carried out rectification, new problems also emerged, mainly market sluggishness, poor markets for goods, and a sharp decline in industrial production. For example, in 1989, the total value of merchandise inventory nationwide reached 150 billion yuan, and the growth rate of total industrial output value slowed down significantly. From the growth rate as described in

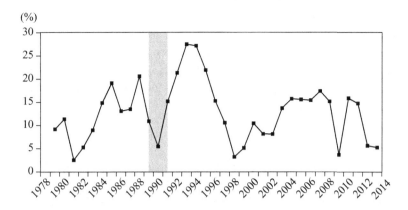

Figure 2.7 Growth rate of China's total industrial output value: 1978–2014.
Source: Calculated by the author based on data published by the National Bureau of Statistics.

Figure 2.7, the growth rate of the value of industrial output in 1989–1991 (shaded part in the figure) fell below 10%, reaching a local minimum in 1990.

Because of this, industrial enterprises were unable to repay each other's debts due to a lack of funding. Mutual arrears constitute a "debt chain." At that time, it formed an intractable debt chain, which further hindered industrial production and blocked the economic cycle. Several attempts by banks to inject start-up funds still failed to solve the problem. In fact, the growth rate of domestic credit supply and money supply in 1989–1991 fell greatly.

In this context, China's economic growth cooled significantly from 1990 to 1993, and the CPI inflation rate fell below 5%. However, Deng Xiaoping's speech in southern China in 1992 brought a historical opportunity for China's new round of economic development. In the context of the government's determination to develop the economy, China once again entered a period of accelerated development. The scale of credit supply and money supply began the rapid recovery since 1993, and China's economic growth entered a new historical development stage. According to the data released by the National Bureau of Statistics, the real GDP growth rate in 1991 stood at 9.2%. In 1992, the real GDP growth rate reached double digits, at 14.2%. In 1993, economic growth picked up speed again, achieving a growth rate of 15.1% in the first quarter and 16.4% in the second quarter. The real GDP growth rate for the whole year reached 13.5%, while the nominal growth rate was up to 31%.

Driven by economic growth, the GPI inflation rate climbed to 10.3% in January 1993, and then rose all the way to 21.1% in January 1994, and further to its peak of 27.7% in October 1994 in this cycle. After the inflation reached a new high in 1994–1995, the state began to take measures to slowly control the ever-rising commodity prices.

2.3.5.2 Causes and characteristics

Compared to the previous inflations after China's reform and opening-up, this inflation from 1990 to 1999 was the longest, lasting 106 months (nearly 9 years), and is the only inflation cycle in which the inflation downward period (55 months) is longer than the rising period (51 months). In addition, the domestic and international economic environment during this inflation had the following characteristics: The non-state-owned economy was ballooning, the prices of most commodities and factors of production were liberalized, the market mechanism became more and more important in regulating the economy, and the foreign exchange mechanism saw great changes.

In order to invigorate large and medium-sized state-owned enterprises, the State Council published 20 important measures at the end of 1991, including lowering interest rates and sending a strong signal of relaxation of monetary policy. As a result, the national credit growth rate reached nearly 50% in 1993. Driven by this, China saw a nationwide real estate boom, a development zone boom, and an investment boom in 1992–1994. In this context, the occurrence mechanism of inflation is mainly reflected in the "double expansion" of investment and consumption.

At that time, in the face of the appealing market mechanism and the rising trend of economic growth, some economists (such as Wu, 1992) predicted with foresight that if the central government did not promote the reform of key sectors such as finance and state-owned enterprises in a timely manner, promoting the role of the market and increasing investment growth nationwide might easily lead to overheating and inflation. Wei et al. (1991) also put forward the idea that to prevent inflation and economic overheating, decision-makers should "fine-tune early on" the macro economy.

However, the views of the economics community and the leadership on economic development were still controversial. In January 1993, the GPI inflation rate climbed to more than 10%, and the RMB exchange rate against the US dollar fell by 45% in half a year. The leadership finally began to implement macroeconomic regulation and control over overheating and inflation. In June 1993, the CPC Central Committee and the State Council jointly issued the "Opinions on the Current Economic Situation and Strengthening Macro-control," which proposed "16" measures to strengthen macro-control, including: (1) strictly control currency issuance and stabilize the financial situation; (2) resolutely correct illegally borrowed funds; (3) flexibly use interest rate leverage to increase savings deposits; (4) resolutely curb all sorts of illegal fund raising; (5) strictly control the total scale of credit; (6) professional banks must guarantee the payment of savings deposits; (7) accelerate the financial reform and strengthen the central bank's financial macro-control capabilities; (8) investment system reforms should be combined with financial system reform; (9) treasury bond issuance shall be completed within deadline; (10) further improve the issuance of securities and regulate market management; (11) improve measures over foreign exchange management and stabilize foreign exchange market prices; (12) strengthen macro management of the real estate market and promote the healthy development of the real estate industry; (13) strengthen tax collection and management, and close the loopholes of tax exemption; (14) queue the projects under construction for audit and strictly control the newly commenced projects; (15) actively and prudently promote commodity price reform to curb the excessive rise in the general price level; (16) strictly control the excessive growth of purchasing power of social groups.

After the introduction of the "16 measures," the credit scale and money supply were controlled to a certain extent. For example, the growth rate of money supply M1 dropped from 32% in 1993 to 27% in 1994, and further dropped to 17% in 1995. The growth rate of money supply M2 also fell from 47% in 1993 to 29% in 1995; the growth rate of domestic credit issue in 1993 approached 50%, and fell by nearly half in 1994 and 1995. At the same time, foreign exchange adjustments changed, as shown in Figure 2.8. After a sharp devaluation in 1993, the exchange rate of the RMB against the US dollar also fell back in 1994–1995 (appreciation of renminbi), which cooled to some extent China's export trade.

But we must see that China's inflation has high inflation inertia (Zhang, 2008b), and economic growth often has inertia. Despite the implementation of tight macroeconomic policies in China in 1993–1995, the time-lag effect of policy is still quite obvious. The time-lag effect of this policy was fully exhibited in the inflation cycle of 1990–1999. Wei (2007) believed that after the austerity policy, the main reason for the sustained rise in domestic commodity prices in 1994–1995 was the lag effect of the excessive money supply in the early period. He also held that another reason is that after the implementation of austerity measures, domestic demand had shrunk significantly. But due to the significant depreciation of the renminbi, the export demand was extremely strong. A wealth of foreign direct investment inflows led to the current account of the international balance of

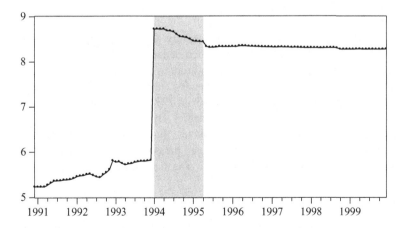

Figure 2.8 Exchange Rate of the RMB against the US dollar: January 1990–December 1999. Source: Federal Reserve St. Louis Branch.

payments having a large surplus. Foreign exchange reserves soared accordingly. The proportion of foreign exchange increased greatly, so the growth rate of the monetary base was up to 30.6%.

Therefore, China's inflation rate of up to 24% in 1994 was also closely related to the sharp rise in foreign exchange reserves at that time. In early 1994, China made great strides in foreign exchange system reform and achieved the integration of the official exchange rate and the market regulated exchange rate. Due to the sharp devaluation of the RMB in 1993–1994, China's export growth reached 32% in 1994, and the trade balance was changed from a deficit of $12.2 billion in 1993 to a surplus of $5.4 billion. As a result, the People's Bank of China's foreign exchange reserves soared from $21.2 billion in early 1994 to $51.62 billion, up by $30.42 billion. The rapid growth of the monetary base led to a corresponding increase in the money supply. It can be said that this is an important reason for China's high inflation in 1994–1995.

Under the comprehensive implementation of the austerity policy, and thanks to the fixed exchange rate mechanism pegged to the US dollar since 1995, China adjusted the "double high" trend of economic growth and inflation in over three years, and gradually embarked on the "austerity and growth" model of high growth and low inflation. China successfully achieved a "soft landing" of the economy, and this nine-year inflation cycle came to an end. However, it should be pointed out that such a long inflation cycle also exerted a considerable influence on China's economic development and national social welfare at that time. This lesson shall be learned for the sake of future economic development.

2.3.6 *1999–2002*

2.3.6.1 *Background*

From 1999 to 2002, China's inflation was chiefly controlled at a low level, and even deflation (negative inflation rates) occurred for a time. Nevertheless, if this period is divided according to the definition of the cyclical nature, a pronounced cyclical change can be seen from Figure 2.2.

If we shift our gaze to the end of the 20th century, China began to take cognizance of deflation in 1998, fearing that continued deflation might have a negative effect on economic development. Therefore, in order to scale up domestic demand and spur the economy, the state adopted a "proactive" fiscal policy and a "prudent" monetary policy focusing on monetary easing from 1998 to 2002. By 2000, China had beaten the shadow of deflation to a certain degree. By mid-2001, different exogenous shocks, such as domestic expansion policies, fluctuations in oil prices, and rises in food prices, gave rise to certain inflationary pressures. However, the peak of inflation in this period did not exceed 2%, and it was moderate overall.

2.3.6.2 *Causes and characteristics*

From the analysis of the background to China's inflation cycle from 1999 to 2002, and the time-lag effect of policy control as mentioned above, we have a basic understanding that the measures taken by China for better macroeconomic control, financial stability, and strong management of fixed asset investment since the late 1990s began to exert an austerity effect at the end of 1998. Due to the long-standing deflation caused by policy inertia and the leadership's concern about the potential adverse effects of long-standing deflation, measures that began to be initiated in 2000, such as expanding domestic demand and stimulating the economy, appropriately pushed the price changes at that time out of deflation for a period of time. The dwindling bank credit supply at the time, and the measures adopted by the financial system and commercial banks such as an unwillingness to grant loans in order to cope with bad debts also contributed to a decrease in inflation after 2001.

This shows that from 1999 to 2002, despite the loose monetary supply, bank credit was still tight, which is also the fundamental reason that inflation in this period remained at a low level.

2.3.7 2002–2006

2.3.7.1 Background

Following high inflation at several times in the 1980s and 1990s, the People's Bank of China gradually showed foresight in coping with inflation in the 21st century. For example, starting from the first quarter of 2001, the People's Bank of China published the "Monetary Policy Report" on its website on a quarterly basis. The paper version was published by China Financial Publishing House and distributed at home and abroad. Therefore, the monetary authorities accurately forecast the inflation cycle from 2002 to 2006, especially the peak inflation period from 2004 to 2005.

The occurrence of this inflation cycle is closely linked with China's deflation that began to emerge in 1998. While deflation eased somewhat in 2001 and slight inflation (less than 2%) occurred, China was still haunted by the specter of deflation. However, it can be seen from Figure 2.9 that the growth rate of broad money (M2) was higher than that of nominal GDP for four years from 2002 to 2006.

In this context, there was investment growth led by local governments at the time, and the prices of assets and property products rose in 2004 and 2005, driving in part CPI's inflation rate to 5% in mid-2004.

2.3.7.2 Causes and characteristics

According to the People's Bank of China's "Monetary Policy Report" in 2003, the overall CPI in China in the first eight months of 2003 saw a slight positive increase year-on-year, and began to rise rapidly from September, reaching a year-on-year increase of 3.2% in December. By 2004, in addition to a rise in the prices of raw materials, outgoing products, and imported commodities, there was accelerated growth in the prices of real estate and fixed asset investment.

The CPI also began to rise from 2003 onwards. From April 2004 to November 2004, the CPI and inflation rate were in excess of 3% for eight straight months,

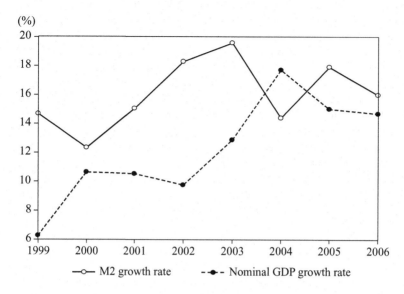

Figure 2.9 Growth rates of China's M2 and nominal GDP: 1999–2006.
Source: International Financial Statistics database, People's Bank of China.

while the CPI and inflation rate from June to September 2004 were above 5%, but began to fall thereafter. Compared to the previous cycles, this inflation cycle was mild in terms of duration, peak value, and volatility.

It should be noted that what is most noteworthy in this inflation cycle is the rise in asset prices such as real estate. Though a rise in real estate prices is not directly manifested in the CPI and inflation rate, a rise in prices of hard assets such as real estate will affect the market's expectations for future inflation, and expectations will surely affect consumption and investment patterns by consumers. Once this transmission mechanism is established, an overall rise in prices inevitably follows. The cyclical changes in China's inflation from 2002 to 2006 were chiefly characterized by moderation, but the "irrational exuberance" driven by sustained asset price inflation after this period was one of the important reasons for the high inflation of 2007 and 2008.

2.3.8 2006–2009

2.3.8.1 Background

Low inflation did not last long in 2006. From the second quarter of 2007, in tandem with a rapid growth of the economy, the CPI and inflation rate showed a month-on-month upward trend, rising from 3.0% in April 2007 to 6.9% in November, and slightly falling (6.5%) in December. Although the rise in CPI and inflation rate in 2007 was less than 5%, it was still mild inflation. The continued rise faced great pressures. It seems on the surface that this is chiefly caused by a shortage of pork and grain supplies, which is difficult to improve in the short term, resulting in the mounting pressure of rising prices. Moreover, due to China's heavy dependence on the international market for oil, the continued high oil prices on the international market caused by the depreciation of the US dollar and the speculation in crude oil futures were a strong driving force for rising prices of energy and raw materials in China.[3]

From the statistical data, in January–November 2007, the purchase prices of raw materials, fuels, and power in China were up 4.1% on a year-on-year basis. The monthly trend of the major price indexes in 2007 shows that China's inflation in food had an obvious trend of affecting other products and services, and the risk of generalized inflation is mounting. As the appreciation of the renminbi against the US dollar picked up and international crude oil prices kept rising, China still faced pronounced inflationary pressure in 2008. At the end of 2007, the Central Economic Working Conference put forward that China's monetary policy would be changed from "prudent" to "tightening" from 2008. In the first five months of 2008, the People's Bank of China raised the required reserve ratio five times, which reached a cumulative 3 percentage points. The required reserve ratio for deposit-taking financial institutions also rose up to 17.5%, and funds totaling upwards of 1.2 trillion yuan were recovered. At the same time, the People's Bank of China also used the central bank bills and window guidance to control loans issued by banks. In September 2008, the subprime mortgage crisis worsened the international financial crisis, and China's inflationary pressures quickly dissipated due to the external negative impact and earlier tightening policies.

2.3.8.2 Causes and characteristics

As China opens wider to the world, changes in global market prices and in the overall prices in China's major trading partners have an increasing impact on changes in the prices of important products and the overall price level in China. Therefore, the rise in the overall price level since 2006 was significantly subject to international influences. In comparison, there was one major difference between this inflation and inflation in the mid-1990s, in that this inflation was not wholly driven by investment demand. The rise in oil, energy, and grain prices on the global market constituted a global supply shock, leading to cost-push inflation to a certain extent. At the same time, as China does not have pricing power for global bulk commodities, the cost of related enterprises in China indeed increased significantly.

What is most noteworthy in the supply shock in 2007–2008 is the international crude oil price. The global crude oil price (world crude oil price with export shares weighting) was less than US$90 per barrel in December 2007, but surpassed US$100/barrel in March 2008, and skyrocketed to an all-time high of US$130 per barrel in June 2008. Figure 2.10 shows the time sequence data on world crude oil prices from 2000 to 2008. The rapid rise in crude oil prices can be clearly seen in Figure 2.10.

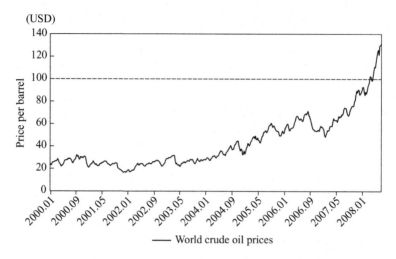

Figure 2.10 World spot prices of crude oil: January 2000–June 2008. Source: US Energy Information Administration.

Due to China's heavy dependence on crude oil energy, the soaring world crude oil prices directly piled on the pressure of inflation in China in 2008. However, changes in energy prices are temporary supply shocks in theory. Studies show (e.g. Zhang et al., 2008) that a supply shock generally does not have a systematic and significant impact on inflation.

In addition to the supply shock, China's inflation problem in 2007 was also attributed to another factor that cannot be overlooked: The reform of the RMB exchange rate mechanism after July 2005. After 2006, the trend of rapid appreciation of the renminbi led to firm expectations for the appreciation of the renminbi, prompting a wealth of international capital to flow into China. Of course, unexpected accidents and disasters in China, such as the snow disaster in southern China in the spring of 2008 and the 2008 Sichuan earthquake resulted in great pressure on price rebounds in the short term. Further details on the relationship between renminbi appreciation and inflation are explained in detail in Chapter 8.

In terms of policy, given the mounting inflationary pressures, the People's Bank of China, from 2007 to May 2008, raised the required reserve ratio and interest rate several times in a row, and issued central bank bills to recoup liquidity, and began to implement tight monetary policy and prudent fiscal policy, and regulated the real estate market and stock market accordingly. However, due to the deflationary effect of the significant appreciation of the renminbi on China's export trade, China's economic growth in 2008 exhibited a downward trend. At this time, rising global energy prices and expectations for further appreciation of the renminbi prompted international liquidity to flow into China, posing grim inflation risks for China. Therefore, the Chinese economy faced the double whammy of economic slowdown and inflation. At the same time, it can be seen that this inflation cycle had its salient international characteristics.

2.3.9 2009–2012

2.3.9.1 Background

In September 2008, the US subprime mortgage crisis further was aggravated by the failure of Lehman Brothers and spread rapidly worldwide. Under the double whammy of the sharply deteriorating international macro environment and the tightening monetary policy in the earlier period, China's economic growth rate saw an accelerated decline from the third quarter of 2008. At the close of 2008, the growth rate of exports and imports slowed down somewhat, but still remained positive. By November and December, the total value of imports and exports in China began to see negative growth. In November 2008, the total value of imports and exports nationwide fell by 9% over the previous year, of which exports fell by 2.2% and imports fell by 17.9%. In December 2008, the total value of imports and exports nationwide plunged by 11.1% over the previous year, of which exports fell by 2.8% and imports fell by 21.3%. As a result of the impact of the adverse environment, high inflation pressure quickly dissipated, CPI nosedived from 8.7% in February 2008 to 1.2% in November 2008, and the growth rate of GDP also fell from 10.6% in the first quarter to 6.8% in the fourth quarter. China's economy faced the risk of a hard landing.

In response to the grim economic landscape, the Chinese government instituted ten measures in November 2008 to expand domestic demand and stimulate stable and rapid economic growth, namely the "Four trillion yuan stimulus package." At the same time, the People's Bank of China also implemented a host of loose monetary policies for support. While having promoted economic recovery, proactive fiscal policy and proactive monetary policy also resulted in considerable inflationary pressures. The inflation rate was rising after it reached a nadir in October 2009, and rose to 5.1% in November 2010. Thereafter, the inflation rate ran at a high level for nearly one year, and did not relax until September 2011.

2.3.9.2 Causes and characteristics

This inflation showed obvious cost-push characteristics and was closely linked to the international financial environment. First, due to the depreciation of the US dollar that followed on the heels of the US quantitative easing policy, the international bulk commodity market prices in US dollars rapidly soared. For example, in 2010, Brent crude oil prices rose by 28.4%, and the Chicago Board of Trade (CBOT) soybean futures price jumped by 29.26%, while Chinese companies relying on imported raw materials were under heavy pressure from rising costs since China did not have a say in the commodity market. Secondly, China took the lead in climbing out of the economic predicament, and the expectation for RMB

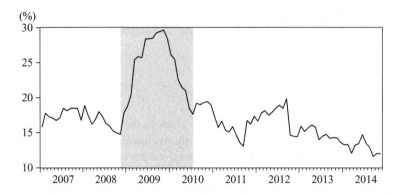

Figure 2.11 Growth rate of China's M2: 2007–2014. Source: Calculated by the author based on data from the National Bureau of Statistics.

appreciation was intense, attracting a wealth of international hot money to China. The hot money engaged in profit-seeking speculation after entering the Chinese market, covering traditional precious metals and real estate, and also agricultural products such as mung beans and garlic, pushing prices further upwards in China. Finally, due to the large-scale stimulus fiscal and monetary policies designed to stabilize the economy, especially the monetary investment in support of infrastructure construction, the inflation rate inevitably rose. Figure 2.11 describes the growth rate of China's M2 from 2007 to 2011. The peak monetary investment brought about by the proactive monetary policy can be clearly seen.

On the whole, the two inflation cycles of 2006–2009 and 2009–2012 show a clear international context. The rapid decline in high inflation in 2008 and the persistently high inflation in 2010–2011 have their reasons in the international environment. Under the wave of globalization, the international economic climate has an intensifying impact on China's macro economy, posing a new challenge to the early warning and governance capabilities of the competent authorities. The impact of globalization on inflation in China is discussed in depth in Chapter 14.

2.3.10 2012–2014

2.3.10.1 Background

Under the influence of proactive fiscal policy and monetary policy, China took the lead in climbing out of the shadow of the new financial crisis that originated in the United States in 2007 and swept the world, and in doing so China spurred the stable development of the national economy. Nevertheless, with the passage of time, the inadequacies of China's potent economic stimulus plan released in 2007–2008 became increasingly apparent: Excessive reliance on infrastructure investment, redundant construction projects in various places, severe overcapacity in some industries, and the original intention of "adjusting the structure" not achieved; economic development is still extensive, and resource waste and environmental pollution increasingly aggravated; with the disappearance of the demographic dividend, the advantages of cheap labor have gradually weakened, but the new competitive advantage has not yet emerged. At the same time, the international macroeconomic environment is still unclear, and European countries have not completely walked out of the shadow of the European debt crisis. Under the impact of multiple factors, the Chinese economy is facing downward pressure, and the GDP growth rate remained below 8% from the first quarter of 2013. Therefore, the inflationary pressures in this cycle are not obvious, and volatility is also low.

2.3.10.2 Causes and characteristics

Inflation in this cycle was relatively moderate, and the interaction between proactive fiscal policy and prudent monetary policy is its main cause. In terms of values, the peak of inflation of 3.2% occurred in October 2013, and most of the time it was between 2% and 3%, which can be regarded as normal fluctuations in economic performance. In the second half of 2014, the inflation rate further declined due to factors such as sluggish macroeconomic growth and the sharp fall in international crude oil prices. In November 2014, inflation was only 1.4%, and there was a risk of entering the deflationary zone. Further, as there is no obvious overheating in the cycle, the characteristics of a "gradual rise and sharp fall" in inflation in the past several cycles are not very obvious, and the rising period and the falling period are basically equal. As inflationary pressures are very small, there is more room for the policy authorities to implement macroeconomic regulation objectively.

2.4 Implications

Since 2007, China's inflation problem has become the focus of concern in all sectors of society in the complicated context of high food prices, rising property prices and stock market, excess liquidity, RMB appreciation, and the US subprime mortgage crisis. In the face of the current overheating risks to China's economy and the rising inflationary pressures, preventing the overheating of the economy and obvious inflation became the top priority in the central government's macroeconomic regulation in 2008. Therefore, studying the dynamic transmission mechanism of China's inflation and conducting scientific predictions of China's inflation trend in the next few years has a bearing on whether it is possible to complete the important task of maintaining price stability and promoting rapid and sound economic development. It is also the key to thoroughly implementing the concept of scientific development in a new era. While recognizing the complexity and arduous task of stabilizing prices, to scientifically and systematically study the dynamic transmission mechanism of China's inflation, and analyze the future trend of inflation from a broad perspective in multiple dimensions has key practical significance for completing the macro control tasks guided by scientific development concepts.

At the same time, as macroeconomic regulation and control in China becomes increasingly standardized and scientific, it is urgent for scientific researchers to make clear the various driving factors of inflation based on the characteristics of current economic development and changes in the domestic and international economic situation with consideration to the national reality. It is necessary to inspect the transmission factors at the macro level from a global perspective, recognize the role of current global high energy prices, excess liquidity, and the pressure of RMB appreciation on China's inflation, and also grasp the more subtle inflation drivers at the micro level, such as market expectations' impact on inflation, so that more comprehensive information is used to accurately predict future inflation trends. This helps the relevant decision-making departments to co-ordinate the requirements of domestic development and opening-up in a timely manner, maintain price stability, and promote sustainable economic development.

In order to adjust price fluctuations timely and effectively and achieve scientific development smoothly, countries worldwide have conducted multi-faceted research into the transmission mechanism and prediction of inflation in recent years. These studies mostly explore the dynamic driving factors and prediction problems of inflation from the perspective of the inflation transmission mechanism based on the econometric model. Some study the dynamic transmission problem of a single price index, and others study the mutual transmission problem between different price indices, analyzing the inflation transmission mechanism from the macro perspective of economic growth and inflation. Still others study the accuracy of inflation forecasting from the angle of different prediction technology. Notwithstanding the different perspectives of these studies and the different depths of analysis, these studies have certain reference significance for studying the dynamic transmission mechanism of inflation and its prediction.

The dynamic transmission mechanism and the prediction of inflation include two aspects: one is the inflation transmission mechanism problem, and the other is the inflation prediction problem. The existing research in China mainly focuses on the former. Some scholars studied the inflation's transmission mechanism at a macro level. For example, He (2003) divided China's policy cycle in 1990–2003 and used the descriptive analysis method to propose that the policy cycle of China's macroeconomic regulation is an important transmission factor of inflation. Gao et al. (2003) and Ma and Tu (2006) used the results of the measurement test to show that economic growth and real GDP gap are significant drivers of inflation based on the Phillips curve model. Zhang (2007a) conducted an in-depth and exhaustive summary and commentary on the dynamic transmission mechanism of inflation from a macro perspective, and supported the transmission effect of economic growth on inflation. However, a study by Gong and Lin (2007) shows that the excessive impact of China's high economic investment rate (as against economic growth itself) is the real reason for the dynamic trend of China's inflation. It is worth noting that Zhang's study (2008a) on the structural transition characteristics of the dynamic path of China's inflation rate shows that the dynamic path of China's inflation underwent a structural change in the mid-to-late 1990s. Although this structural change does not necessarily explain the contradictions found in existing studies, it at least shows that in using historical information to predict the future trend of inflation, structural change factors should also be considered one of the internal factors.

Other domestic scholars chose a relatively micro perspective to analyze the transmission mechanism of inflation. For example, Zhang and Liu (2007) believed that the degree of viscosity of inflation determines its future trend. The research by He (2006), Liu (2007), and Wang (2007) shows that the price changes of upstream products will eventually be passed onto CPI, but there is a long lag period. These studies applied econometric models, but it is a pity that they did not point out how to use the model they set to predict the future trend of China's inflation.

Although domestic research did not analyze in depth how to predict the inflation trend thorough the inflation transmission mechanism, the research by international academic circles on inflation prediction in recent years provides useful inspiration for analyzing the trend of price fluctuations in China. For example, Stock and Watson (1999) systematically expounded the inflation prediction technique, and pointed out that the autoregressive distributed lag (ADL) model can accurately predict the change in US inflation in the 12 months to come. This study is based on a closed economy model and comprehensively compares the forecasting power of economic growth, interest rates, currencies, and other commodity prices on volatility trends of consumer prices. It is found that economic growth has the strongest ability to predict inflation. On the basis of this, Choudhri and Hakura (2006) considered the ability of the exchange rate to predict inflation in an open economy, and found that the domestic price fluctuations in the 71 countries they chose, including China, were significantly affected by exchange rate changes.

It should be noted that with the adjustment of economic development models and economic policies in various countries, the difficulty of predicting inflation increases. For example, Orphanides and Van Noren (2005), and Stock and Watson (2007) found that it became more difficult to predict the inflation trend in the US after 1980 after the comparison of the performance of the US economic indicators in 1980. The main reason is inflation inertia, as well as the greatly reduced fluctuation of its drivers. However, the results of Zhang's (2008b) study show that this conclusion does not apply to China. This just goes to show that inflation prediction needs to be treated differently for specific countries. In particular, it is necessary to consider the actual situation and specific stage of economic development in different countries, and analyze the specific issues in a pragmatic manner.

Overall, the existing research in China provides a certain basis for analyzing the dynamic transmission mechanism of inflation in China, but the perspective of analysis is often limited to a certain aspect at the micro or macro level, without the organic integration of micro and macro aspects. Moreover, there is insufficient analysis of how to scientifically predict the future trend of inflation. In addition, existing research lacks in-depth analysis of how the internal sub-components of China's high-profile CPI are dynamically transmitted to the final consumer prices and how the price chains at different stages exert dynamic influences. Foreign studies are generally based on the economic performance characteristics of their respective countries, and many of their conclusions are often far removed from the reality of China's economic development. However, their methods have a reference value for studying China's inflation prediction problem.

Therefore, the in-depth study of the dynamic transmission mechanism of China's inflation and prediction issues from the comprehensive perspective of micro and macro levels meets the urgent needs of current economic development, and also has a lasting significance for taking a broader view of the application of macroeconomic forecasting theory and promoting the scientific development of national macroeconomic regulation policies. It therefore ensures that the research of this subject has long-term development prospects. These questions will be discussed gradually in subsequent chapters.

2.5 Conclusions

In the four decades of reform and opening-up, China has carried out reform that has attracted worldwide attention to its economic system. As the People's Bank of China began to serve its clearly defined functions, the monetary policy mechanism has undergone tremendous changes. At the same time, the Chinese economy is playing an increasingly important role in the global economy. Correspondingly, the changing world economy is increasingly having an impact on the Chinese economy.

In this process, the problem of inflation is not only a major problem facing the Chinese economy, but also an important issue to be addressed in the future. This chapter divides the dynamic path of China's inflation in 1978–2014 into ten large cycles according to cyclical changes. This chapter analyzes the comprehensive statistical indicators of the inflation cycle, and also expounds the background of each cycle and its causes and characteristics, in order to help readers understand the inflation cycle and its causes after China's reform and opening-up, as well as the characteristics of inflation in each cycle.

It should be noted that in analyzing the causes of inflation, this chapter explains the cyclical changes of inflation based on the basic consensus formed in domestic academic circles, but does not analyze in detail the role of monetary policy and other factors in the formation of inflation. In particular, two consecutive hyperinflations occurred in the 1980s and 1990s. Why did monetary policy not rein in inflation before the formation of hyperinflation at the time? These issues remain to be studied. One possible idea is to think outside of the traditional interpretation framework and analyze the dynamic formation mechanism of inflation after China's reform and opening-up from a wider, multi-faceted, and multi-dimensional perspective. Based on this idea, the subsequent chapters of this book will explain the dynamic formation mechanism of China's inflation from different perspectives, with a view to providing economic strategies and policy recommendations conducive to China's current and future economic development and decision-making.

Notes

1 As it is hard to obtain monthly CPI inflation data before 1981, the annual data for those years are used as the monthly data.
2 If no special explanation is given in the subsequent chapters, the Nth inflation cycle refers to the cyclical sequence starting with the beginning of reform and opening-up.
3 Alan Greenspan, the former Chair of the Federal Reserve of the United States, stated in his memoir *The Age of Turbulence* in 2008 that the root cause for the war in Iraq launched by the Bush administration was oil. Although American President Bush repeatedly denied economic desires in Iraq, the author holds that plundering oil resources was at least one of the key motives for the United States to launch the Iraq war.

3 Inflation dynamics

Internal transmission perspective

Prior to 2008, global economic development saw excessive liquidity, rising energy commodity prices, and over-speculation in financial derivatives on the bulk commodity market, triggering high global inflation. The global financial crisis in 2008 and an increasingly strong US dollar in recent years began to bring down the price of energy such as crude oil worldwide, aggravating global price volatility. In this process, the issue of a dynamic transmission mechanism of inflation which intimately related to the trend of price volatility naturally becomes the focus of policy-makers and academia. As regards the dynamic transmission problem of inflation in China, it is especially worthwhile to note why the CPI inflation rate keeps rising, and what the dynamic factors are that drive the change in the CPI inflation rate.

In view of these issues, Chinese economists have conducted studies of reference value in recent years. For example, Shi et al. (2008) studied the impact of changes in the RMB exchange rate on inflation in China and found that the appreciation of RMB after the reform of the exchange rate system in July 2005 had a material explanatory power for falling domestic inflation. Zhang and Pang (2008) held that the impact of excess liquidity triggered by RMB appreciation on inflation is more significant than the transmission effect of RMB appreciation. The study by Fan (2008) focuses on the impact of changes in money supply and salary growth on inflation, finding that the change in money supply is a principal factor causing inflation. According to the study by Zhang (2008), random monetary policy is an important influencing factor for inflation in China.

The above literature has key theoretical and practical significance for understanding the driving factors and dynamic trends of overall inflation in China. In recent years, foreign literature has begun to turn attention to the importance of the dynamic transmission characteristics of CPI sub-components for the analysis of monetary policy. For instance, the studies by Cecchetti and Debelle et al. (2006) as well as Balke and Wynne (2007) show that the dynamic transmission characteristics of CPI sub-components contain more information than the dynamic mechanism of overall CPI.

This discovery is a key revelation for analyzing the issue of the dynamic mechanism of inflation in China. In particular, an important performance characteristic of its inflation in recent years is that the change in the inflation rate of FOOD is the most prominent one of the eight sub-components of CPI inflation rate. Is the rate of changes in money supply (or changes in exchange rate, etc.) directly transmitted to the overall inflation indicator through its role in the inflation rate of the FOOD category? Or else do the monetary shocks intimately related to changes in the money supply on some sub-components of the CPI inflation rate (such as inflation rate in the FOOD category) raise the overall inflation level? In the meantime, except for a large increase in the inflation rate in the FOOD category among the eight categories for CPI inflation rate, there are relatively mild changes in the other sub-components. Does this mean that there are significant differences in the dynamic transmission characteristics of the sub-components of CPI, and different sub-components have different dynamic transmission effects on the overall CPI inflation rate?

Obviously, scientific analysis of these issues helps us gain an in-depth understanding of the dynamic transmission mechanism of inflation in China. From the perspective of monetary policy analysis, the research into the dynamic transmission mechanism of inflation classification data can provide more detailed information on the formulation of monetary policies. Furthermore, the study of classification data can reveal whether the dynamic transmission characteristics of overall inflation found in the existing literature are led by some sub-components or determined by all the components.

Given this fact, from the internal transmission perspective of price indices, this chapter concentrates on the dynamic transmission mechanism of monthly time series data on eight sub-components of CPI in China (sequence of year-on-year growth rate) from 2001 to 2008. In order to answer the above questions, we conduct a descriptive analysis of the data of eight sub-components of CPI and related statistics in the first section. In the second section, the grid-bootstrap median-unbiased estimation method is adopted to study the dynamic transmission characteristics of CPI sub-components, and shows whether the inertia characteristics of each sub-component are consistent with the overall inflation rate. In the third section, the dynamic vector model is used to analyze the dynamic transmission effect of eight sub-components of CPI on the overall inflation rate. The fourth section adopts the standard inflation–monetary policy analysis model system to compare the transmission effect of monetary policy changes and random monetary policy shocks on the CPI sub-components. The fifth section deals with the analysis of robustness. The sixth section sums up the entire chapter and discusses the implications of the findings for policies in this chapter.

3.1 Time series features of CPI in China

CPI is an aggregate indicator, reflecting the weighted average overall price level. The range of changes reflects the changes in the overall price level of consumer goods and residential services. The classification system of CPI in China was adjusted in 2001. Previously, the retail price index was generally used as an indicator to gauge the overall price level. Since 2001, an eight-category system stipulated by the National Bureau of Statistics was adopted for the CPI index, viz. food, tobacco and beverages, clothes, household and service, medicine and personal supplies, transportation and communication, recreation and education, and residence.

According to the current CPI classification system, this chapter selects the time series data on the eight categories of CPI from January 2001 to August 2008 as the main objects of analysis. The classification data of CPI (month-on-month) are derived from the National Bureau of Statistics and the CEIC database. For the sake of convenience, the eight sub-components (growth rate compared to the same period) of CPI are abbreviated as FOOD, TABACO, CLOTH, HOUSOLD, MEDICINE, TRANS, EDU, and RESIDENCE. Figure 3.1 depicts the time series of the overall CPI inflation rate and its eight major sub-components.

As can be seen from Figure 3.1, the dynamic trends of the eight sub-components of CPI exhibit distinct differences. For example, in 2002, the inflation rate of FOOD and MEDICINE showed a downward trend, while that of TABACO increased; the former increased while the latter decreased in 2003. A detailed observation of the trend since 2008 shows that the decline in inflation rate is most obvious in the FOOD category, and the inflation rate of the MEDICINE and RESIDENCE categories fell slightly, while the inflation rates for other categories increased to different degrees. On the whole, the dynamic trend of inflation rate in the FOOD category is the closest one to the overall CPI inflation rate, while the time lag among other sub-components and with the dynamic path of the overall CPI suggests that the sub-components of CPI may have different dynamic transmission on the overall CPI.

Of course, the weights of the eight sub-components of CPI in the overall CPI vary somewhat. Table 3.1 sums up the weights of the CPI's eight sub-components in the overall CPI as well as the statistics data on inflation rates in the sample including mean and median value. The statistics in Table 3.1 show that the mean (5.6%) and volatility (6.6%) of inflation rate in the FOOD category are the highest. In terms of mean value, the RESIDENCE category ranks second, followed by EDU, TABACO, and MEDICINE. Moreover, according to the weights of the sub-components of CPI inflation rate in Table 3.1, Figure 2.3 depicts the stacked column time series diagram for the weighted sub-components (the percentages in the legend indicate their respective weights). The figure clearly shows the contribution of different sub-components to the overall CPI in each period. The FOOD category contributed the most to the overall CPI in the 2004–2005 and 2007–2008 periods, while the RESIDENCE and EDU categories made the greatest contribution in other periods (Figure 3.2).

It is noteworthy that the difference in the dynamic paths of CPI and its sub-components is reflected not only in the above respects, but also in the statistical distribution characteristics. Figure 3.3 depicts the marginal distribution of CPI and its eight sub-components in a sample with 92 observed values. The probability density function uses the Epanechnikov kernel for the estimation and smoothing process. As can be seen from Figure 3.3, the difference in kurtosis and skewness of the probability density distribution of different sub-components is highly obvious. For example, the FOOD category exhibits an extreme low peak and fat tail, while the traffic category shows a sharp peak and thin tail. The overall CPI is halfway between the two.

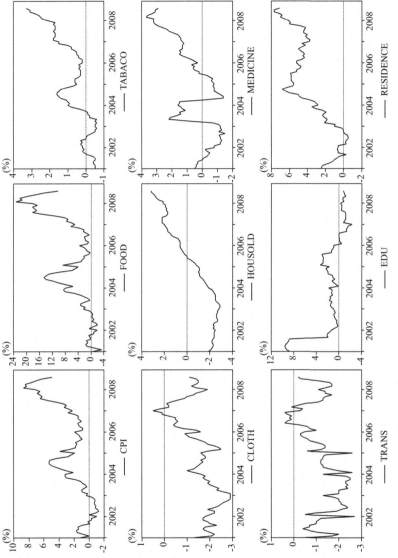

Figure 3.1 Time series of the CPI inflation rate and its eight sub-components.

Table 3.1 Weights of CPI sub-components and statistical information of the sample (%)

	Weight	Mean	Median	Max value	Min value	Standard deviation
FOOD	33.2	5.6	2.6	23.3	−3.3	6.6
TABACO	3.9	0.7	0.4	3.3	−0.6	1.0
CLOTH	9.1	−1.5	−1.7	0.5	−2.9	0.8
HOUSOLD	6.0	−0.5	−1.1	3.2	−2.9	2.0
MEDICINE	10.0	0.6	0.5	3.7	−1.5	1.4
TRANS	10.4	−1.2	−1.3	0.4	−2.7	0.8
EDU	14.2	1.3	0.9	9.6	−2.3	2.7
RESIDENCE	13.2	3.6	4.2	7.7	−0.5	2.3
Overall CPI	100	2.3	1.6	8.7	−1.3	2.5

Note: The sample interval is from January 2001 to August 2008.
Source: National Bureau of Statistics.

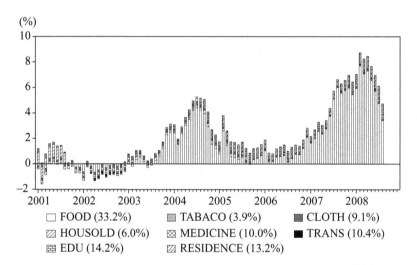

Figure 3.2 Stacked column time series diagram of the eight sub-components of the overall
CPI.

The data analysis above shows that there is a significant difference between the dynamic trend and the statistical characteristics among the CPI classification data and their comparison with the overall CPI. These different characteristics suggest that the information contained in the CPI classification sequence may be richer than the aggregated CPI data. It is therefore necessary to conduct an in-depth study into the dynamic transmission characteristics of CPI sub-components and the transmission mechanism of the overall CPI.

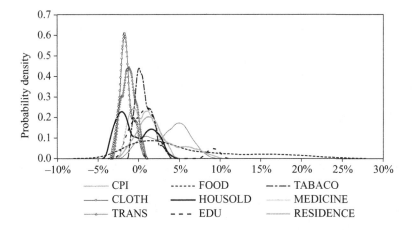

Figure 3.3 Overall CPI inflation rate and marginal distribution of the eight sub-components.

3.2 Internal dynamic transmission mechanism: Univariate model

In analyzing the dynamic transmission characteristics of CPI and its eight sub-components, the inertia characteristics of various types of inflation are particularly noteworthy. This is because the inertia of the inflation rate essentially decides the duration of response after it is subject to random shocks. The greater the inertia is, the longer the duration is. Previous studies (such as Zhang, 2008) show that the overall CPI inflation rate in China has high inertia. We hope that self-transmission differences in inflation rates of different CPI sub-components are compared through the analysis of CPI classification data.

In the field of research on inflation dynamic mechanisms, inflation inertia is generally measured using the coefficient sum of the lagged terms in the dynamic autoregressive model (AR). To this end, we first set up the AR model,

$$w_t = c + \gamma t + \rho(L)w_{t-1} + e_t \tag{3.1}$$

In which w_t represents each inflation sequence; e_t represents the random perturbation term with no serial correlation in order to capture the random shocks on CPI and its sub-components; and $\rho(L)$ represents the lag operator multinomial. The duration of lag is determined by the SIC; t represents the deterministic trend variable; whether the deterministic trend t is included in Equation 3.1 is determined by the corresponding significance test (significance level of 5%).

Under this model design, it is not hard to prove that $\rho(1)$ critically determines the inertia characteristics of inflation through the intrinsic relationship between the cumulative impulse response function and the lagged term coefficient of the AR model with $\rho(1)$. For example, according to the standard time series analysis theory, the cumulative effect (namely cumulative impulse response function (CIRF)) of a unit's random shock on w_t in Equation 3.1 can be expressed as

$$\text{CIRF} = \sum_{i=0}^{\infty} \frac{\partial w_{t+i}}{\partial e_t} = \frac{1}{1 - \rho(1)} \tag{3.2}$$

Obviously, the closer the value of $\rho(1)$ to 1, the greater the cumulative effect of random shock on w_t, and the more difficult it is to constrict CIRF.

While the representation of Equation 3.1 is simple enough, it is not easy to accurately obtain the unbiased estimate of $\rho(1)$. Statistical bias will show in estimates obtained by using traditional ordinary least squares (OLS) estimation methods (Phillips, 1977). The grid-bootstrap unbiased estimation method put forward by Hansen (1999) is adopted here to correct this problem.

In essence, this unbiased estimation method adopts the bootstrap technique to simulate the finite sample distribution of least squares estimations for a slew of possible $\rho(1)$ values, and a grid-searching method is used to compute the confidence interval of $\rho(1)$. For example, the bootstrap quantile function $q_T^*\left(\theta | \rho\right)$ is defined in the set grid-searching field; θ represents the quantile level, and T represents the sample size. The estimation and smoothing of the quantile function can be obtained using kernel regression in non-parametric estimation. Then, the grid-bootstrap confidence interval corresponding to the given confidence level β is defined for $\rho(1)$

$$C = \left\{ \rho \in R : q_T^*\left(\theta_1 | \rho\right) \leq S_T(\rho) \leq q_T^*\left(\theta_2 | \rho\right) \right\} \tag{3.3}$$

Where $\theta_1 = 1 - 0.5(1 - \beta)$, $\theta_2 = 0.5(1 - \beta)$, $S_T(\rho)$ is nondegenerate test statistics. In the actual calculation, 90% of confidence interval of the quantile function structure $\rho(1)$ in compliance with the bootstrap distribution is used, and then the median unbiased estimate of $\rho(1)$ is calculated using the 50% percentile. In the simulation process of grid-bootstrap, the number of grid points is set at 200, and the number of bootstrap simulations is 1999. The Epanechnikov kernel function is used for the estimation of quantile function. The estimation of the 90% confidence interval is corrected using the White heteroscedasticity correction standard.

Based on the above design, Table 3.2 sums up the estimation results of the dynamic inertia indicator of CPI and its classification data. For the sake of comparison, Table 3.2 also reports the estimates of grid-bootstrap and OLS, including point estimates and the 90% unbiased estimate confidence interval. It shall be noted that in order to ensure that the lag period selected for the SIC is sufficient to eliminate the serial correlation of the random perturbation term of the dynamic AR model and to ensure the reliability of results, the Breusch–Godfrey serial correlation LM test is performed on each regression equation. The (p-auto) value of the test statistics, the choice of the deterministic trend in the models, and the optimal lag period are reported in the last three columns of Table 3.2. If the p-auto value is greater than 0.05, it indicates that there is no serial correlation of the disturbance term at the significant level of 5%.

Table 3.2 Estimation results of dynamic inertia of CPI and its sub-components

	Grid-bootstrap		OLS			
	$\hat{\rho}(1)$	90% interval	$\hat{\rho}(1)$ (se)	p-auto	trend	lag
FOOD	0.985	[0.912,1.031]	0.946 (0.032)	0.77	0	2
TABACO	1.013	[0.925,1.028]	0.944 (0.030)	0.35	1	3
CLOTH	0.972	[0.909,1.026]	0.940 (0.031)	0.63	0	2
HOUSOLD	0.981	[0.947,1.010]	0.955 (0.015)	0.67	1	2
MEDICINE	0.935	[0.870,1.010]	0.900 (0.033)	0.71	1	2
TRANS	0.885	[0.772,1.017]	0.842 (0.059)	0.56	0	2
EDU	0.926	[0.737,1.057]	0.896 (0.081)	0.90	0	2
RESIDENCE	1.014	[0.921,1.040]	0.934 (0.032)	0.49	1	1
Overall CPI	1.015	[0.953,1.044]	0.970 (0.028)	0.88	0	1

Note: Trend represents the time trend variable in the AR model (1 means "containing," 0 means "does not contain"); (se) reports the White standard deviation; p-auto refers to the *p*-value of the Breusch–Godfrey serial correlation LM test; lag denotes the optimal lag period determined by the SIC.

It can be seen from the estimation results in Table 3.2 that the unbiased estimation of the overall CPI's inertia coefficient is the largest, reaching 1.015, while the point estimates of the inflation rate of MEDICINE, TRANS, and EDU are relatively small among the eight sub-components. Especially for TRANS, the point estimate is less than 0.9, while that of the MEDICINE and EDU categories are slightly larger than 0.9. The other five categories show relatively high inertia, with a corresponding unbiased estimation close or equal to 1. By comparing the grid-bootstrap and OLS's point estimates, it can be seen that the former is larger than the latter in all regressions, and the correction range of unbiased estimation is generally 3%–7%.

The above results show certain differences in the dynamic transmission characteristics of CPI sub-components. In particular, the self-transmission of inflation rates in the MEDICINE, TRANS, and EDU categories is weaker than that of other components. This shows that the duration of response varies after sub-components of CPI are affected by the shocks of their respective categories. The duration of the impact of random interference factors on the categories of RESIDENCE, TABACO, and FOOD is the longest, while that of the MEDICINE, TRANS, and EDU categories is relatively short. In general, however, whether measured by the median unbiased estimation or by the OLS estimation, the mean of CPI's inertia is higher than that of the inertia index of sub-components, and higher than the respective value of all eight categories. This indicates that there is a certain heterogeneity in self-transmission of the classification data, and the aggregated dynamic inertia characteristics of the CPI cannot reflect the inertia characteristics of the internal sub-components fully and truthfully.

3.3 Internal dynamic transmission mechanism: Vector model

As mentioned above, we have studied the dynamic transmission characteristics of each sub-component of CPI, but without involving the dynamic interaction between sub-components and with the overall CPI. It is known that the overall CPI is an overall indicator obtained from the weighted average of the eight sub-components. Evidently, there is a simple linear weighted identity relationship between CPI and its sub-components in the same statistical period. However, from the relevant data analysis, there seems to be a certain time-lag relationship between the dynamic path of different sub-components and the overall CPI trend, suggesting that there is in all probability a dynamic driving relationship between different sub-components and the overall CPI. The characteristics exhibited by this time series data are consistent with the real laws of economics. A case in point is that when FOOD prices soar after impact during the t period, the market's expectations for future inflation will also rise, thereby affecting the consumer's consumption and investment mode as well as corporate pricing models in the current period. It ultimately leads to a rise in overall CPI in the subsequent $t + 1$ period (or later). Of course, this dynamic effect may also occur between CPI and other sub-components of CPI.

In this part, we establish a dynamic vector model including eight sub-components and CPI to analyze whether there is a dynamic transmission relation between each sub-component and the overall CPI. If so, what is the model of the transmission mechanism? To this end, we establish a non-restrictive vector autoregression model (VAR), namely

$$Y_t = A(L)Y_{t-1} + \varepsilon_t \tag{3.4}$$

Where Y_t denotes a vector containing CPI and its eight major sub-components; $A(L)$ stands for a vector lag operator polynomial; ε_t represents the vector of the white Gaussian noise process consisting of nine perturbation terms; and, moreover, $E(\varepsilon_t) = O$, $var(\varepsilon_t) = \Omega$. It should be noted that variance–covariance matrix Ω is limited as the diagonal matrix, which allows correlation among random disturbance terms corresponding to different classification data and the overall CPI. Such a setting approaches reality, but there is also a certain compromise. Especially when calculating the impulse response function, it is necessary to first orthogonalize the disturbance terms in Equation 3.4 and then calculate the orthogonal impulse response function, rather than using a simple impulse response function. This will be further discussed in the analysis below.

Another key to setting up the non-restrictive VAR model is the variable order-ing. As no clear-cut economic theory exists to show how the variables in the VAR model set-up here should be ordered, the order of the CPI categories (see Table 3.1) is used as the basic order of the position of variables in the vector model. In practice, we also tried other ordering methods. As no sensitive results were found, it is not elaborated here. Thus, according to our research objectives, the dynamic transmission mechanism between the CPI sub-components and the overall CPI is analyzed in terms of impulse response and variance decomposition, respectively.

3.3.1 Impulse response analysis

For starters, whether the shock effect is transmitted to the overall CPI after the eight sub-components of CPI are subject to random shocks is analyzed through the impulse response function. As mentioned above, if a simple impulse response function is used as the basis for analysis in the VAR model, a strong hypothesis is required. Namely, when one of the disturbance term vectors changes, the change in other disturbance terms is 0. This hypothesis essentially requires the variance-covariance matrix of the perturbation terms to be a diagonal matrix. But in gen-eral, this variance-covariance matrix is not a diagonal matrix. In other words, the perturbation terms of the equations in the VAR model may be correlated to each other. Therefore, the orthogonal impulse response function is used. The basic idea of the orthogonal impulse response function is that the perturbation items with correlations are converted into an uncorrelated set of random perturbation items according to the order of the variables in the VAR model, and then the dynamic path of various variables in the model subject to the impact of 1 unit (standard deviation) of orthogonal perturbation term is calculated. The Cholesky decom-position method is used in the calculation process to orthogonalize the impulse response function by the inverse matrix of the Cholesky factor of the residual vector's variance-covariance matrix.

According to this design, Figure 3.4 sums up the dynamic response paths of the overall CPI after being subjected to random perturbation terms by different cor-responding sub-components. It can be seen that the response of CPI to the impact of different sub-components varies greatly. The shocks of the FOOD category have the highest positive impact on the overall CPI, followed by the CLOTH category, but the two have little difference in terms of the range or duration of the impact. In the initial 12 lag periods, the EDU, RESIDENCE, and MEDICINE categories have a positive impact on CPI, but the range of impact of the three categories on CPI is generally less than a quarter of that of the FOOD and CLOTH categories. It is worth noting that the impact of TRANS, TABACO, and HOUSOLD on CPI was mainly negative in the first half of the year. In other words, the random shocks within the three categories of TRANS, TABACO, and HOUSOLD will be reversely transmit-ted to CPI. In terms of the absolute level, however, only the TRANS category has a large impact, while that of the TABACO and HOUSOLD categories is small.

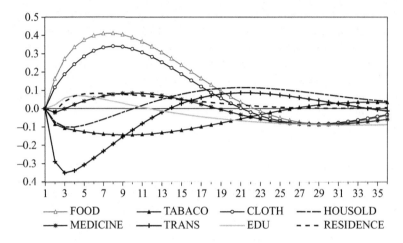

Figure 3.4 Diagram of the impulse response function of the overall CPI after being subjected to its sub-components.

3.3.2 Variance decomposition

The impulse response function can capture the dynamic influence path of one variable's shock on another variable, while the variance decomposition can decompose the forecast variance of a variable in the VAR system into each perturbation term, thus obtaining the dynamic interpretation of different perturbation factors on a certain variable fluctuation. Therefore, the variance decomposition can be used to learn about the extent to which the variance of the impact factor corresponding to the overall CPI can be explained by other random perturbation items, so as to obtain the relative contribution of the perturbation factor of each sub-component to the overall CPI fluctuation range. From this, the relative importance of the impact factor of each sub-component to the overall CPI in the VAR model at different times can be learned.

The calculation of variance decomposition can be realized through the mutual transformation of the VAR model and vector moving–average model (VMA). Essentially, the forecast analytic expression of variable Y in the future h period is obtained by using the vector coefficient matrix in the VAR model. Then, the transformed VMA model is used to obtain the mean square error corresponding to the predicted value of Y in the future h period. Finally, the contribution of the i-th orthogonal disturbance term to the mean square error of the forecast value of Y in the future h period is calculated.

According to such a design, Figure 3.5 depicts the quantified results of the variance decomposition. It can be seen that the forecast variance corresponding to the overall CPI occurs in the first six lag periods. The TRANS category has the strongest forecast explanatory power, followed by the FOOD category. The CLOTH category contributes significantly to the overall CPI's variance decomposition,

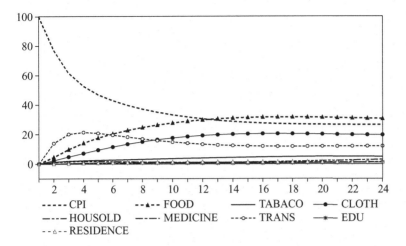

Figure 3.5 Variance decomposition of the overall CPI.

while the contribution of the other five categories is basically negligible. It is noteworthy that the FOOD category contributes more than the TRANS category after the sixth period and maintains the highest contribution rate. After the ninth period, the contribution of the variance decomposition of the TRANS category is further reduced, and is surpassed by that of the CLOTH category. On the whole, the shocks corresponding to the FOOD, CLOTH, and TRANS categories are the main contributing factors for the variance prediction of CPI, while the contribution of other sub-components is small.

3.4 Dynamic transmission mechanism from monetary policy to CPI components

In the above analysis, the transmission mechanism of CPI's internal classification data on the overall CPI's inflation rate is examined. The vector analysis system is established based on the internal sub-components of CPI. In this section, the original vector model is extended to the monetary policy analysis model system, while introducing monetary policy, economic output's growth rate, and other external variables that potentially affect inflation. The dynamic impact of CPI sub-components is analyzed in terms of the changes in monetary policies and the random impact of monetary policies.

To this end, this chapter analyzes whether there is Granger causality between the changes in monetary policies (such as the growth rate of money supply) and the sub-components of CPI in the expanded dynamic vector system. Then, this chapter analyzes how the sub-components of CPI respond to the random impact of monetary policies and the degree of response. As the expanded vector model system increases the monetary policy variable, and also considers other external variables that may affect the inflation rate, the VAR model is correspondingly changed to

$$Y_t = A(L)Y_{t-1} + BX_t + \varepsilon_t \tag{3.5}$$

Where vector Y contains four variables (all variables are in the form of year-on-year growth rate), and follows the order from industrial output's growth rate, inflation rate indicator, growth rate of M2, to the real effective exchange rate. The data on industrial output's growth rate, growth rate of M2, and the real effective exchange rate are obtained from the CEIC database, the People's Bank of China, and the International Financial Statistics.

The core basis for the establishment of Equation 3.5 is the standard IS-LM [investment–saving (IS) and liquidity preference–money supply (LM)] model, a theoretical model for monetary policy analysis. Within this analytical framework, monetary policies act on economic output, which acts on inflation. The change in inflation in turn promotes the monetary authorities to adjust monetary policies, thus forming a dynamic interactive system. For instance, under the loose monetary policy, money supply grows, investment increases, and economic output increases accordingly. The growth rate of economic output substantially reflects the gap between actual output and potential output. The larger the gap is, the greater the inflationary pressure accumulates. A change in inflation will prompt the central bank to adjust monetary policies. When the degree of interest rate liberalization is still relatively low, academic circles generally use the growth rate of money supply as a representative indicator variable of monetary policies. In order to be consistent with the existing literature (such as Fan, 2008) and ensure comparability, this chapter also uses M2 growth rate as a representative of monetary policy variability. In addition, since the exchange rate mechanism in China is not determined by other variables in the system within the sample interval studied herein, the real effective exchange rate can be set as an external variable. Below, this model is used to examine the dynamic transmission mechanism for the random impact of the changes in monetary policy and the monetary policy on the sub-components of CPI.

3.4.1 Dynamic impact of changes in monetary policies on CPI's sub-components

The examination of the dynamic impact of changes in monetary policy on the sub-components of CPI is actually to test whether the lag terms of M2's growth rate in the VAR model has a dynamic driving effect on the inflation rate of all sub-components. The Granger causality test is used for this test. According to the definition of the Granger causality test, the null hypothesis is that the growth rate in M2 is not the Granger causality of the inflation rate. Therefore, if the p-value corresponding to the test statistic is less than the pre-set significance level (such as 1%), the null hypothesis is rejected.

Table 3.3 shows the results of the Granger causality test. From the p-value in the test results, the Granger causality between the growth rate in M2 and the

Table 3.3 Results of Granger causality test of CPI sub-
components with growth rate in M2

Null hypothesis: M2 growth rate is not the Granger cause of the following variables	p-*value*
Inflation rate of FOOD category	0.318
Inflation rate of TABACO category	0.000***
Inflation rate of CLOTH category	0.895
Inflation rate of HOUSOLD category	0.966
Inflation rate of MEDICINE category	0.968
Inflation rate of TRANS category	0.002***
Inflation rate of EDU category	0.394
Inflation rate of RESIDENCE category	0.075

Note: *** indicates that the test results have statistical
significance at the significance level of 1%; the lag period for
each VAR model is determined by the SIC.

inflation of the TABACO and TRANS categories is significant at the significance level of 1%; the impact on the inflation of the RESIDENCE category is only significant at the significance level of 10%, and is not significant for other sub-components of CPI, including the inflation rate in the FOOD category. This shows that the monetary policy is not significant in the Granger causality test of the five sub-components of CPI such as FOOD. The econometric implications of Granger causality deserve special attention here. The Granger causality test does not have statistical significance, indicating that monetary policy has no dynamic forecast effect on the inflation rate of the FOOD category (and inflation rates for other categories). In other words, changes in monetary policies do not provide sufficient forecast information for the future dynamic trend of these sub-indicators, suggesting that the dynamic driving effect of changes in monetary policies is not obvious for sub-components such as FOOD.

3.4.2 *Dynamic impact of monetary policy shock on CPI sub-components*

In analyzing the dynamic impact of the random shocks of monetary policy on the sub-components of CPI, this chapter uses the Cholesky decomposition method to orthogonally decompose the impulse response function. If, after orthogonal decomposition, the orthogonal perturbation factor corresponding to the M2's growth rate is positive, it means the shock of a loose monetary policy; if it is negative, it corresponds to the shock of a tight monetary policy. Therefore, it is possible to analyze the dynamic transmission effect of monetary policy shocks on eight sub-components in inflation through the impulse response functions of the CPI sub-components after being subjected to monetary policy shock. For the sake of comparison, this chapter also reports the dynamic response of the overall CPI after the shock of monetary policy.

Figure 3.6 depicts the dynamic response path of CPI and its eight sub-components after being subjected to random shock of monetary policy. It can be clearly

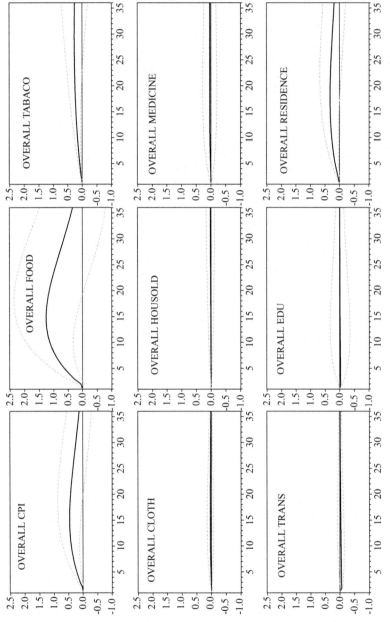

Figure 3.6 Impulse response of the overall CPI and its sub-components upon receiving the impact of the disturbance term of the M2 growth rate.

seen from this that the inflation rate in the FOOD category reacts most strongly after the shock, which gradually weakens after 12 periods. Interestingly, although the overall CPI and inflation rate in the FOOD category show an obvious dynamic response to random monetary policy shocks, the inflation rate of the FOOD category has a higher response than the overall CPI, indicating that unpredictable changes in monetary policy have a higher dynamic transmission effect on the inflation rate of the FOOD category. Further observation of the response of other sub-components of CPI shows that the inflation rate in the RESIDENCE category also has an obvious dynamic response; while the inflation rate of the TABACO category shows a certain response, the response rate is relatively slow; the remaining sub-components have a weak dynamic response to the random shocks of monetary policy.

3.5 Structural change and its effect

In the aforementioned analysis of the dynamic transmission mechanism of inflation, this chapter does not consider whether the model established has structural changes in the research sample. However, studies by Levin and Piger (2004), Cecchetti and Debelle (2006), and Clark (2006) show that if a structural change exists in the sample, the dynamic transmission mechanism of inflation is highly sensitive to this structural change. It is therefore necessary to test whether there is structural change in the model in the research sample. However, it is noted that known breaking points must be assumed for the use of the traditional Chow test. The developments of unknown breaking point stability tests in recent years provide a more rational design for this chapter to analyze whether there is structural change in the dynamic mechanism of inflation. In particular, the unknown breaking point structural change test proposed by Andrews (1993) has sound theoretical development. This chapter uses Andrews' method to judge whether the various dynamic models of inflation as mentioned above have structural changes, thereby judging the robustness of the empirical analysis results in this chapter.

According to Andrews' theory, assuming that the coefficient matrix Φ in $m \times 1$ order represents the parameter in any dynamic model of inflation, there is $\Phi = \Phi_1$ at $t < k$, and there is $\Phi = \Phi_2 (\Phi_1 \neq \Phi_2)$ at $t \geq k$, and it meets the condition $m \leq k \leq T - m$, in which T represents the size of the overall sample. Moreover, assuming that the search domain of the unknown structure breaking point parameter is τ and that the middle 70% of the sample T is usually set, we first calculate a series of Wald test statistic $W_T(\tau_i)$ corresponding to all possible breaking points $k = T\tau_i$ in the region; the null hypothesis of this statistic test is that parameters do not undergo structural change when the structural breaking point is k. It is not difficult to see that for the null hypothesis, this unknown breaking point parameter k does not appear, but appears only under the alternative hypothesis. Such a parameter is called the interference parameter in the statistical test. After $W_T(\tau_i)$ is obtained, the *SupW* statistic is then calculated, namely

$$SupW = SupW_T(\tau_i)\big|\tau_i \in [\tau_{min}, \tau_{max}]$$ (3.6)

If the *SupW* statistic is statistically significant, the time point of its corresponding breakpoint is the change time point when the structural change occurs.

It should be noted that because of the existence of interference parameters, it is necessary to construct the *p*-value calculation function that can capture non-standard distributions in order to obtain the correct concomitant probability in the process of calculating the test statistic of structural change in unknown breaking points. Therefore, Hansen's (1997) non-standard distribution function is used to calculate the *p*-value corresponding to the *SupW* statistic. The progressive *p*-value calculation function corresponding to the test statistic of unknown breaking point under such non-standard distribution conditions can be expressed as

$$p(x|\theta) = 1 - \chi^2\left(\theta_0 + \theta_1 x + \ldots + \theta_m x^m \,\big|\eta\right)$$ (3.7)

Where $x^2(z|\eta)$ represents the cumulative chi-square distribution with a degree of freedom of η, namely

$$x^2(z|\eta) = \int_0^z \frac{\omega^{-1+(\eta/2)} e^{-\omega/2}}{\Gamma(\eta/2) 2^{\eta/2}} \, d\omega$$ (3.8)

The polynomial $\theta_0 + \theta_1 x + \ldots + \theta_m x^m$ is first determined through the quantile estimation method, and the loss function and the quantile function related to the *p*-value is then calculated. In the actual calculation process, the corresponding *p*-value is calculated using the heteroscedasticity correction matrix of the model under unconstrained conditions.

According to the method stated above, Table 3.4 sums up the overall parameter stability test results of three types of dynamic regression models discussed in this

Table 3.4 Stability test result of unknown breaking points in dynamic regression model: *p*-value of SupW statistic

	AR model equations	VAR model equations of CPI sub-components	VAR model equations of monetary policy
FOOD	0.560	1.000	1.000
TABACO	0.939	1.000	0.997
CLOTH	0.680	1.000	1.000
HOUSOLD	0.913	1.000	0.864
MEDICINE	0.656	0.999	0.994
TRANS	0.749	1.000	0.999
EDU	0.840	0.708	1.000
RESIDENCE	0.127	1.000	1.000
Overall CPI	0.106	1.000	1.000

chapter. Judging from the *p*-value corresponding to the test statistic, the *p*-values corresponding to all regression equations are greater than 0.05, indicating that there is no structural change in the tested model at the significance level of 5%, proving the robustness of the empirical results.

In practice, we also examined the impact of increasing the supply shock variable (rate of change in oil prices) on the test results of the monetary policy's VAR model on the basis of the recommendations of Hamilton (1996), but the basic results do not show sensitivity. Moreover, in all dynamic vector model analysis, we check whether the characteristic root of the characteristic equation corresponding to the VAR model meets the condition of the stationary VAR model (the characteristic root is within the unit circle), and the stationary conditions are confirmed.

3.6 Conclusions

Although the dynamic transmission mechanism of overall inflation is important for the analysis of monetary policy, an in-depth understanding of the dynamic transmission characteristics of inflation classification data also has great practical significance for the formulation and implementation of monetary policies. Given that CPI sub-components in China have great differences in dynamic trends in recent years, this chapter focuses on the study of three aspects of the dynamic transmission mechanism of CPI sub-components: Firstly, the dynamic transmission characteristics of CPI's eight sub-components; secondly, the dynamic transmission effect of CPI sub-components on the overall CPI; and thirdly, the dynamic impact of monetary policy and monetary policy shocks on sub-components of CPI. In order to ensure the authenticity and reliability of the research results, this chapter uses the new median-unbiased estimation method and the standard dynamic vector model to explore and analyze the related problems, and performs the robustness test on the research results.

Through the above methods, this chapter draws the conclusions below. Firstly, the inflation inertia of different sub-components of CPI varies, indicating that there is heterogeneity in the dynamic transmission mechanism of the classification data. The self-transmission of the MEDICINE, TRANS, and EDU categories is relatively weak. Secondly, the dynamic transmission effect of CPI sub-components on overall CPI varies. Of these, the FOOD and CLOTH categories have the most obvious positive transmission on the CPI, and also the highest variance forecasting contribution to the changes in CPI. Thirdly, the changes in monetary policies are not significant for a majority of CPI classification data. It is particularly noteworthy that the impact on the inflation rate of the FOOD and RESIDENCE categories is not statistically significant; the random shocks of monetary policies will not significantly affect the inflation rate of the FOOD and RESIDENCE categories in the short term. As the random shocks of monetary policy can be essentially viewed as an unpredictable change in monetary policy, an unexpected loose monetary policy shock will result in a significant increase in the inflation rate of the FOOD and RESIDENCE categories. It only gradually weakens after one year or so.

It is not difficult to see from the above conclusion that although the FOOD category has the greatest weight in the overall CPI in China and is the paramount dynamic driver of CPI's internal transmission, monetary policy per se does not have a significant dynamic driving effect on the inflation rate of the FOOD category. This shows that the change in current monetary policy has a limited transmission effect on inflation. Therefore, judging from the perspective of the effective transmission of monetary policies, the foundation is laid for the effective transmission of monetary policy by accelerating the marketization of interest rates as appropriate and realizing the gradual transition from aggregate regulation to interest rate adjustment.

4 Inflation dynamics

Upstream and downstream transmission perspective

4.1 Price chain transmission mechanism

In recent years, China's CPI has seen obvious fluctuations, and the national economy has been buffeted by fluctuations in the CPI inflation rate to varying degrees in such spheres as production, consumption, and investment. In view of this, CPI attracts the most attention from the public and decision-makers as an inflation indicator, and is also the focus of study in other chapters herein. However, CPI is merely one of the many links in the national economy (namely the consumption link). Change in CPI only mirrors the price trend in the consumption sector, and is the downstream price index in the production–consumption chain. The price indices of other links such as industrial production are equally crucial for national economic development and the formulation of macroeconomic policies.

At the same time, whether there is a dynamic transmission effect among different price indices in the chain from production to consumption has great significance for the dynamic adjustment of macroeconomic policies. For instance, if the upstream producer price index (PPI) has a significant dynamic effect on CPI, and if the PPI is high but the CPI has no significant increase, the decision-makers can determine the future policy orientation according to the dynamic aging and the degree of quantification drive between the two, so as to achieve effective forward-looking policy regulation. Obviously, the dynamic transmission mechanism among price indices at different stages is an important topic for in-depth study in the macroeconomic analysis field.

This problem was recently noticed by some scholars. For example, He (2008) specifically studied the driving orientation between PPI and CPI from 2001 to 2008. The empirical results show that the downstream CPI is the one-way-Granger cause for the upstream PPI. This means that the ebb and flow of consumer prices in China take place before the change in industrial production prices. The change in CPI has a forecasting effect on the dynamic trend of PPI, while the change in PPI has no significant forecasting effect on CPI. It is somewhat surprising that the downstream price is transmitted to the upstream price.

For this, He (2008) explained that this result suggests that the role of the factor at the demand level is greater than that at the supply level in terms of influencing the domestic inflation rate measured by CPI. But this explanation still needs further discussion. Even if the demand factor has dominance in the pricing mechanism, it cannot explain the basic price transmission law. According to the basic law of price transmission, the fluctuations of the overall price level generally occur in the production field first, and then spread midstream and downstream through the industrial chain, and finally to the price of consumer goods. Therefore, the PPI that mirrors the price level of the production link should have a certain dynamic impact on the CPI reflecting the price level of the consumption link.

Of course, as CPI includes the price of the consumer goods, and also the price of services, it is not completely consistent with the PPI in terms of statistical caliber. It is possible that PPI and CPI are temporarily inconsistent. However, if the law of transmission of PPI and CPI continues to be in a state of deviation, it is not in line with the law of price transmission. Moreover, in the dynamic model that analyzes the dynamic transmission of different price indices, the inclusion of PPI and CPI alone may not fully reflect the dynamic interaction effect between price indices at different stages, thus weakening the robustness of empirical results. More importantly, He et al. (2008) ignored the treatment of the non-stationarity of the price sequence in the Granger causality test. The statistical inference of the test statistic is therefore invalid. This will be discussed in detail in the empirical analysis.

Shenyin & Wanguo Institute (2008) also focused on studying the interaction between PPI and CPI, but the conclusions drawn are inconsistent with the results of the study by He et al. (2008). Shenyin & Wanguo Institute holds that the period before 2003 was one of deflation. Therefore, the year 2003 is used as a dividing point, and the simple correlation analysis method is used to judge the transmission relationship between PPI and CPI in 1996–2002 and 2003–2008. It was found that the PPI changed before CPI before 2003, but the change in PPI lagged behind the change in CPI after 2003. The main conclusion is that the impact of changes in PPI on CPI has been reflected in CPI in the current period, with little effect on future CPI. However, it must be noted that the use of deflation or inflation as the division point for the analysis of the dynamic path characteristic of the inflation rate lacks a scientific and rigorous statistical theory basis. Moreover, simple correlation analysis cannot show whether there is a significant dynamic transmission relationship between different price indices. Of course, the analysis by Shenyin & Wanguo Institute also did not fully consider the dynamic effect among prices at different stages.

In order for the research conclusion to be comprehensive, it is necessary to expand and deepen the existing research. As the statistical system for price indices in various links in China improves, there are distinctively different price indices in the different links from purchase, to production, to circulation, to consumption. For example, there is the raw material purchase price index (RMPI) for the raw material purchase link; PPI for the industrial production chain; corporate goods price index (CGPI) for the enterprise commodity wholesale link;

and the familiar CPI for the consumption chain. The price statistics indicators in different links cover the price level of the national economy from the purchase of raw materials, to industrial production, to corporate wholesale, to household consumption, resulting in a relatively complete price statistics index system. The establishment and development of these price indices not only provide an important guarantee for the national economic accounting, but also offer useful information on macroeconomic analysis and the formulation of macroeconomic policies.

For the aforementioned four price indices, the order in the value chain is as follows: Firstly, a company buys raw materials for production, then the products are produced, before entering the commodity transactions and other intermediate circulation links; products finally enter the consumption field. Therefore, RMPI is upstream of PPI, and PPI is upstream of CGPI, while CPI is downstream of the chain. Therefore, the order is as follows: RMPI, PPI, CGPI, and CPI. If the upstream, midstream, and downstream price transmission mechanism follows the traditional hierarchical order, the change in RMPI will cause the PPI to change, and lead to a change in CGPI, and promote the change in CPI. Of course, the dynamic transmission relationship among different prices may not be as simple as we intuitively see. For example, when a specific external shock causes CPI to rise, the market's expectations for the future may significantly affect the pricing of raw materials and industrial products, thus resulting in the reverse dynamic transmission of downstream price CPI to the upstream and midstream price.

It can be seen that there are both conceptual differences and intimate connection between price indices at different stages corresponding to the raw material purchase, corporate production, and household consumption. Therefore, it is possible to provide a reliable scientific basis for determining the future trend of overall price fluctuations by studying whether there is a dynamic transmission relationship between the upstream, midstream, and downstream price indices as well as the driving direction among these. Relevant studies in foreign literature (such as Weinhagen, 2005; Frey and Manera, 2007) also verify this point.

In addition, raw material purchase, corporate production, and household consumption correspond to different stages of production and consumption, but studies are rarely conducted by the academic community on the effects of the driving mechanism of monetary factors on prices at different stages.[1] Whether it is the transmission mechanism among the upstream, midstream, and downstream prices or the driving mechanism of currency for different prices, it is crucial for judging the trend of overall price fluctuations and the direction of monetary policies in the future.

Given this, this chapter carries out a more in-depth study on the dynamic transmission mechanism of multiple price indices at different stages on the basis of the existing research. Specifically, the analyzed inflation indicators are extended to four different types of price indices in the upstream, midstream, and downstream, corresponding to national economic development and four links of consumption, namely raw material purchase, industrial production, corporate commodity wholesale, and consumption. On this basis, this chapter focuses on the following three issues: Firstly, is there a stable dynamic driving relationship between the inflation rates of upstream, midstream, and downstream price indices? Secondly, what is the dynamic prediction and driving mechanism for different price indices? Thirdly, on what types of price index inflation rates does the money supply have a significant direct driving effect?

The answers to these three questions have a direct bearing on how to judge the overall trend of price fluctuations in China in the years to come. At the same time, an in-depth analysis of the above three issues provides decision-makers with information on the dynamic driving effects of various kinds of price index inflation rates in China, thus helping relevant decision-makers better utilize scientific judgment and make decisions in the formulation of policies. Moreover, the driving relationship (namely direct driving and indirect driving) between the money supply and the inflation rate of various price indices provides an important empirical basis for judging the trend of macroeconomic decisions under the current circumstances.

In terms of structural arrangement, the remaining sections of this chapter are organized as follows: Section 4.2 offers a descriptive analysis of the dynamic path of the inflation rates for four different types of price indices in China. Section 4.3 builds the multivariate dynamic model system based on four types of price indices, and carries out the co-integration test, error correction, and Granger causality test. Section 4.4 describes the significance and implications of the empirical results for current macroeconomic governance. The monetary factor is added to the existing dynamic model system. The analysis focuses on different driving effects of the monetary growth rate on the inflation rate of the upstream, midstream, and downstream price indices. Section 4.5 sums up the contents of this chapter.

4.2 Time series features of different price indices

4.2.1 Data description

The four types of price indices examined in this section are RMPI, PPI, CGPI, and CPI. In order to better analyze the dynamic transmission mechanism among various price indices, the authors first briefly introduce the basic composition and connotations of the four types of price indices, and the content and statistical caliber of different indicators.

Firstly, RMPI is calculated based on the prices of the different materials (nearly 500 kinds of products in 9 categories including raw materials, ferrous metals, and non-ferrous materials) consumed in the industrial sector, and is an index that reflects the fluctuations in prices of materials (raw materials purchased) consumed by industrial enterprises for production activities.

Secondly, PPI is calculated based on the ex-factory price of all industrial products, and the accounting basis is the price of raw materials used to manufacture and produce consumer goods. At present, there are over 4,000 kinds of products in 39 industrial sectors covered by the accounting process of China's PPI. PPI is an index that measures the trend and degree of fluctuations in the ex-factory price of industrial products.

Thirdly, CGPI is calculated based on the prices of centralized transactions of commodities between enterprises, and is an index that reflects the changes in the wholesale prices of physical commodity transactions between domestic enterprises.[2]

Fourthly, CPI is a most commonly used price index, and is calculated according to the prices of a given basket of consumer goods (including food, tobacco and beverages, apparel, household equipment and services, medical care and personal products, transportation and communications, recreation, education and cultural goods, and housing). It is an important price index that reflects the prices of products and services related to residents' lives. The rate of change in CPI is an important indicator usually used to observe the overall inflation level of the national economy, and also an important basis for the Chinese government to formulate and adjust macroeconomic policies.

From the above introduction, it can be seen that the four types of price indices are divided according to the upstream, midstream, and downstream levels. RMPI and PPI belong to upstream prices, CGPI can be classified as the midstream price, and CPI belongs to the downstream price. As mentioned above, one of the focuses of this chapter is to explore the dynamic transmission mechanism between these upstream, midstream, and downstream prices, providing a scientific basis for the formulation and analysis of macroeconomic policies.

In terms of sources of data, the raw data for the four types of price indices are obtained from the National Bureau of Statistics and the People's Bank of China, and the sample interval is from January 1998 to June 2009.[3] It needs to be noted that the various statistics of price indices published in China are generally based on the results that the index for the same month or same period in the previous year is 100. The four types of price indices here are essentially the growth rate of the price index (namely inflation), rather than an index indicator in a strict sense. In the discussion below, for the sake of explanation, the authors use RMPI, PPI, CGPI, and CPI to represent the price indices of the above four categories, respectively, and all price indices are in essence in the form of inflation rate. Because the data of all price indices are based on the same month of the previous year (namely year-on-year growth rate), the data are no longer seasonally adjusted in the empirical analysis.

4.2.2 Dynamic path description of sub-components of different price indices

In order to examine the composition of different price indices, Table 4.1 sums up the composition of sub-components in the inflation rate of four price indices as well as the statistics corresponding to the sub-component such as mean, median, maximum value, minimum value, and standard deviation. As can be seen from the basic statistical information reported in Table 4.1, there are quite obvious differences in statistical characteristics among the sub-components of each price index. For instance, of the eight categories of CPI, the food category has the largest price fluctuations (standard deviation), generally three to six times the other sub-components. The sub-components of CPI have big differences in statistics such as mean, maximum value, and minimum value. This difference is also reflected in the other three price indices.

Moreover, the second column in Table 4.1 also describes the weights of each sub-component of different price indices in their respective composition. As there is no official data on weighting, the authors use the simple OLS method to fit the weight coefficient for the four price indices. In the case of CPI, for example, the fitted weighted results show that of the eight sub-components of CPI, the food category ranks first in weight, accounting for 33%, followed by housing (15%), entertainment, education and cultural supplies and services (13.4%), transportation and communications (12.4%), medical care and personal products (9.2%), apparel (8.4%), tobacco and supplies (5.7%), and household equipment and services (2.9%). This result is basically consistent with the information published by the National Bureau of Statistics in 2006.[4] For the other three price indices, the highest weighted of the PPI is the means of production (65.7%), the highest weighted of the CGPI is the price of investment goods (35.9%), and the highest weighted of the RMPI is the price of the fuel and energy category (23.8%).

In order to better observe the dynamic evolution path of sub-components of different price indices, Figure 4.1 depicts the dynamic paths of the four price indices and their respective sub-components (weighted). The dynamic trend of each price index is obviously dominated by the sub-component with the highest weight. For example, the food category price index (in the form of inflation rate) in the CPI leads the overall trend of CPI most of the time.

However, it is noteworthy that the impact of the housing category price on the trend of overall CPI was greatly improved after 2004. Especially in the first half of 2009, the price index of the housing category had a greater impact on the overall CPI than the price in the food category. It is known that the price of the housing category includes the cost of building and decoration materials, rent, property management fees, maintenance fees, and other expenses. This shows that as China's real estate market develops, the impact of housing prices intimately related to the housing market on the dynamic trend of the CPI is becoming increasingly prominent.

From the charts of the dynamic trend of the other three price indices and their sub-components, it can be seen that the overall PPI is chiefly affected by the price index of the means of production. The impact of the price of the means of livelihood and heavy industrial products on the overall PPI increased somewhat after 2008. For CGPI and RMPI, the overall trend is dominated by the respective three to four sub-components, because this is chiefly decided by the weight distribution characteristics of their respective sub-components.

On balance, the classification of the constituent elements of the four price indices shows a common law – the greater the weight of the sub-components,

Table 4.1 Composition of sub-components of the inflation rate for the four price indexes and their statistical description (%)

	Weight	Mean	Median	Max value	Min value	Standard deviation
CPI	100	2.21	1.60	8.70	−1.60	2.51
Food	33	5.35	2.80	23.3	−3.30	6.45
Tobacco and beverages	5.7	0.84	0.50	3.40	−0.60	1.08
Apparel	8.4	−1.58	−1.70	0.50	−2.90	0.76
Household equipment and services	2.9	−0.27	−0.70	3.40	−2.90	2.05
Medical care and personal products	9.2	0.71	0.70	3.70	−1.50	1.41
Transportation and communication	12.4	−1.25	−1.30	0.40	−3.00	0.84
Entertainment, education, cultural goods and services	13.4	1.16	0.80	9.60	−2.30	2.66
Housing	15	3.17	4.00	7.70	−4.80	2.76
PPI	100	2.43	2.87	10.06	−7.20	3.86
Light industry products	0.5	0.46	0.50	4.55	−3.60	2.11
Heavy industry products	6.2	4.28	4.62	15.01	−10.94	5.79
Means of production	65.7	3.18	3.45	11.95	−8.84	4.69
Means of livelihood	27.6	0.34	−0.30	5.48	−2.90	2.11
CGPI	100	2.68	2.30	10.30	−7.60	4.35
Investment products	35.9	2.85	3.20	11.20	−8.90	4.55
Consumer goods	13.9	2.30	0.60	10.80	−4.70	4.33
Agricultural products	11.6	4.42	2.70	18.35	−5.60	6.42
Mineral products	0.7	7.72	9.00	23.50	−15.00	8.33
Coal, oil, and electricity	3.8	8.13	7.74	26.80	−12.90	9.56
Processing industry products	34.1	1.34	1.07	8.00	−7.90	3.63
RMPI	100	4.68	4.88	15.39	−10.37	5.79
Fuel and power category	23.8	7.75	5.90	30.85	−14.47	9.19
Ferrous metal	14.9	6.18	4.00	26.89	−17.58	9.44
Non-ferrous metals and wires	6.2	7.14	6.02	38.79	−31.85	15.30
Chemical raw materials	21.7	2.76	2.99	14.30	−9.85	5.36
Wood and pulp	−4.5	1.83	2.29	6.71	−4.02	2.17
Building materials and non-metallic mines	6.8	2.46	2.30	12.84	−3.00	3.64
Other industrial raw materials	8.2	1.40	1.51	7.10	−3.21	2.68
Agricultural and sideline products	10.7	4.28	4.30	17.50	−8.55	5.96
Textile raw materials	12.2	1.44	1.60	5.80	−3.89	2.53

Note: The sample interval is from January 2001 to June 2009, and the weight is the OLS (non-constant term) estimate with the sum of coefficients limited to 1.

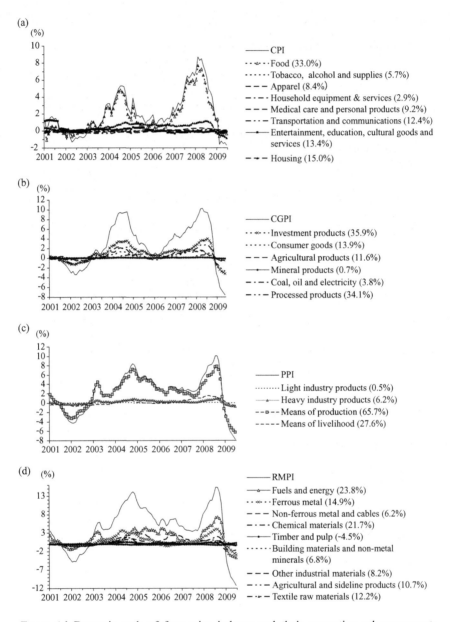

Figure 4.1 Dynamic path of four price indexes and their respective sub-components (weighted): January 2001–June 2009.

the greater the impact of the changes in the sub-components on the trend of the overall price index. From this perspective, it is necessary to focus on the dynamic trend of the components with larger weight in the overall index composition while managing and regulating the overall price level in the future. In this connection, a detailed analysis of the CPI and inflation rate is carried out. An important part for further study in the future is to explore the characteristics of the sub-component's dynamic mechanism in the other three price indices.

4.2.3 Description of overall path of four price indices

The dynamic trend of the sub-components of the overall price index can provide useful information for analyzing the corresponding specific price index. However, the dynamic driving relationship among different price indices is more important for judging the overall inflation trend, and is the focus of this chapter. Therefore, after having examined the composition of the sub-components of different price indices and the corresponding dynamic path, the authors analyze the overall dynamic path of the four price indices. Figure 4.2 shows the comparison of time series charts of CPI, PPI, CGPI, and RMPI data from January 1998 to June 2009. In order to better distinguish the dynamic paths of the different price indices, the authors prepare the column form for CPI for a clearer comparison of the other three price indices with CPI in each period.

From Figure 4.2, it can be seen that there are significant differences in the dynamic paths of different price indices. For instance, PPI, CGPI, and RMPI were generally lower than CPI before 2000, especially RMPI. In 2000–2001, there was a significant change in the dynamic trend of different price indices. PPI and RMPI reached their first peaks in their respective analysis samples in middle and late

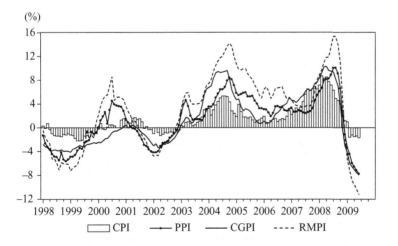

Figure 4.2 Inflation rate of China's four price indexes: January 1998–June 2009.
Source: National Bureau of Statistics, People's Bank of China.

2000, corresponding to 5% and 8%, respectively, while CPI and CGPI were still in a slow climb phase in this period. Although CPI began to show positive growth in early 2000, the highest value did not exceed 2%, while the basic level of CGPI showed a negative number.

It is generally held in the academic community that during this period, the Chinese economy experienced deflation, and the government implemented a proactive fiscal policy and monetary policy on deflation.

Since 2003, however, the dynamic evolution of the upstream, midstream, and downstream price indices sees another noticeable change. A closer observation of Figure 4.2 shows that from 2003 to early 2007, the increase in CPI generally lags behind the other three prices, but the decrease in CPI seems to be earlier than other prices. After 2007, CGPI growth is still ahead of CPI, but the upward trend of PPI and RMPI lagged behind CPI, and this trend continued into early 2008. It is noteworthy that after 2009, the upstream and midstream prices (e.g. RMPI, PPI, and CGPI) fell before CPI, and the decrease far exceeded that of CPI. From the entire sample interval, the range of decrease and increase in upstream product prices (RMPI and PPI) was significantly greater than that of midstream price (CGPI) and downstream price (CPI). This has been verified by volatility indicator (standard deviation) of each price index in Table 4.1.

The dynamic paths of differences shown by the different price indices in Figure 4.2 reflect the changes in prices of different commodities at different stages in different periods. However, from the overall trend, the dynamic evolution of the inflation indicators of the four categories is relatively similar, with troughs in 1999, 2002, 2006, and 2009, and peaks in 2000, 2003, 2005, and 2008. From the mean, maximum value, and minimum value corresponding to the price indices of four categories in Table 4.1, as well as the standard deviation statistic measuring the degree of volatility, we can also see that the mean of RMPI is the highest (4.68%), while the other three price indices are similar (2–3%). The statistical information in Table 4.1 also shows that the maximum value of RMPI reached 15.39% in 1998–2009, followed by CGPI, PPI, and CPI.

4.2.4 Stationary test of data

In addition, we performed the stationarity (unit root) test on the four price indices. In practice, we test whether the inflation rate series of four price indices contain deterministic trends (namely time trend). The traditional ADF unit root test and the Phillips–Peron (PP) test indicate that the time trend hypothesis is rejected. Therefore, the models corresponding to the unit root test do not contain a time trend variable. Table 4.2 summarizes the unit root test results of the four price indices and their first difference items. As the PP test results are wholly consistent with the ADF test results, Table 4.2 only reports the results of the ADF test.

As can be seen from Table 4.2, the ADF unit root test is performed on the original sequence of the four price indices, which shows that the *p*-values of the corresponding statistics are all greater than 5% (ADF test in the first column).

Table 4.2 Unit root test results of China's four price indexes: January 1998–June 2009

ADF test		ADF test		Conclusion
CPI	0.488	ΔCPI	0.000	CPI is I(1)
PPI	0.221	ΔPPI	0.000	PPI is I(1)
CGPI	0.054	ΔCGPI	0.013	CGPI is I(1)
RMPI	0.135	ΔRMPI	0.000	RMPI is I(1)

Note: The null hypothesis of the ADF test is that the variable contains a unit root; the table reports the concomitant probability (*p*-value) corresponding to the test statistic, and I(1) represents the integrated of order one.

indicating that the null hypothesis that each price index contains a unit root cannot be rejected at the significance level of 5%.[5] After the first difference and unit root test are performed on each price index sequence, the *p*-value corresponding to the test statistic (ADF test in the second column) is less than 5%, and these values are less than 1% except ΔCGPI, indicating that the first difference of price indices does not contain the unit root. Based on the above test results, it can be determined that the four price indices are integrated of order one (non-stationary). Based on the characteristics of the non-stationarity of price index data, the cointegration and error correction model is used to analyze the dynamic transmission mechanism between price indices.

4.3 Long-term equilibrium analysis of price chain transmission mechanism

4.3.1 Cointegration test

A multivariate dynamic model system needs to be established for analyzing the dynamic transmission mechanism of different price indices. In general, if the variable under study is stationary, a vector autoregression model (VAR) can be established directly, such as

$$\Phi(L)Y_t = C + \varepsilon_t \tag{4.1}$$

Analysis results are obtained using the traditional estimation and inference methods. In Equation 4.1, C denotes the constant term; $\Phi(L)$ denotes the lagged operator polynomial in the form of a vector; ε_t denotes a white noise vector process.

However, the data analysis in the second section shows that the four prices studied in this chapter are non-stationary series. To analyze the dynamic transmission mechanism of the non-stationary series system with multiple integrated of order one, it is necessary to first use the Johansen cointegration analysis method to test whether there is a long-term equilibrium relationship among variables.

Therefore, the establishment of a multiple-variable dynamic model requires the further conversion of Equation 4.1. The VAR(p) model with n variables is rewritten in the following form:

$$\Phi^*(L)\Delta Y_t = C + \Pi Y_{t-1} + \varepsilon_t \qquad (4.2)$$

Where

$$
\begin{cases}
\Pi = -\Phi(1) = \sum_{i=1}^{p} \Phi_i - I_n \\
\Phi^*(L) = I_n - \sum_{i=1}^{p-1} \varphi_i L^i \\
\varphi_i = -\sum_{j=i}^{p} \Phi_j
\end{cases}
\qquad (4.3)
$$

In the actual regression process, the optimal lagged order p in the VAR(p) model needs to be determined by two basic diagnostic tests: One is the coefficient exclusion test; the other is the serial correlation test of the residual of the VAR model. It is worthy of special note that when regression estimation is performed on a dynamic system such as the VAR model, the selection of the lag order of the model must pass the coefficient exclusion test and also should meet the condition that the residual does not have serial correlation, in order to ensure that the estimation result and subsequent various tests (such as the Granger causality test) are valid.

In the above definition, the attribute of Π in the nth-order matrix is the core of the Johansen cointegration test. Simply put, Johansen's cointegration analysis method is in fact a cyclical test process, starting with testing the first general hypothesis $r = \text{rank}(\Pi) = 0$ (rank represents the rank of the matrix). Corresponding to this hypothesis is that all variables in the VAR system are non-stationary and there is no cointegration relationship. Next, $r = \text{rank}(\Pi) = 1$ is re-tested, and so on, until a stationary system corresponds to $r = \text{rank}(\Pi) = n$. This cyclical process can be used to test how many cointegration relationships there are in the vector system. When this process stops at the point H_{0r} that cannot be rejected, the estimated value of the corresponding cointegration relationship is r.

According to the Johansen cointegration analysis method, if the characteristic root of the matrix Π is $\lambda_i (i = 1, 2, \ldots, n)$, then the following two statistics can be used to test the number of vector cointegration relationships, namely

$$\text{Trace statistic} = -T \sum_{i=r+1}^{k} \ln\left(1 - \hat{\lambda}_i\right), r = 0, 1, \ldots, n-1 \qquad (4.4)$$

$$\text{Maximum eigenvalue} = -T \ln\left(1 - \hat{\lambda}_{r+1}\right), r = 0, 1, \ldots, n-1 \qquad (4.5)$$

Where, $\hat{\lambda_i}$ refers to the estimated value of the characteristic value of the matrix Π, and T is the effective sample size. If the statistical significance of the trace statistic or the maximum eigenvalue is not zero, then the corresponding null hypothesis H_{0r} is rejected. It needs to be noted that the traditional hypothesis test results of these two statistics cannot be directly used for statistical inference. This is because the distribution of relevant statistics is different from the traditional distribution under the conditions of null hypothesis. The root of the problem is that the traditional statistical inference assumes that the variable is a stationary sequence. Under the conditions of the null hypothesis, the variable is non-stationary. Therefore, in the actual test process, the simulation method by MacKinnon et al. (1999) is used to calculate the p-value of the corresponding statistic.

According to the method described above, Table 4.3 reports the results of the Johansen cointegration test.[6] It is not difficult to see that whether it is the trace statistic or the maximum characteristic root statistic, the p-value corresponding to the first round of the cyclical test (namely under the null hypothesis that the number of cointegration is 0) is less than 5%, indicating that the null hypothesis without a cointegration relationship is rejected at the traditional significance level. For the null hypothesis with at most one cointegration relationship, the p-values of the corresponding statistics are relatively high (greater than 10%), indicating that the null hypothesis with one cointegration relationship in the four categories of prices cannot be rejected.

For the sake of comparison, Table 4.3 also reports the third round of the cyclical test, namely the test result of the null hypothesis with at most two cointegration relationships. It is not difficult to see that at the traditional significance level, the null hypothesis with at most two cointegration relationships cannot be rejected. However, based on the order of the cyclical hypothesis test and the stop principle, it is determined here that there is a cointegration relationship in RMPI, PPI, CGPI, and CPI.

The results reported in Table 3.4 indicate that there is a long-term equilibrium relationship among the upstream, midstream, and downstream prices in China. The so-called long-term equilibrium relationship means that there is a stable one-to-one trade-off relationship between different prices in the long term. Therefore, even if the relationship among different prices deviates from this equilibrium

Table 4.3 Test results on the number of Johansen cointegration relations for four price indexes

Null hypothesis (number of cointegration relationships)	Trace statistic (p-value)	Maximum characteristic root statistic (p-value)
None	0.035**	0.005***
At most 1	0.736	0.897
At most 2	0.363	0.743

Note: ** and *** indicate that the corresponding statistics are statistically significant at the significance level of 5% and 1%, respectively.

in the short term, the time series formed by such deviation is still a stationary sequence, and the degree of positive and negative deviations is offset mutually in the long term (expected value is 0).

Of course, the above process only examines whether there is a cointegration relationship between the upstream, midstream, and downstream prices as well as the number of cointegration relationships, and does not reflect the specific characteristics of the cointegration relationship. To characterize this long-term equilibrium relationship, it is necessary to estimate the error correction model that shows the characteristics of the cointegration relationship. Detailed elaboration is given below.

4.3.2 Error correction model

The establishment and estimation of the error correction model chiefly involves the cointegration vector and adjustment coefficient. The former characterizes the long-term equilibrium relationship between the variables in the system, and the latter reflects the correction characteristics of the cointegration system following the deviation from the equilibrium state. For the sake of explanation, according to the standard time series analysis theory, Equation 4.2 is re-written as

$$\Phi(L)\Delta Y_t = C + \Pi Y_{t-1} + \varepsilon_t = C + AB'Y_{t-1} + \varepsilon_t \tag{4.6}$$

Where matrix B represents the cointegration vector (B' represents the transposed matrix) and A represents the matrix of adjustment coefficients.

Under such a definition framework, if $Z_{t-1} = B'Y_{t-1}$, it is not difficult to see that the vector Z_{t-1} is the error sequence formed by vector Y_{t-1} (containing four price indices) through the role of the cointegration vector B. After this error (namely deviation from the long-term equilibrium state) occurs in the $t-1$ period, the cointegration system will correct this in the next period (namely the t period) to ensure the stable existence of the long-term equilibrium relationship. What is the range of correction? This is what the adjustment coefficient matrix A reflects as defined in Equation 4.6. Therefore, the error correction model reflects a dynamic correction mechanism.

In fact, after the number r in the vector cointegration relationship is tested, the estimation of the cointegration vector B and the adjustment coefficient matrix A is a byproduct in the Johansen cointegration analysis process. Therefore, following the estimation of the characteristic root λ_i through the Johansen cointegration analysis method as described above, the column of matrix B is the corresponding characteristic root vector. Thus, r elements corresponding to $Z_t = B'Y_t$ can be estimated.

Based on the above description, the error correction model can be written as

$$\Phi(L)\Delta Y_t = C + AZ_{t-1} + \varepsilon_t \tag{4.7}$$

Traditional statistical inference can be applied to the adjustment coefficient matrix A, and also to the dynamic coefficient matrix $\Phi(L)$, due to the fact that Z_{t-1} in the error correction model system is a stationary sequence.

Based on the above theoretical analysis, Table 4.1 reports the empirical results of the estimation of the Johansen error correction model. The result includes an estimate of the cointegration vector B and the adjustment coefficient matrix A. It should be noted that since the cointegration vector B needs to be identified, the coefficient corresponding to the first variable (RMPI) in the model system is standardized as 1. Thus, $B' = (1 -1.404 -0.551\ 0.849)$ characterizes the long-term equilibrium relationship between the four price indices in China, and this equilibrium relationship is statistically significant at a significance level of 1%. (Table 4.4).

For the adjustment coefficient matrix, $A' = (-0.139\ 0.085 -0.018 -0.201)$ indicates that when there is a positive non-equilibrium state (positive deviation error) among the variables in the system in the short term, PPI will be corrected in the same direction, but the correction range is not large (0.085) and not statistically significant. The other three types of prices will have a reverse correction; of these, CPI has the largest correction range (−0.201), followed by RMPI and CGPI.

According to the estimation results of the adjustment coefficient, when the long-term equilibrium relationship between the upstream, midstream, and downstream prices temporarily deviates, the reverse correction of the bottom downstream price (CPI) and the top upstream price (RMPI) is the most obvious. The two dominate the dynamic mechanism in which the model system is adjusted from temporary disequilibrium to long-term equilibrium. This also suggests to some extent a possible significant dynamic interaction between the upstream and downstream prices. Of course, this dynamic interaction may also involve other prices between the two. To clarify this dynamic transmission mechanism among different prices, the Granger causality test needs to be performed on the basis of the error correction model.[7]

4.3.3 Granger causality test

In the framework of cointegration analysis, the Granger causality test is the corresponding significance test based on the established error correction model. Of course, to perform this test, Equation 4.7 needs to be properly deformed, namely

$$\Delta Y_t = C + AZ_{t-1} + \Phi'(L)\Delta Y_{t-1} + \varepsilon_t \tag{4.8}$$

Table 4.4 Estimation results of Johansen error correction model (standard deviation in parentheses)

	RMPI	PPI	CGPI	CPI
Cointegration vector B	1.000	−1.404***	−0.551***	0.849***
		(0.083)	(0.124)	(0.166)
Adjustment coefficient matrix A	−0.139*	0.085	−0.018	−0.201***
	(0.089)	(0.062)	(0.049)	(0.054)

Note: * and *** indicate that the corresponding statistics are statistically significant at the significance levels of 10% and 1%, respectively.

Where $\Phi(L) = I - \Phi'(L)L$. Thus, the Granger causality test performs a test on the joint significance level of the corresponding coefficients in matrix $\Phi'(L)$. In the case of taking ΔCPI_t in ΔY_t as the dependent variable, the reason for testing whether the other price index is the Granger cause is to test whether the respective lagged term coefficient of the other prices on the right-hand side of the test Equation 4.8 is 0.

According to the test principle explained above, Table 4.5 reports the Granger causality test results based on Equation 4.8, where lag(ΔCPI) represents the lagged term of ΔCPI on the right side of the regression equation, and the definitions of the other symbols are similar. The second column in Table 4.5 reports the results of the test in which CPI is the dependent variable. From the results of the second column, at the significance level of 5%, the null hypothesis that PPI, CGPI, and RMPI are not the Granger causes of the CPI can be rejected. In other words, the other three kinds of prices are Granger causes for CPI. The upstream and midstream price indices have a significant predictive effect on the dynamic trend of downstream CPI.

The third column in Table 4.5 reports which price indices are the Granger causes for PPI. The results show that the midstream price CGPI is the Granger cause of PPI, while the upstream RMPI and the most downstream CPI are not Granger causes for PPI. From a prediction perspective, CGPI has a predictive effect on the dynamic trend of PPI, but RMPI and CPI have no predictive effect on the trend of PPI. Under the same logic, the results of the fourth column show that CPI has a predictive effect on CGPI, whereas RMPI and PPI do not have a significant predictive effect on CGPI. The results of the last column indicate that PPI and CGPI are predictive of RMPI, but CPI has no predictive effect on the dynamic trend of RMPI.

Based on the test results of Table 4.5, it is found that while there is no general transmission law (such as one-way or two-way) of a particular model among upstream, midstream, and downstream prices, the following results are noteworthy: Firstly, the transmission of upstream and midstream prices (RMPI, PPI, and

Table 4.5 Granger causality test results of four kinds of price indexes

	ΔCPI_t	ΔPPI_t	$\Delta CGPI_t$	$\Delta RMPI_t$
lag(ΔCPI)		0.321	0.000***	0.220
lag($\Delta CGPI$)	0.026**	0.028**		0.031**
lag(ΔPPI)	0.000***		0.923	0.001***
lag($\Delta RMPI$)	0.008***	0.271	0.643	

Note: The optimal lag order of the VAR model on which the test is based is 2 as determined by the serial correlation test of the residual of VAR model and the coefficient exclusion test (maximum number is 6); lag (ΔCPI) represents the lag length of all ΔCPI terms on the right side of the equation in the Granger causality test (representations of other price index are similar); the null hypothesis is that there is no Granger causality; the table reports the p-value of the Wald significance test statistic; *** and ** represent statistical significance at the significance levels of 1% and 5%, respectively.

CGPI) on downstream price (CPI) is significant; secondly, downstream price CPI only has a reverse transmission effect on the midstream price CGPI (namely from downstream to midstream and upstream), but has no reverse transmission effect on other prices; thirdly, the midstream price CGPI has a reverse transmission effect on the upstream PPI and RMPI; fourthly, PPI has a reverse transmission effect on RMPI.

Our first finding is significantly different from that of He et al. (2008). The reason lies not in the nuances of the analysis samples, but in the processing of non-stationary sequences in the Granger causality test. Although He (2008) made a correct judgment of the non-stationary nature of China's price variables, the horizontal value of the price series was still used for statistical tests in the Granger causality test. The analysis of this paper is fully aware of the non-stationarity of the price series. The Granger causality test is performed on the basis of the correct establishment of the error correction model. The empirical results of this paper are therefore more robust.

4.4 Monetary effects on the price chain transmission mechanism

As mentioned above, RMPI, PPI, CGPI, and CPI are incorporated into a dynamic vector model system for analyzing the dynamic transmission mechanism between the upstream, midstream, and downstream prices. The preceding analysis focused on the analysis of interaction between prices, with no consideration for the impact of monetary factors on the price transmission mechanism. However, from the perspective of historical development experience, the view that the money growth rate is closely related to the inflation rate (such as Friedman's view that "inflation is always and everywhere a monetary phenomenon") is of inspirational significance for the study of the price transmission mechanism.

To this end, China's M2 growth rate (year-on-year) is included in the existing VAR model to judge the dynamic driving effect of the money supply growth rate on upstream, midstream, and downstream prices in China and to test which price indices are directly driven by the money supply factors through empirical analysis similar to the preceding one. At the same time, the analysis of the augmentation model in which the money supply factor is added can also examine whether the preceding analysis results are robust.

Before performing regression analysis, it is necessary to first explain the data source and stationary characteristics of the M2 growth rate (M2GR). The original data on M2GR are obtained from the People's Bank of China, and the sample interval is consistent with the price index range, from January 1998 to June 2009 (see Figure 4.3). In this sample interval, the ADF unit root test is performed on the M2GR and its first-order difference form. The p-values corresponding to the statistics are 0.13 and 0.000, respectively. This indicates that at the traditional significance level, it can be determined that the M2 growth rate is a first-order non-stationary sequence, namely an $I(1)$ sequence. This provides a feasible theoretical foundation for the cointegration analysis below. Besides, it has been explained at

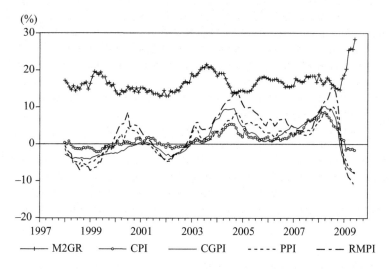

Figure 4.3 M2 growth rate and price index inflation rate: January 1998–June 2009.
Source: National Bureau of Statistics, People's Bank of China.

the beginning of this chapter that all price indices are substantially in the form of a growth rate (inflation rate). Therefore, using the M2 growth rate and the four kinds of price series to establish the VAR model is in line with the consistency principle of variable indicator data processing.

Based on the above analysis of M2GR data, the authors conducted a cointegration test on the VAR model consisting of four price indices and M2GR according to the Johansen cointegration test as described in Section 4.3. The results are reported in Table 4.6. It can be seen from this that for the null hypothesis without cointegration, the *p*-values corresponding to the trace test and the maximum eigenvalue are 0.061 and 0.069, respectively. This indicates that although the null hypothesis that the vector system consisting of four kinds of price indices and M2GR does not have a cointegration relationship cannot be rejected at

Table 4.6 Results of test on the number of Johansen cointegration relationships of the augmentation model

Null hypothesis (number of cointegration relationships)	Trace statistic (p-value)	Maximum eigenvalue (p-value)
None	0.061*	0.069*
At most 1	0.394	0.589
At most 2	0.483	0.865

Note: The establishment of the cointegration model is consistent with the process as described in Table 4.3; * indicates that the corresponding statistics are statistically significant at the significance level of 10%.

the significance level of 5%, it can still be rejected at the significance level of 10%. For the second round of tests on the number of cointegration relationships, the null hypothesis that there is at most one cointegration relationship cannot be rejected at the traditional significance level.

On the whole, the test results in Table 4.6 indicate that there is one cointegration relationship between China's money supply growth rate and prices in the sample interval from 1998 to 2009. Based on such a long-term equilibrium relationship, it is possible to further perform the Granger causality test on the variables in the model system, and then examine the driving characteristics between the money supply factors and the prices at different stages, and judge whether there is a change in the transmission mechanism between the upstream, midstream, and downstream prices after the addition of the money supply growth rate.

According to such an idea, the authors perform the Granger causality test on the four types of price indices and M2GR as per the error correction model system corresponding to the cointegration test. Table 4.7 sums up the Granger causality test results corresponding to the augmentation model with the addition of M2GR (the test process is identical to the process corresponding to Table 4.5). Based on the research objective in this section, the following three points in Table 4.7 are worthy of special attention: Firstly, M2GR does not have statistical significance for midstream and downstream CPI and CGPI according to the Granger causality test, but M2GR has significance for upstream RMPI and PPI according to the Granger causality test (see line 2 of Table 4.7). Secondly, compared with Table 4.5, the augmentation model of M2GR is added to the test. Except that RMPI's Granger causality on CPI changed from significant to insignificant (column 3 of Table 4.7), the dynamic transmission effects among the upstream, midstream, and downstream prices did not change significantly. Thirdly, all prices are not significant for the money supply growth rate according to the Granger causality test (column 2 of Table 4.7).

The above results have important implications in three respects. For starters, the money supply growth rate has a direct dynamic driving effect on China's downstream prices, but has no significant direct dynamic transmission on the midstream and downstream prices. This finding is consistent with the conclusion given in Chapter 4, which means that systematic monetary policy changes are not

Table 4.7 Granger causality test results augmentation model with the addition of M2GR

	$\Delta M2GR$	ΔCPI	$\Delta CGPI$	ΔPPI	$\Delta RMPI$
lag(ΔM2GR)		0.816	0.297	0.003***	0.018**
lag(ΔCPI)	0.733		0.001***	0.431	0.452
lag(ΔCGPI)	0.406	0.001***		0.001***	0.001***
lag(ΔPPI)	0.896	0.048**	0.820		0.002***
lag(ΔRMPI)	0.261	0.238	0.303	0.922	

Note: The optimal lag order of the VAR model is 4 as determined by the serial correlation test of the residual of VAR model and the coefficient exclusion test (maximum number is 6).

directly reflected in downstream CPI. But the results of the study in this chapter go one step further. It can be seen that the dynamic transmission of the money supply growth rate on the upstream price is significant, while the upstream price has a significant transmission effect on the CPI. From this perspective, the money supply growth rate has a direct driving effect on upstream prices, while midstream and downstream prices have an indirect driving role.

Secondly, from the perspective of the dynamic transmission mechanism of different prices, the addition of the money supply growth rate variable only has a subtle impact on the Granger causality relationship between RMPI and CPI, possibly because the increase in the independent variables in the vector model system affects the degree of freedom and collinearity in the regression estimation. However, taken as a whole, the results of the augmentation model do not basically change the preceding research conclusions. Therefore, the transmission of upstream, midstream, and downstream prices found in this chapter is robust. In particular, the price transmission direction is exactly identical with the results in the third section.

Finally, the dynamic impact of price changes on China's monetary policy adjustment is not significant. This suggests that when the People's Bank of China adjusts the intermediate targets (such as M2) of monetary policy, more attention is paid to economic growth among the information set consisting of factors such as price and economic growth. Of course, this is consistent with the significant number of people to be employed in China every year. Only by ensuring a certain level of economic growth is it possible to effectively create employment and rationally curb the unemployment rate.

4.5 Conclusions

This chapter conducts empirical analysis of the transmission mechanism of upstream, midstream, and downstream prices in China from January 1998 to June 2009, and examines the driving effect of monetary factors on different prices. Through the cointegration test, error correction, and Granger causality test of the dynamic models, this chapter answers three important questions: Firstly, is there a stable dynamic driving relationship between the upstream, midstream, and downstream price indices and inflation rates? Secondly, what is the dynamic prediction and driving mechanism among the indices? Third, on what price index and inflation rate does the money supply have a significant direct driving effect?

Judging from the results of the study, our answer to the first question is positive. There is a long-term equilibrium relationship among the purchase price of raw materials, producer prices, commodity trading prices, and consumer prices in China. This indicates that the dynamic driving mechanism for the upstream, midstream, and downstream prices is stable.

On this basis, we analyze the dynamic transmission mechanism among different prices. The empirical results indicate that the upstream, midstream, and downstream prices have a significant dynamic transmission effect on the downstream prices, while the downstream prices only have a reverse transmission effect on the midstream prices. Moreover, the midstream prices have a reverse transmission effect on the upstream prices, while the upstream PPI has a reverse transmission effect on RMPI. These transmissions are unidirectional.

For the third question, the authors add the money supply growth rate to the vector system consisting of four price indices. The empirical test shows that the dynamic driving effect of the currency factor on the upstream prices is most significant, but it is not directly transmitted to downstream prices. The significant impact and direct driving role of the money supply on upstream prices suggest that although the current changes in monetary policy may not be directly reflected in the changes in downstream consumer prices for a period of time, they can be transmitted to downstream prices by affecting upstream prices. This indirect dynamic transmission effect may make the inflation effect of the money supply imperceptible in the short run, but it will show in the end after a period of time.

The results of these studies in this chapter have important implications for the accurate judgment of inflation trends and the scientific regulation of macroeconomic policies in the future. Special attention should be paid to the fact that although the year-on-year growth rate of various prices in China continues to be negative in 2009 after the global financial crisis, the prices of global energy and bulk commodities see greater fluctuation, and the entry and exit of international working capital fluctuated in lockstep with the volatility of US dollar, causing considerable uncertainty in the trend of domestic upstream prices. From the results of the transmission law of China's upstream, midstream, and downstream prices in this chapter, the dynamic trend of downstream prices will highly likely see great fluctuations in the coming period. Therefore, China's risks in inflation in the few years to come should not be ignored. Of course, curbing inflation is not the only goal of macroeconomic policy regulation. Especially in the current situation, with the lack of fundamental improvement in the economic development of major countries, how to boost the sustainability of China's economic growth is a major issue to which leaders should pay close attention.

Finally, given the dynamic effect of money supply on price transmission, dynamic adjustment is a realistic strategy worth considering in macro-control when decision-makers balance the prevention and control of inflation and growth stimulus. Of course, for the desired effect of dynamic policy adjustment, a lot of basic work remains to be done, such as building a comprehensive scientific economic forecasting system and introducing more dynamic random general equilibrium analysis mechanisms to the macroeconomic policy analysis framework, and so on. In setting up the forecasting system, the dynamic transmission law of the upstream, midstream. and downstream prices provides a favorable information channel for forecasting the overall dynamic trend of prices. In this way, the improvement in macroeconomic policy regulation and forecasting mechanism will provide an important guarantee for the healthy and stable development of the Chinese economy.

Notes

1   Zhao and Wang (2005) found that there is a cointegration relationship between China's currency stock and price level, but Chen et al. (2009) held that China's monetary factors have no effect on changes in price. But these studies did not consider the dynamic relationship between currency and upstream, midstream, and downstream prices.

2   CGPI is a statistical price index established and organized by the People's Bank of China with the approval of the National Bureau of Statistics. The predecessor of CGPI was the domestic wholesale price index (WPI) compiled on a pilot basis as from January 1994. However, as the intermediate wholesale link is shortening, the purchase price link of this price survey gradually tends towards the producers. Further, as it is easy to confuse the "wholesale" in the wholesale price index and general "commodity wholesale" and it cannot fully reflect the essence of its comprehensive price index, the domestic WPI was later renamed the commodity trading price index.

3   In terms of data on sub-component of each price index, the sample interval is from January 2001 to June 2009 due to limited data availability.

4   The National Bureau of Statistics first disclosed the composition of the weight of CPI in China at the time in June 2006 (Oriental Morning Post, June 15, 2006). Food accounted for 33.2%, tobacco and alcohol accounted for 3.9%, apparel accounted for 9.1%, household equipment and services accounted for 6%, medical care and personal products accounted for 10%, transportation and communications accounted for 10.4%, entertainment, education and cultural products and services accounted for 14.2%, and housing accounted for 13.2%. Of course, like other price indices, the weight of CPI is adjusted at regular intervals (such as five years). Therefore, the OLS estimation results of the weights of price index sub-components may not be accurate. This degree of inaccuracy is further compromised by the number of classification components (loss of degree of freedom in regression). For example, in the classification weight of RMPI in Table 4.1, the weight estimate result of wood and pulp is negative (−4.5%), which may be due to the weight adjustment in the sample interval and the high number of RMPI sub-components.

5   As mentioned above, the price index in the text is essentially in the form of the inflation rate.

6   In the Johansen cointegration model, according to the criteria set by Zhang (2008c) for the deterministic trend in the analysis model, it is assumed that the constituent variables of the VAR model system do not contain deterministic trends, but the cointegration vector contains deterministic trends.

7   It needs to be pointed out that due to historical reasons in the development of econometrics, Granger causality uses the name of its founder Granger in the classic literature. But this name does not refer to the "causal relationship" in a general sense. Actually, Granger causality tests whether there is dynamic predictive relationship between variables, namely whether the historical information of a variable is statistically significant for predicting the future trend of another variable, rather than a causal relationship in a general sense.

5 Inflation dynamics

Industry tide perspective

5.1 Foundation for industry tide and inflation dynamics

The global new financial crisis that raged in recent years stemmed from the American real estate market bubble and spread rapidly worldwide through financial derivatives. In the panicked climate, bulk commodity prices fluctuate frequently. At the same time, quantitative easing policies are common in various countries. A host of factors have periodically promoted global price increases. In the face of the global financial crisis and the cyclical volatility of the world economy, China's economic stimulus policies led by state investment have shown effect. Such industries as automobile, high-end equipment manufacturing, and new energy have developed rapidly. China still maintains a high economic growth rate on the whole.

However, as industry focuses continue to emerge, China's inflation has increasingly become an aggravated problem. The influx of funds in the recovery plan has pushed up the price levels of various industries rapidly. Joking media expressions on garlic, mung bean, and ginger graphically describe the rising prices of general consumer goods, and also reflect the real problems of capital cycle movement and industry tides in various agricultural product sectors. More typical of industry tide than the agricultural industry is the real estate industry. In recent years, China's real estate market has developed apace, with the real estate sector evolving from an early labor-intensive industry to a capital- and information-intensive industry. The frequent emergence of "the most expensive land" in real estate across the country suggests an influx of financial capital into the real estate industry, driving the housing prices in large and medium-sized cities. In this context, the market has strong expectations for future inflation.

The tidal development of real estate and agricultural products industries is only a representative of the tide in domestic industry development. Many other industries have also seen the tide phenomenon (Lin, 2007). In fact, as China is still at a stage of rapid development, the industries are facing upgrade and adjustment. In this course, national capital and private capital prefer the industries with high returns. Therefore, there are cyclical investment cycle movements of capital in different industries during the cyclical changes in industry development, resulting in wave upon wave of industry tide development models. In each wave of industry tide development, capital accumulation and tide are evidently obvious. However, in the wake of the peak of development in a particular industry, there will be a whole host of problems such as overcapacity and capital flows to other industries. Correspondingly, the price of products in the tide industry will also fluctuate greatly according to the cyclical fluctuations of the tide phenomenon. This not only affects the dynamic trend of inflation in China and increases the cyclical fluctuations of inflation, but also poses great challenges to the management of domestic inflation. Therefore, it is of great practical significance to reinterpret China's inflation problems from the angle of the tide phenomenon.

The academic research on the tide phenomenon began to be carried out not long ago, and it mainly focuses on the tide phenomenon and the production capacity of enterprises as well as the cyclical swings of the macro economy. For example, Lin (2007) and Lin et al. (2010) proposed that the tide phenomenon often occurs in the development of enterprises in developing countries, culminating in overcapacity. Yuan and Zhang (2009) analyzed the tide phenomenon in conjunction with state control and cyclical economic fluctuations, and found that industry tide can explain China's macroeconomic fluctuations. Wan et al. (2009) focused the research on the alternative changes between investment tides and domestic inflation and deflation, holding that tide will intensify inflation in the short run but induce deflation in the long run. The analytical framework of this study is based on the traditional division of industry and agriculture. While the traditional division of industry and agriculture is representative and crucially important, the typical facts of domestic capital cycle movement and industry tides in recent years have been manifested in the industry tides and capital cycle movement of real capital goods (such as real estate) and general consumer goods to a greater extent. As a result, the alternative occurrence of inflation change in industrial and agricultural products becomes more and more inconspicuous, and the difference in price changes and the dynamic transmission relationship in industry and agriculture becomes obscure (He et al., 2008; Zhang, 2010).

This chapter differs from existing research. National industry is divided into real capital goods and general consumer goods based on the standard theory of the modern monetarist school (such as Meltzer, 1995). With the inherent relationship between the tide phenomenon of real capital goods and general consumer goods sectors and inflation as the research goal, the authors re-examine the industry tide phenomenon and the current inflation problem in China, and explore the linkage between the two. The main outcome of this chapter is to innovate the theoretical model of the inflation-driving mechanism under the industry tide mode. Specifically, on the basis of competitive equilibrium, the authors simplify the multi-level and complex industry development into two parts, the real capital goods industry and the general consumer goods industry (real capital goods are represented by real estate), and the tide development characteristics of different industry sectors are introduced into the macro-equilibrium model of the two sectors. By exploring the internal relationship between industry tide and inflation through the model, the authors obtain the driving factor of inflation under this model, and then validate this through empirical analysis.

It needs to be noted that the research in this chapter is premised on the periodic cycle movement of China's financial capital and the reality of fierce and frequent industry tides. While the tide phenomenon is intimately linked to problems such as overcapacity, what is more important is that it will exert a significant impact on the cyclical changes in inflation. Furthermore, the theoretical model constructed in this chapter does not deny existing inflation theory, but supplements and corrects the existing theories on the basis of changes in the inflation-driving mechanism in China in the dozen years following 1998. After the theoretical model analysis in this chapter, the authors further use real data to empirically analyze the dynamic interaction mechanism between industry tide and inflation, in an attempt to explain inflation since 1998 from the perspective of industry tide.

In view of this, this chapter is arranged as follows: Section 5.2 describes the typical facts of capital cycle movement, the tide phenomenon, and the dynamic evolution of inflation in China in recent years. Section 5.3 deals with the theoretical model. The authors construct an inflation model of real capital goods and general consumer goods, and discuss the changes and driving mechanisms of inflation in China on the basis of the theoretical model. In the fourth section of this chapter, the theoretical model is changed into an econometric model, and the relevant data from 1998 to 2010 are used for an empirical analysis, and the implications of relevant policy are explored. Section 5.5 sums up the contents of this chapter.

5.2 Capital cycle movement, industry tide, and inflation

5.2.1 Capital cycle movement and industry tide

The so-called capital cycle movement refers to the periodic capital flows into different industries for cycle movement. Although it is not easy to obtain the micro time sequence data on capital cycle movement, the industry tide phenomenon under capital cycle movement in recent years is prominent in the actual economic performance in China. For example, the sale prices of garlic, ginger, mung bean, and even apples in recent years have shown great fluctuations in different periods. One of the key reasons behind this price volatility is various types of capital surge into the corresponding industries in different times (Li and Chen, 2010). By reviewing other various product markets in recent years, there seems to be a cycle movement of capital in different industries and its corresponding industry tide. For example, according to media exposure, speculative capital has made frequent entries into such industries as Pu'er tea, Dahongpao tea, vintage wine, Fengzhu textiles, bloodstones, and jade, and even cemeteries, for speculation, ultimately ending in great cyclical fluctuations in the prices of products.

In recent years, capital cycle movement and industry tides have become more prominent in the real estate sector. Looking back at the development of China's real estate sector in a dozen years since 2000, there is a cyclical movement of capital and industry tide. In 1998, the State Council issued the "Circular on Deepening the Reform of Urban Housing System and Speeding up Housing Construction."

China began to cease the distribution of housing and real objects, and gradually implemented the monetization of housing distribution. It vigorously developed housing finance and cultivated the housing trading market on the basis of a multi-level urban housing supply system. This marks the beginning of the new development of the real estate sector in China. Under the impetus of state control, China's real estate sector has developed rapidly, and its proportion in the national economy is increasing, and it has even become a pillar industry in the national economy.

From the perspective of investment of industry capital, the growth rate of real estate development investment shows typical cyclical changes, and its trajectory of changes is highly consistent with the cyclical changes in China's CPI and inflation rate (year-on-year) from 1998 to 2010 (see Figure 5.1). Judging from the specific data, the average growth rate of real estate development investment in China from 1998 to 2010 was 23%, far higher than the average annual growth rate of about 13% for nominal GDP in the same period. Judging from the changes in time points, the investment growth rate soared from 8.8% to more than 20% in one year after the introduction of the new real estate policy in 1998; it fell somewhat at the end of 1999 under the impact of the Asian financial crisis, but the investment growth rate began to rise under stimulus such as a real estate-related tax reduction and exemption policies implemented in 2001. By the end of 2004, the development of China's real estate sector reached one climax after another, and the investment growth rate also reached a cyclical peak, at more than 34%.

Thereafter, the People's Bank of China announced in October 2004 a hike in the benchmark interest rate for deposits and loans. When the preferential policies for housing loans were rescinded in April 2005, the growth rate of investment in

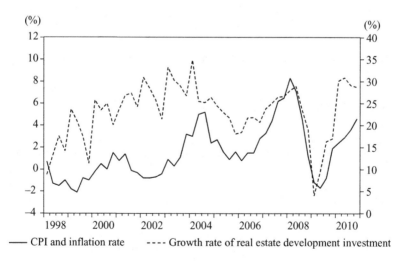

Figure 5.1 Growth rate of China's real estate development investment and CPI and inflation rate (year-on-year): Q1 of 1998–Q4 of 2010. Source: CEIC database and calculations by the authors.

the real estate sector began to slow down; however, there is a wide consensus on the high returns of financial capital in the real estate industry, and as a result the growth rate of investment in real estate development bottomed out in 2006 and reached another cyclical high in 2007. Of course, the new global crisis that raged in 2007–2008 had a temporary suppressing effect on capital influx into the real estate industry. In early 2009, the investment rate fell to the lowest level in ten years (less than 5%), but after 2010, the investment rate showed an upward trend. The upward trend eased somewhat thereafter, mainly owing to the impact of austerity measures such as purchase limitations in the real estate sector. The fact that the evolution path of the growth rate of investment in real estate development dovetails with the path of CPI and the inflation rate once again implies that there is an internal linkage mechanism between industry tide and inflation.

In the capital cycle movement in the real estate sector, the driving effect on related industries is also evidently obvious. According to the calculation by Liu (2010), China's real estate development investment has a nearly double driving effect on connected industries. In other words, for every 10 billion yuan of investment in real estate development, the total output of its related industries will reach 16 billion yuan after the deduction of land acquisition fees (about 20% of investment in real estate development). Moreover, with the additional increase of 24 billion yuan in output, coupled with consumer demand of 3 billion yuan, it can lead to an increase of 7.8 billion yuan in total output in various industries. The sum of the total output of related industries in the above two aspects is 23.8 billion yuan. Calculated at an average growth rate of 33%, it will lead to an increase of 7.9 billion yuan in value added, about 80% of the initial increase in investment in real estate development. These typical facts show that the development of real capital goods (the real estate industry) drives the sector of general consumer goods. At the same time, general consumer goods essentially provide intermediate product support for the production of the real capital goods sector. This is also the real basis for the assumed conditions of the theoretical model below.

Similarly, the specific industry tide resulting from capital cycle movement will dominate the price trend of products in an industry, and also bring about price changes in other related industries. For example, the tide development of the real estate industry obviously affects the price of products in its upstream industries, and affects the prices of parallel or downstream industries, and ultimately leads to changes in the overall price level. This transmission mechanism can be seen from the dynamic evolution path between the change rate in real estate sale price and the overall inflation rate as described in the section below. From this transmission mechanism, industry tide is indeed intimately related to the inflation problem.

However, the industry tide phenomenon was not used to interpret China's inflation problem in the early days of discussions in academia (such as Lin, 2007). This problem was analyzed from the perspective of the industrial development cycle and economic cycles. However, it has come to our notice that the industry tide proposed by Lin Yifu and the innovative interpretation of the unbalanced industry development behind this phenomenon are of great significance for understanding China's inflation problem in recent years. It is known that one of the characteristics of industrial development in developed countries is that all industries are at the forefront of the global industrial chain. For the next new industry deserving capital investment in the national economy, each enterprise holds different views in most cases and there is generally no social consensus. The government is generally unlikely to obtain more accurate information than enterprises. Therefore, the government generally does not formulate harmonized industrial policies, nor interfere unduly with the investment of enterprises.

However, for a rapidly developing country, especially in the course of industrial upgrading and restructuring, a majority of enterprises (or financial capital) choose to invest in an industry with supply and demand imbalance and high returns. For enterprises that have been involved in various product markets in China for many years, with rich investment and speculation experience, and which possess huge financial capital, it is easy to reach consensus on which industries are new and have a high rate of return. There is mostly likely an industry tide phenomenon in investment, namely wave upon wave of companies invest in the same industry.

Of course, financial capital consists of private capital and state-owned capital. Different capital entities have different market information and market resources. State-owned capital (especially the financial capital possessed by state-owned enterprises) can dominate industries with policy advantages and clear returns faster. For instance, the abundant funds of state-owned enterprises enter the real estate market, giving an impetus to the rapid prosperity of the real estate sector. Private capital is more sensitive to opportunities in the dynamic imbalance of market supply and demand at the micro level, such as the continuous investment of private capital in some products in the agricultural market.

Regardless of the nature and form of capital, each company has high expectations for return on their investment when each tide emerges in the course of industry tide. There is a strong impulse for financial capital to invest in these industries under the influence of the "herd effect." However, after the investment climax and hype by each enterprise or industry, absolute surplus or relative surplus of production capacity results inevitably, and the price of industrial products will also fall accordingly. When the price of existing industry products falls, industry profits shrink significantly. In the absence of a sound market mechanism at this time, investment impulse which does not follow rules will develop a new industry starting point, and the industry tide may continue. When this price fluctuation in local industries has a scale effect, it exerts a potential impact on inflation expectations and is ultimately transmitted to fluctuations at the overall inflation level.

From this, it can be seen that there is an urgent need to study the mechanism of action between the tide phenomenon and inflation in China under the capital cycle movement, so as to provide a scientific reference for decision-makers to fine-tune the industrial structure in the process of formulating macroeconomic policies, maintaining the structurally balanced development of the national economy, and achieving the goal of effectively curbing inflation. Because the focus of this chapter is industry tide and inflation, the characteristics of inflation operation under industry tide in China are explained below.

5.2.2 Inflation under industry tide

For a market economy, the change in price level (or inflation equivalently speaking) is essentially determined by the relationship between supply and demand. However, for the current inflation operation mechanism in China, it is obviously far from sufficient to judge the driving factors of inflation from the supply and demand relationship of commodity markets alone, in that when the supply and demand relationship sees a short-term imbalance at the dynamic level during rapid national economy development, there is no perfect automatic regulation mechanism. At this time, financial capital will enter an industry and form the capital cycle movement mechanism as mentioned above, thus spurring the emergence of the industry tide phenomenon and affecting the law of changes in price levels.

Industry tide affects the price of the respective industry products first, and is then transmitted to other industries and ultimately affects overall inflation. The typical facts at this level can still be seen from the price changes in the real estate industry and the changes in the overall prices. Figure 5.2 shows the dynamic time series of the growth rate of China's housing sale prices (70 large and medium-sized cities) and CPI and the inflation rate from the first quarter of 1998 to the fourth quarter of 2010. Figure 5.2 clearly shows that the growth rate of sale prices of housing is generally higher than the overall inflation rate, and the two show high consistency in terms of the evolution rule and cyclical changes of the dynamic path. In this chapter, the authors hold that this high degree of consistency is not a coincidence, but a specific manifestation of the linkage between industry tide and inflation.

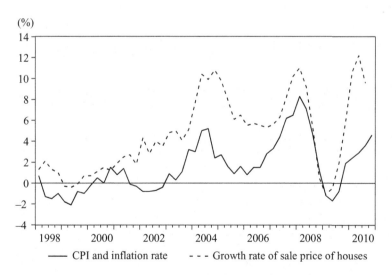

Figure 5.2 Growth rate of housing sale price and CPI and inflation rate (both year-on-year): Q1 of 1998–Q4 of 2010. Source: CEIC database and calculations by the authors.

In practice, we also compare the change path of the price growth rate of the other industries with the tide phenomenon (such as agricultural products) and the overall inflation rate in recent years. The results show that the growth rate of product prices in the industries with a tide phenomenon is generally higher than the overall inflation. The fluctuation range is also significantly larger than that of the overall inflation rate, and is consistent with the law of cyclical change in the overall inflation rate. By this token, when the industry tide phenomenon reaches a scale, the price change in a corresponding industry will have a cumulative effect on the overall price, and ultimately will form the dominant factor driving the overall price change, and affect the law of cyclical change in inflation. From the perspective of the microscopic transmission mechanism, the industry tide is by and large driven by industry profit margins. Capital floods into industries with high profit margins, and new investment will lead to prosperity in the respective industry. When the gap in profit margin between this industry and other industries widens, the other industries will also raise prices to increase their profit levels. Workers will also demand wages in line with high-profit industries. The rise in wages and prices in individual industries will be transmitted to the changes in the overall price level.

Of course, different entry points can be chosen for the analysis of industry tide and inflation. The selection of real capital goods (real estate) in this chapter as the typical representative is based on two considerations. Firstly, in the past dozen years since 2000, China's real estate sector has experienced a typical industry tide development. Since 1998, the central and local governments have focused on the development of real capital goods through the planning, organization, and distribution of some economic resources, thus promoting fast economic growth. In particular, state control over the supply of land and natural resources has greatly reduced the production cost of land and natural resources in the real capital goods sector. This is appealing to the financial capital, thereby promoting industry tide development. Secondly, existing theories provide a key basis for the division of real capital goods and general consumer goods. In particular, the important literature of Meltzer (1995) regards real estate as the representative of real capital goods when describing the composition of the economic structure. While Meltzer's (1995) research focuses on the transmission mechanism of monetary policy, it lays the foundation for the authors to set up a theoretical model to analyze current industry tide and inflation in China.

Given the above understanding, this chapter divides the sector economic structure into the real capital goods sector represented by real estate and the general consumer goods sector. This division is similar to the classification method in Marx's economic reproduction theory. Marx divides the production of aggregate social products into two major categories: The first category is the production of goods that must enter productive consumption; the other is the production of goods for personal consumption in the capitalist class and the working class. The output of the first category enters the reproduction of the two categories in the form of constant capital, and the output of the second category exists in the form of consumer goods. Under Marx's reproduction theory framework, the means of production produced by the first category include both fixed capital, such as machines, tools, and buildings, which are consumed in part and whose value is transferred to the product, and also the flowing capital and constant capital such as raw materials, auxiliary materials, and semi-finished products which are consumed in full and whose value is transferred to the products. From the perspective of Marx's reproduction theory, this chapter combines the first category that produces the flowing and constant capital for the whole society and the second category that produces consumer goods (collectively the general consumer goods sector) based on the real economic development model, while the capital goods production sector in the sense of fixed capital is classified as real capital goods sector.

5.3 Real capital goods and consumer goods: Dual sector model

In this section, a two-sector model is established to explain the industry tide and inflation issues as introduced earlier. Based on the above, the following assumptions are put forward: Firstly, the state economy can be divided into the real capital goods sector and the general consumer goods sector. The general consumer goods sector provides intermediate product support for the production of the real capital goods sector. Secondly, the labor force can flow between the two sectors, but there is an access threshold. Thirdly, industry profits and policy support (such as strong state control) will lead to a tide movement from resources such as financial capital, intermediate products, and human capital to the real capital goods sector. On the basis of competitive equilibrium, the authors analyze the determining factors of China's inflation from the perspective of industry tide.

5.3.1 Benchmark framework: Supply, demand, and macroscopic equilibrium

It is supposed that the state economy consists of the real capital goods sector (represented by RA) and the general consumer goods sector, C. The Cobb–Douglas production function is used for the two sectors. The production function of manufacturers in the real capital goods sector is $Y_{RA} = A_{RA}L_{RA}^{1-\alpha}X^{\alpha}$, where $0 < \alpha < 1$; Y_{RA}, L_{RA}, and X represent the output, labor, and intermediate products in the real capital sector, respectively. A_{RA} represents the technical level of the real capital goods sector. Since the technology gap in the world will not disappear in the near future, technological progress in the real capital goods sector is long-standing, namely $\dot{A}_{RA}/A_{RA} \geq 0$; at the same time, along with the one-way flow of the supply of resources such as labor, capital, and land, $\dot{X}/X \geq 0$ and $\dot{L}_{RA}/L_{RA} \geq 0$. Further, the production function of manufacturers in the general consumer goods sector is set as $Y_C = A_C L_C$, where Y_C and L_C stand for the output and labor input in the general consumer goods sector, respectively, and A_C is the technical level established by the general consumer goods sector under spontaneous conditions.

In order to describe the important influence of strong state control over macroeconomic performance, the intermediate product variable X is introduced into the model. Supposing that each unit Y_C can be converted to X of $1/\kappa$ units, then κ is the price of general consumer goods relative to intermediate products. This relative price implies an important assumption that there is an intermediate product market (or a circular flow system for the national economy). Y_C can be converted into an intermediate consumption product X produced by the real capital goods sector. Assuming that there is an equilibrium price κ^* in a fully competitive market, the number of κ relative to κ^* reflects the strength of state control: (1) when $\kappa < \kappa^*$, the relative price of general consumer goods is lower than the market equilibrium price, indicating that the state depresses the market price of the intermediate product of Y_C in support of the development of the real capital goods sector, namely the so-called "scissors difference"; (2) when $\kappa = \kappa^*$, the price of general consumer goods is equal to the market equilibrium price, and the various sectors of the national economy have balanced development; (3) when $\kappa > \kappa^*$, the price of general consumer goods is higher than the market equilibrium price, indicating that the state supports the development of the general consumer goods sector through control. Therefore, κ is a simple abstraction of the national economic development strategy orientation and intention of macroeconomic control, indicating strong state control over the factor market (Yuan, 2009).

Representative manufacturers of the real capital goods sector choose labor input and inputs of intermediate products to maximize profits, namely

$$\max_{X, L_{RA}} \left\{ P_{RA} A_{RA} L_{RA}^{1-\alpha} X^\alpha - \kappa X - w_{RA} L_{RA} \right\} \tag{5.1}$$

Where P_{RA} is the price of real capital goods. Manufacturers in the real capital goods sector require κX units of Y_{RA} in exchange for X units of intermediate products. Similar to the case in which Restuccia et al. (2008) studied the dual structure of developing economies, the authors assume that there are certain institutional barriers to the flow of labor between the two sectors. Let the wage level in the real capital goods sector be w_{RA}, and the wage level in the general consumer goods sector be w_C, then the first-order condition obtained after the derivation of X and L_{RA} is

$$w_{RA} = P_{RA}(1-\alpha) \frac{Y_{RA}}{L_{RA}} \tag{5.2}$$

$$\kappa P_C = P_{RA} \alpha \frac{Y_{RA}}{X} \tag{5.3}$$

From this, the intermediate product representing the industry tide is $X = (P_{RA} \alpha A_{RA} / \kappa P_C)^{\frac{1}{1-\alpha}} L_{RA}$. Let $i = \kappa P_C / P_{RA}$ be the actual interest rate, there is $X = (\alpha A_{RA} / i)^{\frac{1}{1-\alpha}} L_{RA}$. In other words, the strength of the industry tide is inversely proportional to the real interest rate, which is consistent with traditional economic theory. From the derivation of X, there is

$$\frac{dX}{X} = \frac{1}{1-\alpha}\left(\frac{dP_{RA}}{P_{RA}} + \frac{dA_{RA}}{A_{RA}} - \frac{dP_C}{P_C} - \frac{d\kappa}{\kappa}\right) + \frac{dL_{RA}}{L_{RA}} \tag{5.4}$$

It can be seen that the price growth rate in the real capital goods sector exceeds the price growth rate of the general consumer goods sector. The faster technological progress in the real capital goods sector, the strengthening state control, and the acceleration of labor transfer are likely to drive the resource tide with intermediate product X as the carrier, thus accumulating production capacity in the sector. Jones (2002) interprets intermediate products as the primary form of capital. Our model endows X with more meaning. It can be a physical product produced by the general consumer goods sector, or a financial capital flow established after exchange in the product market. The influence of the strong state control power κ on the former is shown in a slew of control policies, such as price guidance for some commodities and price control over resources and land; its influence on the latter is shown in the implementation of policies of cheap finance (Gong and Lin, 2007). Of course, strong state control is ultimately for promoting the transfer of resources to the real capital sector.

Moreover, the first-order condition of the optimum behavior of representative manufacturers in the general consumer goods sector can be written as

$$w_C = A_C P_C \tag{5.5}$$

As real capital goods represented by real estate can only be consumed in the domestic country, consideration is given only to the closed economy. Assuming the national economy consists of a fixed number of N households, the utility function of representative households can be written as

$$U = a\log(C_C) + (1-a)\log(C_{RA}), \ 0 \le a < 1 \tag{5.6}$$

Where C_C and C_{RA} stand for the consumption of general consumer goods and real capital goods by representative households, respectively, while a is the weight given to the two consumer goods in the utility function. Assuming that the household income is y, then $y = bw_{RA} + (1-b)w_C$, in which b is the weight of salary in household income in each sector; given $0 < b < 1$, and the constraint condition of $P_{RA}C_{RA} + P_C C_C \le y$, the demand function under the optimum behavior of households can be obtained from the first-order condition

$$C_C = ayP_C^{-1} \tag{5.7}$$

$$C_{RA} = (1-a)P_{RA}^{-1}y \tag{5.8}$$

In the closed economy, the market clearing conditions are obtained, namely the labor market's equilibrium condition $L_{RA} + L_C = N$, the real capital market's equilibrium condition $Y_{RA} = NC_{RA}$, and the general consumer goods market's equilibrium condition $Y_C = NC_C + \kappa X$. The above two-sector model based upon the basic characteristics of the Chinese economy has a solid microfoundation, providing a clear benchmark framework for analyzing China's inflation issue.

5.3.2 Inflation-driving model

According to market clearing conditions, the following can be obtained

$$P_C = \frac{ay}{C_C} = \frac{ayN}{Y_C - \kappa X} = \frac{ayN}{G} \tag{5.9}$$

$G = Y_C - \kappa X$ defined here is used to represent the effective supply of the general consumer goods sector. The size of G indicates the production capacity of the general consumer goods sector. The larger the G, the larger the production capacity and vice versa. From the definition of G, it can be seen that when X rapidly grows, G will be greatly cut, resulting in a supply and demand gap; when $G < NC_C$, the production capacity of the general consumer goods sector cannot meet the total demand of society. At this time, P_C inevitably rises. According to

$$\frac{dP_C}{P_C} = \frac{dy}{y} + \frac{dN}{N} - \frac{dG}{G} \tag{5.10}$$

It can be seen that when the growth rate of the domestic population and the income of residents are stable, the changes in price of the general consumer goods sector are mainly affected by the effective supply G.

Further, from the market clearing conditions of the real capital goods sector, the following can be obtained

$$\frac{dP_{RA}}{P_{RA}} = \frac{dy}{y} + \frac{dN}{N} - \frac{dY_{RA}}{Y_{RA}} \tag{5.11}$$

Supposing that the inflation rate is expressed as Π, then $\Pi_C = dP_C/P_C$, $\Pi_{RA} = dP_{RA}/P_{RA}$. According to the design of the theoretical framework, the overall inflation rate is the weighted mean of the inflation rate of the two sectors. Let λ be the weight of Π_C, then there is

$$\Pi = \lambda\Pi_C + (1 - \lambda)\Pi_{RA} = \frac{dy}{y} + \frac{dN}{N} - (1 - \lambda)\frac{dY_{RA}}{Y_{RA}} - \lambda\frac{dG}{G} \tag{5.12}$$

According to the definition of G, it is known that $dG = dY_C - \kappa dX - Xd\kappa$. It is not difficult to see that the tide phenomenon will drive the rapid accumulation of intermediate products X. The rapid reduction in effective supply will result in an increase in the prices of general consumer goods, culminating in an increase in inflation. When the time interval observed becomes longer, intermediate inputs have been converted into the production capacity of the real capital goods sector, and the production capacity of real capital goods is greatly enhanced. When the output rate rises, the inflation rate will fall. This forms cyclical changes in the inflation rate from high to low. Therefore, the prosperity of the real capital goods sector and rising prices brought about by the tide phenomenon mark the beginning; the inadequate effective supply of general consumer goods and the subsequent price rises are the medium-term performance; and the cyclical changes in the overall inflation rate are the result. This forms the dynamic evolution path of inflation experienced by China in recent years.

5.4 Inflation dynamics under industry tide: An empirical analysis

5.4.1 Proposition to be tested and conversion of econometric model

The above section illustrates the theoretical mechanism of inflation under industry tide and the resulting inflation-driving equation. To perform an empirical test on the above theoretical mechanism, it is necessary to first establish the corresponding proposition to be tested. According to the theoretical model and analysis as mentioned above, the propositions to be tested empirically can be divided into two parts: Firstly, whether the inflation transmission mechanism under the industry tide mode exists, namely whether the actual data support the transmission of the growth rate of real capital goods prices to the change rate of prices of general consumer goods and the overall inflation rate. Secondly, whether the econometric model corresponding to the inflation theory model is supported by empirical test results.

For the first proposition, this paper examines the interaction mechanism between the growth rate of real capital goods prices, the change rate of prices of general consumer goods, and the overall inflation level. If the industry tide is indeed linked to the formation mechanism of inflation, it should be seen that the growth rate of real capital goods prices drives the change rate of the prices of general consumer goods and the overall inflation rate. The test of this proposition can be performed by setting up the vector autoregressive model containing indicators of the relevant price change rate, and performing the standard Granger causality test.

Regarding the price indicator variables involved, the growth rate of real capital goods prices can be represented by the growth rate of real estate sale prices. The prices of general consumer goods can be represented by the change rate of retail commodity prices. The overall inflation level can be represented by CPI and the inflation rate. In the empirical analysis, the VAR model can be written as

$$Z_t = \Phi(L)Z_{t-1} + e_t, e_t \sim \text{VGW}(0, \Omega_e) \tag{5.13}$$

Where Z represents the variable vector, and $\Phi(L)$ represents the vector lagged operator polynomial. Lag order can be selected according to AIC, and e_t represents the vector Gaussian noise (VGW). According to the estimation results of the VAR model and the relevant Granger causality test, it is possible to ascertain the driving mode between the growth rate of real capital goods prices, the change rate of prices of general consumer goods, and the overall inflation rate.

For the second proposition, the quantitative regression model can be established. The dependent variable is the overall inflation rate, and the independent variables include the income growth rate of residents, the growth rate of output of the real estate sector, and the growth rate of effective supply, while supposing that the population growth rate is insignificant and can be incorporated into the constant term. For the sake of simplicity, π_t, $\tilde{y}_t$, $\tilde{Y}_t^{RA}$, and $\tilde{G}_t$ are used to represent the overall inflation rate, the income growth rate of residents, the growth rate of the output of the real estate sector, and the growth rate of effective supply. c represents the constant term. Then the econometric model can be written as

$$\pi_t = c + \alpha_y \tilde{y}_t + \alpha_{RA} \tilde{Y}_t^{RA} + \alpha_G \tilde{G}_t + \varepsilon_t \tag{5.14}$$

Where ε_t is the disturbing term of the econometric model, and its distribution allows for non-spherical characteristics. The coefficients in the measurement model, Equation 5.14, should theoretically meet the conditions $\alpha_y > 0$, $\alpha_{RA} < 0$, $\alpha_G < 0$.

Based on the above analysis, the measurement models to be estimated and tested that correspond to the empirical part of this chapter are Equation 5.13 and Equation 5.14. The specific data, estimation methods, and estimation results involved in the two econometric models are described hereunder separately.

5.4.2 Data description

According to the degree of consistency with the theoretical model and the data availability, the authors explain the variable selection and corresponding data. Firstly, as empirical analysis is based on quarterly frequency (subject to the highest frequency available for data related to real estate), monthly frequency data need to be converted into quarterly data. Quarterly data are obtained from the observed value of the last month of the corresponding quarter in the corresponding sequence, in order to avoid additional sequence correlation caused by data conversion.

Secondly, the econometric model, Equation 5.13, involves three variables, namely the overall inflation rate, the growth rate of prices of general consumer goods, and the growth rate of prices of real capital goods. The overall inflation rate is expressed as the year-on-year growth rate of CPI commonly used in China, and the data are obtained from the National Bureau of Statistics. The growth rate of prices of general consumer goods is expressed as the retail price index (RPI), and the data are derived from the year-on-year growth rate of the RPI published by the National Bureau of Statistics. The growth rate of prices of real capital goods is expressed as the housing price index (HPI), and the data are obtained from the CEIC database. Since the data ending the third quarter of 2010 are available for HPI, the sample interval in Equation 5.13 runs from the first quarter of 1998 to the third quarter of 2010.

Thirdly, the econometric model, Equation 5.14, involves four variables, namely, the overall inflation rate, the income growth rate of residents, the growth rate of real capital goods output, and the growth rate of effective supply. The data on the overall inflation rate is the same as the data used in Equation 5.13. The income growth rate of residents is expressed as the growth rate of per capita income of urban residents. This variable includes information on operating income, income from transfer, and income from property, and is relatively consistent with the establishment of the theoretical model in this chapter. Based on data availability, the starting and ending dates for the data on the income growth rate of residents are the first quarter of 2003 and the fourth quarter of 2010. The growth rate of the output of real capital goods is expressed as the growth rate of the size of completed real estate. This variable of effective supply is expressed as the products of the general consumer goods sector less the consumption of intermediate products. This variable reflects the effective supply capacity of the general consumer goods sector to supply products as consumer goods. Not only does it reflect the consumption of intermediate products by the real capital goods sector, it also shows the production capacity of the general consumer goods sector. For specific indicators, it has been noted that the total retail sales of consumer goods is the total output value of general consumer goods on the market after deducting the consumption of intermediates. It is therefore used as a measure indicator of effective supply, and its year-on-year growth rate is used as a growth rate of effective supply. The raw data of the above variables are obtained from the CEIC database.

The results of the unit root test performed on the above data show that except for the growth rate of the total retail sales of consumer goods having trend stationary sequence, all other sequences are confirmed as stationary sequences at the traditional significance level. For trend stationary sequences, the authors use the standard time trend removal method to obtain the corresponding stationary sequence for regression analysis. According to the above design, the regression estimate of each model and empirical results of related tests are discussed below.

5.4.3 Regression results

5.4.3.1 Estimation results of Equation 5.13

In order to use the VAR model, Equation 5.13, to test the interaction mechanism between the growth rate of prices of real capital goods, the change rate of prices of general consumer goods, and the overall inflation level, the authors perform the Granger causality test under the framework of the VAR model. The Granger causality test is performed to test the joint significance level of the corresponding coefficients of coefficient matrix Φ in Equation 5.13. In the case of the equation in which CPI in the VAR model is the dependent variable, testing whether there is Granger causality between HPI and RPI is to test whether the respective lag coefficients of HPI and RPI are 0.

According to the test principle described above, Table 5.1 reports the Granger causality test results based on Equation 5.13, where lag(HPI) stands for the lagged term of HPI on the right side of the regression equation, and the definitions of

Table 5.1 Granger causality test results of VAR model, Equation 5.13

	HPI	RPI	CPI
lag(HPI)		0.015**	0.018**
lag(RPI)	0.165		0.057*
lag(CPI)	0.104	0.032**	

Note: The optimal lag order of the VAR model on which the test is based is 4 as determined by AIC; lag(HPI) represents the lag period of all HPI terms on the right side of the equation in the Granger causality test (other representations are similar); the null hypothesis is that there is no Granger causality; the table reports the *p*-value of the Wald significance test statistic; ** and * show that the results are statistically significant at the significance levels of 5% and 10%, respectively.

other symbols are similar. Table 5.1 shows the test results of HPI as the dependent variable in the second column. From the results in the second column, the null hypothesis that CPI and RPI are not the Granger causes of HPI can still be rejected even at the significance level of 10%. In other words, the overall inflation rate and the inflation rate of general consumer goods are not the Granger causes for the growth rate of real estate prices. CPI and RPI have no significant forecast effect on the dynamic trend of the rate of change in real estate prices.

The third column in Table 5.1 reports whether HPI and CPI are Granger causes for RPI. The results show that HPI and CPI are the Granger causes for RPI at the significance level of 5%. From a predictive perspective, the rate of change in real estate prices and the overall inflation rate have a forecast effect on the dynamic trend of the growth rate of prices of general consumer goods. According to the same logic, the results of the fourth column show that at the traditional significance level, HPI is the Granger cause for CPI, and RPI also has a significant dynamic driving effect on CPI (at the level of 10%).

Based on the test results of Table 5.1, the following points are found to be noteworthy: Firstly, the transmission of the growth rate of real estate prices to the change rate of prices of general consumer goods and CPI and the inflation rate is significant. Secondly, the reverse transmission from the growth rate of prices of general consumer goods and CPI and the inflation rate to the growth rate of real estate prices is not significant. Thirdly, there is a two-way driving effect between the change rate of prices of general consumer goods and the CPI and inflation rate.

Overall, the results of the Granger causality test show that in 1998–2010, the growth rate of real estate prices in China indeed affected the trend of the change rate of general consumer prices and the overall inflation rate, while the latter two did not have a reverse driving mechanism for the former. The results verify the inflation transmission mechanism under the industry tide mode as proposed in this chapter. In other words, the tide phenomenon drives the prosperity of the real capital goods sector and rising prices, resulting in inadequate effective supply of general consumer goods and subsequent price rises, and ultimately affecting the cyclical changes in the overall inflation rate.

5.4.3.2 Estimation results of Equation 5.14

While Equation 5.14 is not complex in the form of expression, it is not easy to make an estimation and obtain scientific estimation results, chiefly because the disturbing term affecting the current inflation rate in the model will in all probability affect the current independent variable, and there is heteroscedasticity and sequence correlation (this is why non-spherical characteristics are allowed for its distribution in the measurement model settings). Therefore, before estimating the parameters, the following necessary explanations will be made from the perspective of measurement methods.

First of all, as the independent variables in the model may be non-orthogonal with the disturbing term (namely there is an inherent problem), the Durbin–Wu–Hausman test (based on the heteroscedasticity-sequence correlation correction standard deviation) is used to confirm that the null hypothesis that "least squares estimation has statistical consistency" is rejected at the traditional significance level. To this end, in the regression process of the model, it is necessary to use instrumental variables and use the generalized method of moments (GMM) to obtain the point estimates of parameters and the corresponding standard deviation. It should be noted that the basic idea of the Durbin–Wu–Hausman test is to compare the parameter estimation vectors under least squares estimation and instrumental variable estimation, and construct the statistic in line with chi-square distribution for the test. Of course, in practice, hypothesis testing is performed based on the projection matrix combination of independent variables and instrumental variables and the standard Frisch–Waugh–Lovell principle in econometric analysis. For the specific process, refer to Durbin (1954), Wu (1973), Hausman (1978), and Davidson and MacKinnon (1989).

Secondly, in the course of establishing the econometric model based on the economic model, the random disturbing terms introduced may have sequence correlation and heteroscedasticity. Newey–West variance–covariance correction matrix (HAC) is used to correct the variance of the estimated residual term in the regression estimation process. The HAC correction matrix uses the standard Bartlett's method (Newey–West fixed bandwidth), and the lag term of the weight matrix in HAC is automatically selected through AIC. It should be noted that the weighting algorithms of the objective functions to be optimized in GMM estimation are different, and the corresponding results may also vary. To ensure the robustness of the estimation results, the iterative convergence method and the continuous updating method are used to estimate the weight matrix.

Moreover, the instrumental variables in GMM estimation need to be related to the independent variables, and the over-identification constraint conditions need to be satisfied. Over-identification constraints are confirmed using Hansen's (1982) J test, with the null hypothesis that "all instrumental variables are exogenous." If the null hypothesis cannot be rejected, it shows that the choice of instrumental variables is reasonable. Accordingly, four variables in the model as well as the first lag term of the M2 growth rate are selected as the instrumental variables (data on M2 are obtained from the People's Bank of China, and its growth rate is verified as a stationary sequence).

According to the above design, Table 5.1 summarizes the GMM estimation results based on the iterative convergence and continuous updating methods. The following points merit special explanation. First of all, GMM estimation results given by the iterative convergence method and the continuous updating method are basically the same, indicating that the GMM estimation results of Equation 5.14 are relatively robust, and the effect of different algorithms on the estimation results is not great. Secondly, the coefficient estimate value corresponding to the variables on the right side of Equation 5.14 (income growth rate of residents, growth rate of real capital goods output, and growth rate of effective supply) are positive, negative, and negative, respectively. It is identical with the theoretical assumptions. Judging from the point estimates (in the case of iterative convergence method), α_y, α_{RA}, and α_G are 0.376, −0.102, and −0.130, respectively; the former two are significant at the level of 1%, and the latter is significant at the level of 10%. This indicates that, conditions being the same, the total inflation rate will rise markedly by nearly 0.4 percentage points for every 1 percentage point increase in residents' income. On the contrary, inflation rate will fall significantly by approximately 0.1 percentage points respectively for every 1 percentage point increase in the output of real capital goods and effective supply. Finally, from the results of Hansen's (1982) J test, the choice of instrumental variables is reasonable (Table 5.2).

The above results indicate that the growth rate of residents' income in China has a positive driving effect on the overall inflation rate, while the growth rate of the output of the real capital goods sector and the growth rate of effective supply have a suppressing effect on the inflation rate. From the statistical characteristics of the empirical results, the growth rate of the output of the real capital goods sector has a significantly higher repressing effect on the overall inflation rate than the growth rate of effective supply. It is noteworthy that residents' income includes operating income, income from transfer, and income from property, but not pure

Table 5.2 GMM estimation results of Equation 5.14

	Iterative convergence			Continuous updating		
	α_y	α_{RA}	α_G	α_y	α_{RA}	α_G
Estimated value	0.376***	−0.102***	−0.130*	0.363***	−0.106***	−0.144*
Standard deviation	(0.071)	(0.035)	(0.069)	(0.073)	(0.035)	(0.071)
p-value of J test	0.825			0.841		

Note: The p-value of J test refers to the p-value corresponding to Hansen's J test (1982) (the null hypothesis is that all instrumental variables are exogenous); the standard deviation in parentheses is the Newey-West corrected standard deviation; the Marquardt algorithm is used for the optimization algorithm in GMM estimation (the results remain unchanged with the BHHH algorithm).

salary income. This may imply that residents' consumption and investment patterns may change when the income increases significantly. For instance, marginal propensity to consumption and willingness to invest will increase sharply, affecting the overall economic output through the aggregation effect and ultimately affecting the overall price level. Generally speaking, the theoretical model of China's inflation established in this chapter has been verified by real data. The growth rate of residents' income, the growth rate of real capital goods output, and the growth rate of effective supply of consumer goods are the significant driving factors behind China's inflation. The former positively affects the inflation rate, while the latter two have an effect of suppressing inflation.

5.5 Conclusions

In this chapter, the Chinese inflation theory model is constructed from the perspective of the industry tide under the capital cycle movement to explain the inflation formation mechanism in China since 1998. On the basis of competitive equilibrium, and with the industry tide phenomenon under capital cycle movement as the main thread and with the change in inflation rate driven by the industry tide as the theme, the authors introduce the industry tide factor into the two-sector macro equilibrium model, and find an intrinsic connection between industry tide and inflation in the theoretical model. Realistic data are used in a rigorous quantitative analysis and statistical test on the two related theory propositions, in an attempt to conduct an in-depth theoretical interpretation and empirical analysis of the typical facts of related issues in China.

Based on theoretical logic, the real capital goods sector will have significant industry tide characteristics after securing a wealth of financial capital with the support of relevant policies. During the stage of industry development and prosperity, the growth rate of prices of the real capital goods sector exceeds that of the general consumer goods sector, while tightening state control and the accelerated transfer of other resources will add to the industry tide. At this time, more capital and intermediate products will favor the real capital goods sector, causing a rapid decline in effective supply. This will inevitably cause an increase in the price of general consumer goods, driving the overall inflation upward. When the industry tide reaches a certain level, the intermediate inputs have been effectively converted into the production capacity of the real capital goods sector. The supply of real capital goods gradually increases, causing a significant reduction in price. At this time, it will bring down the overall inflation level. The industry tide is cyclical, thus resulting in the cyclical changes in inflation.

From the results of empirical analysis, the growth rate of real estate prices in China has a significant driving effect on the overall inflation rate and the rate of change in prices of general consumer goods. This indicates that the change from capital inflow to industry tide to changes in prices of real capital goods is the driving chain of the change in the overall inflation rate in China in recent years. It also verifies the linkage mechanism between industry tide and inflation. At the same time, empirical results also show that the growth rate of residents' income including income from property is a positive driving factor behind inflation, while the effective supply of real estate and general consumer goods is an important factor in suppressing inflation. These research findings provide a key reference for managing China's inflation.

For the decision-makers, the current inflation expectations and inflation management should consider shifting the focus from extensive macroeconomic regulation of fiscal policy and monetary policy to focusing on tide phenomena in key industries as well as the adjustment of residents' income, and the supply of real capital goods and general consumer goods. Firstly, in terms of adjusting residents' income, the adjustment of residents' income in a general sense may be more important than the adjustment of wage income in inflation governance. The decision-makers can consider further extending the tax adjustment policy for salary income to the wider income of residents, especially greater tax adjustment for income from property, with a view to governing inflation while improving the strategy of structural adjustment of residents' income. Secondly, consideration is given to increasing the supply of real capital goods as appropriate at a time of high inflation, so as to significantly suppress prices. Of course, the supply of real estate involves a host of issues such as the land ownership transfer mechanism and the planning and use of land. Further research is required to provide more reference in this respect.

Another important implication of the findings of this chapter is to reasonably increase the effective supply of general consumer goods. In the past, the management of demand had always been the focus of macroscopic management. But from the perspective of inflation governance, supply-level management is more important. In particular, when supporting the general consumer goods sector, relevant policies should not focus on the demand level alone, and we should not place over-reliance on the policies of domestic demand expansion to drive industrial prosperity. At the same time, it is necessary to pay attention to the supply level and rationally step up support for the broader general consumer goods sector closely related to the people's livelihood, such as agriculture and the food manufacturing industry. Only by focusing on demand and supply management and narrowing the gap in the supply of general consumer goods is it possible to suppress overall prices and reduce the risk of a hard landing in the economy while maintaining steady economic growth.

6 Inflation dynamics

Goods financialization perspective

6.1 Goods financialization: Definition

As mentioned in the previous chapters, economic and financial crises have been frequent occurrences worldwide in recent years. The American financial problems, European debt restructuring, and Japan's economic stagnation exert a large negative impact on global economic development. Due to the sluggish external economic development, China's economic growth rate is also experiencing a staged downward trend. In this context, quantitative easing policies are frequently unveiled in various countries, and China also unveiled an investment-led economic stimulus plan. While there is no large-scale concentrated investment like the "4 trillion yuan" in 2008, the funds invested by the central government and local governments in recent years have been considerable. These loose policies pushed up the market's inflation expectations for economic recovery to a certain extent, and brought great inflationary pressures to the real economic performance. Besides, as funds flood into different industries, the price fluctuations of many general commodities intensify. Joking media expressions about garlic, mung bean, and ginger graphically describe the rising prices of general consumer goods, and also imply the deep problems of the financialization trend in ordinary commodities in China.

There is currently no single standard for a strict definition of commodity financialization. In fact, there is even no consensus on the definition of "financialization." Relevant documents often use the expression "financialization" in analyzing various respects of the "financial rise," but the definitions and the meanings given vary. Some literature uses "financialization" to refer to the capital market overtaking the banking system to have a dominant position in the financial system (Phillips, 2002), and other literature limits "financialization" to the rise in shareholders' value in corporate governance (Engelen, 2002; Froud et al., 2000; Lazonick and O'Sullivan, 2000; Williams, 2000). Others use the expression "financialization" to describe the rapid expansion of innovation and transactions of financial products (Phillips, 1996).

However, the definition of "financialization" in this literature is not mutually inclusive. Some scholars therefore use a more general definition that covers the above situations, namely the trend that profit is increasingly accumulated through financial channels rather than through commodity transactions and production is called "financialization" (Arrighi, 1994; Krippner, 2005; Aalbers, 2008). This chapter also inclines to this definition, and agrees with the view of Aalbers (2008) that "financialization" can be largely characterized as excessive capitalization of real production. The goal of market operation is no longer production and consumption, but speculation and profit. Therefore, the commodity price in essence runs counter to the original price operation law (namely no longer determined solely by supply and demand on the commodity market), and there are similar and related phenomena with financial products in terms of capital aggregation and price fluctuation models. This is called the financialization of the commodity.

The underlying products in economic transactions can be divided into two categories: Financial products and commodities. Financial products include stocks, bonds, and derivatives. Commodities are sub-divided into capital goods and ordinary goods. Capital goods include real estate, large machinery and equipment, collectibles, etc. These goods generally have sound trading mechanisms, large market scale, and high capital investment. Therefore, they show some characteristics of financial products. Investment value and use value are equally important in their main attributes, and investment value is even more important. By and large, general merchandise does not have a large-scale market, with little capital investment, and the use value is its principal attribute.

Commodity financialization goes back a long way. The "tulip bubble" that occurred in the Netherlands in the 17th century is a typical case in point.[1] From the beginning of the 21st century, commodity financialization has been showing an intensifying trend in China. Products in many industries and capital goods (especially real estate) show similar trends in different periods. This is connected to the adequacy of financial capital in China in recent years. Because financial capital has a profit-driven nature, there is capital accumulation and capital cycle movement (namely periodic entry into different industries) once it captures the profit-seeking space in the cyclical changes in commodity prices, promoting the emergence of financialization characteristics in various commodities and causing large fluctuations in the prices of industrial products.

Obviously, understanding the law of price changes in financial products at different levels and exploring the regularity of the price changes affecting inflation in the financialization of various commodities are of great significance for boosting the effectiveness of macroeconomic regulation. At present, the financialization issue discussed in the academic world is chiefly concerned with economic financialization (Krippner, 2005; Palley, 2008; Zalewski and Whalen, 2010) and bulk commodity financialization (i.e. Tang and Xiong, 2010, United Nations, 2011; Shi, 2011) or the impact of commodity financialization on the financial derivatives market (i.e. Yin, 2008). It rarely covers the financialization of commodities including general commodities, nor does it distinguish the level of commodity financialization and its impact on inflation.

In view of this, this chapter analyzes the price formation mechanism of commodities with different levels of financialization and its driving mechanism of inflation based on the typical facts of commodity financialization in China, with a view to obtaining a more targeted macro-regulation path and providing a useful reference for decision-makers to guide the reasonable flow of industrial capital. Based on the theoretical hypothesis of the endogenous economic cycle theory and the multiplier–accelerator model, the authors obtain the price formation mechanism of commodities with different levels of financialization, and further analyze how the price fluctuations of commodities with different levels of financialization drive inflation. For the division of financialization levels of commodities, two complementary approaches are used: One is to use factor analysis to automatically classify the information in the variable sequence; the other is to give a prior definition based on actual experience, namely selecting the housing products with the highest capital concentration as high-financialization commodities, the commodities with futures trading as middle-financialization commodities, and the general commodities without futures trading as low-financialization commodities.

According to the above explanation, this chapter has a structure as follows: The second section describes the typical facts of commodity financialization in China; the third section explains the price formation mechanism of commodities with different levels of financialization based on the multiplier–accelerator model and its logical relationship with the overall price; the fourth section empirically analyzes how price fluctuations of products with different levels of financialization affect inflation, and uses factor analysis dimensionality reduction technology to solve the model identification problem caused by too many commodity varieties in the system, and uses the corresponding results to establish, estimate, and test the VAR model; the fifth section is a summary.

6.2 The evolution from goods to capital goods and financial products

Judging from historical price information, commodities with large price fluctuations are chiefly capital goods, such as precious metals like gold and silver and antiques like artworks. The price fluctuation characteristics and trading characteristics of this type of commodities are more like those of financial products. Traders tend to have the mentality of following winners, and prices are often subject to large cyclical fluctuations. General merchandise is traditionally for consumption, and its price is generally determined by supply and demand. The price should not be subject to wild fluctuations under normal circumstances as long as the supply and demand on the commodity market is stable. In recent years, however, the prices of many general consumer goods in China have experienced obvious large fluctuations. Typical examples are garlic, ginger, tea, and caterpillar fungus. Capital speculation can be seen behind the price shocks of such consumer goods. The sources of capital are increasingly diversified, and the prices of hyped goods generally experience roller-coaster changes.

By way of illustration, the authors describe and explain the characteristics of price changes of general merchandise and capital goods separately. For general consumer goods, eight commodities most closely related to the consumption and lives of residents are chosen as the representatives for description. These eight commodities are corn, cotton, soybean, sugar, green onions, garlic, ginger, and eggs.[2] At the same time, in order to fully portray the real problems, the authors also glean the data on the prices of representative products of Chinese herbal medicines, tea, and jade products that experienced wild fluctuations in recent years, through the Genius database, the Yimutian agricultural product e-commerce platform, and sporadic media reports. The basic attributes of these commodities should mean they belong to general consumer goods, but their actual price fluctuations obviously run counter to the characteristics of the price formation mechanism of general consumer goods. They have obvious financialization features due to the rapid influx and outflow of capital. For capital goods, real estate and the steel industry are chosen as the representatives. Real estate has the highest capital concentration, and in recent years, the use of real estate transactions for value preservation and appreciation has become more pronounced (real estate has become an important tool for value preservation and appreciation for the public). Therefore, real estate has an increasing degree of financialization; steel is a futures trading product, and has obvious characteristics of financialization.

Firstly, Figure 6.1 depicts the changes in time sequence of the price growth rate of eight agricultural products – green onions, garlic, ginger, egg, corn, cotton, soybean, and white sugar from February 2001 to March 2012. Although the lines in Figure 6.1 seem at first glance to be chaotic, a closer inspection shows two noteworthy regularity features. Firstly, the peaks and troughs of each sequence in Figure 6.1 do not overlap much but emerge alternatively, suggesting that the prices of different agricultural products do not rise or fall simultaneously. In periods of rapid price increase of certain agricultural products, the growth rate of other agricultural products is low or even falls. For example, in February–April

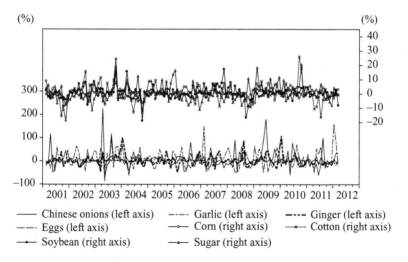

Figure 6.1 Price growth rate of eight representative agricultural products (month-on-month): February 2001–March 2012. Source: Wind database.

2001, garlic prices rose sharply, with a growth rate close to 100%, while the price of green onions fell by 33% in the same period. Similar phenomena occurred in 2006, 2009, and 2011. From the perspective of transaction attributes, these two commodities are agricultural products without futures trading, with a low degree of financialization. In reality, occasional speculation in these products is generally short in duration and discontinuous. Secondly, it can be seen from Figure 6.1 that the commodities with wild fluctuations of price growth rates are mainly general commodities without futures trading and a low degree of financialization (i.e. garlic, green onion, ginger, and egg), while the other four commodities with futures trading (corn, cotton, soybean, and white sugar) have relatively little fluctuation in price change rate. Intuitively, this contrast in the price change rate may be linked to the investment characteristics of the futures market. Due to the existence of bull and bear futures markets, the market will have a reverse change expectation when a commodity price rises, and then the reverse position building will be performed. This mechanism suppresses the price fluctuations of commodities with a higher level of financialization to a certain extent.

In order to compare the differences in price changes of agricultural products with and without futures markets, the authors illustrate by way of garlic and sugar. Garlic has no futures trading, low capital concentration and financialization levels, and generally small trading volumes. White sugar has a futures trading market, high capital concentration and financialization levels, and a larger transactions size. From Figure 6.1, it can be seen that garlic experienced many large fluctuations in the price change rate, and in recent years this was most obvious near 2009. In fact, the price of garlic soared from 0.5 yuan/kg to 12 yuan/kg from April 2009 to September 2010. During this period, the media reported many times the fact of capital speculation on garlic. Of course, the size of this capital is much smaller than that of the futures market. Later, as it is easy to predict the expanding scale of garlic cultivation in the following year, capital began a quick exit from garlic products, with the result that the price of garlic fell to below 2 yuan/kg in 2011. From the information implied in the price data, for these agricultural products with a small scale, hot money generally speculates in the years when the yield is low, because the total yield is small and it is easy to manipulate the market. The time span for speculation is generally one year or one and a half years. As agricultural products cannot be stored for long periods, commodities are generally shipped in the current year, and the capital makes an exit from the industry in the second year.

By comparison, the price fluctuation model of white sugar is markedly different. From 2001 to the first half of 2009, the price of white sugar saw little fluctuation. From the second half of 2009, the price of white sugar rose rapidly. However, as distinguished from the price of garlic, the price of white sugar did not have a sharp drop immediately after the significant rise, but began to fall slightly from the second half of 2011. From Figure 6.1, the prices of other commodities with futures trading (those with a high degree of financialization) also show characteristics similar to the trend of the price change of white sugar. This difference may be due to the fact that China's general agricultural products such as garlic mainly rely on domestic production. Thus, it is easy for hot money to speculate on and stockpile the goods, pushing up the prices. Prices fall rapidly after the exit of the hot money. Products such as sugar feature huge import, and the price is subject to the international market. Coupled with the futures market trading mechanism, the investment scale will not fluctuate wildly in the short term, and thus the price rises and falls stably.

Secondly, Figure 6.2 depicts the prices of several representative products including Chinese herbal medicine, tea, and jade products, including Tienchi ginseng, caterpillar fungus, Pu'er tea, Dahongpao tea, *Pterocarpus indicus*, and Hotan jade (*Pterocarpus indicus* is raw material for precious furniture and high-grade crafts, and Hotan jade is the raw material for jade products).[3] Due to the value of storage and collection, these products have attracted considerable capital inflow in recent years, and their attribute as capital goods has gradually replaced their attribute as consumer goods, with an increasing degree of financialization. In reality, these commodities experienced capital speculation and the prices fluctuated wildly accordingly. In gleaning the data, the authors found that medium- and high-frequency continuous price data are lacking for these products, and it is hard to calculate the corresponding price change rate. For this reason, the price level values of each variable are used to roughly gauge the characteristics of the price fluctuation of these commodities. From Figure 6.2, it can be seen that the prices of the above six commodities rose significantly from 2007, and dropped briefly in 2008–2009. Since then, there was a sharp increase again, and there is a clear trend of simultaneous rise and fall. Based on the changes in the capital market (rising

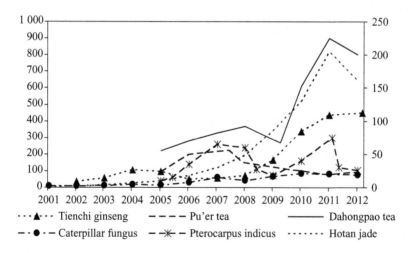

Figure 6.2 Prices of representative Chinese herbal medicines, tea, and jade products: 2001–2012. Note: The prices of Tienchi ginseng, Pu'er tea, and Dahongpao tea (yuan/kg) correspond to the left axis; Hotan jade (10,000 yuan/kg), *Pterocarpus indicus* (10,000 yuan/ton), and caterpillar fungus (10,000 yuan/kg) correspond to the right axis. Source: Genius Database, Yimutian agricultural product e-commerce platform.

again from 2009 to the first half of 2011, and falling after 2011), it can be seen that the price fluctuation of these commodities tends to be the same as the changes in prices of financial products in the capital market.

As can be seen from the characteristics of the specific price changes in Figure 6.2, the prices of Chinese herbal medicine generally show a continuous upward trend, and there is rarely price collapse. In the case of the price of Tienchi ginseng, its price continued to rise from 2001, and only declined slightly in 2011. This characteristic is obviously different from that of agricultural products, mainly because Chinese herbal medicines and agricultural products have different storage characteristics: Agricultural products can only be consumed in the current year, and their quality will be compromised in the next year. Therefore, capital will generally exit after profit in the current year, resulting in a sharp fall in the prices of the corresponding product after a rapid rise; as Chinese herbal medicines can be stored and resold in the next year, capital will enter as long as investors have good market expectations, thus affecting the market supply and demand and price trends.

Tea products represented by Pu'er tea and Dahongpao tea were also one of the consumer products subject to capital hype. From Figure 6.2, it can be seen that the characteristics of their price changes are similar to those of Chinese herbal medicines. In fact, tea products entered the commodity fields early in China due to the long history of tea products. In recent years, the price fluctuations in tea products have been particularly obvious. Pu'er tea experienced a period of rapid price rise in 2005–2007, jumping from 190 yuan/kg to a high of 450 yuan/kg. Afterward, the price began to decline, falling to some 160 yuan/kg in 2011. As capital is invested in different products in the same industry at different times (capital cycle movement), the price fluctuation period of Dahongpao tea is different from that of Pu'er tea. The price of Dahongpao tea rose rapidly from 2009 and only began to fall in 2011. Capital cycle movement can be seen from the time difference for the price fluctuation cycles of Pu'er tea and Dahongpao tea. Different commodities (even products of the same category) obviously have price fluctuation in different periods. While the price of a commodity rises, the prices of other commodities rise slightly or even fall. This characteristic is highly consistent with the characteristic of the different price cycles of different agricultural products as shown in Figure 6.1 (the chaotic lines in Figure 6.1 reflect this characteristic). The alternating fluctuations of the hot industry areas and corresponding prices under this capital cycle movement mean that the price change rate at each time point is not high after all relevant commodity prices are added. This is an important reason for the modest overall inflation of China in the past dozen years since 2000.

Hotan jade and *Pterocarpus indicus* in Figure 6.2 have weaker consumption attributes, and tend to be capital goods, being more characteristic of financialization than tea products. Taking the price of *Pterocarpus indicus* for instance, there were two peaks of a similar height in 2007 and 2011, which is more similar to the price trend of financial products such as stocks. From Figure 6.2, the price of *Pterocarpus indicus* reached a local high of 650,000 yuan/ton in 2007. The investment volume fell sharply thereafter due to the financial crisis, and the price dropped sharply. The average price dropped to 180,000 yuan/ton in 2009, but the price began to rise shortly afterwards, reaching a high of 750,000 yuan/ton in early 2011. From the second half of 2011, the price of *Pterocarpus indicus* fell sharply again due to the reduction in investment, reaching some 260,000 yuan/ton in early 2012. From the basic attributes of commodities, the wood *Pterocarpus indicus* was originally used as a general consumer product for the production of products such as furniture. However, due to capital entry and speculation, it has gradually evolved into a capital product, with the increasingly obvious characteristics of financialization.

Finally, Figure 6.3 compares the price growth rate of real estate and steel with an increasing level of financialization in recent years and growth rates of their respective corresponding industry investment (investment data are available for corresponding commodities in Figure 6.1 and Figure 6.2, so it is not explained). The growth rate of real estate prices is expressed as the growth rate of average sales prices of housing, and the investment growth rate is the growth rate of investment in residential real estate development; the investment data in the steel industry are represented by the fixed asset investment of the ferrous metal smelting industry. As ferrous metals include iron, manganese, and chromium, fixed asset investment in the ferrous metal smelting industry can represent the fixed asset investment in the steel industry. From the perspective of industry capital investment, the investment growth rates of both real estate development and the steel industry show typical periodical changes, and the investment change trajectory is highly consistent with the periodical change trend of the growth rate of respective industry prices. This indicates that the growth rate of the capital goods investment is highly consistent with the evolution path of its price growth rate.

From the analysis of the price volatility characteristics of different commodities with different levels of financialization, the authors conclude that commodity financialization can be divided into two stages: The first stage is the transition from general merchandise to capital goods; the second stage is the transition from capital goods to financial products. In the first stage, the price of general merchandise is still subject to the relationship between supply and demand, but due to the entry of investment capital, market demand has shifted from simple consumer demand to the coexistence of consumer demand and investment demand. As investment gradually grows, the financialization characteristics of commodities become gradually more pronounced. This stage can also be subdivided into the low-level stage and high-level stage. Commodities in the low-level stage include green onions, garlic, and ginger, and their prices are mainly determined by the supply and demand relationship. There is no large-scale, single market, with few market participants, but the commodity price is prone to be manipulated by a small amount of capital. Wild price fluctuations come with capital influx and exit. Commodities at the high-level stage include cotton, sugar, and high-grade tea, and these are highly subject to investment. They have formed large-scale trading markets, such as the futures market or large-scale trading markets in major producing areas. Market transactions are active, and these are affected by the external market in part. A small amount of funds can hardly control such commodity markets, and their prices often show moderate, sustained increase, with occasional staged decrease.

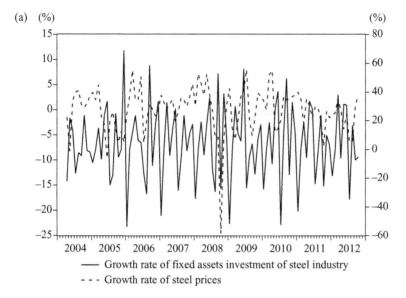

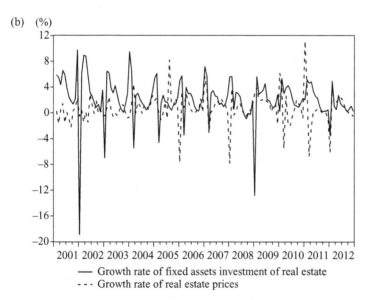

Figure 6.3 Growth rate of fixed assets investment of real estate and steel industry and its price growth rate (month-on-month ratio). Source: CEIC database.

In the second phase, capital goods transition to financial products, and the representative commodities include *Pterocarpus indicus*, jade, and real estate. While commodities at this stage still have physical attributes, the consumption function is not obvious. The commodity attribute is in large measure dominated by investment and speculative attributes, and the transaction behavior is chiefly determined by investment or speculative motives. The impact on the price of commodities at this stage shifts from supply and demand to investment and expectations. The market capital environment has a huge impact on the trading behavior, and the price fluctuations show the volatility regularity consistent with the financial markets such as the stock market and bond market. When funds are abundantly available on the market, the price rises sharply. When there is financial strain, the price falls. It can be seen that the higher the level of financialization of goods, the greater the impact of investment on prices.

Of course, the characteristics of price fluctuations corresponding to commodities with different levels of financialization are also markedly different. From the typical facts, it can be seen that the regularity (such as the time when the peaks and valleys occur) for change rates of prices of various commodities at different levels of financialization differ greatly. This difference may mean that the change rate in the prices of commodities at different levels of financialization has a different impact on the rate of change in overall prices. Therefore, differentiating the driving effect of the price of goods at different levels of financialization on the overall price helps in understanding the dynamic trend of overall inflation. It is possible to reflect the development and guidance of commodity financialization through the characteristics of the driving mechanism obtained. The author first explains the logic in price changes of commodities at different levels of financialization and their relationship with the overall price from the perspective of capital cycle movement, and then performs empirical analysis on the change rate of prices of commodities at different degrees of financialization and their mechanism of interaction with the overall inflation rate.

6.3 Goods financialization and pricing mechanism

According to the traditional theory framework, commodity prices are subject to supply and demand. But the traditional model cannot capture the impact of capital speculation (or investment) on different commodity markets. When financial capital floods into a specific commodity market, for instance, it will result in a rising demand and rising prices. Following the price rises, market demand will have a positive response to the price. In view of this, the multiplier–accelerator model is used to depict the commodity markets with different levels of financialization, and explain the relationship between various commodity prices and the overall price in this context (i.e. the context of commodity financialization levels). The multiplier–accelerator model was first proposed and systematically elaborated by Samuelson (1939). Recent studies include those by Rosser (2000), Westerhoff (2006), and Karpetis and Varelas (2012). The model was originally used to analyze economic cycle issues. The basic idea is that investment constitutes a part of aggregate demand. Therefore, investment growth will raise the total social output through the multiplier effect, while the increase in total output will promote a greater increase in investment through the increase in total income, thus contributing to economic prosperity.

Similarly, it can be observed in real life that when a commodity is favored by capital and the investment volume of the industry increases sharply, its price will increase rapidly correspondingly. The price rise will attract more investment, thereby driving an increase in demand, pushing up the price of goods. In such a cycle, there is a mutual relationship and also an acceleration relationship between price and investment. Therefore, the authors use the theoretical framework of the multiplier–accelerator model and extend it to explain the commodity financialization issue as described above.

According to the case studies, there are differences in the levels of financialization of commodities in the market. For the sake of feasible analysis of the problem and explanation, it is assumed that the degree of financialization of goods can be divided into three levels: High, medium, and low, and subscripts $j = 1, 2$, and 3 are used to indicate the commodities in the high, medium, and low categories, respectively. It is further assumed that the average price of a certain commodity at the specific financialization level of the t-stage is P_{jt}, and the demand for such commodities is divided into two parts: One is the demand D_{jt} due to the real consumption demand, and the other is the investment demand I_{jt}. Moreover, given that government bodies often intervene in the price of specific commodities during macroeconomic performance (especially prices of agricultural products), it is tentatively assumed that government intervention influences demand by acquiring or selling corresponding commodities, and the government regulation quantity is set as G_{jt}. Therefore, the demand function for such a commodity can be written as

$$AD_{jt} = f(D_{jt}, I_{jt}, G_{jt}) \tag{6.1}$$

For convenience of explanation, it can be written as the simplest addition form

$$AD_{jt} = D_{jt} + I_{jt} + G_{jt} \tag{6.2}$$

It is known that the real consumption demand D_{jt} has the nature of the general demand function and has an inverse relationship with the price. Therefore, D_{jt} can be written as

$$D_{jt} = c_j - m_j P_{jt} \tag{6.3}$$

Where m_j represents the proportional coefficient of the demand reduction for 1 unit price increase, and $m_j > 0$ represents the market demand when the price is 0.

Investment demand is related to two factors: One is the actual change in price, and the other is the expected change in price. This is because in the course of commodity financialization, capital is more concerned with the price change range rather than the absolute value of commodity prices. At the same time, the greater the expected price increase, the greater the increase in investment. As investors generally judge from existing information, what affects investment demand is the historical data of actual price change (it is represented by $\Delta P_{j,t-1}$, Δ represents the difference). The expected price change is represented by ΔP_{jt}^e. Therefore, the investment demand I_{jt} can be written as

$$I_{jt} = a_j \Delta P_{j,t-1} + b_j \Delta P_{jt}^e \tag{6.4}$$

The values of the coefficients a_j and b_j can be used to depict the financialization level of different commodities. In general, the higher the financialization levels of commodities, the greater the two factors. Such goods have developed markets, with many investors. The price changes of the same range can attract more investors to make a response, thus resulting in greater changes in investment demand.

Regarding the government regulation variable G_{jt}, if it is assumed that the government's equilibrium price for a certain commodity is judged as P_{j0}, G_{jt} will be affected when the prices P_{jt} and P_{j0} on the market differ. Thus, G_{jt} can be expressed as

$$G_{jt} = -k_j(P_{jt} - P_{j0}) \tag{6.5}$$

Where, coefficient $k_j > 0$.

By integrating the Equations 6.1–6.5, the following expression can be obtained:

$$AD_{jt} = D_{jt} + I_{jt} + G_{jt}$$
$$= (c_j - m_j P_{jt}) + I_{jt} - k_j(P_{jt} - P_{j0}) \tag{6.6}$$

For the total supply, a simple linear model is used as an example, namely

$$AS_{jt} = d_j + \lambda_j P_{jt} \tag{6.7}$$

The coefficient λ_j is used to reflect the reaction intensity of the supply side when products with different levels of financialization are subject to the same range of price change. It will also vary according to the level of financialization.

According to the market clearing conditions, the following can be obtained

$$P_{jt} = \frac{I_{jt} + c_j + k_j P_{j0} - d_j}{\lambda_j + m_j + k_j} \tag{6.8}$$

Equation (6.8) clearly shows that the coefficient I_{jt} is a positive value ($\lambda_j + m_j + k_j > 0$).

Equations 6.4 and 6.8 show the formation mechanism of prices of various commodities under commodity financialization. It can be seen from Equation 6.4 that when the price of a commodity rises rapidly (namely $\Delta P_{j,t-1}$ increases), capital will flood into the production industry of this product, thereby driving the increase in investment demand I_{jt}. Then, from Equation 6.8, it can be seen that if other conditions are tentatively unchanged, the increase I_{jt} will cause the current price P_{jt} to rise, increasing $\Delta P_{j,t-1}$ and further pushing up $\Delta I_{j,t+1}$. In this way, the increase of $\Delta P_{j,t+1}$ will be greater than before, thus pushing up the price. This process is reflected as the interaction of investment and price and accelerated increase.

At the same time, Equation 6.4 also shows that when the expected price increases (namely ΔP_{jt}^e increases), the investment demand I_{jt} will also increase, causing an increase in P_{jt}. The rapid rise of spot prices will further increase the next expected price, namely $\Delta P_{j,t+1}^e$ increases, thereby pushing up the price. When the price rise reaches a certain level, the rate of price increase begins to slow down, and investment demand may also fall. At this time, the price P_{jt} also falls accordingly, and there is a surplus supply of goods. If the investment demand for a certain commodity falls sharply, the price of such commodities may plummet sharply. Of course, after exiting from a certain industry, capital will find another commodity with investment value or room for speculation, leading to the cyclical fluctuation of prices of different types of commodities. The hot industry areas emerge one after another, forming the different levels of commodity financial stratification.

On the whole, if we can obtain prices of commodities with different levels of financialization, then the overall price P_t can be written as the sum of the prices of products with various levels of financialization

$$P_t = \sum_{j=1}^{m} \omega_j P_{jt} \tag{6.9}$$

It can be seen from Equation 6.9 that if commodities with different levels of financialization have different price fluctuation cycles, the overall price after aggregation may also show stable performance at any given time point (static), even if the prices of various commodities in different periods rise rapidly. Of course, in real life, the dynamic impact of prices of commodities with different levels of financialization on overall prices deserves more attention. Therefore, the dynamic impact of prices of commodities at all levels on the overall price can be written as

$$P_t = \sum_{j=1}^{m} \varpi_j(L) P_{jt-1} \tag{6.10}$$

Where $\varpi_j(L) = \varpi_{j0} + \varpi_{j1}L + \varpi_{j2}L^2 + \ldots + \varpi_{jp}L^p$ indicates the lag operator polynomial.

Of course, to analyze the driving mechanism of the prices of commodities with different levels of financialization on the overall price according to the above theoretical logic, it is first necessary to solve the problem of the stratification of commodity financialization, namely separating the indicator variables of commodities with different levels of financialization from a wealth of commodities. It is also necessary to consider the possible feedback effect of the overall price on the prices of commodities with different levels of financialization. To this end, in the empirical analysis below, factor analysis dimensionality reduction technology is used to obtain a price index sequence of commodities at the three levels of financialization. This also solves the model identification problem caused by excessive commodity sequences. The possible interaction mechanism between the prices of commodities with different levels of financialization and the overall price is captured through the VAR model in the empirical analysis.

6.4 Price-driving mechanism under goods financialization

6.4.1 Model setting and data description

This section tests the driving mechanism between the change rate of prices of various commodities under the different levels of financialization and the change rate of overall price (namely inflation rate). To this end, a VAR model is set up:

$$Z_t = C + \Phi(L)Z_{t-1} + e_t, e_t \sim \text{Vector White Noise}(0, \Omega_e) \tag{6.11}$$

Where C represents a constant vector, Z represents a variable vector, and $\Phi(L)$ represents vector lag operator polynomial. Generally, e_t represents vector white noise.

If, according to the basic attribute of the VAR model, Equation 6.11, the individual sequences in the vector Z can be ascertained, the interaction characteristics between the sequences can be analyzed through the standard Granger causality test and the impulse response function (IRF), thereby judging the dynamic relationship between variables. However, for a VAR model with a lag order of p, the coefficient to be estimated will increase radically as the number of variables n increases (namely $pn^2 + n$). The content to be analyzed now involves a variety of commodities. Thus, even if only a representative number of commodities are selected, the number of variables combined is huge. Moreover, subject to the availability of data on variable sequence, the number of observations available for empirical analysis is also relatively limited (sample interval runs from January 2001 to March 2012). Therefore, it is not feasible to estimate and test the VAR model by directly using the price sequences of various commodities. At the same time, if empirical analysis is performed using the price sequence of various commodities, it is hard to clearly define the financialization levels of each commodity. It is thus impossible to test the interaction between the change rate of prices of commodities with different levels of financialization and the overall inflation rate.

Factor analysis can single out common features for many sequences. Multiple sequences with high correlation levels among the price sequences of many commodities can be classified through factor analysis. Therefore, this chapter uses the factor analysis method to perform dimensionality reduction on the price sequences of many representative commodities, in order to extract the common factor of commodities with different levels of financialization, and give an interpretation of the financialization level corresponding to the common factor. On this basis, the common factor sequence containing information on different financialization levels is used to estimate and test the VAR model, so as to obtain the interaction relationship between the change rate of prices of various commodities with different financialization levels and the overall inflation rate.

For the data in empirical analysis, the authors select the change rate of prices of ten commodities with continuously observed values, covering different financialization levels, including corn, cotton, soybean, sugar, green onion, garlic, ginger, egg, polyethylene film, and real estate (housing)[4] and the growth rate of CPI is used as an indicator of overall inflation. The raw data are derived from the Wind and CEIC databases. Subject to the needs of the verification model and the availability of actual data, the sample interval is set between January 2001 and March 2012. The price on the last day of the month is used as the current month's observed value. If the last day is not a trading day or the data are missing, the price on the trading day nearest the end of the corresponding month is used as the current month's observed value. All price growth rate sequences in the empirical analysis are month-on-month growth rates and are confirmed as stationary sequences by the ADF unit root test.

It should be noted that as real estate is a capital product, the capital concentration is especially high. In recent years its characteristics as a financial product (namely speculation and investment characteristics) become increasingly obvious. Therefore, real estate is used as a product with a high financialization level in the empirical analysis. The price sequences of other commodities have no distinctive characteristics. Dimensionality reduction and classification are performed using factor analysis, so as to obtain the price indices of the medium financialization level and low financialization level.

6.4.2 Factor analysis

Factor analysis is performed on the price sequences of nine commodities including white sugar, corn, cotton, green onion, garlic, soybean, ginger, polyethylene film, and egg. It is hoped that these commodities are divided into the medium financialization level and the low financialization level through factor analysis. As a representative commodity with a high financialization level, real estate is not involved in factor analysis. It should be noted that since the authors want to obtain two factors corresponding to the commodities with a medium financialization level and a low financialization level, the factor analysis obtains the target factors by limiting the number of factors coupled with the eigenvalue evaluation index. Moreover, since the analysis involves the choice of factor rotation method, the varimax rotation method is used to maximize the sum of maximum variance of each factor and to enhance the explanatory capacity of the extracted factors.

Table 6.1 summarizes the eigenvalue in the factor analysis and the results of the factor rotation method. It can be seen from the table that the two extracted factors have a common explanatory ability of more than 37%. This result is acceptable for issues such as price study affected by multiple factors. Furthermore, judging from the initial eigenvalues, the eigenvalues of the first two factors drop rapidly, while the eigenvalues for the factors starting with the third factor decrease slowly. This indicates a large fault at the third factor. Thus, the factor extracted by the method of limiting the number of factors is reasonable. From the evaluation index of eigenvalues, the result of two factors also carries conviction. On the whole, the results in Table 6.1 show that the analyzed commodities with different levels of financialization have the characteristics of classification and accumulation in the sequence of the price growth rate.

Table 6.1 Eigenvalues of factor analysis and rotation factors

Composition	Initial eigenvalue			Sum of squares of factor loading extracted after rotation		
	Eigenvalue	Variance contribution rate (%)	Cumulative variance contribution rate (%)	Eigenvalue	Variance contribution rate (%)	Cumulative variance contribution rate (%)
1	1.93	21.48	21.48	1.86	20.62	20.62
2	1.42	15.76	37.24	1.50	16.62	37.24
3	1.09	12.11	49.34			
4	0.95	10.52	59.86			
5	0.92	10.22	70.08			
6	0.86	9.53	79.61			
7	0.79	8.75	88.36			
8	0.58	6.45	94.80			
9	0.47	5.20	100.00			

After separating the factors, it is necessary to further analyze the strength of financialization of the commodities represented by each factor based on the factor loading. To this end, Table 6.2 reports the factor loading matrix after rotation. Figure 6.4 shows a more intuitive factor load scatter diagram corresponding to this result. The meaning of each factor can be seen from Table 6.2 and Figure 6.4. The distinction between the two factors is highly obvious. Factor 1 has a stronger correlation with white sugar, corn, cotton, soybean, and polyethylene film. These commodities can be traded on the futures market, with capital concentration and large market scale. The trading price is often affected by capital inflows and

Table 6.2 Factor load matrix (after rotation)

Commodity or indicator	Factor	
	1	*2*
White sugar	0.561	−0.133
Corn	0.685	0.182
Cotton	0.629	−0.144
Soybean	0.699	0.168
Garlic	0.089	0.683
Green onion	0.082	0.334
Ginger	0.031	0.580
Egg	0.408	0.180
Polyethylene film	0.074	0.670

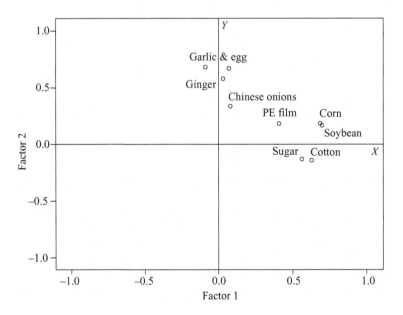

Figure 6.4 Scatter diagram of factor load in the rotated space.

outflows. The futures market significantly raises the degree of financialization of the spot market. Factor 2 has a stronger correlation with garlic, green onion, ginger, and egg. It can be seen from Figure 6.4 that factor 1 of these commodities approaches zero (namely concentrated near the Y axis in Figure 6.4). It is not difficult to see that these commodities with a strong correlation with factor 2 are daily necessities, featuring a lack of concentrated trading market, relatively scattered investment, and sluggish trading activity. Therefore, the degree of financialization of commodities represented by factor 1 is higher than that of factor 2, namely factor 1 represents the growth rate sequence of prices of commodities with a medium financialization level, and factor 2 represents the growth rate sequence of prices of commodities with a low financialization level.

6.4.3 VAR model analysis

Based on the factor analysis, the authors combine the factor 1 sequence (factor 1 represents commodities with a medium financialization level) and the factor 2 sequence (factor 2 represents commodities with a low financialization level) and the growth rate of prices of real estate (house) previously selected (house represents commodities with a high financialization level) to establish the reduced VAR model in order to examine the interaction between the sequences of the price growth rate of commodities representing three different levels of financialization and the CPI and inflation rate, and to explore the inflation-driving mechanism under the different levels of commodity financialization. To this end, a judgment is made using the standard Granger causality test. It is noteworthy that the Granger causality test based on the VAR model is simple from a technical viewpoint, but it is not easy to make a correct choice on the lag order in the model setting, and this directly affects the test results and conclusions. This detail has not received sufficient attention in the empirical literature on dynamic time sequence analysis. In particular, a clear explanation is lacking for the highest order on which information criteria are based, whether the model residual has sequence correlation, and others. This detail is just the key factor that may lead to sensitivity. Regarding dynamic models such as VAR, if there is sequence correlation of residuals, statistical inference such as model estimation and the Granger causality test will have neither unbiasedness nor consistency. Therefore, the description of this detail herein (and in other similar studies) cannot be omitted.

According to the standard time sequence analysis theory (Zhang, 2012), the dynamic time sequence model needs to secure accurate and effective statistical inference. What is most important is that the model has simplicity but no sequence correlation: The disturbing items that meet the model under the simplest model design have no significant sequence correlation. Therefore, the authors use the double constraint method in the choice of the lag order for the VAR model, namely using the AIC and VAR-LM sequence correlation test to jointly determine the optimum lag order. Setting up a model in this way can ensure that the model residuals have no significant sequence correlation, and can meet the simplicity requirements of econometric modeling as far as possible. Specifically, under the given maximum lag order of 8, AIC is used to determine the optimal lag order, and then the VAR-LM sequence correlation test is used to determine whether it has sequence correlation. If the test results show no significant sequence correlation, then this lag order is optimal; if there is sequence correlation, the sequence correlation of the corresponding model is tested from the eighth order downwards based on the general-to-special model setting principle. The lag order corresponding to the minimum AIC chosen in the group without sequence correlation is optimal.

Based on the above design, Granger causality test is performed on the established VAR model. According to the definition, the Granger causality test is used to test the joint significance level of the corresponding coefficients in the matrix $\Phi(L)$ in Equation 6.11. For instance, in the equation in the VAR model in which CPI and inflation rate are dependent variable, testing whether house is the Granger cause or not is to test whether all the lag term coefficients of house on the right side of the regression equation are 0 at the same time. According to this test principle, Table 6.3 reports the corresponding test results, where lag(CPI) indicates the lag term of the CPI on the right side of the regression equation and the definitions of other symbols are similar to this.

The p-value in the second column in Table 6.3 is the Granger causality test result with CPI and inflation rate as dependent variables, which indicates that factor 1 and the growth rate of real estate prices are statistically significant at the traditional significance level, namely both have a significant driving (prediction) effect on CPI and inflation rate; factor 2 is not the Granger cause of CPI and inflation rate, namely factor 2 has no significant driving (prediction) effect on the overall inflation rate. In other words, the growth rate of prices of commodities with medium- and high-level financialization has a significant driving effect on the overall inflation rate, while the growth rate of prices of commodities with low-level financialization has no significant impact on CPI and inflation rate.

From the results of the other columns in Table 6.1, it can be seen that at the traditional significance level, the dynamic drive of factor 1 on CPI and inflation rate is unidirectional (namely factor 1 is the Granger cause of CPI and inflation

Table 6.3 Granger causality test results (p-value)

	CPI	*House*	*Factor 1*	*Factor 2*
lag(CPI)		0.069	0.619	0.018
lag(House)	0.000		0.117	0.411
lag(Factor1)	0.003	0.598		0.021
lag(Factor2)	0.170	0.997	0.083	

Note: The table reports the p-value of the Wald significance test statistic (the null hypothesis has no Granger causality); the VAR model's optimal lag order is determined by the vector residual sequence correlation test (VAR-LM, including lagged 4 phase) and AIC (maximum 8); lag(CPI) represents lag phases of all CPI terms on the right side of the equation in the Granger causality test (other representations are similar).

rate, but CPI and inflation rate are not the Granger cause of factor 1); the interaction between growth rate of real estate price and CPI is two-way (mutual Granger cause). Moreover, factor 1 and factor 2 also have a two-way interaction mechanism (factor 2 has significant Granger causality with factor 1 at the level of 10%), while there is no significant interaction between factor 1 and factor 2 on the one hand and the growth rate of real estate prices on the other hand.

The above results have important implications in several respects. First of all, the multiplier–accelerator effect as explained in the theoretical model is more obvious for the commodities with a higher level of financialization. In other words, the price rise of goods with a high level of financialization will drive CPI upwards, which contributes to the speculation atmosphere and raises investors' profit expectations. As a result, the price of goods with a high level of financialization rises obviously faster. This phenomenon may be because goods with a high level of financialization have characteristics of financial products and are subject to speculative moods and market capital conditions to a greater extent. Therefore, rising CPI may be a clear signal for investors of these commodities – driving the rapid rise of prices of such commodities. Further, as the representative of goods with a high level of financialization is real estate, it has a considerable weight in the CPI. Since the consumption due to housing demand accounts for a large proportion of the total household consumption, the impact on consumers is also significant. Because of this, both consumers and investors regard the price increase of commodities with a high level of financialization as an important signal. Therefore, such commodities have a significant driving effect on CPI, and there is a two-way interaction mechanism.

Secondly, the growth rate of prices of commodities with a medium level of financialization is the Granger cause of CPI and the inflation rate, while CPI and the inflation rate have a weaker reverse driving effect on it, possibly because commodities with a medium level of financialization are often basic production materials, raw materials, or basic agricultural products with large transaction volumes. There are often few substitutes for such products, and the demand is rigid. The price increase will greatly enhance consumers' inflation expectations, thus driving up CPI. Conversely, commodities with a medium level of financialization mostly have centralized trading mechanisms (such as the futures market). Due to this trading mechanism, the price is not only determined by the physical market, but also is obviously subject to the influence of the financial market. The rise and fall of the financial market (such as the rise and fall of the futures index and the rise and fall of the stock market) will affect the price trend of such commodities. In this context, it is not hard to understand the unidirectional driving result of factor 1 on CPI and the inflation rate.

In addition, the growth rate of prices of commodities with a low level of financialization is not the Granger cause of CPI and the inflation rate, while CPI and the inflation rate have a reverse driving effect on it, probably because such products generally lack a large trading market. It is hard for these commodities to change hands, and there is limited space for appreciation in the long run. Therefore, even if there is capital hype, its cycle will not be very long. Because there is frequent capital cycle movement between such commodity markets, general price increases in the category of commodities are few and far between. Overall, the impact of such commodities on the overall price changes is likely to be insignificant. On the contrary, it is just because of a low level of financialization that such goods are little affected by financial markets. There is no overlapping effect of other markets, and they are mainly affected by the real economy. Therefore, CPI and the inflation rate indicator have a significant predictive effect on the changes in their prices.

It deserves special attention that while goods with a medium and high level of financialization have a significant driving effect on CPI and the inflation rate, the corresponding two-way impact mechanism is wholly different. The goods with a high level of financialization and CPI have two-way interaction. This is the form of investment-price spiral escalation brought about by the financialization of commodities, and is the product of advanced financialization. Commodities with a medium level of financialization cannot show this spiral escalation trajectory overall. At the same time, commodities with a low level of financialization are only affected by CPI, but have no driving effect on CPI. This also reflects the small influence of the trading market of such commodities, and the financialization mechanism does not have an obvious role in such commodities.

On balance, the results of the Granger causality test show that the increase in prices of commodities with a high financialization level represented by real estate in China has a significant driving effect on the increase in CPI and inflation rate, and there is a reverse driving relationship. Commodities with a medium financialization level have a driving effect on CPI, but the reverse driving effect is weak. The impact of commodities with a low financialization level on CPI is insignificant, but CPI has a significant impact on the prices of commodities with a low financialization level. This shows that the level of financialization is an important factor for the commodity price changes to affect CPI. The higher the level of financialization, the greater the impact on CPI. Meanwhile, this finding is consistent with the multiplier–accelerator model for the commodity price increase under the capital cycle movement mechanism as proposed in this chapter.

6.4.4 Robustness analysis

In the above analysis, in addition to the real estate price, the authors select the nine representative price sequences with continuous data for the calculation. Commodities are automatically divided into two categories of medium and low financialization levels according to factor analysis. Analysis shows that factor analysis has a strong capacity to extract the common change trend of the sequences, and the extraction method for a limited number of factors is consistent with the result corresponding to the eigenvalue index. However, the types of goods that can be added to the model in the foregoing analysis are limited. If too many types of goods are added, there emerges the problem that the explanatory power of the factor analysis is significantly reduced. The explanatory power of the initial two factors will drop below 30%, thus lowering the feasibility of problem analysis. At the same time, the addition of too many commodities will result in a conflict between the results given by the eigenvalue method and the results given by the quantification method of the number of factors. Moreover, when the number of load matrix dimensions increases in this case, its nature becomes more complicated, and it is hard to define the naming and meaning of the factors.

In order to address the above problems, this section does not put all the commodities together to extract the factors. Instead, it first classifies the high, medium, and low financialization levels according to the financialization characteristics of various commodities in reality, extracts one factor for each category, and then uses this factor as a representative of this category of commodity. In this way, the types of commodities can be increased significantly, and the number of factors is fixed (three). The factor extraction method of principal component analysis (PCA) can be used to improve the explanatory ability of the factors. To this end, the authors use the growth rate sequence corresponding to the house sales price, sales price of commodity housing, and gold price to extract the factor of the high financialization level; the ten price growth rate sequences corresponding to white sugar, corn, cotton, soybean, rapeseed oil, polyethylene film, soybean oil, copper, early indica rice, and wires (steel) are used to extract the factor of the medium financialization level; the low financialization factor is extracted using the five price growth rate sequences corresponding to garlic, green onion, ginger, egg, and flat glass.

Thus, the price sequences involved in the calculation number 18, thus enriching the commodity categories and enhancing the representativeness of various commodities. Commodities with a high financialization level include both real estate and typical capital goods like gold, increasing the representative characteristic of such commodities. At the same time, commodities with a medium financialization level include commodities that are transitioning to capital goods and have shown the nature of capital goods such as copper and steel. These include metal materials that play an important role in industry. Moreover, the goods with a low financialization level include not only agricultural products, but also non-futures goods such as plate glass.

By way of illustration, the authors calculate the percentage of variance that can be explained by the first factor in the three factors' extraction process. The factors extracted from goods with a high financialization level can explain 67% of the serial variance; the first factor extracted from goods with a medium financialization level can explain 32% of the serial variance; the first factor extracted from goods with a low financialization level can explain 31% of the serial variance. The explanatory ability of the three factors is above 30%, indicating sound representativeness. However, if all the sequences are clustered for factor analysis according to the main model approach, the initial two factors will have a low common explanatory ability, and eight factors will be selected according to the eigenvalue indicator, thus compromising the feasibility of subsequent analysis.

After the extraction of factors, the authors establish, estimate, and test the VAR model according to a process similar to the aforementioned one. Table 6.4 reports the Granger causality test results for the corresponding VAR model, where High,

Medium, and Low represent the factor sequence corresponding to high, medium, and low financialization levels. The comparison of the results given in Table 6.3 and Table 6.4 shows that in terms of the dynamic impact of the three factors on CPI, the results here are consistent with the conclusions of the above analysis. In other words, the higher the level of financialization, the more significant the impact of its price change rate on CPI and inflation rate. The change rate of prices of commodities with a low financialization level has no significant driving effect on the overall inflation rate. This result once again indicates that the rise in the financialization level of commodities will significantly increase the impact of price changes in corresponding commodities on the overall inflation rate. This implies that the trend of commodity financialization exerts a great impact on the overall economy. Besides, while the results of the dynamic impact between the price growth rates of goods with different financialization levels are not consistent with the results in Table 6.3, the meaning of the corresponding results and their orientation are still consistent. For instance, although CPI and inflation rate have no significant reverse driving effect on the growth rate of prices of goods at three financialization levels, the p-value of the Granger causality test for goods with a high financialization level is the lowest. At the same time, the change rate of price of goods with a medium financialization level has a significant dynamic effect on the change rate of prices of goods with a low financialization level, but the reverse effect is weak (not significant).

6.5 Conclusions

This chapter focuses on the financialization levels of commodities in China and financialization's impact on the inflation-driving mechanism. Although commodity financialization traditionally appears in capital goods, some general commodities also have had the characteristics and trends of financialization in recent years with the capital influx into many industries, posing new challenges to the overall control of inflation. This chapter studies the financialization levels of commodities and the inflation-driving mechanism from the perspective of theory and practice.

According to the theoretical logic, there is a mutual acceleration relationship between commodity prices and capital investment demand. The commodity prices rise sharply because the price increases lead to an increase in capital investment. Once the rate of return drops, the capital may shift, causing a reduction in the absolute investment in corresponding commodities. Of course, the characteristics of price changes for commodities with different levels of financialization are different, and the change rate of prices of commodities with different levels of financialization has a different driving mechanism for the overall inflation rate. According to the empirical results, factor analysis automatically classifies commodities at different levels of financialization, and the higher the level of financialization, the more obvious the driving effect of the price change rate of the commodities on inflation. From the perspective of the dynamic impact mechanism, there is two-way interaction between the change rate of prices of goods with a high financialization level and inflation. The change rate of prices of goods

Table 6.4 Granger causality test results of the robustness test model

	CPI	High	Medium	Low
lag(CPI)		0.135	0.843	0.204
lag(High)	0.000		0.156	0.702
lag(Medium)	0.001	0.997		0.039
lag(Low)	0.212	0.944	0.557	

Note: High, Medium, and Low represent the growth rates of prices of commodities at high, medium, and low financialization levels, respectively, and the explanation for the rest is the same as that shown in Table 6.3.

with a medium financialization level has a one-way impact on inflation, while the change rate of prices of commodities with a low financialization level has no significant driving effect on inflation.

Based on the significance of the research results, the overall control and management of inflation needs to be treated differently according to the financialization levels of various commodities, and targeted adjustment should be made to price increases of different commodities. Specifically, as general commodities with a low financialization level have a weak driving effect on CPI, it is not necessary to adopt the overall macro-monetary policy to adjust the price increases of one or two types of general commodities with a low financialization level, in order to avoid the possible resulting distortion effect on other industries. From the producer's viewpoint, commodities with a low financialization level are subject to greater price fluctuations before and after capital speculation, with more uncertainties. The risks are therefore greater. The government may consider the dynamic regulation of the supply and demand of such goods, and tighten the regulation.

In the long run, general commodities, especially those with a low financialization level, are characterized by small market size and ease of price rigging, and are prone to become the preferred industry for capital cycle movement. The trend of financialization of general commodities may intensify day by day. In the future, more commodities may be subject to moderate and continuous price increase, and the influence of the investment fund flow will become increasingly obvious. Therefore, it is necessary to consider increasing the trading varieties on the futures market as appropriate, so as to guide the separation of financial demand and consumer demand, and prevent the possible impact of excessive financialization of general commodities on smooth economic performance.

Notes

1 "Tulip bubble," aka the tulip effect, is said to be the first recorded financial bubble in human history. In the mid-16th century, people had a craze for the tulip when it was introduced to Europe. By the early 17th century, some precious tulips were sold at extraordinarily high prices, and the wealthy class vied to showcase the latest and rarest varieties in their gardens. By the early 1630s, this fashion culminated in a classic

speculative craze, and even led to a futures trade for tulips. People bought tulips not for their intrinsic value or enjoyment, but in expectation of value appreciation for gain. Therefore, the tulip, a common commodity, became a financial product, showing a key feature of financialization.

2   These eight commodities are chosen not only for their close relationship with the people, but also for the availability of time series data. At the same time, the choice can cover the commodities of different levels with futures and with no futures, thus laying the foundation for distinguishing financialization levels below.

3   In practice, attention is paid to the price trends of commodities favored by capital hype in recent years such as bloodstone seals, dark red enameled pottery, mahogany furniture, and Hotan jade. However, the price of finished goods of this category is subject to many aspects such as producers of collectibles, appraisers, and tenderers, and it is hard to obtain continuous price data directly from the existing information channels. Therefore, the raw materials corresponding to the finished products are chosen for analysis (the average price of collectibles is basically consistent with the trend of raw material prices).

4   In order to cover the relevant information in the industrial product industry, the data on prices of polyethylene film, an important industrial intermediate product, are added (the price of industrial intermediate products is intimately linked to the raw materials and finished product market).

7 Inflation dynamics

Equilibrium of goods and asset markets perspective

7.1 Background

As discussed in the previous chapters, China experienced two periods of severe inflation in the late 1980s and mid-1990s. Especially in the study on the inflation cycle in the second chapter, the authors use the year-on-year growth rate of CPI as an indicator of the inflation rate, and portray the dynamic evolution path of CPI and the inflation rate in China from 1978 to 2014 (see Figure 2.1 in Chapter 2). From Figure 2.1, it can be clearly seen that CPI and the inflation rate peaked in 1989 and 1995 after the reform and opening-up, both above a high level of 25%. After 1995, the inflation level began to decline gradually, and China experienced brief deflation (namely a negative inflation rate) in 1998–2000, 2002–2003, and 2009.

For the two inflation peak periods represented by 1989 and 1995 and the dynamic changes in inflation before the 21st century, the chief driving factors are clear: The high inflation in 1989 was mainly driven by the "price breakthrough" in the transition from the planned economy to the market economy, while the high inflation in 1995 was driven by the nationwide real estate boom, development zone boom, and investment boom in the context of loose credit aimed at invigorating large and medium-sized state-owned enterprises (Zhang, 2009a). In the late 1990s, the measures adopted by China to tighten macroeconomic regulation, stabilize the financial order, and manage fixed asset investment, as well as the Asian financial crisis that occurred in 1997 gradually began to show a suppressing effect on inflation at the end of 1998.

Although China has not experienced the same high inflation as that of 1989 and 1995 since the mid-to-late 1990s, inflationary pressures in economic performance have indeed existed in recent years. From Figure 2.2 in Chapter 2, it can be seen that since 1996, China experienced three obvious cyclical peaks of inflation (2004–2005, 2007–2008, and 2010-to-present), and the three inflation periods seem to show a ladder-type upward trend. What is more noteworthy is that despite a general consensus on the inflationary pressures on economic development in China in recent years, there are still wildly different views on the main drivers of inflation in recent years. Academia and the relevant decision-makers are far from agreement on this issue.

At present, there is increasingly heated discussion on the causes of inflation in recent years. The representative views can be summed up into three categories: One is structural inflation theory (Wu and Tian, 2008); the second is cost push theory (Chen, 2011); the third is the currency push theory (Fan, 2008; Zhang, 2009a). For structural inflation theory, Huo (2008) and Zhang et al. (2010) have made a detailed rebuttal. However, the reasons given in these two articles against the structural inflation hypothesis are not the same. The former holds that structural inflation cannot explain the driving effect of money growth on inflation, while the latter argues that the skyrocketing prices of primary products triggered by financial speculation are the main reason for inflation in recent years. For cost push theory, it can be divided into two respects: Labor costs push inflation and resource costs push inflation. The study by Fan (2008) shows that labor costs (such as wage increases) have not been the main drivers of inflation in China since 2000. The increase in the price of resource products with a supply shock nature (such as the increase in prices of bulk commodities) does not seem to be a systemic driver of inflation in China (Zhang, 2009b). For the money-push inflation theory, existing studies have mostly studied the direct driving effect of the money growth rate on inflation, but rarely focus on the transmission effect of monetary expansion to overall inflation through changes in real estate prices, and lack theoretical framework analysis of such transmission effects.

Unlike existing research, this chapter proposes the real estate price-push mechanism for inflation in the context of monetary expansion. This is an in-depth study of the dynamic relationship between typical representatives (i.e. real estate) and inflation in the context of industry tide on the basis of research in Chapter 5. To this end, based on the Meltzer's (1995) new monetary analysis framework, with reference to the ideas on the two-sector model for real capital goods and general consumer goods in Chapter 5, the authors establish an extended AS–AD model with a supply and demand two-way structural imbalance. This model is used to analyze the linkage mechanism between asset market equilibrium and commodity market equilibrium, thereby examining the linkage mechanism among money growth, real estate prices, and inflation.

It is noteworthy that although Friedman (1956, 1968) and Meltzer (1995) are typical representatives of the monetarist school, their theoretical analysis frameworks are not the same.[1] Friedman's quantity theory of money (QTM) mainly describes the direct link between the money growth rate and the inflation rate. Meltzer's theory of monetarism establishes an analytical framework for the indirect relationship between money growth and inflation based on the prices of real capital goods (as it is new, it is called new monetarism in this chapter). Meltzer's theoretical framework was originally used to analyze the transmission mechanism of monetary policies, giving prominence to the interaction between monetary assets, securities assets, and real capital goods assets. Because China's real estate market has gradually evolved into a crucial real capital goods market since the mid-to-late 20th century, the authors hold that the real estate market is an important medium between China's money growth and inflation.

From the perspective of structure, the second section of this chapter introduces the new monetarism's theoretical framework based on the linkage mechanism between the asset market and the commodity market; the third section explains the data used in the empirical analysis, and performs the empirical analysis and test; the fourth section sums up the contents of this chapter and points out the policy implications and ramifications of the relevant results.

7.2 Monetary theory frame based on interactions between the asset market and the goods market

In order to study the dynamic driving mechanism between the money growth rate, the change rate of real estate prices, and the overall price change rate (i.e. inflation rate), the theoretical analysis framework in this chapter is based on two central parts, namely, Meltzer's (1995) monetarism theory's asset market equilibrium analysis framework and the aggregate supply and aggregate demand framework of an expanded commodity market. In the asset market equilibrium analysis, the asset market equilibrium model proposed by Meltzer is used as the theoretical basis; in the aggregate supply and aggregate demand analysis, the authors introduce the real structural supply and demand imbalance based on the standard AS–AD model in conjunction with the characteristics of China's overall economic performance mechanism, and analyze the linkage mechanism between commodity market prices and the asset price changes under this expanded AS–AD framework.

First of all, in the asset market equilibrium analysis framework, the asset categories considered are consistent with standard monetarism theory, including monetary assets, securities assets, and real capital goods assets. Based on the reality of China, these three assets are representative. The monetary assets mainly correspond to the money market and are intimately linked to the Central Bank's monetary policies. The securities assets correspond to the bond market and the securities market, and the demand and interest rates are closely linked to prices of other assets. Real capital goods assets mainly correspond to the real estate market. These of course also include production plants, equipment, and consumer durable goods. For the sake of a simple explanation, real estate can be used as a representative of real capital goods assets, and P is used to denote its price. Obviously, both individuals and institutions consider how to arrange these three financial assets for optimization. Therefore, changing the weights of the three assets under different market conditions is not necessarily an act of financial speculation. In most cases, this should be seen as a rational choice.

Under this condition, the markets of three different assets can be harmonized into a comprehensive asset market equilibrium framework. Figure 7.1 demonstrates the basic logic of this asset market equilibrium analysis. First of all, in the coordinates system in which the horizontal axis represents the price of real assets (namely, real estate) P, and the vertical axis represents the interest rate level r, the money market equilibrium line MM and the securities market equilibrium line

SM intersect at the point (P_0, r_0), which indicates the corresponding real estate prices and interest rates when the markets of three assets reach equilibrium simultaneously. Secondly, the positions of the lines MM and SM are linked to factors such as the holding of different assets, the performance of the real economy, commodity prices, and market expectations. On the whole, real estate prices and interest rates in the state of equilibrium are determined by the market supply and demand for different assets.

For the line MM, if the interest rate level and the corresponding real estate price are given, the slope of the line MM indicates the market's willingness to hold monetary assets. When the interest rate rises, the market demand for money will fall. Therefore, when the entire asset market returns to equilibrium at this time, it is necessary to cut down the amount of real capital goods held by raising the real estate prices, thereby stimulating the market demand for monetary assets, and finally entering a new equilibrium state. Therefore, the line MM inclines upwards (the slope is positive). For the line SM, when the interest rate rises, the market demand for securities products such as bonds will increase. Therefore, the entire asset market returns to equilibrium on the condition that asset holders are encouraged to increase the holding of real capital goods in their portfolio through the decrease in real estate prices. This mechanism determines the opposite direction of the slope of line SM and the line MM.

Supposing that the expansionary monetary policy makes the curve MM move to the right to MM1, wealth owners have more monetary assets and use the added money to buy securities and real capital goods, lowering interest rates and pushing asset prices upwards. As the curve MM moves, the curve SM also shifts. As shown in Figure 7.1, when interest rates decline and asset prices rise, the holding of securities falls, and SM moves to the left to SM1. The new equilibrium also moves from the intersection (P_0, r_0) of the curve MM and the curve SM to the intersection (P_1, r_1) of MM1 and SM1. The increase in the quantity of money and the decline in demand for securities lead to a decrease in interest rates. At the

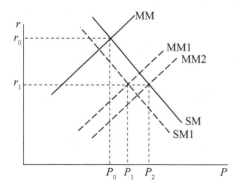

Figure 7.1 Asset market equilibrium analysis framework.

new equilibrium point, the interest rate is lower than the initial level (namely $r_0 >$ r_1). Since the asset price level is affected in two opposite directions, it is not easy to determine the direction of change. However, when interest rates are regulated (such as when the central bank maintains interest rate levels at r_1), the outward expansion of the curve MM1 will cause asset prices to rise from P_1 to P_2.

Secondly, the movement of equilibrium points in the asset market also leads to fluctuations in the commodity market. As the equilibrium point of the asset market moves, the aggregate supply and aggregate demand on the commodity market change accordingly. However, it has been noted that the traditional aggregate supply and aggregate demand (AS–AD) analysis framework is based on the developed economies and cannot accurately characterize the structural imbalances that may exist in developing countries during periods of high economic growth. In reality, this structural imbalance can be reflected as a structural demand or a structural supply problem, and also as the two-way imbalance between supply and demand. Because of this, based on the expanded AS–AD model framework, the authors portray the evolution path of equilibrium price changes in the domestic commodity market following changes in the asset market equilibrium in Figure 7.2 (the price level on the commodity market is expressed as p and the real economic output as Y).

It needs to be noted that the AS–AD model framework described in Figure 7.2 is obtained based on the standard AS–AD model theory, in conjunction with the typical facts of different market operating characteristics of real capital goods (such as real estate) and general consumer goods in China. For the sake of a simple explanation, the model framework shown in Figure 7.2 is explained based on the characteristics of aggregate demand and aggregate supply.[2] Under the benchmark framework of the overall supply and demand, it is possible to deduce the aggregate demand function with a microfoundation based on the demand function, assuming the residents' optimal behavior and the clearing conditions that differentiate real capital goods and general consumer goods markets. It can be proved that this model has important developments in two respects on the basis of the existing macroeconomic analysis theory, thus better reflecting the reality of the Chinese economy. Firstly, the income gap structure has a negative impact on national consumption. As the income gap expands, aggregate social demand will fall due to the decrease in social purchasing power. Secondly, state control exerts an important impact on aggregate social demand. Strong support from the state (and local governments) for the real capital goods sector will contribute to industry tide and further investment, resulting in an increase in aggregate demand (Yuan and Zhang, 2009).

In this way, the three characteristic phases of the aggregate demand function can be obtained: Firstly, the smooth performance phase (segment AB). If the macro economy runs in a healthy state, namely the aggregate demand as the decreasing function of the price p, then this characteristic is consistent with the existing macroeconomic theory. However, the two stages of severe overcapacity (namely economic slump) and serious demand structure imbalance (namely the overheated economy) often occur during periods of high economic growth in China. This is clearly outside the scope of existing macroeconomic theory. It is therefore necessary to expand the classical theory and build the aggregate demand function in the context of overcapacity and demand structure imbalance. The second is the overcapacity phase during the economic downturn (segment AM). This phase is caused by a significant decrease in the price of real capital goods, and the aggregate demand function has a relatively flat line. This phase is also the starting point of the next round of market boom in real capital goods. The third is the demand structure imbalance phase during the overheated economy period (segment BY1). As the rapid development of the real capital goods sector causes the income gap to widen rapidly, the aggregate demand function has a relatively straight line. Thus, segment MABY1 in Figure 7.2 shows the shape of the aggregate demand curve of the expanded AS–AD frame.

Based on the above expanded AS–AD framework, it is possible to examine the linkage relationship between asset market equilibrium and commodity market equilibrium, and then analyze the overall price changes in the commodity markets. When the asset market equilibrium moves from P_1 to P_2, the market's enthusiasm for and pursuit of real capital goods stimulate the consumption of related products, leading to an increase in aggregate demand. From Figure 7.2, the aggregate demand curve expands outward (curve AD1), and the equilibrium point of the corresponding overall price level must be higher than the original equilibrium point p_0. Therefore, from the linkage mechanism between the asset market equilibrium and the commodity market equilibrium as summarized in Figure 7.1 and Figure 7.2, the changes in the total quantity of money affect the price of real capital goods, while the changes in the prices of real capital goods will eventually be transmitted to the changes in the overall price level.

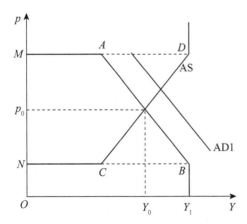

Figure 7.2 Extended AS–AD analysis framework based on asset market equilibrium.

7.3 Empirical tests of asset market equilibrium

7.3.1 Data description

The empirical analysis in this chapter chiefly concerns three variables, viz., the growth rate of the monetary aggregate, the inflation rate, and the rate of change in real estate prices. The authors use M2 as a measure indicator of the monetary aggregate, M2's year-on-year growth rate as the growth rate of the monetary aggregate, and year-on-year growth rate of CPI as an indicator of the inflation rate. The year-on-year growth rate of sales prices of commodity housing (yuan/square meter, cumulative average, and national total) is used to measure the rate of change in real estate prices. Raw data are obtained from the CEIC database. The sample interval is from the fourth quarter of 1996 to the first quarter of 2012 (the starting point of the sample is subject to the data on real estate prices). For the sake of explanation, ΔM2, ΔCPI, and ΔHPI are used to represent the growth rate of the monetary aggregate, the year-on-year growth rate of CPI (namely, CPI and inflation rate), and the change rate of HPI (namely, the rate of change in real estate prices).

Figure 7.3 portrays the dynamic evolution path of M2 growth rate, CPI and inflation rate, and the change rate of HPI in China from 1996 to 2012. Based on the statistical data, the average cumulative increase in M2 in the sample interval in China approaches 300%, the average cumulative increase in the sales prices of commodity housing exceeds 120%, and the average cumulative increase in the CPI and inflation rate approaches 30%. Moreover, Figure 7.3 shows that the change characteristics of the three variables are different at specific time points, but there are similarities in the overall fluctuation trend. Specifically, as ΔM2

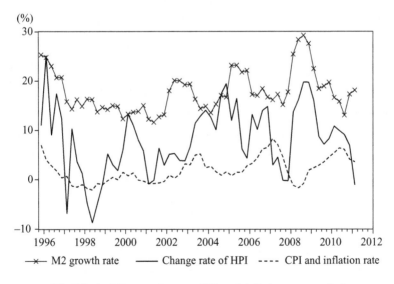

Figure 7.3 China's M2 growth rate, CPI and inflation rate, and change rate in HPI (year-on-year).

decreased from the end of 1996 (from 25% in 1996 to below 15% in 2002), ΔHPI and ΔCPI also showed a downward trend, and this continued until 2002. During this period, the leapfrogging change in ΔHPI was more frequent and obvious (especially a transient local high peak in 2001), while ΔCPI and ΔM2 were relatively stable. After 2002, the three are more similar in terms of characteristics of cyclical changes, but for the most part of the period, ΔM2 seems to be ahead of ΔHPI by about one year, while ΔHPI is ahead of ΔCPI by about one year. Judging from the time sequence evolution path of these three growth rate variables, there may be a high dynamic correlation among the three. Whether this dynamic correlation suggests a dynamic driving relationship among variables (such as Granger causality) requires further rigorous measurement testing. The analysis of this will be performed in the fourth section.

Regarding the above sequence of variables, the empirical analysis below first judges its stationarity. To this end, a unit root test is performed on ΔM2, ΔCPI, and ΔHPI, respectively. In order to ensure the robustness of the results of the unit root test, the authors use standard ADF, PP and KPSS unit root tests. The null hypotheses of the first two tests are the same (namely, "the sequence to be tested contains unit roots"), while the null hypothesis of the KPSS test is "the sequence to be tested is a stationary sequence." According to the basic definition and graphical characteristics of the variables, the authors assume that the models corresponding to the unit root tests do not contain time trend variables (but all contain constant terms). Moreover, the optimal lag phase in the ADF test is determined by the AIC (maximum of eight phases is given), and Newey–West method is used for the variance estimation correction process in the KPSS test (Bartlett kernel).

Table 7.1 sums up the different results of the unit root test for the three variables. From the test results, the *p*-values of the ADF and PP tests corresponding to ΔM2 and ΔCPI are less than 5%, and the KPSS statistic is not significant at the level of 5% (corresponding to the "stationarity" null hypothesis). Therefore, ΔM2 and ΔCPI can be judged as stationary sequences. For ΔHPI, the ADF test shows that the null hypothesis that this variable contains a unit root cannot be rejected at the level of 5%, but both the PP and KPSS tests show it to be a stationary sequence. These seemingly inconsistent test conclusions are not surprising. On the one hand, the basic principles of the different tests are different. On the other hand, the power of unit root tests (especially the ADF test) is relatively low. Where the results of different tests differ, the researchers need to make active judgments on

Table 7.1 Unit root test results of variables

	ADF (p-value)	*PP (p-value)*	*KPSS (statistics)*
ΔCPI	0.013**	0.047**	0.455*
ΔM2	0.041**	0.032**	0.244
ΔHPI	0.227	0.004***	0.251

Note: *, **, and *** indicate that it is statistically significant at the levels of 10%, 5%, and 1%, respectively.

the basic definition of the sample characteristics and sequences (rather than judgments passively determined by statistical results). Based on the above description, it is reasonable to judge ΔM2, ΔCPI, and ΔHPI as stationary sequences.

7.3.2 Model estimation results

In order to test whether monetary growth and inflation lead to an indirect driving relationship through real estate prices, the authors set up the vector autoregression (VAR) model system for the Granger causality test. The standard VAR model can be written as

$$X_t = \Phi(L)X_{t-1} + \varepsilon_t \qquad (7.1)$$

Where X_t is a time sequence vector containing endogenous variables; $\Phi(L)$ represents the vector polynomial of the lag operator; optimal lag order is determined by the information criteria and the VAR sequence correlation test (VAR-LM); ε_t is the vector disturbing item.

Regarding the analysis, the authors set up three VAR model systems. The first VAR model contains three variables of ΔM2, ΔHPI, and ΔCPI; the second VAR model contains ΔM2 and ΔHPI; and the third VAR model contains ΔHPI and ΔCPI. The general dynamic driving relationship that may exist among the three variables is examined by estimating and testing the first VAR model. By analyzing the second and third VAR models, the authors can study the two-way interaction between the monetary growth rate and the housing price growth rate, and between the housing price growth rate and the inflation rate. At the same time, by establishing the second and third VAR models, it is possible to reduce the impact of potential collinearity between the price growth variables (namely, the housing price growth rate and inflation rate) on the estimation results.

The VAR model-based Granger causality test is relatively simple from a technical viewpoint, but it is not easy to correctly choose the lag order in the model setting, and this directly affects the test results and conclusions. It has been noted that for dynamic models such as VAR, in case of sequence correlation of residuals, statistical inferences such as model estimates and the Granger causality test have neither unbiasedness nor consistency. Therefore, this chapter adopts the double constraint method in the choice of the model lag order, namely, jointly judging the optimal lag order based on the information criterion and the VAR-LM sequence correlation test. Setting up the model in this way has the advantages of ensuring that the model residuals have no significant sequence correlation, and also meeting the simplicity requirements of econometric modeling as far as possible. Specifically, given that the maximum lag order is eight, the AIC is used to determine the optimal lag order, and then the VAR-LM sequence correlation test is performed to determine whether there is sequence correlation.[3] If the test results show a lack of significant sequence correlation, the lag order is optimal. If there is sequence correlation, the sequence correlation of the corresponding model is tested from the eighth order downwards based on the general-to-model setting principle. The lag order corresponding to the minimum AIC chosen in the group without sequence correlation is optimal.

Based on the above design, the authors perform the Granger causality test on the basic model. According to the definition, the Granger causality test is performed to test the joint significance level of the matrix $\Phi(L)$ corresponding coefficient in Equation 7.1. For instance, in the equation with ΔCPI as the dependent variable, testing whether ΔM2 has Granger cause with this is to test whether all the lag term coefficients of ΔCPI on the right side of the regression equation are 0 at the same time. According to this test principle, Table 7.2 reports the Granger causality test results based on Equation 7.1. In this, lag(ΔCPI) represents the lag term of ΔCPI on the right side of the regression equation, and the definitions of the other symbols are similar to this.

Firstly, for the first VAR model (containing ΔM2, ΔHPI, and ΔCPI), the authors examine the causal relationship between any two of the three variables. The third column reports the causality result with ΔM2 as the dependent variable. It can be seen that at the traditional significance level, the null hypothesis that ΔHPI and ΔM2 have no Granger causality cannot be rejected (p-value = 0.622), but the null hypothesis that ΔCPI and ΔM2 have no Granger causal relationship is rejected (p-value = 0.000). In other words, the change rate of HPI does not have a dynamic driving effect on the monetary growth rate, whereas the CPI and inflation rate have a significant dynamic driving effect on the monetary growth rate. This is fully consistent with China's monetary policy response equation (the inflation rate is the main target of the central bank's regulation policy on the monetary aggregate). The subsequent two columns are Granger causality test results with ΔHPI and ΔCPI as dependent variables, respectively. As for ΔHPI, the results show that it has a Granger causal relationship with the M2 growth rate and CPI and inflation

Table 7.2 Results of Granger causality test based on Meltzer model

		ΔM2	ΔHPI	ΔCPI
VAR:[ΔM2,ΔHPI,ΔCPI]	lag(ΔM2)		0.010**	0.023**
Optimal lag = 7	lag(ΔHPI)	0.622		0.211
VAR-LM(p-value) = 0.417	lag(ΔCPI)	0.000***	0.025**	
VAR:[ΔM2,ΔHPI]		ΔM2	ΔHPI	
Optimal lag = 1	lag(ΔM2)		0.056*	
VAR-LM(p-value) = 0.227	lag(ΔHPI)	0.612		
VAR:[ΔHPI,ΔCPI]		ΔHPI	ΔCPI	
Optimal lag = 8	lag(ΔHPI)		0.017**	
VAR-LM(p-value) = 0.122	lag(ΔCPI)	0.111		

Note: The sample interval is from the fourth quarter of 1996 to the first quarter of 2012 (before the adjustment of the lag phase); the table reports the p-value of the Wald significance test statistic (the null hypothesis shows no Granger causality); the optimal lag order of the VAR model is determined by the vector residual's sequence correlation test (VAR-LM, lag phase 1) and the information criterion (maximum of 8); lag(ΔCPI) represents the lag phase of all CPI terms on the right side of the equation in the Granger causality test (other representations are similar).

rate; for ΔCPI, the growth rate of M2 has a significant dynamic driving effect on it, but ΔHPI does not seem to indicate a significant driving effect.

Secondly, the authors further examine the results of the Granger causality test corresponding to the second and third VAR models reported in Table 7.2. The test results of the second VAR model indicate that ΔM2 has a unidirectional significant driving effect on ΔHPI (significant at the level of 10%). The test results of the third VAR model show that ΔHPI has a unidirectional significant driving effect on ΔCPI. It is not difficult to see that the results of the Granger causality test on the second and third VAR models are not fully consistent with the test results corresponding to the first VAR model, especially the difference between the mutual driving results of ΔCPI and ΔHPI. As mentioned earlier, this may be due to the high collinearity between the rate of change of the price index (namely ΔCPI and ΔHPI) and ΔM2. However, in conjunction with the test results of these three VAR models, it can still be seen that the dynamic driving effect of ΔM2 on ΔCPI is significant, and the unidirectional driving effect of ΔM2 on ΔHPI and the unidirectional driving effect of ΔHPI on ΔCPI are also significant. In other words, not only does the monetary growth rate have a direct dynamic driving effect on the CPI and inflation rate, it can also be transmitted to the CPI and inflation rate through the price of real estate (rate of change). This indirect transmission mechanism has been significantly present in at least the past dozen years since 2000. It is noteworthy that, based on the results of the sequence correlation test (the original hypothesis is "there is sequence correlation for the residuals of VAR model"), the choice of lag phase in all VAR models ensures that the model has no sequence correlation (p-values are greater than 10%). This also guarantees scientific and reliable results of the empirical analysis.

7.4　Conclusions

Based on the new monetarism theory proposed by Meltzer (1995), this chapter proposes an expanded AS–AD model with a two-way structural supply and demand imbalance. It is used to analyze the driving mechanism of inflation in China from 1996 to 2012. The results of the research show that since the mid-to-late 1990s, the increase in real estate prices has been a fundamental driving factor for overall inflation in the context of monetary expansion. From the perspective of theoretical logic, when interest rates are subject to regulation and cannot float freely, the direct effect of monetary expansion is the rise of prices of real capital goods represented by real estate (on the asset market), and then the overall price level is raised through the linkage with the commodity market. This in turn leads to the formation of the real estate price (or asset price) driving mechanism of inflation.

From the perspective of the characteristics of real economic performance, expansionary monetary policy for ensuring rapid economic growth, the increase in funds outstanding for foreign exchange under the mandatory foreign exchange settlement and sale system, and the excess liquidity brought by the expectations for appreciation of the renminbi in recent years are expressed as the rapid expansion of money supply. As the savings deposit rates are relatively low under the currency expansion, private capital and state-owned capital inevitably seek to invest in industries with high return. At this time, the real capital goods market (mainly the real estate market in China) will see rapid development, resulting in a sharp rise in real estate prices and promoting the market to form high inflation expectations. Once the market expects that future prices will continue to rise, consumers will find it easier to accept price increases in the commodity market. The pricing behavior of manufacturers will change, with the result that the rise in commodity prices far exceeds that of the cost of raw materials. This chain leads to a dynamic driving relationship between the rate of change in the real estate price (and monetary growth rate) and the fluctuating inflation.

From the perspective of financial system arrangements, the non-market-oriented interest rate determination mechanism and interest rate regulation constitute the basis of the financial system that forms the current driving mechanism from monetary expansion to real estate prices to inflation in China. Therefore, a change of the non-market-oriented interest rate determination mechanism is one of the fundamental measures to achieve stable real estate prices and overall prices in China. As China's market economy rapidly develops, the non-market-oriented interest rate system arrangement is increasingly in conflict with the development efficiency of the national economy, and has an increasingly negative impact on the dynamic trend of core macroeconomic variables such as inflation. Under the progressive reform model, decision-makers need to consider speeding up the interest rate marketization. While the development of the money market has played an important role in promoting the interest rate marketization in recent years, the regulation of the benchmark interest rate of loans is still the main bottleneck which restricts the full realization of interest rate marketization.

Based on the extended significance of the research in this chapter, eliminating the existing model dominated by demand management and the balanced management of supply and demand is an institutional choice worthy of consideration at present. For a long time to come, the balanced management of supply and demand on the real estate market is a top priority. While the promotion of affordable housing, housing with double limitations, and low-rent housing helps to ease demand pressure in the short run, the construction of affordable housing that provides private property rights should be phased out of the market from the perspective of long-term sustainable development. It may be a better choice to step up the supply of policy housing such as low-rent housing without the granting of property rights. We should be aware that the excessive development of policy low-income housing will occupy limited land resources and the supply space of general commodity housing. In the long run, it is of no benefit to urban planning and the improvement of human settlements, and may even result in a vicious circle of exhaustion of land resources and deterioration of the urban environment. Of course, the real estate market and urban planning is a complicated systematic undertaking. More scientific research and system planning are urgently needed in this respect.

Notes

1   Milton Friedman, Anna Schwartz, Karl Brunner, and Allan Meltzer are representatives of the monetarist school. Continuous and in-depth research on the theory of monetarism has been conducted. On balance, the general consensus of the monetarist school is as follows: Firstly, currency is neutral in the long run. Secondly, currency is non-neutral in the short run. Thirdly, the nominal interest rate and real interest rate should be differentiated in the relevant economic analysis. Fourthly, monetary aggregate occupies an important place in policy analysis.

2   Refer to Chapter 5 for the deduction process of the theoretical model corresponding to Figure 7.2.

3   The choice of information criteria and maximum lag phase needs to be set according to the sample size. Generally, when the sample is relatively large, it is reasonable to use AIC and the maximum eight lag phases (for quarterly data) as the basis for judging the optimal lag phase, because the eighth highest lag corresponds to two years. The lag effect of economic variables should be released within two years. If the sample is small in special cases, consideration is given to using SIC (or AIC and SIC) and a maximum of four phases as the basis, but there is a need to balance sequence correlation and model simplicity.

8 Inflation dynamics

A compromise perspective between monetarism and New Keynesianism

8.1 Literature review

Since the reform and opening-up in 1978, inflation and economic growth have always been the most pivotal economic indicators for China's macroeconomic regulation, while the money supply growth rate is regarded as the main policy medium for regulating inflation and economic growth. The Executive Report on Monetary Policy published by the People's Bank of China clearly pointed out that the growth rate of money supply is the most important intermediary target for the People's Bank of China. Therefore, the mechanism of interaction between inflation, economic growth, and money supply has received much attention in domestic academic circles and decision-makers. For China, conducting in-depth research into the interaction mechanism between relevant variables since the reform and opening-up, exploring how the monetary growth rate affects inflation rate and economic growth rate under a certain basic theoretical framework, and carrying out targeted short-term and medium- and long-term overall strategy adjustment on this basis are of great significance for promoting the stable transition of China's economic growth model and thus achieving sustainable economic development.

Due to the above reasons, a slew of empirical studies on this issue have been carried out in academic circles in China as the data on China's economy accumulate. However, following a dozen years of research, the mechanism of interaction between inflation, economic growth, and money supply has become increasingly blurred instead and no broad consensus has been reached. This has without a doubt brought great confusion to decision-making on the overall economy. From the existing literature, there is the conclusion of monetary neutrality (namely, that the monetary growth rate has no effect on the economic growth rate, the conclusion of the non-neutrality of money; the conclusion that the growth rate of money significantly drives inflation (Yang Liping et al., 2008); and the conclusion that the monetary growth rate is not a significant driver of the inflation rate.

On the surface, the different conclusions of existing studies may be caused by different data sample intervals, definitions of relevant indicators, and different quantitative methods. However, a careful perusal of the relevant literature shows that the nub of the problem is the dislocation between the macro-theoretical framework and the empirical quantitative analysis. Specifically, the existing research on the mechanism of interaction between inflation, economic growth, and money supply mainly performs corresponding variable choice and quantitative regression on the statistical nature (stationarity) of the data sequence, but lacks the constraints of a general macro-theoretical model framework. For example, for the analysis of the relationship between money supply and inflation, the variable sequences for regression in some literature are the monetary growth rate and inflation rate, while other literature performs the regression relationship between the increase in the monetary growth rate and the increase in the inflation rate (such as Liu Jinquan et al., 2004). Even if the data on variables are processed in the same way, the number of variables selected for the econometric model in the same literature is different. Thus, relevant conclusions are prone to high sensitivity to the sample interval and definitions of indicators.

In fact, the issue of the mechanism of interaction between inflation, economic growth, and money supply is not merely an empirical problem. Constraints on the macroscopic theoretical model (especially the choice of variable forms) and the rigorous quantitative analysis are of equal importance. From the perspective of the development of basic theory, the 1970s and 1980s became the watershed for the transition from monetarism to Keynesian theory. Before the 1980s, studies on inflation and economic growth issues were mostly based on the monetarism theory framework represented by Friedman's (1956) quantity theory of money (QTM). The relationship between money and price or between the monetary growth rate and the inflation rate (namely price growth rate) became the focus of research. However, with the combination of New Keynesian sticky-price theory represented by Calvo (1983) and dynamic stochastic general equilibrium modeling (DSGE) and as the Western countries represented by the United States began to use interest rates instead of monetary aggregate as a monetary policy medium after 1982, monetarism theory, which stresses the importance of monetary indicators, gradually faded out of the macroeconomic analysis framework. To date, an analysis framework that contains the real economic output, inflation rate, and interest rate (rather than currency) has become the mainstream model of modern macroeconomic analysis. As the model system is simple and can portray the dynamic relationships of the main macroeconomic indicators comprehensively, it is also called the toy model of modern macroeconomic analysis.

The New Keynesian macroeconomic model is a mainstream theory. However, due to the different stages of development, the growth rate of money supply still occupies an important place in China's macroeconomic development. Therefore, it is unreasonable to use Keynesian theory to analyze China's issues. Likewise, analysis based on traditional monetarism theory alone ignores the endogenous problem of China's money supply mechanism (the monetarism theory supposes that money supply is an exogenous variable). In view of this, this chapter integrates China's endogenous monetary supply mechanism into the monetarism theory model, and rigorous empirical analysis is carried out under the constraints of the basic theoretical framework, with a view to detecting the interaction between inflation, economic growth, and money supply.

This chapter makes contributions in two aspects: Firstly, the dynamic model system is set up based on monetarism theory under the endogenous money supply mechanism to explain its internal relationship with the New Keynesian macro model, and the relevant variables are selected for empirical analysis under the constraints of the theoretical framework. Secondly, a detailed examination of issues such as dynamic model setting and sequence correlation is carried out under the empirical analysis, and the short-term dynamics and long-term equilibrium mechanism of the core variables are comprehensively analyzed. The general law of interaction mechanism for China's inflation, economic growth, and money supply since the reform and opening-up is obtained based on the multi-dimensional robustness test. It can be seen that this law does not vary with changes in sample intervals and definitions of variables. This is the main contribution of this chapter.

In terms of structure, the second section of this chapter sets up a monetarism theory model under the endogenous money supply mechanism, and clarifies its internal connection with the New Keynesian modern macro model and its applicability to the analysis of China's problems. The third section deals with data analysis and an explanation of typical facts. The fourth and fifth sections analyze the short-term dynamic mechanism and long-term equilibrium mechanism of the model system established. The sixth section explains the policy implications of the empirical results and gives a summary of this chapter.

8.2 Internal consistencies between monetarism and New Keynesianism

The most influential theory analysis framework for the interaction between inflation, economic growth, and money supply is the famous quantity theory of money (QTM) proposed by Friedman (1956). In the equilibrium state, according to this theory, the following equation applies to the relationship between the monetary stock M, the price P, and the real economic output Y:

$$M = kPY \tag{8.1}$$

Where k measures the ratio of the currency that people are willing to hold to their nominal income, and its reciprocal $V = 1/k$ denotes the speed of currency circulation. According to Equation 8.1, the monetarist school argues that if there is a change in the monetary stock, such as a sudden increase, aggregate demand is highly likely to increase due to stimulation in the short term, and aggregate output may increase accordingly. However, due to the restriction of production capacity, enterprises pursuing maximum profit will raise the prices of their products. In this way, the growth effect of the monetary stock is mainly reflected in the rise of prices, without substantially promoting an increase in real economic output. In extreme cases (the speed of money circulation is basically constant), the rate of change of M is identical to the rate of change of P, namely the growth rate of monetary stock is equal to the inflation rate. There is no change in real economic output at this time.

Equation 8.1 is the basis for understanding the central theory of traditional monetarism. If the logarithm at both sides of Equation 8.1 is taken for difference processing, it can be re-written as follows:

$$\Delta M_t + \Delta V_t = \Delta P_t + \Delta Y_t \tag{8.2}$$

Where ΔM_t represents the growth rate of the monetary stock, and the definitions of other variables are similar. Assuming that the speed of money circulation is basically stable, Equation 8.2 can be rewritten as

$$\Delta P_t = \Delta M_t - \Delta Y_t \tag{8.3}$$

In the view of the monetarist school, Equation 8.3 suggests that the rate of change in prices (namely, inflation rate) and the monetary growth rate will change with the same proportion in the long term. Even if the monetary growth rate has a positive impact on economic output, this effect only exists in the short-term, and will certainly disappear in the long run. This is the so-called monetary neutrality theory.

However, the theoretical setting in Equation 8.3 is highly stylized. It is not easy to accurately portray the reality. In particular, if monthly or quarterly data are used for empirical modeling, consideration must be given to the duration of the price contract in the real world and the dynamic impact among variables. In fact, this static theoretical equation can hardly capture the time-lag effects brought by cognition, understanding, and adjustment in the real world. Therefore, given the time lag effect in the real world, it is reasonable to introduce the lag effect into Equation 8.3, namely

$$\Delta P_t = \alpha(L)\Delta M_{t-1} - \beta(L)\Delta Y_{t-1} \tag{8.4}$$

Where $\alpha(L) = \alpha_1 + \alpha_2 L + \alpha_3 L^2 + \ldots + \alpha_n L^{n-1}$ is a lag operator polynomial, and n is the optimal lag order. In practice, it can be determined using the corresponding information criteria. The definition of $\beta(L)$ is similar.

Although Equation 8.4 considers the lag effect mechanism of the monetary growth rate and economic growth rate on the inflation rate, this one-way equation still cannot fully characterize the relevant variable role mechanism in China. Since monetarism theory emphasizes that the central bank can effectively regulate the money supply without resorting to excessive constraints, the policy interpretation of the Equation 8.4 is that the money supply is exogenous. However, China's money supply is affected by economic output, the inflation rate, and funds outstanding for foreign exchange under the mandatory foreign exchange settlement and sales system, and has obvious endogenous features. This endogenous nature is the reaction of banks and the public to economic changes, and its formation mechanism is linked to institutional reform.

Therefore, the core variables in Equation 8.4 (namely, ΔP_t, ΔM_t, and ΔY_t) are in fact endogenously determined mutually in a dynamic interaction system. It should be noted that in this dynamic system, the endogenous nature of money supply does not mean that the central bank cannot exercise macroeconomic regulation by adjusting the money supply, only that such regulation must be subject to the constraints of the relevant variable impact mechanism. Based on the above considerations, the mechanism of interaction between the real economic growth rate, the inflation rate, and the growth rate of money supply can be summarized using vector autoregression (VAR) system, namely

$$X_t = \Phi(L)X_{t-1} + e_t \tag{8.5}$$

Where, $X_t = (\Delta P_t \quad \Delta M_t \quad \Delta Y_t)'$ represents the time sequence vector of the endogenous variable; $\Phi(L)$ represents the vector lag operator polynomial; e_t is the impact vector.

In fact, there is an intrinsic relationship between Equation 8.5 and the New Keynesian toy model as summarized by Blanchard (2009). In the New Keynesian model system, the investment savings (IS) equation, the Phillips curve equation, and the Taylor rule-based monetary policy response equation are three core elements. If i_t is used to represent the nominal interest rate and other variable symbols in Equation 8.5 are followed, the stylized form of the New Keynesian model system can be expressed as[1]

$$\Delta Y_t = \alpha_{11}(i_t - \Delta P_t) + \varepsilon_{yt} \tag{8.6}$$

$$\Delta P_t = \beta_{21}\Delta Y_t + \varepsilon_{pt} \tag{8.7}$$

$$i_t = \gamma_{31}\Delta Y_t + \gamma_{32}\Delta P_t + \varepsilon_{it} \tag{8.8}$$

Where the Equation 8.6 describes the IS model; Equation 8.7 portrays the Phillips curve; Equation 8.8 is the monetary policy response equation (Taylor rule). The disturbance term ε in the equation represents demand shock, supply shock, and monetary policy shock in turn.

This system portrays the interaction logic of interest rate-based monetary policy and economic development. Specifically, the decrease in the real interest rate (namely, the nominal interest rate minus inflation rate) will stimulate investment, thereby speeding up the growth of real economic output (Equation 8.6), while the increase in economic output growth rate will bring inflation pressures (Equation 8.7). At this time decision-makers will adjust the interest rate according to the change in the inflation rate and economic growth rate (Equation 8.8), while the interest rate will act on the real economic output through Equation 8.6 after changes. In this way, the economic growth rate, inflation rate, and interest rate form a clear dynamic transmission mechanism.

The New Keynesian toy model is widely recognized in macroeconomic analysis. However, since the economic performance mechanisms in different countries differ from each other, special attention should be paid to differences in monetary policy tools in the course of analyzing the interaction mechanism for China's macroeconomic variables. While growing importance is attached to the role of price tools in China's monetary policy transmission mechanism in recent years, there is still a huge gap between China and Western developed countries in terms of the degree of interest rate marketization. The People's Bank of China also clearly states that China's monetary policy mainly takes money supply as the intermediary goal. Therefore, the money demand function[2] can be used (namely, the LM relationship, where M, P, and Y represent the monetary aggregate, the total price level, and the real economic output, and f($\cdot$) represents the functional relationship):

$$\frac{M_t}{P_t} = f(Y_t, i_t) \tag{8.9}$$

After logarithmic linearization, linear difference, and combination with Equations 8.6–8.8, the growth rate of money supply can be introduced into the dynamic system. At the same time, since the economic variables in the system generally exhibit inertia (smoothness) characteristics and there is lag effect on the mutual influence of economic variables in reality, the right side of each equation in the model system generally has a lag term. The following model system can be obtained accordingly:

$$\Delta Y_t = a_{11}\Delta M_t + a_{12}\Delta P_t + \text{lags} + \varepsilon_{yt} \tag{8.10}$$

$$\Delta P_t = b_{21}E_t\Delta P_{t+1} + b_{22}\Delta Y_t + \text{lags} + \varepsilon_{pt} \tag{8.11}$$

$$\Delta M_t = c_{31}\Delta Y_t + c_{32}\Delta P_t + \text{lags} + \varepsilon_{mt} \tag{8.12}$$

The "lags" in each equation represents the lag term of each variable (specific order can be determined by the information criteria) for capturing the dynamic effect that exists objectively in reality. It is easy to see that if $E_t\Delta P_{t+1}$ is replaced by ΔP_{t+1} (an extra random disturbance term is introduced), then Equations 8.10–8.12 actually constitute a typical structural vector autoregression (SVAR) model, namely

$$A_0X_t = A(L)X_{t-1} + \varepsilon_t, \varepsilon_t \sim (0, \Omega) \tag{8.13}$$

Where ε_t represents a structural random disturbance term composed of the mutually orthogonal supply shock, demand shock, and monetary policy shock. The variance–covariance matrix Ω is a diagonal matrix.

According to the standard time sequence analysis theory, it is possible to add a certain constraint condition to the coefficient matrix A_0 (for example, set as lower triangular matrix) so that it meets the identification condition of SVAR in order to obtain the estimation results. But whether SVAR is used depends on the purpose of the study rather than the VAR model. Equation 8.13 can be converted into a reduced VAR model through the conversion between the structural formula and reduced formula of the VAR model,

$$X_t = \Phi(L)X_{t-1} + e_t, e_t \sim (0, \Omega_e) \tag{8.14}$$

Where $\Phi(L) = A_0^{-1}(\sum_{i=1}^{n} A_i L^{i-1}), e_t = A_0^{-1}\varepsilon_t, \Omega_e = A_0^{-1}\Omega(A_0^{-1})'$.

Obviously, Equation 8.14 derived based on the New Keynesian model framework is fully consistent with the monetarism school model, Equation 8.5, that allows the endogenous currency. Therefore, whether it is based on the monetarism analysis framework or the New Keynesian modern macro model, the VAR model system containing the real economic growth rate, inflation rate, and growth rate of the monetary aggregate can be used as a basic model to analyze the interaction between the three. Of course, in an open economic environment, especially for the non-free floating of the RMB exchange rate, consideration can be given to including the exchange rate variable in this model system. This will be examined in a series of robustness analyses in the fourth section.

8.3 Stylized facts of monetary growth and inflation interactions

8.3.1 Data description

The sample interval for empirical analysis in this chapter is from the first quarter of 1978 to the fourth quarter of 2011. The data used for the analysis are based on the model as introduced in the second section, and also include a series of data sequences for robustness analysis. In summary, the empirical analysis involves four variables, namely, a real economic output variable, a price variable, a currency variable, and an exchange rate variable. In the basic analysis of the model, the authors use GDP as the indicator of real economic output, CPI as the price indicator, M2 as the indicator of the monetary aggregate, and the real effective exchange rate (REER) as the exchange rate indicator. In the robustness test, the authors also use the implicit price deflator (GDP IP), the total narrow money M1, and the US dollar to the renminbi exchange rate (USCH, direct quotation method) as a measure of price, currency, and exchange rate.

Since there is both short-term dynamic analysis and long-term equilibrium analysis in the empirical analysis, the variable data involve both the growth rate and the horizontal value sequence. Therefore, it is necessary to further explain the original form of specific sequences and data processing, among others. First of all, we will discuss the real GDP. Since China has only released the quarterly data on nominal GDP since the first quarter of 1992 and the constant price growth rate (namely, the real GDP growth rate) in the corresponding period, the authors first calculated the actual GDP level from the first quarter of 1992 to the fourth quarter of 2011 based on the data on these two sequences since the benchmark year 1997, and then used Abeysinghe and Gulasekaran's methods (2004) to break down the real GDP data published by the National Bureau of Statistics before 1992 into the quarterly data, thus obtaining a complete sequence of real GDP data from the first quarter of 1978 to the fourth quarter of 2011.

In terms of the price indicator, we obtained the year-on-year and month-on-month growth rates (data on month-on-month figures are available since January 1995) of the CPI from January 1978 to December 2011 from the National Bureau of Statistics and the China Monthly Economic Indicators. Then the consumer price index is converted in the order of year-on-year and month-on-month data based on the benchmark period of October 1995, and the CPI level value used in the long-term equilibrium analysis is obtained. The quarterly frequency data used in the empirical analysis is obtained from the conversion of the monthly average in the corresponding quarter. Another variable of the price indicator, namely the GDP deflator, is obtained based on the nominal GDP (converted from the seasonal average of the annual data used before 1992) and the real GDP level. Its year-on-year growth rate is the inflation rate of the GDP deflator.

For the indicator of the monetary aggregate, the quarterly data on the M2 and M1 levels are taken from the international financial statistics database, and their respective year-on-year growth rates are used as variables of the corresponding currency growth rate. For the exchange rate indicator, the REER is an important indicator commonly used to examine the overall change in the exchange rate of the RMB against a basket of currencies. The US dollar to the RMB exchange rate is the most important exchange rate in bilateral relations. Thereafter, this chapter considers these two exchange rates when analyzing stability in an open environment. The raw data of these two exchange rates are also obtained from the international financial statistics database, and their respective year-on-year growth rates are used in the empirical analysis of the short-term dynamic mechanism.

For all data as introduced above, the horizontal value sequences are seasonally adjusted by the Census X12 and are in the form of natural logarithms. As the growth rate sequence is in the year-on-year form, there is no need to make a seasonal adjustment. For the sake of explanation, the analysis below uses ΔCPI to represent the year-on-year growth rate of CPI (inflation rate), and other variables containing the differential sign Δ are similar to this. Moreover, while the dynamic system of the theoretical model, Equation 8.5, or Equation 8.14 shows that the short-term dynamic mechanism of the core variables is based on the growth rate of each variable (namely, economic growth rate, inflation rate, and money growth rate), it is still necessary to test and determine the stationary characteristics of each variable before performing the empirical analysis. To this end, the authors performed two unit root tests of ADF and PP on all variables (the null hypothesis contains unit roots).

Table 8.1 reports the unit root test results (*p*-value) for the horizontal values of all variables and the corresponding year-on-year growth rate sequence. For the horizontal value sequences, the results of the ADF and PP tests are identical, and the null hypothesis that the sequences contain unit roots at the traditional significance level cannot be rejected. For growth rate sequences, the null hypothesis containing unit roots is generally rejected. Although the test results of ΔM2 are in conflict

Table 8.1 Unit root test results for related variables: First quarter of 1978–fourth quarter of 2011

Horizontal value (natural logarithm)	ADF(p-value)	PP(p-value)	Growth rate (year-on-year)	ADF(p-value)	PP(p-value)
CPI	0.617	0.658	ΔCPI	0.036	0.075
M2	0.513	0.347	ΔM2	0.137	0.026
M1	0.610	0.565	ΔM1	0.037	0.007
GDPIP	0.905	0.929	ΔGDPIP	0.062	0.055
REER	0.070	0.072	ΔREER	0.001	0.014
USCH	0.212	0.289	ΔUSCH	0.024	0.019
GDP	0.887	0.973	ΔGDP	0.005	0.014

Note: The lag order in the ADF test is determined by AIC (maximum of 8); the Bartlett kernel estimation method and the Newey–West automatic bandwidth are used for the PP test; the *p*-value reported in the table is calculated according to MacKinnon (1996).

(the *p*-value of the ADF test is >10%, and the *p*-value of the PP test is <5%), it is relatively reasonable to judge the M2 growth rate as the stationary sequence, in that the power of the ADF test is relatively low, and the PP test is more robust for the sequence test results with structural changes for the marginal distribution.

8.3.2 Typical facts

Since the reform and opening-up, China's economic growth rate, inflation rate, and currency growth rate have always exhibited typical interaction character-istics. Figure 8.1 portrays the time sequence path of China's real GDP growth rate, CPI and inflation rate, and monetary growth rate from 1978 to 2011. It can be seen from the figure that although the time sequence paths of the three cen-tral variables are not identical, the overall evolution trend is similar, and there seems to be regular change in the occurrence of the peaks and troughs of each variable. Another similarity is the huge fluctuation of the monetary growth rate in the 1980s and 1990s in lockstep with the violent fluctuations of the inflation rate and economic growth rate. After the 1990s, the fluctuation of the three vari-ables became significantly subdued, but there was a significant increase after the new global financial crisis in 2007–2008, especially in the monetary growth rate and inflation rate.

From the perspective of the time sequence path of the inflation rate and mon-etary growth rate, the CPI and inflation rate saw peaks and troughs in lockstep with the rise and fall of the monetary growth rate. Most of the time, the monetary growth rate is ahead of CPI and inflation by one to two years. In the 1980s and 1990s, the period of time when the monetary growth rate was ahead of the CPI and inflation rate significantly exceeded that of the subsequent periods, possibly indicating that the lag effect of China's monetary policy improved significantly after the 1990s. At the same time, the similarity between the monetary growth rate and the inflation rate in the change trend suggests a possible high dynamic correlation between the two.

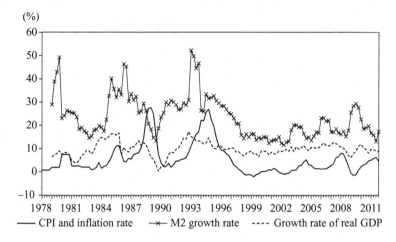

Figure 8.1 China's real GDP growth rate, CPI and inflation rate, and growth rate of M2: First quarter of 1978–fourth quarter of 2011.

From the perspective of the time sequence path of economic growth rate and monetary growth rate, there seems to be high correlation between the two, and this correlation was more obvious before the end of the 1990s. For example, the two dropped almost simultaneously in 1987–1990, and almost simultaneously reached a local low in 1990, after which the two rose simultaneously. However, the two rebounded to the next peak at different time points. The growth rate of GDP peaked in 1993, while the growth rate of M2 did not reach the local peak level until 1994. Further comparison of the evolution paths of the two in other time periods shows that the growth rate of GDP seems to be ahead of the monetary growth rate in many periods.

On the whole, Figure 8.1 initially portrays the dynamic (sequential) change relationship between China's real economic growth rate, inflation rate, and monetary growth rate, but more importantly, it implies the high correlation of the three in the real economic performance. Of course, strictly speaking, correlation does not necessarily mean that there must be a driving relationship between variables, or a "causal" relationship in a dynamic system. Therefore, below is a rigorous quantitative test of the driving relationship between the economic growth rate, inflation rate, and monetary growth rate.

8.4 Short-term dynamic mechanism

8.4.1 Basic results

For the short-term dynamic mechanism of the central variables, the authors use the VAR model to first test the Granger causality among the economic growth rate, inflation rate, and monetary growth rate in the basic model (without consideration of the open environment). The impact of exchange rate factor in the open environment and other sensitivity tests will be discussed in the subsequent robustness analysis. The Granger causality test based on the VAR model is simple from a technical viewpoint, but it is not easy to choose the correct lag order in the model setting, and the choice of the lag order directly affects the test results and conclusions. This has not received enough attention in the existing research. In particular, there is a lack of explicit explanations in terms of the highest order on which the information criteria are based, whether the model residual has sequence correlation, and others. This is precisely one of the key reasons that may lead to different conclusions. If, for dynamic models such as VAR, the residual has sequence correlation, statistical inferences such as model estimation and the Granger causality test will have neither unbiasedness nor consistency. The description of this detail here (and in other similar studies) cannot be omitted. Otherwise, we may be under the misunderstanding that "whatever conclusion is desired can be obtained."

According to the standard time sequence analysis theory (Zhang, 2012), for the dynamic time sequence model to obtain accurate and effective statistical inference, what is most important is that the model has simplicity but no sequence correlation: Satisfy the condition that the model's disturbance term has no significant sequence correlation in the minimalist model design. Therefore, this chapter uses the double constraint measure in the choice of the lag order for the model, namely using the AIC and VAR-LM sequence correlation test to jointly determine the optimal lag order. Setting up the model in this way can ensure that the model residuals have no significant sequence correlation, and also meet the simplicity requirements for econometric modeling as far as possible. Specifically, under the given maximum lag order of 8, AIC is used to determine the optimal lag order, and then the VAR-LM sequence correlation test is used to determine whether it has sequence correlation. If the test results show no significant sequence correlation, then this lag order is optimal; if there is sequence correlation, the sequence correlation of the corresponding model is tested from the eighth order downwards based on the general-to-special model setting principle. The lag order corresponding to the minimum AIC chosen in the group without sequence correlation is optimal.

Based on the above design, the authors perform the Granger causality test on the basic model. According to the definition, the Granger causality test is performed to test the joint significance level of the matrix $\Phi(L)$ corresponding coefficients in Equation 8.5. For example, in the equation with ΔCPI_t as the dependent variable, to test whether ΔGDP_t has Granger causality with this is to test whether all the lag term coefficients of ΔGDP_t on the right side of the regression equation are 0 at the same time. According to this test principle, Table 8.2 reports the Granger causality test results based on Equation 8.5. lag(ΔCPI_t) represents the lag term of ΔCPI_t on the right side of the regression equation, and the definitions of other symbols are similar to this. In order to test whether different sample intervals affect the results, Table 8.2 reports the test results of the entire sample interval from 1978 to 2011, and also reports the corresponding results before and after 2000.

Table 8.2 Results of the Granger causality test (*p*-value) of the basic model

	1978Q1–2011Q4			1978Q1–1999Q4			2000Q1–2011Q4		
	$\Delta GDP_t(1)$	$\Delta CPI_t(2)$	$\Delta M2_t(3)$	$\Delta GDP_t(1)$	$\Delta CPI_t(2)$	$\Delta M2_t(3)$	$\Delta GDP_t(1)$	$\Delta CPI_t(2)$	$\Delta M2_t(3)$
lag(ΔGDP_t)		0.677	0.019		0.685	0.088		0.259	0.102
lag(ΔCPI_t)	0.058		0.025	0.006		0.603	0.008		0.000
lag($\Delta M2_t$)	0.870	0.000		0.845	0.001		0.988	0.009	
VAR-LM	0.540			0.057			0.072		

Note: The table reports the *p*-value of the Wald significance test statistic (the null hypothesis has no Granger causality); the VAR model's optimal lag order is determined by the vector residual sequence correlation test (VAR-LM, including lagged 4 phase) and AIC (maximum 8); lag(CPIt) represents lag phases of all CPI terms on the right side of the equation in the Granger causality test (other representations are similar).

Firstly, the authors examine the test results of the entire sample interval. The second column reports the results of the causality test with ΔGDP_t as the dependent variable. It can be seen from this that at the traditional significance level, the null hypothesis that the monetary growth rate is not the Granger cause of the real GDP growth rate cannot be rejected, but the null hypothesis that the inflation rate is not the Granger cause of the real GDP growth rate can be rejected (at the level of 10%). In other words, the monetary growth rate does not have a dynamic driving effect on real economic growth, and the inflation rate has a significant dynamic driving effect on the real economic growth. The subsequent two columns are the results of the Granger causality test with ΔCPI_t and $\Delta M2_t$ as dependent variables, respectively. For the CPI and inflation rate, the results show that the growth rate of M2 is its Granger cause, while the real GDP growth rate is not its Granger cause; for the growth rate of M2, the economic growth rate and the inflation rate are both Granger causes.

Secondly, the authors further examine the test results of the corresponding subsample intervals before and after 2000 in Table 8.2. A comparison with the results of the entire sample interval shows that with ΔGDP_t and ΔCPI_t as the dependent variables, the conclusion of the Granger causality test is fully consistent with the conclusion of the entire sample interval (the dynamic driving effect of ΔCPI_t on ΔGDP_t has more obvious significance). With the $\Delta M2_t$ as the dependent variable, the results of the Granger causality test before and after 2000 are not fully consistent with the results of the entire sample interval: The entire sample intervals ΔGDP_t and ΔCPI_t are the Granger causes of $\Delta M2_t$, while in the subsample interval before and after 2000, ΔGDP_t and ΔCPI_t are the Granger causes of $\Delta M2_t$ respectively (but not simultaneously).

Since the regression equation with $\Delta M2_t$ as the dependent variable can be viewed as a form of monetary policy response equation ($\Delta M2_t$ is the main medium of China's monetary policy), the inconsistency of the subsample's results in the monetary policy response mechanism shows the consistency between the information contained in the data and China's economic development law. This implies a subtle change in the weight of policy objectives in economic growth and inflation in China's economic development process. This result is highly consistent with the semantic connotations of the monetary policy objective of "maintaining the stability of the currency value and promoting economic growth based on this" which was stipulated in the "Law of the People's Bank of China" 1995 – namely "stability of currency value" is the paramount goal (this is the case at least after 1995). From the perspective of realistic responsibility, after the People's Bank of China was designated as the central bank by legislation, its response to inflation was inevitably more resolute than the response to economic growth. After all, economic growth is viewed as the efforts of different departments, but if prices rise too fast, the central bank can hardly be blameless.

Based on the test results in Table 8.2, the following general rules deserve special attention: Firstly, the monetary growth rate significantly drives the inflation rate, but has no significant driving effect on the real economic growth rate. Secondly, the driving effect of inflation rate on the real economic growth rate is significant. Thirdly, the driving effect of the inflation rate and the real economic growth rate on the monetary growth rate changes somewhat in different periods. In the 20th century, the currency rate had a one-way driving effect on inflation rate, but in recent years, the two-way driving effect of the inflation rate on the monetary growth rate is more significant. It is noteworthy that, whether it be the entire sample interval estimation or different subsample interval estimations, the choice of the VAR model's lag term ensures that the residual matrix of the corresponding model has no sequence correlation at the significance level of 5%, thus guaranteeing the credibility of these general laws.

8.4.2 Robustness analysis

In order to check whether the above conclusions are robust, six robustness tests are performed, which consider the impact of the exchange rate factor in the open environment and the sensitivity of core variables to different measurement indicators. According to the similar VAR model setting and Granger causality test process, Table 8.3 reports the results of the Granger causality test for six robustness tests. For the sake of explanation, the letters A–F are

Table 8.3 Robustness test results (p-value of Granger causality test)

		ΔGDP_t	ΔCPI_t	$\Delta M2_t$	$\Delta REER_t$
A	lag(ΔGDP_t)		0.887	0.001	0.145
	lag(ΔCPI_t)	0.057		0.030	0.011
	lag($\Delta M2_t$)	0.923	0.009		0.000
	lag($\Delta REER_t$)	0.554	0.007	0.013	
		ΔGDP_t	ΔCPI_t	$\Delta M2_t$	$\Delta USCH_t$
B	lag(ΔGDP_t)		0.478	0.005	0.013
	lag(ΔCPI_t)	0.117		0.014	0.006
	lag($\Delta M2_t$)	0.987	0.000		0.000
	lag($\Delta USCH_t$)	0.203	0.032	0.050	
C		$HPGAP_t$	ΔCPI_t	$\Delta M2_t$	
	lag($HPGAP_t$)		0.412	0.002	
	lag(ΔCPI_t)	0.009		0.055	
	lag($\Delta M2_t$)	0.677	0.001		
D		$LDGAP_t$	ΔCPI_t	$\Delta M2_t$	
	lag($LDGAP_t$)		0.498	0.000	
	lag(ΔCPI_t)	0.001		0.007	
	lag($\Delta M2_t$)	0.697	0.001		
E		ΔGDP_t	$\Delta GDPIP_t$	$\Delta M2_t$	
	lag(ΔGDP_t)		0.000	0.144	
	lag($\Delta GDPIP_t$)	0.488		0.103	
	lag($\Delta M2_t$)	0.615	0.010		
F		ΔGDP_t	ΔCPI_t	$\Delta M1_t$	
	lag(ΔGDP_t)		0.259	0.021	
	lag(ΔCPI_t)	0.005		0.013	
	lag($\Delta M1_t$)	0.232	0.007		

Note: The relevant description is the same as that in Table 8.2.

used to identify the VAR models corresponding to the six tests. Firstly, A and B are model systems that extend the basic model to an open environment. Given the possible interaction between the exchange rate factor and the economic growth rate, and between the inflation rate and the currency growth rate, the exchange rate variable uses the REER and the year-on-year growth rate sequence corresponding to the US dollar against the RMB exchange rate (direct quotation method). Secondly, since the GDP gap is often used instead of the GDP growth rate in the New Keynesian toy model to portray real economic performance, C and D in Table 8.3 use the HP filter (penalty coefficient is 1600) and the linear time trend elimination method to obtain the real GDP gap (represented by HPGAP and LDGAP) instead of the growth rate of GDP in order to test the sensitivity of the basic conclusions. Finally, E and F, respectively, correspond to the test results of using the GDP deflator inflation rate instead of the CPI inflation rate and using the growth rate of the narrow money M1 instead of the growth rate of M2.

For all robustness tests, of most concern is whether the general rules in Table 8.2 will change. Firstly, the dynamic impact of the monetary growth rate on the economic growth rate and inflation rate. According to the results in Table 8.3, whether it is the addition of the exchange rate factor or the use of different real economic variables, inflation rate indicators, or the monetary aggregate indicator, the test results show that the monetary growth rate exerts no driving effect on real economic output, but will significantly drive the inflation rate. Secondly, the driving effect of the inflation rate on real economic output is still significant in most cases (except B and E). Finally, except E, the driving effect of the inflation rate and real economic growth rate on the monetary growth rate is significant, namely, the monetary growth rate has a significant feedback mechanism for the historical performance of inflation and economic growth. In conjunction with analyses of the short-term dynamic mechanism, the above three general laws have high robustness. In particular, the neutrality of the monetary growth rate for the economic growth and its significant driving effect on the inflation rate are tenable in all cases.

8.5 Long-term equilibrium mechanism

8.5.1 Cointegration test

The sequence of long-term equilibrium analysis is the horizontal values of price, real economic output, and monetary aggregate (natural logarithm). Long-term equilibrium mechanism analysis shows that the authors can test whether there is a long-term equilibrium relationship between related variables, and also obtain the mechanism of interaction of variable growth rates based on the error correction model under the correction system of the long-term equilibrium model. A Granger causality test similar to that in the fourth section is performed. For the analysis of the long-term equilibrium mechanism under the vector system, the authors first use the standard Johansen cointegration analysis method to test whether there is a long-term equilibrium relationship among the variables. In view of this, the VAR model, Equation 8.5, with n variables can be rewritten in the following form:

$$\Phi^*(L)\Delta X_t = C + \Pi X_{t-1} + \varepsilon_t \tag{8.15}$$

At this time, X_t represents the vector composed of the horizontal value sequence of variables, and

$$\begin{cases} \Pi = -\Phi(1) = \sum_{i=1}^{p} \Phi_i - I_n \\ \Phi^*(L) = I_n - \sum_{i=1}^{p-1}\left(-\sum_{j=i}^{p}\Phi_j\right)L^i \end{cases} \tag{8.16}$$

In the above definition, the attribute of the n matrix Π is the core of the Johansen cointegration test. Simply put, the Johansen cointegration test is in fact a cyclical test process. Starting with testing the first overall hypothesis $r = \text{rank}(\Pi) = 0$ (rank represents the order of the matrix), all the variables in the VAR system corresponding to this hypothesis are all non-stationary and there is no cointegration relationship. $r = \text{rank}(\Pi) = 1$ is tested next, and so on until $r = \text{rank}(\Pi) = n$ corresponding to a stationary system. This cyclical process is used to check whether there is a vector system and the number of cointegration relationships. When this process progresses until the null hypothesis H_{0r} cannot be rejected, the estimated number of corresponding cointegration relations is r.

It should be noted that under the Johansen cointegration analysis method, the trace statistic based on the matrix Π eigenvalue and maximum eigenvalue statistic can be used to test the cointegration relationship, but the trace statistic is relatively more accurate. Furthermore, since the distribution of relevant statistics differs from the traditional distribution under the null hypothesis, the results of the traditional hypothesis test cannot be directly used for statistical inference. The root cause of the problem is that the traditional statistical inference assumes the variable to be a stationary sequence, but the variable is non-stationary under the null hypothesis here. Therefore, in the actual test process, it is necessary to use the p-value of the corresponding statistic calculated by MacKinnon et al. (1999) through the simulation method.

According to the method as introduced above, Table 8.4 reports the results of Johansen cointegration test.[3] In order to ensure the robustness of results, the authors consider the three-variable basic model in a closed environment and the four-variable extension model with an effective exchange rate in an open economy. It is not difficult to see that in the first round of the cyclical test (namely, the null hypothesis that the total number is 0), the corresponding p-values are less than 5%, whether the basic model or the extended model is used. This indicates that the null hypothesis that there is no cointegration relationship is rejected at the traditional significance level. For the null hypothesis that there is at most one cointegration relationship, the p-value of the corresponding statistic is significantly

Table 8.4 Results of Johansen cointegration test

Null hypothesis (number of cointegration relationships)	(GDP CPI M2)	(GDP CPI M2 REER)
None	0.000	0.005
At most 1	0.503	0.317
At most 2	0.266	0.499
VAR-LM	0.086	0.056

Note: The table reports the p-value of the trace statistic; each variable and the cointegration vector do not have a deterministic trend; the setting process of the lag order of each model is the same as Table 8.2.

higher than 10%, indicating that this null hypothesis cannot be rejected. For the sake of comparison, Table 8.4 also reports the results of the third round of cyclical test, namely, the test results of the null hypothesis that there are at most two cointegration relationships. It is not difficult to see that at the traditional significance level, the null hypothesis that there are at most two cointegration relationships cannot be rejected. However, based on the order and stop principle of the cyclical hypothesis test, it is reasonable to judge that there is one cointegration relationship in the relevant variables.

The results in Table 8.4 show that there is a long-term equilibrium relationship between prices, economic output, and monetary aggregate (and the effective exchange rate). The long-term equilibrium relationship means that there is a stable one-to-one exchange relationship between these variables in the long term. Thus, even if the relationship between the variables diverges from the equilibrium state in a short time, the time sequence formed by such deviation is stable, and the numbers of positive and negative deviations cancel each other out (expected value is 0). Of course, the above process only tests whether there is a cointegration relationship between prices, economic output, and currency, and the number of cointegration relationships, without reflecting the specific characteristics of the cointegration relationship. To characterize this long-term equilibrium mechanism, it is also necessary to estimate the error correction model that shows the characteristics of the cointegration relationship. After obtaining the error correction model, the Granger causality test on the variable difference form can then be performed. Detailed elaboration is given below.

8.5.2 Error correction and Granger causality

The setting and estimation of the error correction model mainly involve the cointegration vector and the adjustment coefficient. The former characterizes the long-term equilibrium relationship among the variables in the system, and the latter shows the correction features of the cointegration system following deviation from the equilibrium state. For the sake of explanation, Equation 8.15 is rewritten according to the standard time sequence analysis theory.

$$\Phi^*(L)\Delta X_t = C + \Pi X_{t-1} + \varepsilon_t = C + AB'X_{t-1} + \varepsilon_t \tag{8.17}$$

Where matrix B represents the cointegration vector (B' represents matrix transposition), and A denotes the adjustment coefficient matrix. Under this definition framework, if $Z_{t-1} = B'Y_{t-1}$, it is easy to see that the vector Z_{t-1} is the error sequence formed by the vector Y_{t-1} through the cointegration vector B. When such an error occurs in the $t-1$ period (namely, deviating from the long-term equilibrium state), the cointegration system will correct this in the subsequent period (namely, period t) to ensure the stable existence of the long-term equilibrium relationship. How large is the correction? This is what the adjustment coefficient matrix A reflects as defined in Equation 8.17. Therefore, the error correction model reflects a dynamic correction mechanism. In fact, as long as the number r of the vector cointegration relationship has been verified, the estimation of the cointegration vector B and the adjustment coefficient matrix A is a byproduct of the Johansen cointegration analysis. Therefore, through the Johansen cointegration analysis method as introduced above, the column of matrix B is the corresponding characteristic root vector after estimating the characteristic root. Traditional statistical inference can be used for the adjustment coefficient matrix A and also for the dynamic coefficient matrix $\Phi(L)$. This is because that Z_{t-1} in the error correction model system is a stationary sequence.

According to the above theoretical analysis, Table 8.5 reports the empirical results of the estimation of Johansen error correction model, including the estimated values of the cointegration vector B and the adjustment coefficient matrix A. It should be noted that in order to identify the cointegration vector B, the coefficient corresponding to the first variable in the model system is standardized to 1. In the case of a three-variable basic model, $B' = (10.808 \quad -0.667)$ portrays the long-term equilibrium relationship between the real economic output, price index, and monetary aggregate, and this equilibrium relationship is statistically significant at the significance level of 1%. For the adjustment coefficient matrix $A' = (-0.039 \quad -0.114 \quad -0.043)$, it indicates that when there is a positive non-equilibrium state (positive deviation

Table 8.5 Estimation results of the Johansen error correction model (standard deviation is reported in parentheses)

	GDP	CPI	M2	
Cointegration vector B	1	0.808***	−0.667***	
		(0.067)	(0.015)	
Adjustment coefficient matrix A	−0.039	−0.114***	−0.043	
	(0.028)	(0.024)	(0.085)	
	GDP	CPI	M2	REER
Cointegration vector B	1	0.633***	−0.633***	−0.067
		(0.076)	(0.014)	(0.038)
Adjustment coefficient matrix A	−0.050*	−0.119***	0.056	−0.433***
	(0.027)	(0.025)	(0.095)	(0.123)

Note: *, **, and *** indicate that the corresponding statistics are statistically significant at the significance levels of 10%, 5%, and 1%, respectively.

Table 8.6 Results of Granger causality test based on cointegration model

	ΔGDP_t	ΔCPI_t	$\Delta M2_t$	
lag(ΔGDP_t)		0.269	0.039	
lag(ΔCPI_t)	0.007		0.044	
lag($\Delta M2_t$)	0.400	0.005		

	ΔGDP_t	ΔCPI_t	$\Delta M2_t$	$\Delta REER_t$
lag(ΔGDP_t)		0.302	0.010	0.340
lag(ΔCPI_t)	0.277		0.051	0.075
lag($\Delta M2_t$)	0.852	0.015		0.003
lag($\Delta REER_t$)	0.575	0.073	0.149	

Note: The table reports the p-values of the Granger causality test based on the cointegration model.

error) among the variables in the system in the short run, the three will be reversely corrected. The CPI has the largest and most significant degree of correction. In other words, CPI dominates the dynamic mechanism of the model system from temporary non-equilibrium to long-term equilibrium.

Under the framework of cointegration analysis, the Granger causality test performs a corresponding significance test based on the established error correction model. Table 8.6 reports the results of the Granger causality test based on the error correction model. According to Table 8.6, several basic conclusions drawn from the short-term dynamic mechanism model in this chapter are still tenable: The monetary growth rate significantly drives the inflation rate under either the closed framework or the open framework; the monetary growth rate does not have a significant driving effect on real economic growth rate; the inflation rate and real economic growth rate affect the adjustment of the monetary growth rate dynamically.

8.6 Conclusions

This chapter studies the mechanism of interaction between China's inflation, economic growth, and money supply since the reform and opening-up. This chapter makes fundamental contributions in two respects in terms of theoretical model expansion and empirical analysis. Firstly, in terms of construction of the theoretical framework, this chapter does not simply select theoretical models from different schools. Rather, it finds the intrinsic logical relationship from the basic models of the monetarism and New Keynesian theory, and gives full consideration to the characteristics of the endogenous mechanisms of China's money supply in such a logical relationship, thereby setting up a dynamic model system. Secondly, in the empirical analysis of the dynamic model system, this chapter clarifies the dual constraint mechanism in the selection of the lag order of the dynamic time sequence model, namely combining the information criteria with the sequence correlation test and determining the basic rules of the maximum initial lag period according to the data frequency (quarterly data generally have eight phases). Moreover, it is necessary to be fully aware that in the dynamic time sequence analysis based on economic and financial theory, the unit root test is merely a routine diagnostic test, and it is not acceptable to completely and passively rely on the unit root test results to determine the stationarity of variables and ignore the economic meaning of variables and the constraints of the macro-theoretical model. Otherwise, it is prone to fall into the dilemma of drawing different conclusions from different samples, different frequencies, and different test methods.

Through the regulation of the theoretical model framework and the rigorous dynamic time sequence analysis, this chapter portrays the characteristics of the mechanism of interaction between China's inflation, economic growth, and money supply: The monetary growth rate significantly drives the inflation rate, but has no significant driving effect on the real economic growth; the inflation rate and real economic growth rate affect the adjustment of the monetary growth rate, and in recent years, the impact of the inflation rate on the adjustment of the monetary growth rate is more significant. Through the analysis of the short-term dynamic mechanism and long-term equilibrium mechanism and other various sensitivity analyses, this chapter finds that the above conclusions remain unchanged despite changes in sample intervals, variable definitions, and long- and short-term analysis frameworks. Therefore, these conclusions are general rules that deserve the attention of decision-makers and have policy reference value.

From the policy implications of the conclusions, the adjustment of the money supply mechanism clearly holds the key to managing China's inflation. However, since the adjustment of the monetary growth rate does not play a significant role in promoting economic growth, it may be necessary to change the monetary policy implementation currently dominated by aggregate regulation in order to effectively regulate the real economic growth. This implies that in the course of policy implementation, we must draw on the idea of using the money supply to regulate inflation in monetarism theory, and attach importance to the conclusion of New Keynesianism about price rigidity and the regulation of the macro economy through the interest rate, while the compromise between and integration of monetarism and New Keynesianism may be an effective path for future macroeconomic policy adjustment. Of course, whether the interest rate has a better regulation effect on economic output than the monetary aggregate remains to be studied and explored further, at least as far as China is concerned. Moreover, it is necessary to note that in recent years, financial innovation has picked up speed, and the accuracy of the currency in predicting the trend of inflation may be affected. Obviously, this raises new requirements for China to speed up marketization of the interest rate and implement the transition to macro-policy based on price-based regulation.

Notes

1   In a complete market environment, it is feasible to introduce the relationship between currency and interest rate into the toy model through the money demand function, but it is noteworthy that the situation is more complicated in terms of the specific mode of China's regulation of monetary policies. At present, China is implementing a combined

quantitative and price-based regulation model. Quantitative means include window guidance and macroprudential management. In this pattern, the variables corresponding to these regulation measures may also be involved in the exchange relationship between money and interest rate. Therefore, it may be inaccurate to explain the money supply through the interest rate. However, if the above indicators are introduced into the theoretical expressions, the model system corresponding to the monetarist theory also needs to consider similar problems. Therefore, it is also possible to clarify the consistency between the New Keynesian model framework and the monetarist model system. In the actual analysis process, since it is hard to obtain the data on such variable indicators (especially quarterly data), empirical analysis will encounter difficulty. To simplify the problem, the relationship between money and interest rates is considered based on the traditional money demand function.

2 Note that Equations 8.6–8.8 are highly stylized expressions, and are used herein to explain the relationship between the core variables. Under general settings, lags of variables are often added to the model to capture typical characteristics such as inflation persistence and smoothness of interest rate. However, even under this general setting, the internal consistency of the monetarist model and Neo-Keynesianism model can still be proved.

3 In the setup of the Johansen cointegration model, based on the criteria set by Zhang (2012) for the establishment of deterministic trend in the cointegration analysis model, it is assumed that the constituent variables in the VAR model system and the cointegration vector do not contain deterministic trends.

9 Target mismatch and dynamic mechanism of inflation

This chapter studies the mismatch of inflation goals in China, with a view to finding out the deep implications of the differences in the dynamic nature of different inflation indicators for the choice and implementation of monetary policy (especially counter-cyclical policy) and what can be learned from this. In view of this, this chapter analyzes the differences in the dynamic nature of China's CPI inflation rate and GDP deflator inflation rate as well as its difference with the linkage with monetary policy; the chapter also explains the real problems for current inflation management due to the inflation goal mismatch which takes CPI as the single inflation target, and, based on this, puts forward specific suggestions for the current management of inflation in China, with a view to providing a scientific reference for decision-makers to develop targeted and forward-looking counter-cyclical policies.

The structure of this chapter is as follows: The first section discusses the difference between consumer prices and generalized prices, and compares the characteristics of the dynamic time sequence paths of different inflation indicators. The second section uses the unobserved components stochastic volatility (UCSV) to capture and compare the dynamic nature of inflation expectations of different inflation indicators. The third section explores the impact of monetary policy on the dynamic features of different inflation indicators by comparing simulation experiments. The fourth section deals with the analysis of policy implications. The fifth section summarizes this chapter and introduces the relevant implications of the research results.

9.1 Differences between consumer price and broad price

9.1.1 Comparison of concept and connotations

In recent years, China's monetary policies have been plagued by a complicated and changing domestic and international economic situation. In particular, as the economic and financial situation changes, there is significant alternation of inflation and deflation in China. In 2007, prices rose significantly, and the continuous rise in CPI made inflation the focus of attention in the year. In 2008, the economic growth rate slowed down somewhat as a result of the global financial crisis sparked by the American subprime mortgage crisis. In this context, the CPI inflation rate began to show a downward trend, and even saw a negative value. From the end of 2009 to the first half of 2010, the CPI inflation rate rose somewhat in the context of China's strong economic stimulus to cope with the global financial crisis, but the peak stood only at 3%. Therefore, from the perspective of CPI, domestic inflation is still at a moderate level.

In marked contrast to the inflation level measured by CPI is the perception of a marked rise in overall prices and the strong inflation expectations that emerge gradually in this context. Although the public, the market, and the media pay close attention to the CPI inflation rate published monthly, there is increasing public dissatisfaction with the inflation level reflected by the CPI, especially casting doubt on the weight of real estate-related price factors in the CPI.[1] Therefore, it seems that CPI, as an inflation indicator, is facing a dilemma of inconsistency between statistics and reality.

Since the traditional inflation indicator has such a dilemma, is it possible to solve the problem of the measurement distortion of inflation by greatly re-adjusting the weights of each sub-component in China's CPI basket (for example, referring to the weights in developed countries)? The answer is no according to the findings in this chapter. More importantly, the empirical results in this chapter also imply that, since the monetary authorities have used the CPI as a single inflation target for a long time, the more extensive generalized price indicator – the GDP deflator inflation rate – is ignored, resulting in the problem of serious inflation target mismatch. This constitutes great challenges to the effective management of real inflation.

China's inflation issue has always attracted great academic attention, but the literature mainly focuses on the analysis of the driving factors of inflation in recent years. For example, Fan (2008) argues that the main driver of inflation in China is the money supply rather than excess wage increases. Wu and Tian (2008) propose that China's inflation is mainly triggered by structural drivers, but Huo (2008) considers that the structural factor is not the main cause of inflation in China, and that excessively loose monetary policy is the main cause for domestic inflation. The research by Zhang (2009b) and Yang (2009) analyzes the causes of inflation from the perspective of excess liquidity, holding that inflation in China in recent years is chiefly a monetary phenomenon.

There is no doubt that these studies are of important practical significance for understanding the dynamic trend of China's current inflation and macroeconomic policy regulation. However, it is noteworthy that the existing research takes CPI as the only inflation indicator, and few studies focus on the broader GDP deflator, much less the differences in the dynamic nature of different inflation indicators and their deep implications for the management of inflation targets. As an important indicator for gauging the inflation level, the GDP deflator differs from the information contained in CPI : CPI mainly reflects the price changes in consumer goods purchased by urban and rural residents and the price changes in services in a certain period of time, while the GDP deflator is a generalized price indicator. Because the GDP deflator is calculated based on GDP (nominal GDP) with price changes and GDP (real GDP) without price changes, the accounting basis better covers the overall prices in the economy, and prices associated with investment (such as real estate prices) have greater weight in this indicator. Therefore, the GDP deflator can better reflect the overall state of inflation in China.

As far as China's current economic environment is concerned, the dynamic trend of generalized price indices may be more important for managing inflation. It is known that since the reform and opening-up, both the economic system and the macroeconomic policies have seen profound changes. Especially after the State Council issued the "Circular on Deepening the Reform of Urban Housing System and Accelerating Construction of Housing" in 1998, the change of housing distribution and real estate marketization have exerted a major impact on China's price formation mechanism in the past dozen years since 2000. From the follow-up analysis in this chapter, it can be seen that this effect is reflected in the continuous difference in the dynamic trend of the CPI inflation indicator and the GDP deflator (for example, the CPI inflation rate was consistently lower than the GDP deflation after 1998). This difference is rare in other countries.

9.1.2 Actual performance

The overall inflation level can be gauged through different price indices, such as the respective rates of change in CPI and the GDP deflator. Since the reform and opening-up, however, China has chiefly adopted CPI as a measure of the inflation rate, and the monetary authorities have principally adopted CPI as the central goal of inflation management and policy adjustment. Although more information is available on price changes covered by the GDP deflator's inflation rate, it does not receive widespread attention. This chapter comprehensively analyzes the differences in dynamic characteristics of these two different inflation indicators. By studying the dynamic changes in inflation indicators containing different information, the authors portray the characteristic changes in China's overall inflation as comprehensively as possible since the reform and opening-up as well as its intrinsic relationship with monetary policy, so that the policy recommendations of the research findings have more reference value.

To ensure the accuracy of the empirical analysis and the reliability of results, the data used herein are described and analyzed. The raw data (month-on-month) on the CPI inflation rate are from the National Bureau of Statistics and the China Monthly Economic Indicators. The data on quarterly frequency are converted from the monthly average in the corresponding quarter. The quarterly data on the GDP deflator's inflation rate are calculated based on the nominal GDP and real GDP. Since China has only released the quarterly data on nominal GDP since 1992 and the constant price growth rate (namely, the real GDP growth rate) in the corresponding period, the authors first calculated the actual GDP level from the first quarter of 1992 to the fourth quarter of 2011 based on the data on these two sequences with the year 1997 as the benchmark year, and then use Abeysinghe and Gulasekaran's methods (2004) to break down the data on real GDP published by the National Bureau of Statistics before 1992 into quarterly data, thus obtaining a complete sequence of real GDP from the first quarter of 1978 to the fourth quarter of 2011. The nominal GDP sequence before 1992 was obtained by using the quarterly average of the annual data. In this way, the GDP deflator sequence in 1978–2010 was obtained according to the basic definition of the GDP deflator (nominal GDP/real GDP), and its year-on-year growth rate is the GDP deflator's inflation rate (expressed as GDPDI).

According to the above explanation, Figure 9.1 shows the dynamic time sequence path of China's two inflation rate indicators from the first quarter of 1979 to the first quarter of 2010. On balance, the overall dynamic trend of the two inflation indicator variables is fundamentally the same. For example, each inflation variable showed a strong growth trend in the late 1980s and mid-1990s. Since the late 1990s, the degree of price change decreased significantly. Compared to the previous period, the two inflation indicators showed a certain degree of decline. However, based on the details, there are obvious differences in the dynamic path of the inflation rate based on different price indicators. This difference is reflected not only in the horizontal values of different indicators at different time points, but also in the statistical nature of the two indicators in different periods.

As can be seen from Figure 9.1, the inflation rate measured by the CPI was higher than the GDP deflator's inflation rate in most of the period before 1998, and the fluctuation range of the CPI inflation rate was significantly greater than the latter. However, after 1998, this situation was reversed. The GDP deflator's inflation rate was higher than the CPI inflation rate for ten years, and its fluctuation was also significantly higher than the CPI inflation rate.

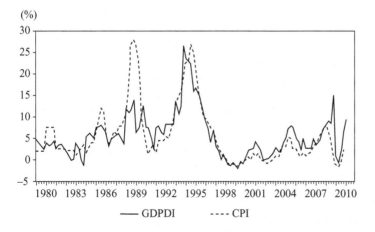

Figure 9.1 China's CPI inflation rate and GDP deflator's inflation rate (year-on-year): First quarter of 1979–first quarter of 2010.

Table 9.1 Comparison of statistical attributes of different inflation rate indicators in China

	Average inflation level		Inflation volatility		Inflation persistence	
	CPI	GDPDI	CPI	GDPDI	CPI	GDPDI
1979–2010	5.62	5.59	6.89	5.28	0.92	0.85
1979–1989	7.14	5.09	7.00	3.48	0.84	0.78
1990–1999	8.78	7.89	8.29	7.52	0.90	0.91
2000–2010	1.87	3.99	2.41	3.27	0.82	0.58

Note: Inflation persistence is measured using the estimated value of the sum of lag term coefficients of the autoregressive model

For a clearer comparison of the dynamic changes of the statistical characteristics of different inflation indicators, Table 9.1 sums up the average inflation level, inflation volatility, and persistence of inflation corresponding to the two indicators during the overall sample interval and each decade since 1979. The inflation persistence measures the time it takes for the inflation rate to return to its static level after an exogenous shock. Firstly, from the comparison of average inflation levels, the GDP deflator's inflation rate was lower than the CPI inflation rate by 1–2% in the 20 years before 1999. However, the situation changed significantly from 2000 to 2010. On average, GDP deflator's inflation rate was higher than the CPI inflation rate by over 2 percentage points. Secondly, from the perspective of inflation fluctuation, the fluctuation of the GDP deflator's inflation rate after 2000 was significantly higher than that of the CPI inflation rate, but the situation in the previous period was just the opposite. Finally, from the comparison of inflation persistence, the decline in the persistence of the GDP deflator's inflation rate from 2000 to 2010 was greater than the CPI inflation rate.

On balance, the information stated in Table 9.1 shows that the statistical characteristics of China's CPI inflation rate and GDP deflator's inflation rate vary significantly at different stages, and the difference characteristics at different stages also vary significantly. Moreover, judging from the changes in the dynamic time sequence attributive character of the two inflation indicators, the dynamic mechanism of inflation may have undergone significant structural changes in 30 years from 1979 to the present. Whether there are differences in the structural change characteristics of different indicators and whether the driving factors of their respective changes are the same have a bearing on the choice of inflation target of monetary policies and the effect of inflation management. A detailed analysis of these issues is given below.

9.2 Stochastic volatility: Long-term trend fluctuations of different price indices

Inflation expectations have important implications for the dynamic trend of real inflation, and increasingly become a core factor for decision-makers in the issue of inflation management. At the same time, the fluctuation of inflation expectations has a critical impact on the dynamic trend of real inflation. Therefore, it is possible to explore whether there is a difference in the dynamic trend of different inflation indicators by comparing the fluctuation of the sequence different inflation indicator sequences.

But it is not easy to accurately measure inflation expectations and their volatility. The existing methods to measure inflation expectations include consumer surveys (such as China's survey on urban savings income and price diffusion index), professional economist surveys (such as the Federal Reserve Bank of Philadelphia's professional forecast survey), and the rational expectation measurement of inflation rate, among others. These measures have their respective characteristics: The expectation sequence obtained through the survey data better reflects the reality of life, but it may be restricted by the respondents; the rational expectation measure is simple and intuitive, but extra noise information is introduced into the econometric analysis (Zhang et al., 2009). Therefore, which inflation expectation measure will be used depends on the nature and needs of the specific research.

Since this chapter aims to compare the differences in the dynamic characteristics (especially volatility) of inflation expectation sequences corresponding to different inflation indicators, the above three measurement methods of inflation expectation cannot meet the research needs. To calculate the inflation expectation volatility corresponding to each time point while obtaining the sequences of inflation expectation levels, this chapter uses the unobserved components stochastic volatility (UCSV) to capture the dynamic evolution path of China's inflation expectations and its volatility. The central idea of the UCSV model is to break down the inflation time sequence (without mean value) into a long-term trend component and a short-term periodic component, and also allow random variability (subject to the random walk process) of the variance of the two components. Therefore, the basic form of the UCSV model can be set as

$$
\begin{cases}
\pi_t = \tau_t + \eta_t, (\eta_t = \sigma_{\eta,t}\xi_{\eta,t}) \\
\tau_t = \tau_{t-1} + \varepsilon_t, (\varepsilon_t = \sigma_{\varepsilon,t}\xi_{\varepsilon,t}) \\
\ln \sigma_{\eta,t}^2 = \ln \sigma_{\eta,t-1}^2 + \omega_{\eta,t} \\
\ln \sigma_{\varepsilon,t}^2 = \ln \sigma_{\varepsilon,t-1}^2 + \omega_{\varepsilon,t}
\end{cases}
\tag{9.1}
$$

In the above model, τ_t represents the long-term trend component and follows the random walk process; η_t is a short-term periodic component unrelated to the sequence; ξ represents the standard Gaussian independent identical distribution (i.i.d.N(0,1)); ω represents Gaussian independence identical distribution (i.i.d.N(0,γ)), where the parameter γ controls the smoothness of the random volatility process.

From the model setting, it is not difficult to see that the long-term trend component τ_t characterizes the long-term trend of the dynamic path of inflation and can be used to capture inflation expectations (Stock and Watson, 2007; Mishkin, 2007b). After the long-term trend component (namely inflation expectations) is affected by random shocks, its impact will last, and therefore will affect the long-term inflation dynamic trend. On the other hand, the short-term periodic component only causes temporary fluctuations without a long-term effect on the inflation trend following the random shocks. In this way, by comparing the dynamic trend of the stochastic volatility sequence corresponding to the long-term trend component and the short-term periodic component (represented by SV_trend and SV_trans respectively), it is possible to examine which of the two components of the inflation sequence is dominant, thereby judging the overall trend of future inflation. If the volatility of the long-term trend component is clearly dominant compared to the short-term periodic component, it implies that there is a great increase in the risk of future inflation. On the contrary, if the volatility of the short-term periodic component is dominant, the fluctuating real inflation is only temporary. In this case, since the volatility of inflation expectations is relatively small, inflation will not increase significantly in the long term, and the risk of high inflation in the future is not high.

According to Equation 9.1, Figure 9.2 portrays the results of the stochastic volatility estimation of the long-term trend component and the short-term periodic component corresponding to the CPI inflation rate and the GDP deflator's inflation rate. It can be seen from Figure 9.1 that the stochastic volatility level of the long-term trend components of the two inflation indicators in 2000–2010 is higher than the volatility of their respective short-term periodic components, implying that China's inflation may have a large increase in risk in the future, no matter which inflation indicator is used as the benchmark.

At the same time, it has been noted that there is a significant difference in the trend of inflation expectation volatility of different inflation indicators (this issue is of the most concern to this chapter). A closer inspection of the time sequence of the long-term trend component volatility of CPI and GDPDI in Figure 9.2 shows that although the volatility of the expectation of the CPI inflation rate increased somewhat after 2007, its growth rate is not large compared to that in the 1980s and 1990s. There were signs of a significant decrease after 2009. In marked contrast to this is the volatility of the expectation component of the GDP deflator's inflation rate. The expectation volatility of the GDP deflator's inflation rate generally increased in 2001–2010, and the volatility of the long-term trend component has a more obvious dominant status compared to the volatility of the short-term periodic component. In addition, the volatility of the long-term trend component of GDPDI after 2009 showed a stronger rising trend.

The above analysis has important implications for China's inflation management in two respects. Firstly, as the volatility of inflation expectations calculated by the GDP deflator has increased significantly in recent years, an upward trend of the change rate of overall price in China is a high possibility. More importantly, the volatility of inflation expectations corresponding to different inflation indicators has significant differences in terms of dynamic trend. In particular, the inflation expectation volatility calculated based on the GDP deflator is significantly higher than that calculated based on CPI. This means that if decision-makers continue to use CPI as a single inflation target for policy mix, they will neglect the information on inflation reflected by generalized price indicators that cover a wider range and are more intimately linked to the current national economic reality, resulting in the problem of a mismatch of inflation targets that cannot be ignored.

(a)

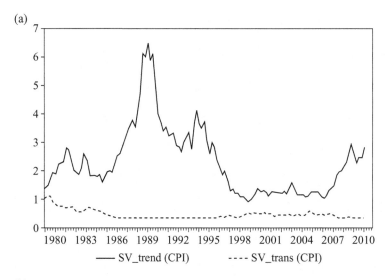

(b)

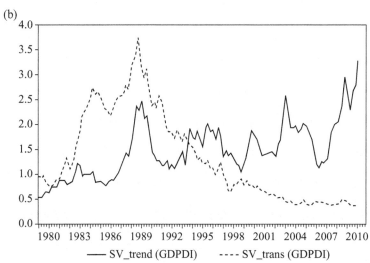

Figure 9.2 Comparison of stochastic volatility of long-term trend component and short-term periodic component corresponding to China's CPI inflation rate and GDP deflator's inflation rate.

Therefore, if the inflation target chosen by the central bank in the policymaking process cannot fully reflect the real price changes, the mismatch of inflation targets will occur. This problem brings real difficulties to the effective management of inflation. Since CPI has served as the only inflation management target for a long time, the inflation management effect of monetary policies since the reform and opening-up is chiefly reflected in the CPI inflation rate, while the GDP deflator's inflation rate is ignored in policy management, resulting in increasing volatility (uncertainty) of the inflation rate of the generalized price indicators. The monetary policies have huge differences in explaining the persistence of different inflation indicators.

9.3 The characteristic transformation of inflation dynamics mechanism: Counterfactual simulation experiment

9.3.1 Structural changes in inflation persistence and volatility

Inflation persistence and volatility are crucial for inflation management. Whether there is structural change in inflation persistence and volatility and how much this change is related to monetary policies are of great significance for the effects of inflation management. For the persistence of inflation, the definition given herein is consistent with the standard literature in the academic world, namely using the sum of lag term coefficients in the autoregressive model for measurement. According to this definition, inflation persistence measures the time it takes for an inflation rate to return to a static level after being impacted by one unit of random shock. It is not difficult to see that if monetary policy has a high contribution (interpretation) power on the change in inflation persistence, it implies that monetary policy is highly effective in managing inflation; if the opposite, it shows the poor effectiveness of policy measures for inflation management. In the actual estimation, the optimal lag orders of the AR model corresponding to the CPI inflation rate and the GDP deflator's inflation rate are determined by AIC, which are six phases and one phase, respectively.

For the inflation volatility, the stochastic volatility (SV) model is used to calculate the instantaneous volatility of the inflation rate at each time point, and then examine whether there is structural change in the time sequence of inflation volatility. The stochastic volatility model is established based on the autoregressive dynamic process of the time sequence parameter. For the sake of explanation, h_t is used to represent the instantaneous standard deviation of the sequence y_t at time t. The stochastic volatility model of time sequence parameter can be written as

$$\begin{cases} \pi_t = \theta_t(L)\pi_{t-1} + h_t\varepsilon_t \\ \theta_t(L) = \theta_{1t} + \theta_{2t}L + \ldots + \theta_{pt}L^{p-1} \\ \theta_{it} = \theta_{it-1} + c_i\eta_{it}, i = 1, 2, \ldots, p \\ \ln h_t^2 = \ln h_{t-1}^2 + \zeta_t \end{cases} \tag{9.2}$$

Where L represents the lag operator; p represents the optimal lag order determined by AIC; the stochastic disturbance terms ε_t and η_t obey the Gaussian independent identical distribution with a mean of 0 and a variance of 1; ζ_t is orthogonal to other disturbance terms. It should be noted that in order to accurately reflect the volatility change of the inflation rate at each time point, the distribution of the stochastic disturbance term ζ_t is combined according to different probability forms; in other words, at the probability of m = 95% $\zeta_t \sim N(0,h_1^2)$; at the probability of $(1 - m)$, $\zeta_t \sim N(0,h_2^2)$, and $h_2^2 = 25, h_1^2 = 0.04$. Such a setting allows for a large change in the instantaneous variance at different times, thereby helping the capture of the characteristics of the change in inflation volatility. A standard Markov chain Monte Carlo (MCMC) simulation method is used in the estimation process of time sequence parameters.

Based on the above design, the authors can test whether there is structural change in inflation persistence and instantaneous volatility in the entire sample interval. The test of structural change in econometrics dates back to the Chow test developed in the 1960s, but the Chow test must assume known breaking points. The development of test methods for structural change in unknown breaking points in recent years provides a more rational design for the analysis of structural change in inflation persistence. The theory proposed by Andrews and Ploberger (1994) on the test of structural changes in unknown breaking points is particularly sound. Hansen (1997) provides the *p*-value for calculating the corresponding test statistic based on this theory. Therefore, Andrews and Ploberger's methods are used to obtain the unknown breaking points of structural changes in inflation persistence and volatility.

According to Andrews and Ploberger's theory, it is assumed that the $m \times 1$ coefficient matrix Φ represents the parameter matrix to be tested; $\Phi = \Phi_1$ if $t < k$, and $\Phi = \Phi_2(\Phi_1 \neq \Phi_2)$ if $t \geq k$, and it meets the condition $m \leq k \leq T - m$, where T represents the size of the full sample. Moreover, assuming that the search domain of the breaking point parameter of the unknown structure is τ, a series of Wald test statistic $W_T(\tau_i)$ corresponding to all possible breaking points $k = T\tau_i$ in the domain are calculated first. The null hypothesis of this statistic test is that the parameters in the model do not have structural changes when the structural breaking point is k. After $W_T(\tau_i)$ is obtained, the maximum Wald statistic can be further calculated. If the SupW statistic is statistically significant, its corresponding breaking point is the transition time point at which structural change occurs.

Andrews and Ploberger further proposed two other test statistics with optimal characteristics for testing structural changes in the presence of interference parameters, namely the Exponential Wald and the Average Wald statistics. Andrews and Ploberger's study shows that even under asymptotic conditions, the above three test statistics correspond to non-standard statistical distribution. Therefore, while calculating the test statistics of the structural change in unknown breaking points, the authors use the non-standard distribution function proposed by Hansen (1997) to calculate the *p*-value corresponding to each statistic (p-sup, p-exp and p-ave, respectively) in order to obtain the correct accompanying probability. According to the method introduced above, the authors perform the test of structural change in unknown breaking points in the persistence and volatility of the CPI inflation rate and the GDP deflator's inflation rate from the first quarter of 1979 to the first quarter of 2010, respectively, so as to judge whether there are structural changes and the specific time point of structural changes. After the structural breaking points are identified, the samples are segmented by breaking

Table 9.2 Results of test of structural changes in inflation persistence and volatility

	p-sup	*p-exp*	*p-ave*	*Breaking point*	*Estimated value before and after the breaking point*
CPI inflation rate					
Persistence	0.108	0.069	0.059	1996Q3	0.88/0.81↓
Volatility	0.000	0.000	0.000	1998Q1	7.43/2.52↓
GDP deflator's inflation rate					
Persistence	0.012	0.040	0.228	1995Q4	0.85/0.68↓
Volatility	0.000	0.000	0.000	1987Q4	2.30/5.96↑

points and the changes in inflation persistence and volatility in different periods are examined.

Table 9.2 reports the results of the test of structural changes. It can be seen that although the significance of the *p*-value corresponding to Andrews and Ploberger's three different statistics is not identical in the test of structural change in inflation persistence, the test results still show that the persistence of the CPI inflation rate and GDP deflator's inflation rate has undergone significant structural changes (at the significance levels of 10% and 5% respectively). The time point for change in the persistence of the CPI inflation rate was the third quarter of 1996. The time point for change in the persistence of the GDP deflator's inflation rate was at the end of 1995. From the direction of change (as indicated by the arrow in the last column of Table 9.2), the persistence of both inflation indicators is significantly reduced. Moreover, the test of structural changes in inflation volatility shows that at the significance level of 1%, the volatility of the two inflation indicators underwent structural changes. However, it is noteworthy that the volatility of the CPI inflation rate dropped significantly after the structural breaking point (in early 1998), while the GDP deflator's inflation rate is just the opposite, and the volatility rose significantly after the structural breaking point (at the end of 1987).

In order to analyze the contribution of China's changing monetary policies to the structural changes in inflation persistence and volatility, this chapter designs the counterfactual comparative simulation experiment. By comparing the differences in the contribution of monetary policies to the persistence and volatility of different inflation indicators, the authors further clarify the real problems brought to China's inflation management by the inflation target mismatch caused by the single inflation indicator (namely, the CPI inflation rate).

9.3.2 Counterfactual comparative simulation experiment

The basis of the counterfactual comparative simulation experiment is to construct a multivariate model system that can capture the dynamic relationship between inflation and its related economic variables, and then the parameter estimation results of the multivariate model system in different sample intervals (including the variance–covariance matrix of the stochastic disturbance items in the system) serve as the basis of the data generation. Then comparative simulation is performed through the parameter matching in different sample intervals to obtain the simulation data on the inflation rate under different combinations, thus estimating the persistence and volatility of inflation. In this way, the driving factors of the change in persistence and volatility can be determined by comparing the estimation results corresponding to the simulation data under different parameter matching.

The construction of a multivariate dynamic model system is the key in the comparative simulation analysis. Such a model system should reflect the impact of changes in real economic output on inflation, and also captures the dynamic interaction between macroeconomic policy adjustment on the one hand and real economic output and inflation on the other. Since the dynamic transmission mechanism of the short-term inflation rate is chiefly reflected in the macroeconomic policy, especially monetary policy, the authors first take the growth rate of M2 (M2GR) as the monetary policy indicator variable according to the main intermediary target of monetary policies released in the "Executive Report on Monetary Policy" by the People's Bank of China over the years. The real economic output variable is measured by the real GDP growth rate (RGDPGR). In this way, the authors set up the structured vector autoregressive model (SVAR):

$$A(L)Y_t = \varepsilon_t, \varepsilon_t \sim (0, \Omega_\varepsilon) \tag{9.3}$$

Where $Y_t = (\text{RGDPGR} \quad \text{CPI} \quad \text{M2GR})'$, $A(L) = A_0 - \sum_{i=1}^{p} A_i L^i$ and matrix A_0 is used to capture the instantaneous relationship between variables; L represents the lag operator; p represents the optimal lag order selected according to AIC; ε_t represents the Gaussian noise of vector.

According to the standard time sequence analysis theory, the estimation of the SVAR model can meet the SVAR identification condition by adding constraints to the coefficient matrix A_0 (such as the lower triangular matrix), thus obtaining the estimation results. Since the SVAR model here is used to perform simulation analysis, the simulation data can be obtained through the conversion between the structural formula and the reduced formula in the VAR model. Specifically, Equation 9.3 can be rewritten as

$$Y_t = \Phi(L)Y_{t-1} + e_t, e_t \sim (0, \Omega_e) \tag{9.4}$$

Where $\Phi(L) = A_0^{-1} \left(\sum_{i=1}^{p} A_i L^{i-1} \right)$, $e_t = A_0^{-1} \varepsilon_t$. By comparing Equation 9.3 and Equation 9.4, it is not difficult to obtain the variance–covariance matrix $\Omega_e = A_0^{-1} \Omega_\varepsilon \left(A_0^{-1} \right)'$ of the disturbance term in the reduced formula. In this way, the authors use Equation 9.4 as the data generation process for simulation by means of the relationship between the structural model and the reduced model, thus examining the persistence and volatility exhibited by the inflation data generated by the mutual matching combination of Φ and Ω_e in different sample intervals. In the simulation process, the coefficients of the reduced VAR model use the results of the fitting of least squares estimation. The identification and estimation of the A_0 and the variance of the disturbance term in SVAR are obtained by the Wald causal chain constraints. The initial value of the simulation process uses the actually observed value corresponding to the VAR model. The generated sample size is consistent with that of the actually examined sample interval, and the first 100 simulation values in the generated data are eliminated to avoid sensitivity possibly brought by the initial values.

For the sake of explanation, the authors use $\left(\hat{\Phi}_1, \hat{\Omega}_1\right)$ and $\left(\hat{\Phi}_2, \hat{\Omega}_2\right)$ to represent the portfolio combination of the variance–covariance matrix of the model coefficient matrix and the structured disturbance vector in the sample interval before and after the structural change. $\left(\hat{\Phi}_1, \hat{\Omega}_2\right)$ represents the portfolio combination of the variance–covariance matrix of the model coefficient matrix before the structural change, and the structural disturbance vector after the structural change, and $\left(\hat{\Phi}_2, \hat{\Omega}_1\right)$ and $\left(\hat{\Phi}_1, \hat{\Omega}_2\right)$ have similar meanings. In this way, the authors can simulate and generate inflation sequences consistent with the respective sample sizes through four different combinations, and then use the generated simulation data to estimate the persistence and volatility of inflation. Because the change in coefficient matrix in the VAR model represents the systematic change caused by the changes in monetary policy, and the different variance–covariance matrix of the disturbance term before and after the structural change represents the change in random shocks, the simulation comparison experiment can determine the extent to which monetary policies contribute to the structural changes in inflation persistence and volatility.

According to the above model building and comparative simulation, Table 9.3 summarizes the comparative simulation results of the four matching cases of the VAR model coefficient matrix and the variance–covariance matrix of disturbance terms. In each case, the point estimates of the persistence and volatility of different inflation indicators are reported. The contribution of monetary policies before and after structural changes is calculated in each case, with the results summarized in the last column of Table 9.3. The results of the comparative simulation experiment are analyzed below.

First, Table 9.3 shows that the persistence of the CPI inflation rate before and after the breaking points calculated by the parameters estimated in the VAR

Table 9.3 Results of counterfactual comparative simulation experiment

		$\left(\hat{\Phi}_1, \hat{\Omega}_1\right)$	$\left(\hat{\Phi}_2, \hat{\Omega}_2\right)$	$\left(\hat{\Phi}_1, \hat{\Omega}_2\right)$	$\left(\hat{\Phi}_2, \hat{\Omega}_1\right)$	*Degree of policy contribution (%)*
Persistence	CPI	0.865	0.807	0.877	0.742	100
	GDPDI	0.889	0.564	0.840	0.733	48
Volatility	CPI	7.636	2.540	3.905	4.741	57
	GDPDI	2.496	6.354	3.611	8.811	0

model is 0.865 and 0.807, respectively, and the persistence of the GDP deflator's inflation rate is 0.889 and 0.564, respectively. The two sets of estimates are basically consistent with the inflation persistence calculated by directly using the actual samples. From a closer inspection of the simulation experiment results of the volatility of the inflation rate before and after the breaking points (CPI and GDPDI are 7.636 and 2.540 as well as 2.496 and 6.354, respectively), it can be seen that it is very close to the results calculated by the actual samples. This shows that the SVAR model system established can portray the dynamic relationship between China's real economy, inflation, and monetary policy.

Secondly, Table 9.3 reports the inflation persistence and volatility calculated from the counterfactual matching based on the SVAR coefficient matrix and the disturbance term's variance–covariance matrix before and after the breaking points. From the perspective of inflation persistence, if the coefficient matrix remains unchanged and the variance–covariance matrix of the structural shock term is changed to the result corresponding to the second sample (namely $\left(\hat{\Phi}_1, \hat{\Omega}_2\right)$), then the persistence of CPI is changed from 0.865 to 0.877; if the coefficient matrix is changed to the result corresponding to the second sample and the variance–covariance matrix of the structural shock term remains unchanged (namely $\left(\hat{\Phi}_2, \hat{\Omega}_1\right)$), then the CPI persistence level falls to 0.742. The results of this comparative simulation show that the change in the persistence of CPI inflation rate can be explained by systematic improvement in monetary policies. Through similar investigation, the authors can calculate the contribution rate of monetary policy to the change in the GDP deflator's inflation rate to be 48%. This shows that the change in the persistence of the inflation rate of the generalized price index is chiefly caused by the change in the nature of exogenous shock, while the degree of interpretation of monetary policy is less than half.

Moreover, according to the results of comparative simulation of inflation volatility (the results corresponding to the final two rows in Table 9.3), the volatility of CPI's inflation rate significantly weakens after the structural breaking point, and monetary policy has a high contribution (57%) to this reduction. Contrary to the results of the CPI's inflation indicator, the volatility of GDPDI does not weaken after the structural breaking point, but instead intensifies. Therefore, monetary policy does not have a positive contribution to the volatility of the GDP deflator's inflation rate (namely, without weakening the volatility of the generalized inflation indicator). In fact, according to the simulation results, monetary policy did not weaken the inflation volatility calculated by the GDP deflator in the past 20 years, but instead intensified the volatility of the inflation rate of this generalized price index.

9.4 Decision selections: Weight adjustment or target adjustment

The above analysis results provide an important reference for China's inflation management in the new era, with special significance and implications for inflation target matching and selection for monetary policy. Firstly, according to the sustained differences in inflation levels measured by CPI and GDP deflator in recent years, the CPI's inflation rate significantly underestimated the increase in overall prices. This result may explain why China's CPI-based inflation has been moderate in recent years, but the inflationary pressure felt by the public and the markets is mounting significantly. It has come to our notice that it is in this context that some domestic studies have begun to explore the problems in the preparation of CPI in China, especially casting doubt on the weighting of sub-components of CPI. For example, Wang (2008) argues that China should cut the proportion of food in the eight sub-components of CPI. Gao (2009) proposes that China needs to shorten the updating time of weights in the preparation of CPI. Some news media called for increasing the weight of housing expenditures in the CPI system.

In reality, the weights of CPI sub-components in China are indeed very different to those in other countries, especially developed countries like the United States. In the United States, for example, the weight of housing in CPI exceeds 40%, while this figure is only 15% in China. To further illustrate the problem, Table 9.4 compares the weights of the sub-components of CPI in China and the United States. The weights of CPI sub-components in China are estimated according to the recursive least squares (RLS) method. The American data are from the US Department of Labor. It can be seen from the figures in Table 9.4 that China and the United States indeed have obvious difference in the weights of CPI sub-components, with an especially marked contrast in the three categories of food, tobacco and alcohol and supplies, and housing. In the United States, the weight of the two categories of food, and tobacco and alcohol and supplies is only 15%, while this figure is 38.3% in China.

Does the combination of the above analysis and the findings of this chapter suggest that a significant adjustment in the weights of CPI can solve the problem of significant differences between the CPI inflation rate and the GDP deflator's

Table 9.4 Comparison of weights of sub-components of CPI's inflation rate between China and the US

	Chinese weight	American weight
Overall CPI	100	100
Food	33	15
Tobacco, alcohol, and supplies	5.3	
Apparel	9.3	3.7
Household equipment and services	3.8	3.5
Medical care and personal products and services	8.4	6.3
Transportation and communications	11.4	17.2
Entertainment, education, cultural goods and services	13.8	11.6
Housing	15	42.7

Note: China's weights are the RLS estimates (Jan. 2001–Jun. 2010), and the American weights are from the US Department of Labor.

inflation rate? To answer this question, the authors re-calculate the CPI inflation rate in China from January 2001 to June 2010 according to the American weights, and compare it with the dynamic trajectory of the raw data on China's CPI inflation rate in Figure 9.3. It can be seen from Figure 9.3 that through the re-calculation of China's CPI based on the weights of the CPI components in the US, the new CPI time sequence trajectory is basically consistent with the original data. Although the new CPI for several years is slightly higher (in 2006) or slightly lower (in 2008) than the raw data, the deviation is generally not more than 1%.

From the above analysis, it is not difficult to see that even the new significant adjustment to the weights of sub-components of China's CPI basket cannot completely solve the problem of underestimation of the overall inflation by China's CPI indicators. Therefore, regarding inflation management, decision-makers should shift the focus of attention from the adjustment of CPI weights to the correct selection and matching of inflation target variables, especially paying attention to the fact that CDP deflator's inflation rate is higher than the CPI inflation rate in the long term. In fact, according to the experience of developed countries, the phenomenon that the GDP deflator's inflation rate is persistently higher than the CPI's inflation rate is rare. Figure 9.4 compares the time sequence trajectories of the CPI inflation rate and the GDP deflator's inflation rate in the United States and Japan in 1980–2010. It can be seen that although the inflation levels measured by different inflation indicators in the US and Japan differ in individual periods, the difference is small, and the CPI inflation rate is higher than the GDP deflator's inflation rate in the majority of cases. This is just the opposite of the case in China. It can be seen that the special phenomenon that the current GDP deflator's inflation rate in China is consistently higher than the CPI inflation rate deserves the special attention of decision-makers.

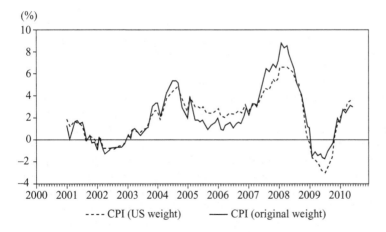

Figure 9.3 Comparison of CPI inflation rate and CPI's original sequence re-calculated according to the American weights.

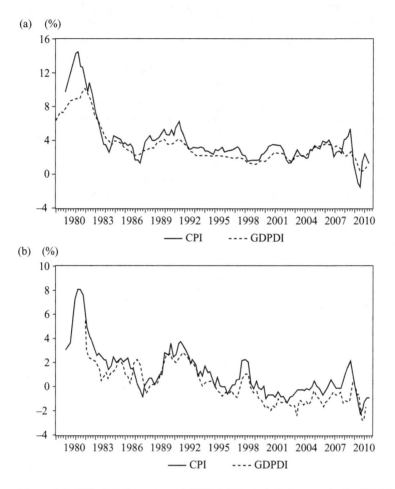

Figure 9.4 CPI's inflation rate and GDP deflator's inflation rate in the US (above) and Japan (below): First quarter of 1980–second quarter of 2010.

Besides, the continuous rise in China's real estate prices in recent years reflects the strong demand of the public for housing, but also reflects the public's concern about the depreciation of monetary assets on the other hand. This shows strong demand for investment for value preservation (not housing). According to the research findings in this chapter, the inflation level measured by China's GDP deflator in recent years is usually significantly higher than the inflation level measured by CPI. As a result, although the CPI-based real interest rate (without the interest rate of inflation factor) is positive in some periods, the real interest rate based on the GDP deflator is negative. This can be verified by Figure 9.5: The one year fixed term deposit rate (expressed as r-CPI) based on CPI's inflation rate was positive in 2001, 2003, and 2005–2007, but the real interest rate (expressed as r-GDPDI) based on the GDP deflator's inflation rate is negative in these periods.

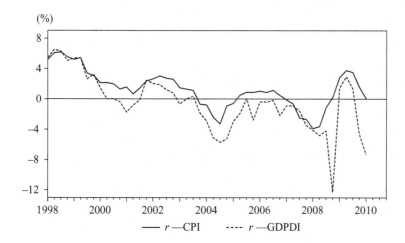

Figure 9.5 China's real interest rate (one-year fixed-term deposit rate): First quarter of 1998–second quarter of 2010.

In this case, the public naturally prefer hard assets that can maintain value in the long run, especially real estate.

Therefore, more attention should be paid to the dynamic trend of generalized prices for the adjustment of monetary policy, especially the adjustment of interest rate policy. Although CPI is an important indicator for measuring inflation, the current dynamic trend of CPI is insufficient to serve as an effective inflation indicator to warn against the systemic and structural risks of the economy according to the findings of this chapter. Therefore, changing the practice of using CPI as a single inflation target and improving the information content on the inflation rate of the generalized price index are important measures for the prevention and resolution of financial risks and effective maintenance of economic and financial stability in the current period.

9.5 Conclusions

Whether the monetary policy can choose the correct inflation target for matching has a direct bearing on whether the ultimate goal of policy adjustment can be achieved. Because the overall economic performance mechanism of China has undergone significant structural changes in the late 1990s since the reform and opening-up, there has been a significant continuous difference between the consumer expenditure-based inflation index and the inflation rate of generalized price indices. This difference is of great significance for current inflation management in China.

In view of this, this chapter focuses on studying the differences in dynamic characteristics of China's CPI inflation rate and GDP deflator's inflation rate. It is found that the GDP deflator's inflation rate has been significantly higher than the

CPI inflation rate in recent years, and there are significant differences in the interpretation of the persistence and volatility of different inflation indicators by the monetary policies. Monetary policies make greater contribution to the persistence and volatility of the CPI inflation rate than GDP deflator's inflation rate. These results imply that due to the use of CPI as a single inflation target in the long term in China, there is a lack of active monitoring, response, and management of generalized price indices, with the result that monetary policy is unable to interpret the dynamic mechanism of the inflation rate of generalized price indices.

The findings of this chapter show that the GDP deflator's inflation rate indicator urgently needs to be incorporated into the decision-making information database in order to evaluate the dynamic trend of domestic inflation and to determine the timing of the policy on inflation prevention, and the intensity of implementation. Since CPI reflects only the price fluctuations of consumer goods, it cannot fully cover the price changes in broader fields such as real estate. Therefore, for the formulation of monetary policy, it is impossible to judge the trend of overall inflation based on the change in CPI. It is also necessary to pay attention to the dynamic change in the GDP deflator's inflation rate. Especially in the current situation, the regulation of real estate prices reaches a critical period, and the post-crisis macroprudential supervision system remains to be established and improved. Therefore, the correct selection and matching of inflation targets will be the decisive factor for smooth national economic performance in the future.

In summary, to achieve the ideal target of effective inflation management, it is necessary to perform much basic work, such as building a comprehensive scientific economic forecasting system, introducing scientific analysis mechanisms into macroeconomic policy analysis framework, in addition to the need to correctly understand the current mismatch problem of inflation targets. In the actual work of building the forecasting system, the statistical accounting of generalized price indices, currency-driven price transmission mechanism, and the dynamic transmission law of upstream, midstream, and downstream prices in China provide beneficial information channels for predicting the dynamic trend of the overall prices. Only by following the laws of real economic performance for forward-looking dynamic adjustment of macroeconomic policy can we guarantee the healthy and stable development of the Chinese economy.

Note

1   Some even think that China needs to incorporate real estate prices in the statistical system of CPI. However, it should be noted that CPI is a statistical indicator of the consumer price system. When it is not easy to define the consumption and investment properties of real estate, the inclusion of real estate price in CPI has problem in terms of basic concept.

10 Inflation expectations and its dynamic mechanism

10.1 Types of inflation expectations

Inflation expectations are an important variable in the modern macroeconomic analysis framework. In particular, the micro-based New Keynesian Phillips curve model developed in recent years highlights the impact of inflation expectations on real inflation (such as Gali and Gertler, 1999). However, in the macroeconomic analysis framework, inflation expectations are generally obtained using the rational expectations or the adaptive expectations hypothesis. Therefore, inflation expectations are only statistically variable indicators in such an analysis framework, but not public expectations of inflation in reality.

The problem of inflation expectations management has always been the focus of general concern, and relevant theoretical research and applied research have yielded rich results. Although existing studies differ in terms of analytical perspectives, analytical methods, and analytical priorities, it is generally believed that the sound management of inflation expectations is a central task for central bank to suppress inflation. Existing studies have shown that rising inflation expectations can increase aggregate demand while cutting aggregate supply, leading to a rise in overall price levels. In fact, panic buying in the 1980s in China and the excessive boom in the domestic stock market and real estate market before the 2007–2008 global financial crisis are all related to inflation expectations to a certain extent. Because inflation expectations can affect the public's consumption and investment modes and affect the overall economic performance, stable inflation expectations help monetary policy to play a better role, and the stability of inflation expectations is of central significance for the inflation trend and overall economic performance (Mishkin, 2007a).

The academic community and decision-makers attach great importance to the inflation expectations issue and see inflation expectations as a key factor in understanding the inflation formation mechanism. However, since it is difficult to directly observe public expectations and it is hard to obtain the information implicit in public behavior patterns, little is known about how the public's inflation expectations are formed. Existing research has three main ideas on the analysis of the formation mechanism of inflation expectations: The first is to suppose that public expectations follow the full rational expectation model, and public expectation sequence can be obtained through the real inflation rate one stage in advance. The second is to obtain the inflation expectation sequence through time sequence estimation methods and further analyze its dynamic characteristics. The third is the forms of public expectations, which is the closest to the reality, but it is harder to obtain accurate observation data on public expectations.

The first form of inflation expectations (namely the rational expectations hypothesis) is widely used in the existing research. For instance, Chari et al. (1998) and Albanesi et al. (2003) used the limited participation model (LPM) to study the effects of monetary policy under the rational expectations hypothesis, and found that the mechanical monetary policy response function cannot adequately reflect the relationship between the monetary policy credibility and inflation expectations, and the central bank's commitment mechanism is conducive to the prevention of the "expectation trap" problem (namely, the central bank cannot effectively guide the public). Moreover, Gali and Gertler et al. (1999) performed empirical analysis of the micro-based inflation dynamic mechanism model based on the rational expectations hypothesis on inflation. The second form of inflation expectations separates the inflation expectations component of the relevant data mainly based on the time sequence analysis method. A more representative estimation method is the unobserved components stochastic volatility (UCSV) used by Stock and Watson (2007). By applying the stochastic volatility model to discrete time sequence analysis and combining it with the time-varying parameter dynamic model, it is possible to obtain the long-term trend component implied in the corresponding sequences, namely the expectation component.

Although the inflation expectation sequence and the formation mechanism of expectations corresponding to the above two methods are crucially important, the formation pattern of public expectations is not necessarily similar to the modeled mathematical calculation process in reality. Therefore, the first two expectation forms cannot be used to capture and characterize the public expectations in the real economic performance, and it is impossible to analyze the formation mechanism of public expectations. Therefore, this chapter focuses on the formation mechanism of the third type of inflation expectations, namely the public inflation expectations in reality. For public expectations, it has come to our notice that the formation of public inflation expectations will be affected by media opinion in all probability, especially with extensive media coverage. The formation of public expectations is more closely related to media opinion, as evidenced by a few typical events that occurred in recent years.

For example, in a media interview in late March 2011, the person in charge of Unilever (China) Co., Ltd. commented on an upcoming price rise in household chemicals. Accordingly, the news media reported many times that the prices of household chemicals of such brands as Unilever would rise in April 2011. This sparked widespread public concern and increased consumers' price expectations, triggering the panic buying of household chemicals in some cities. As another example, on June 14, 2011, Xinhuanet forwarded the news of Singapore's Lianhe Zaobao entitled "salary increase of 1,000 yuan lower than small change in property prices." This piece of news was feverishly forwarded, triggering a heated public debate on rising prices. This increased public perceptions and expectations of currency depreciation and inflation to some extent. Although it is a normal phenomenon that a salary increase of 1,000 yuan is less than the small change in property prices, the news media publishing negative news significantly exaggerated the impact of price increases. This effect is built by the impact of media opinion on public expectations.

It is not difficult to see from the above cases that the impact of public expectations on the real inflation rate cannot be ignored. Indeed, Goodfriend (1993) pointed out that unstable inflation expectations and the panic about accompanying cyclical inflation were the root causes of stagflation in Western countries in the 1970s. Li (1994) and Shi (2000) hold that the main triggering factors of high inflation in China in 1988 and 1993 were inflation expectations. Moreover, the New Keynesian Phillips curve model developed in recent years also highlights the impact of inflation expectations on real inflation (such as Gali and Gertler, 1999).

It can be seen that media opinion is closely linked to the influence mechanism of public expectations and the dynamic mechanism of inflation, and deserves further study. At present, the research into the relationship between media opinion and public expectations chiefly focuses on areas of securities investment such as investor sentiment and stock yield, as well as unemployment, deficits, and others. There are relatively few studies on media opinion and public inflation expectations. Carroll's (2003) study of macroeconomic expectations is more representative. This study points out that the higher the frequency of media coverage on inflation, the higher the probability that consumers will read the information, and the more accurate the consumer expectations. Therefore, the probability of updating rational expectations through comprehensive information is higher. Reis (2006) further proves that consumers chiefly gain macroeconomic cognition through media information, rather than spending a lot of time in continuously tracking current data in order to judge the macroeconomic trend. However, Carroll (2003) and Reis (2006) focus on the relationship between media reports and rational expectations, rather than on whether the number and tone of media reports significantly affect public expectations, nor do they offer an interpretation of the power of media reports regarding changes in public expectations.

In recent years, the research on China's inflation expectations issue has been mainly geared to the characterization model of expectations (Wang and Zhao, 2006; Xu, 2009; Zhang and Wang, 2012) and the econometric estimation of the dynamic mechanism of inflation (Zhang, 2008; Yang, 2009) and other issues, but the relevant studies did not include media opinion in the analysis of the formation mechanism of inflation expectations and inflation's dynamic mechanism. From the reality of China, the frequency (quantity) of media coverage on "price" or "inflation" and the trend of change in inflation show obvious consistency. As an example, Figure 10.1 portrays the number of reports from the first quarter of 2001 to the first quarter of 2012 on inflation by the major media units as included in GENIUS database. Figure 10.1 shows that during the period when China's inflation rate was low, before 2007, the number of media reports

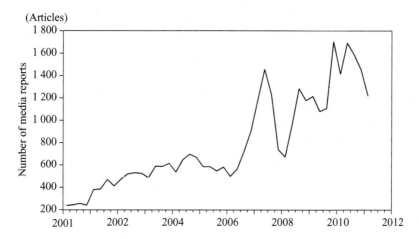

(Articles)

Number of media reports

Figure 10.1 Statistics on media coverage of inflation (first quarter of 2001–first quarter of 2012).

was relatively small. After 2007, the number of media reports rose significantly, and this period saw a significant rise in China's inflation rate. The consistency between media reports and the trend of real inflation shows that the media opinion may drive the same trend change in the real inflation rate through the impact on inflation expectations.

In view of this, this chapter studies media opinion, public expectations, and the dynamic mechanism of China's inflation in a combined manner, and innovatively differentiates the tone of media coverage. Firstly, the relevant reports of the mainstream news media are quantified to calculate the number of reports on prices and inflation by the major media units from the first quarter of 2001 to the first quarter of 2012. The authors have noticed that media opinion can send different signals affecting consumers' expectations through the tone of news reports. Therefore, in statistics, it is not sufficient simply to make sums; it is necessary to carefully peruse the content of relevant reports, and divide the tones into positive, neutral, and negative in order to calculate the net value of the number of media reports. Then, we obtained the public expectations of the inflation rate based on the data of "People's Bank of China Questionnaire on Quarterly National Urban Depositor" and "Weekly on Stocks," thus analyzing whether media opinion significantly affects public expectations. On this basis, this chapter examines the influence mechanism of inflation expectations on real inflation based on the micro-based inflation's dynamic mechanism model. Through the above design, the authors hope to discover the influence mechanism between Chinese media opinion, public expectations, and real inflation, with a view to providing a reference for decision-makers to fully consider the media impact on public expectations in macroeconomic management.

10.2 Inflation expectations measurement: Micro-groups

Many statistical measurement methods are available for inflation expectations, including rational expectations, adaptive expectations, and multivariate dynamic model prediction. Since this chapter focuses on the impact of media coverage on public expectations, the authors use survey data on inflation expectations. The survey data directly or indirectly provides the expected inflation rate through feedback from the public, thus reflecting the real expectations of the public. Two different types of expectation survey data are used in this chapter to obtain the expected inflation rate: Firstly, the raw index on the public expectations is obtained through the "future price expectation index" in the "table on urban savings income and price diffusion index" published by the People's Bank of China. The standard difference statistics method is used to calculate the inflation rate expected by the public. The second is to directly obtain data on inflation expectations according to the "China Macroeconomic Forecast" published by the Weekly on Stocks.[1]

The first set of data is from the questionnaires conducted by the People's Bank of China. The question of the questionnaire is "How do you think the prices of the next stage (quarter) will change?" The options include "rise," "fall," and "remain unchanged." Based on the number of people choosing the different options, commodity price can be converted to the expected inflation rate using the difference statistics method. According to the questionnaires by the People's Bank of China, the publicly expected inflation rate obtained by the difference statistics method is equivalent to the quarterly year-on-year growth rate. It should be noted that the People's Bank of China adopted a new method to calculate the depositor's income and price index in the third quarter of 2009. By adding 100%, the original difference is divided by 2 to be converted into an index value fluctuating near 50%. The data before and after the use of new method are harmonized, so that the obtained data on expectation are consistent.

For the sake of explanation, the authors use R_t to indicate the percentage of respondents choosing "the price in the next stage will rise" at the $t - 1$ phase; F_t to indicate the percentage of respondents choosing "the price in the next stage will fall"; and N_t to indicate the percentage of respondents choosing "the price in the next stage will remain unchanged." In this way, the authors can calculate and obtain the inflation expectation sequence using the standard difference statistics method (of course, the regression method and the probability method can also be used, but only the difference statistics method can be used to calculate the available data information published by the People's Bank of China). Specifically, let $B_t = R_t - F_t$, where B_t represents the net difference, namely the difference between the percentage of people who think that the price will rise in the next stage and the percentage of people who think that the price will fall in the next stage, which depicts the strength of consumers' expectations. The net difference is between -1 and 1. When the net difference is greater than zero, the inflation expectations are rising. Conversely, if the net difference is less than zero, the inflation expectations are falling. In this way, the expected inflation rate can be directly calculated based on the net difference B_t, namely, $\pi_t^e = \beta B_t$, where the coefficient β is calculated based on $\beta = \sum_{t=1}^{T} \pi_t / \sum_{t=1}^{T} B_t$ (π_t represents the inflation rate, as measured by the CPI inflation rate).

The second set of forecast data used in this chapter is from the "China Macroeconomic Forecast" competition (aka "Vision Cup") organized by Weekly on Stocks. According to the relevant design, Weekly on Stocks invited 27 domestic institutions to make forecasts, and released several pieces of macroeconomic forecast data including CPI's inflation rate (year-on-year) on a quarterly basis.[2] The "Vision Cup" competition measures the accuracy of forecasts made by various organizations. Weekly on Stocks reports the forecast results of participating institutions on a quarterly basis. We average the forecast values of the CPI inflation rate given by all the institutions and calculate the second set of data on the expected inflation rate used in this chapter.

For the actual inflation rate, the authors use the CPI's year-on-year growth rate published by the National Bureau of Statistics as the representative. The original sample interval is from January 2001 to March 2012. The data of the last month corresponding to each quarter are used as the data on quarterly inflation rate to avoid introducing extra sequence correlation due to data frequency conversion. Based on the above data, Figure 10.2 gives the time sequence of the publicly expected inflation rate and the real CPI inflation rate. For the sake of comparison, Figure 10.2 also portrays the media coverage sequence of GENIUS. It has come to our notice that the number of media reports is highly similar to the publicly expected inflation rate and the real inflation rate with respect to the characteristics of cyclical changes, and that the changes are far ahead of the publicly expected inflation rate most of the time, while the publicly expected inflation rate is ahead of the real inflation rate. Of course, the relationship between media public media, public expectations, and real inflation rate cannot be accurately judged from Figure 10.2 alone. The quantitative regression method is used below for further analysis.

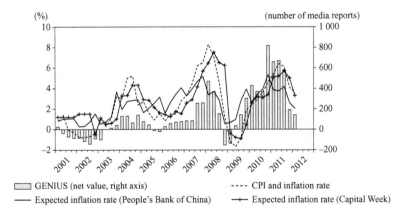

Figure 10.2 Publicly expected inflation rate and number of media reports (net value reported by GENIUS).

10.3 Inflation expectations dynamics mechanism: Media perspective

10.3.1 Source of data reported by the media

The sample interval for study in this chapter is from the first quarter of 2001 to the first quarter of 2012 (subject to the frequency of survey data and sample interval of public expectations). To comprehensively and accurately obtain the data on inflation-related reports by Chinese news media during this period, this chapter selects four different databases for search statistics according to circulation rankings, influence, and reach. The first and second groups of data are news statistics of a single media newspaper or magazine, which are Reference News and People's Daily, respectively; the third and fourth groups of data are from the comprehensive statistics from the media "news pool" composed of various newspapers and magazines. The databases are GENIUS FINANCE's financial services platform database (hereinafter GENIUS FINANCE) and WiseNews Search Database (hereinafter WiseNews).

As the source of the first group of data, Reference News is the daily newspaper with the highest circulation in China since 2004, and also one of the only two newspapers in China that can legally and directly publish foreign news. It features both major current events in China and major news from around the world.[3] As the source of the second group of data, People's Daily is the daily newspaper with the second largest circulation in China since 2004, and is recognized by UNESCO and the World Association of Newspapers and News Publishers as one of the top ten newspapers in the world. It has obvious characteristics as the newspaper of the Party – keeping to positive reporting of national guidelines and policies, and timely dissemination of information on various fields at home and abroad.

Given that a newspaper has a fixed readership, it may not fully reflect the impact of media opinion on public expectations, resulting in biased results of subsequent econometric analysis. Therefore, the authors use the "news pool" from various newspapers and magazines in the broad-based GENIUS FINANCE and WiseNews database for relevant report retrieval and statistics. The authors select 15 widely recognized influential newspapers and magazines from GENIUS FINANCE, including national newspapers and regional newspapers, comprehensive newspapers, and financial newspapers. At the same time, it is guaranteed that the full text of these 15 newspapers and magazines is included for the sample interval we studied.[4] The "news pool" of WiseNews consists of 20 different types of newspapers with greater coverage, including China's most influential comprehensive newspapers,[5] important central Party newspapers,[6] and the most influential financial newspapers.[7] At the same time, it is guaranteed that the full text of all newspapers is included for the sample interval studied.

10.3.2 Number and tone of media reports

On the basis of the four databases, the authors conducted relevant searches, quantity, and tone identification on the news in the media, thus obtaining accurate quantitative information on media opinion. Firstly, the authors selected from the media databases the articles related to price and inflation that may have an impact on consumer expectations of inflation. The first step is to search the topic and the full text of articles. The search keywords are inflation, deflation, price of commodities, price, CPI, PPI, consumer price index, wholesale price index, and others. Any article or title that contains one of the above keywords is selected and recorded.

News reports that are unrelated to inflation in China may be selected or related reports may be omitted due to the sole dependence on keyword search. Therefore, the second step is to review the articles through manual reading. The review mainly includes: (1) selecting reports related to the overall price levels in China or the world, and excluding articles that solely report the price level and inflation in other countries; (2) excluding articles on the changes in prices of non-typical non-common goods such as stock prices and gold prices; (3) checking whether the content of articles reports or comments on the current commodity prices and information (avoiding statistical omissions) when their titles do not contain keywords. Through electronic retrieval and manual reading, the authors obtained the total number of relevant media reports from the four data sources (see Figure 10.3).

Based on the above four sets of data, Figure 10.3 describes time sequence data on the number of reports by Chinese media from the first quarter of 2001 to the first quarter of 2012. From Figure 10.3, it can be seen that the number of reports by different media in different periods and the peaks and valleys of the number of reports vary slightly, but the number of reports by the four types of media has similarities in the overall trend: Before 2007, the number of reports on related topics such as inflation by various types of media was relatively stable, but the number of reports by various types of media increased significantly thereafter. There was a brief decline in 2009–2010, and the number reached a historical high in 2011 and declined slightly after 2012.

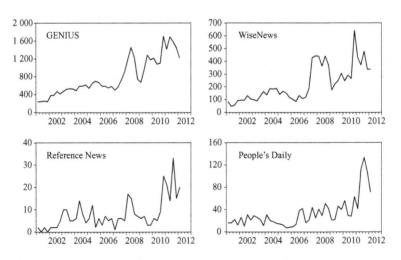

Figure 10.3 Total number of media reports on inflation, etc.

Secondly, because of the different content and commentary angles in different articles, the impact on public expectations of inflation may be different. Therefore, the content of the reports is differentiated on the basis of establishing the number of articles. Through reading of the full text and judgment of the tone, the authors divide news reports into three categories (based on the basic content, tone, and conventional logic of the original text): (1) News that positively affects the public expectations of inflation is recorded as +1. Such articles mainly state that the price level is currently high or the price levels have a rising trend in the future, or the government is implementing proactive monetary policy, and so on. Titles commonly used are "national CPI hit a record high according to National Bureau of Statistics" and "central bank lowers the required reserve ratio again." (2) News that may have a negative impact on public expectations of inflation is recorded as −1. Such reports are broadly divided into two categories: Firstly, direct reports on the decline in price level or deflation in China, and secondly, reports of government measures to curb inflation or of the change in price levels in the context of positive inflation. Titles commonly used are "CPI hit a new low in 22 months" and "the central bank raises the required reserve ratio for financial institutions for the fifth time in fight against inflation and deflation," and so on. (3) News that has a neutral impact on public expectations of inflation is recorded as zero. Such reports are generally free from biased reporting, and only give descriptive reports on the real economic situation, such as "prudent currency assists the stable and healthy economy."

In this way, the authors calculate the net value of the number of media reports according to the number of reports with different tones, namely the number of reports with a positive tone minus the number of reports with a negative tone (neutral tone is recorded as 0). For the sake of demonstration, Figure 10.4 depicts

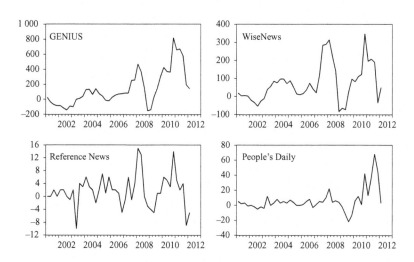

Figure 10.4 Net value of the number of media reports after the tones are differentiated.

the number of media reports with differentiated tones. Since the number of media reports with differentiated tones can more scientifically reflect the real information of media opinion, the empirical analysis uses the net value of the number of media reports described in Figure 10.4.

10.3.3 Stationarity test of data

In addition to inflation expectations and the real inflation rate, this chapter also uses the M2's growth rate and the real GDP gap in the analysis of the dynamic mechanism model of inflation. The original quarterly data on M2 is derived from the People's Bank of China. In order to maintain a consistent caliber of data, the year-on-year growth rate of M2 is used in empirical analysis. The real GDP gap is based on the quarterly data on real GDP and is obtained using the standard HP filter (namely, the natural logarithm difference between real GDP and HP filtered trend components, expressed as GAP). Real GDP data are obtained based on the quarterly data on the nominal GDP published by the National Bureau of Statistics since the first quarter of 1992 and the constant price growth rate (namely, the growth rate of real GDP) in the corresponding period. For the sake of explanation, the authors use ΔCPI to express the year-on-year growth rate of CPI (namely, inflation rate) in the analysis below, and other variables with the differential sign Δ are similar to this. Moreover, the authors use EXP to indicate the publicly expected inflation rate (using the suffixes _YH and _ZQ to represent "central bank" and "securities" to differentiate the data on two types of expectations), and use JL, HK, CK, and RM to represent the number of reports corresponding to GENIUS FINANCE, WiseNews, Reference News, and People's Daily.

Before carrying out empirical analysis, it is necessary to test and determine the stationary characteristics of each variable. To this end, the authors performed the ADF unit root test on all variables (the null hypothesis is that the sequence contains unit roots). Table 10.1 reports the *p*-values of the ADF test on all variables. Except for the sequence of number of reports by GENIUS FINANCE, the *p*-values of the ADF test of other sequences are mostly less than 5% (the *p*-values corresponding to EXP_YH and ΔCPI are less than 10%). Therefore, the null hypothesis that the sequence contains unit roots is rejected, namely these sequences are stationary sequences. For the indicators of the number of reports on GENIUS FINANCE, the authors further use the KPSS test (the null hypothesis is a stationary sequence) for verification and find that the test statistic is not

Table 10.1 Results of unit root test of related variables

Sequence	EXP_YH	EXP_ZQ	JL	HK	CK	RM	ΔCPI	ΔM2	GAP
ADF(*p*-value)	0.08	0.005	0.313	0.006	0.001	0.007	0.06	0.029	0.024

Note: The sample interval is from the first quarter of 2001 to the first quarter of 2012; the ADF test does not include the time trend item (including the intercept term), and the lag order is determined by AIC (maximum of 8); the *p*-value reported in the table is calculated according to MacKinnon (1996).

significant at the significance levels of 5% and 10% (cannot reject the null hypothesis on stationary sequence). Given that the unit root test has relatively inefficient power in the case of a small data sample, it is relatively reasonable to judge it to be a stationary sequence.

10.3.4 Impact of media opinion on public expectations

Through the above research, the authors find that news reports may affect public expectations of inflation to a certain extent, thus affecting the real inflation rate. To this end, the authors start with the simplest single regression equation to explore whether there is a driving relationship between the two. The authors use the net value variable (expressed as VOL) of the number of media reports as the explanatory variable, and the publicly expected inflation rate (EXP) as the explanatory variable for simple regression, namely

$$EXP_t = c + \beta VOL_t + u_t \qquad (10.1)$$

Where c is the intercept term and u_t is the stochastic disturbance term, allowing non-spherical features for its distribution. It should be noted that since other stochastic factors that affect public expectations (namely, stochastic disturbance items) may be non-orthogonal to the media report variables in a quarter, the estimation of Equation 10.1 requires the use of two-stage least squares (2SLS), and the instrumental variable uses the lag term with one to four phases of the VOL. Of course, another alternative modeling method (often used in the literature) is to perform the regression of the lag terms of the media report variables by the publicly expected inflation rate, namely

$$EXP_t = c + \beta VOL_{t-1} + u_t \qquad (10.2)$$

Although the regression estimate of Equation 10.2 is easier than that of Equation 10.1 (only ordinary method of least squares), the impact of any media opinion on public expectations will be felt in part (even if not fully) within one quarter to some extent. Because the frequency of data analyzed in this paper is on a quarterly basis, the possible impact of current media opinion on public expectations during the same period cannot be ignored, even if the lag effect is considered.

Based on the above description and with full consideration to the possible impact of the media opinion in the current and lag phases, the authors separately perform the regression estimation on Equation 10.1 and Equation 10.2, with the estimation results reported in Table 10.2. It should be noted that in order to make the estimates of coefficient points of the media variables comparable, the levels of media report variables in the regression should be standardized (namely, the original value of the number of reports divided by the number of newspapers included in the corresponding media). After the standardization of levels, it is easier to interpret the meaning of the coefficient β, indicating the degree of impact of each additional report in a single newspaper on the public expectations. According to

Table 10.2 Estimation results of Equations 10.1 and 10.2

EXP_YH	GENIUS FINANCE		WiseNews		Reference News		People's Daily	
	2SLS	OLS	2SLS	OLS	2SLS	OLS	2SLS	OLS
β	0.06***	0.05***	0.20***	0.16***	0.21***	0.10***	0.03	0.01
	(0.01)	(0.01)	(0.03)	(0.03)	(0.08)	(0.08)	(0.05)	(0.01)
$\bar{R}^2$	0.52	0.36	0.62	0.33	0.02	0.10	0.14	0.003
EXP_ZQ								
β	0.12***	0.10***	0.41***	0.36***	0.25	0.23***	0.12***	0.07***
	(0.02)	(0.03)	(0.03)	(0.04)	(0.15)	(0.02)	(0.01)	
$\bar{R}^2$	0.15	0.54	0.18	0.79	0.03	0.03	0.20	0.24

Note: The 2SLS instrumental variable is the lag term 1–4 phases of the variable of reports by the respective media units. The parentheses report the Newey–West HAC correction standard deviation (Bartlett automatic bandwidth); *** indicates it is significant at the significance level of 1%; the media report variables in the regression are subjected to the level standardization (namely, the original number of the number of reports divided by the number of newspapers included in the corresponding media) to make the point estimates comparable.

the results reported in Table 10.2, the estimates of the coefficient β are all positive in both Equation 10.1 and Equation 10.2, and are statistically significant in the majority of cases (below the level of 1%). This shows that media opinion has a significant positive driving effect on public expectations. The more the media reports on price increases and similar, the stronger the public expectations of a rising inflation level in the future.

Based on the concrete estimation results, the estimates of the coefficient β points corresponding to Equation 10.1 and Equation 10.2 are close with respect to the same public expectation index. For example, regarding the data on expectations issued by the People's Bank of China, the estimated coefficients of the number of reports on GENIUS FINANCE are 0.06 and 0.05 respectively; the estimated coefficients of the number of reports on WiseNews are 0.20 and 0.16 respectively. The estimated values corresponding to Reference News are 0.21 and 0.10, respectively; the corresponding results of the People's Daily are 0.03 and 0.01 respectively (not significant). In other words, the significant degree of impact of media opinion on the public expectations of inflation surveyed by the People's Bank of China is 0.05–0.20. That is, for one additional article on price increases for each newspaper, the public expectation of the inflation rate (based on the survey by the People's Bank of China) may rise by up to 0.20%. For the data expectations released by the Weekly on Stocks, the estimates of coefficient β points corresponding to the media reports are higher than the results corresponding to the data on expectations released by the People's Bank of China. The coefficient of the People's Bank of China is significant in the regression of this inflation expectation variable (the point estimate value also increases somewhat).

The difference in the impact of different media opinion on the same inflation expectations may be caused by the different levels of richness and comprehensiveness of the relevant information covered by different media databases. The same media opinion can have a different impact and interpretation power on different data on expectations, perhaps because of the different sources and influence ranges of the two types of survey data. However, according to the average degree, the 2SLS estimation results corresponding to Equation 10.1 show that the mean of β estimates corresponding to the data on expectations released by the People's Bank of China is about 0.13, namely $(0.06 + 0.20 + 0.21 + 0.03)/4$. The mean of the corrected $R^2(\bar{R}^2)$ is about 0.33, namely $(0.52 + 0.62 + 0.02 + 0.14)/4$. The estimated mean of β corresponding to the data on expectations released by Weekly on Stocks is about 0.23, and the mean of the corrected R^2 is 0.14. The OLS estimation results corresponding to Equation 10.2 indicate that the estimated mean of β corresponding to the data on expectations released by the People's Bank of China is 0.08, and the mean of the corrected R^2 is 0.20; the estimated mean of β corresponding to the data on expectations released by Weekly on Stocks is 0.19, and the mean of the corrected R^2 is 0.40.

On the whole, the index of the media opinion's impact on public expectations corresponding to the survey data of the People's Bank of China is about 0.11 on average, namely $(0.13 + 0.08)/2$. The impact parameter for the data on expectations released by the Weekly on Stocks is 0.21 on average. Judging from the media opinion's interpretation of changes in public expectations (corrected R^2), the figure corresponding to the data on expectations released by the People's Bank of China is about 0.27, namely $(0.33 + 0.20)/2$, and the corresponding figure of the Weekly on Stocks is also 0.27. In other words, in the formation of public expectations, media opinion contributes 27%. For every extra report on price increases in each newspaper, the public expects rises by 0.1–0.2 percentage points. Of course, the average result of the above calculation is obtained using Equation 10.1 and Equation 10.2 as the division criteria. The average results corresponding to the two types of data on expectations can be differentiated. The estimated mean of β and the mean of corrected R^2 are very close to the above comprehensive average (the β values corresponding to the data on expectation released by the People's Bank of China and Weekly on Stocks are 0.10 and 0.21, and the corrected R^2 values are 0.26 and 0.27, respectively).

10.4 Inflation expectations and the New Keynesian Phillips curve

10.4.1 Theoretical framework

For the micro-based dynamic mechanism model of inflation (especially the New Keynesian Phillips curve model), the research represented by Roberts (1995) and Gali and Gertler (1999) provides an epoch-making theoretical basis. Based on the existing literature, this chapter considers the lag effect in real pricing based on the microscopic theory, and incorporates a richer dynamic model of inflation into the microscopic vendor pricing mechanism, thereby building the dynamic mechanism model of inflation. In constructing the theoretical model, the authors prevent the ossified dynamic mechanism from causing a sequence correlation problem to the empirical model without being divorced from the basic theoretical assumptions. In empirical analysis, this chapter chiefly focuses on the impact of public expectations about inflation on the real inflation rate, and considers the possibility of a non-orthogonal (namely endogenous) relationship between public expectations and stochastic disturbance items in model settings.

In the analysis of the impact of inflation expectations on inflation, it is critical to build a model with a rigorous theoretical basis. Such a model reflects the impact of inflation expectations and other relevant factors on the real inflation rate at the level of the macro mechanism without being separated from the microfoundation of the modern dynamic mechanism theory of inflation. To this end, in the building of the theoretical model, the authors deduce the dynamic mechanism model of inflation in line with China's price formation mechanism based on the New Keynesian sticky-price theory, so that the macroscopic theoretical model obtained has a solid microfoundation. As can be seen below, this model is essentially the New Keynesian Phillips curve (NKPC) model widely used in modern macroeconomic analysis, but this chapter carries out prudent and rational expansion in the specific form of the dynamic mechanism in the model. This expansion makes the results of empirical analysis below more scientific and reliable.

Specifically, the classic sticky-price theory is used as the basis, but there are critical differences in the specific pricing models of micro-enterprises. In the traditional sticky-price theory model, it is generally assumed that micro-enterprises only concentrate on future inflation and real economic performance in the pricing of products, namely the so-called "forward-looking" pricing model. While Gali and Gertler (1999) innovatively divide corporate pricing into "forward-looking" and "backward-looking" types, the data on historical inflation rate considered by firms in the model lag by one phase, and differ greatly from the reality. This problem means the final macro-theoretical model derived is too ossified, causing significant sequence correlation in the empirical model, thus rendering the subsequent econometric analysis invalid. Therefore, based on the traditional sticky-price theory, the authors not only consider the "forward-looking" and "backward-looking" corporate pricing models, but also allow "backward-looking" enterprises to consider the average weighting of historical inflation rates in multiple periods in pricing, so that the theoretical hypothesis is closer to reality.

Based on the above explanation, the authors assume that enterprises at the micro level have pricing power for their products in a monopolistic competitive economic environment. At the same time, it is assumed that all enterprises maintain fixed price levels for a certain period of time and only consider re-pricing after being impacted by some stochastic signals. In this way, price adjustment has "stickiness." At the same time, when enterprises price a product, they consider the price levels set by other relevant companies. This means that enterprises will consider the previous prices when formulating the current product prices. It is now assumed that the probability that an enterprise will change its prices in any given period is $1 - \theta (0 < \theta < 1)$. If p_t expresses the total price level at the t period (form of natural logarithm, the same below), the price is determined by the weighted sum of the overall price level in the previous phase and the price level (expressed as p_t^*) newly set by all enterprises at the t period, namely

$$p_t = \theta p_{t-1} + (1-\theta)p_t^* \tag{10.3}$$

In the original model of Calvo (1983), all enterprises were assumed to be "forward-looking" in the pricing process, namely the price wholly depends on the company's rational expectations for future domestic economic performance. However, since the end of the 20th century, academic circles have reached a basic consensus. In the economic performance, there are always a certain number of enterprises that adopt "backward-looking" pricing methods. They will refer to the previous industry pricing standards in the pricing process, and will consider correcting the prices based on the previous inflation rate level. Therefore, the authors assume that enterprises with a ratio of ω adopt the "backward-looking" pricing model, with the price p_t^B; enterprises with a ratio of $(1-\omega)$ adopt "forward-looking" pricing mechanisms, with the price p_t^F. Thus, the new price level (relative to overall price level) determined by all enterprises at the t period can be expressed as

$$p_t^* = (1-\omega)p_t^F + \omega p_t^B \tag{10.4}$$

The price level p_t^F set by "forward-looking" enterprises is generally in the traditional sticky-price theory as the discounted sum (such as Gali and Gertler, 1999) of the expected total output gap (namely, the natural logarithm difference between real GDP and potential GDP) and the inflation rate. Therefore, the pricing model of "forward-looking" enterprises can be written as follows:

$$p_t^F = \theta\beta \sum_{s=0}^{\infty}(\theta\beta)^s E_t\pi_{t+s+1} + (1-\theta\beta)\sum_{s=0}^{\infty}(\theta\beta)^s E_t(\zeta y_{t+s}^d) \tag{10.5}$$

Where π_t represents the inflation rate; $E_t\pi_{t+1}$ represents the forecast sequence of the inflation rate at the t period and previous $t+1$ period for information set; β represents the subjective discount factor; ζ is the structural parameters introduced during the logarithmic linearization process (ζ has economic implications, see Woodford, 2003). Moreover, y_t^d represents the domestic output gap. Through repeated iterations, the pricing model of "forward-looking" enterprises can be rewritten as follows:

$$p_t^F = \theta\beta E_t\pi_{t+1} + (1-\theta\beta)\zeta y_t^d + \theta\beta E_t p_{t+1}^F \tag{10.6}$$

For the pricing mechanism by "backward-thinking" enterprises, the authors extend the one-phase lag of inflation rate in the traditional literature to the form of a lag operator polynomial, namely

$$p_t^B = p_{t-1}^* + \pi_{t-1} + \rho^*(L)\Delta\pi_{t-1} \tag{10.7}$$

Where $\rho^*(L) = \rho_1^* + \rho_2^* L + \rho_3^* L^2 + \ldots + \rho_q^* L^{q-1}$ represents the lag operator polynomial; and q represents the lag order. In the empirical analysis, the value of q needs to be determined by AIC and sequence correlation test.

According to the substitution deduction of Equations 10.3 to 10.7, the dynamic mechanism model of macro-inflation based on the pricing mechanism of micro-enterprises can be obtained, namely

$$\pi_t = c + \gamma_e E_t \pi_{t+1} + \gamma_b \pi_{t-1} + \sum_{i=1}^{q-1} \alpha_i \Delta \pi_{t-i} + \delta_d y_t^d + \eta_t \tag{10.8}$$

Where c is a constant term, η_t represents a stochastic disturbance term, and the remaining coefficients have more intuitive interpretation power in Equation 10.8. These coefficients are the combination of underlying structural parameters in the micro model of Equations 10.1 to 10.8. Compared to the existing literature, the dynamic model for inflation, Equation 10.8, derived from the micro-based expansion has the basic characteristics of the New Keynesian Phillips curve model, and richer dynamic mechanisms are added. This expansion is more in line with reality and avoids the sequence correlation arising from the stylized model. It can be used as a benchmark model for analyzing the dynamic mechanism of inflation in China.

It should be noted that the coefficients γ_e and γ_b in Equation 10.8 gauge the degree of impact of inflation expectations and inflation inertia on the current inflation rate. From the perspective of New Keynesian economics, if γ_b is not zero, it indicates that the price level is rigid and the inflation rate itself is sticky. For the comparison of the size of γ_e and γ_e, the mainstream research represented by Gali and Gertler (1999) holds that the expectation factor in the New Keynesian Phillips curve model should be dominant, namely γ_e is far larger than γ_b. However, regarding whether this conclusion applies to China, there is no convincing research conclusion. Besides, the coefficient δ_d corresponding to the output gap in China measures the pressure of the domestic output gap on the current inflation rate. If δ_d is significantly larger than 0, it shows that the impact of domestic real economic performance on the level of domestic inflation cannot be ignored. Of course, the specific values of the above parameters need to be determined according to empirical analysis.

10.4.2 Endogenous nature and sequence correlation

Because Equation 10.8 contains inflation expectations and a spot output gap variable, the endogenous issue of the model must be considered. Specifically, since inflation expectations are based on the forecast of all relevant information at the t phase and before, the random factors that affect the spot inflation rate (such as supply shocks caused by changes in international oil prices) are likely to affect the inflation expectations. At the same time, according to the standard macroeconomic analysis framework (such as Stock and Watson, 2002), random factors affecting the spot inflation rate may also affect the spot output gap. Therefore, the disturbance term and the independent variable in Equation 10.8 may have a non-orthogonal relationship, namely there is an endogenous problem.

In practice, the authors use Durbin–Wu–Hausman test to confirm that the null hypothesis that "least squares estimation is statistically consistent" is rejected at the traditional significance level (Durbin, 1954; Wu, 1973; Hausman, 1978). To this end, the regression estimation of Equation 10.8 requires the use of the instrumental variable estimation methods to obtain the point estimates of the parameters and the corresponding standard deviation.

For the choice of instrumental variables, it is necessary to consider the economic relationship between the instrumental variables and the respective variables in the model, and to consider the rationality of the number of instrumental variables relative to the sample size, and also to ensure that instrumental variables are unrelated to disturbance items. To this end, the authors choose the output gap and the lag terms of one to four phases corresponding to the year-on-year growth rate of M2 as instrumental variables. Moreover, the constant terms and the all lag terms for the inflation rate on the right side of the model (in practice, jointly determined by AIC and the sequence correlation test described below) are also included in the instrumental variable set. The rationality of choice of instrumental variables is further determined by Hansen's (1982) J test. The null hypothesis of this test is that all instrumental variables are exogenous. If the null hypothesis is not rejected, the choice of instrumental variables is relatively reasonable.

Moreover, as mentioned above, another key issue in whether Equation 10.8) can obtain reliable estimation results is sequence correlation. For the dynamic model of Equation 10.8, if there is sequence correlation in the disturbance terms, it means that the lag terms of inflation are non-orthogonal with the disturbance terms. As a result, the lag terms of other relevant time sequence variables are related to the disturbance terms. At this time, even if the regression of instrumental variables is adopted, the results are not statistically consistent and are biased. Therefore, while estimating Equation 10.8, it must be tested whether there is sequence correlation in the model. However, traditional sequence correlation tests (such as the Breusch–Godfrey test) are invalid under the instrumental variable estimation mode. To this end, the authors perform a sequence correlation test on Equation 10.8 according to the sequence correlation test methods proposed by Godfrey (1994) under the instrumental variable estimation.

10.4.3 Results of model estimation

Table 10.3 reports the results of model estimation corresponding to different expectation sequences. First of all, what the authors are most concerned about is the estimation results corresponding to public expectations. It can be seen from the results of the first group in Table 10.3 that the publicly expected inflation rate based on the survey data by the People's Bank of China significantly drives the real CPI inflation rate, and the point estimate value (0.70) is higher than the estimate value of inflation inertia (0.48). Although the estimated value of the corresponding output gap coefficient is not statistically significant at the traditional significance level, the size and direction of the point estimates are consistent with the basic theory. For the results of the second group (corresponding to the data on

expectations released by Weekly on Stocks), the point estimate of expected inflation (0.69) is basically the same as the results of the first group, and is also significantly larger than the inflation inertia estimate (0.09). Although the estimates
of the corresponding output gap coefficient are not statistically significant (point
estimates are relatively small), the coefficient value is still positive.

From the diagnostic tests corresponding to the results of the two groups, the
extended model of Equation 10.8 in this chapter can remove the sequence correlation (the *p*-value of the sequence correlation test is greater than 10%), and
the choice of instrument variables is relatively reasonable. The joint significance
test of the lag term coefficients after the first phase is significant at the traditional
level, which proves that the model expansion of the dynamic lag terms is reasonable. From the perspective of goodness of fit, the corrected R^2 of the regression
results of the survey data from the People's Bank of China is greater than the corresponding results in the survey data from Weekly on Stocks. From the absolute
level, however, the goodness of fit between the two sets of regression results is
relatively high (not less than 75%).

On the whole, although the use of different inflation expectation measure indicators has a certain influence on the estimation results of various parameters in
the model, there is a significant positive influence on the real inflation rate from
the perspective of the impact of inflation expectations, whether it is based on the
inflation expectations surveyed by the People's Bank of China or those surveyed
by Weekly on Stocks. Because the significant impact of media opinion on public
expectations has been explained above, the results here indicate that public expectations indeed significantly drive inflation. Therefore, the impact of media opinion
on the real inflation rate cannot be ignored.

It is noteworthy that the results stated in Table 10.3 show that the impact of the
domestic output gap on the real inflation rate is not significant without exception.

Table 10.3 Results of NKPC model estimation (2SLS) using different data on inflation
expectations

Expectation indicator	γ_e	γ_b	δ_d	$p(\alpha)$	p-auto	p-J	$\bar{R}^2$	Lag phase
EXP_YH	0.70*** (0.23)	0.48*** (0.10)	0.20 (0.24)	0.008***	0.80	0.999	0.90	6
EXP_ZQ	0.69 (2.23)	0.09 (1.82)	0.04 (0.55)	0.06*	0.15	0.15	0.75	6

Note: The sample interval is from the first quarter of 2001 to the first quarter of 2012; the optimal lag
order of the model is determined jointly by AIC and the sequence correlation test (optional maximum
order of 8); the instrumental variables are the all lag terms of inflation rate and the lag terms of 1 to 4
phases of the output gap in the regression model. p(αi) indicates the *p*-value corresponding to the joint
significance test of all lag terms of the inflation rate after the first phase; p-auto refers to the *p*-value of
the sequence correlation test of instrumental variables by Godfrey (1994) (the null hypothesis is there
is no sequence correlation); p-J refers to the *p*-value corresponding to Hansen's (1982) J test (the null
hypothesis is that all instrumental variables are exogenous); the parentheses report the White corrected
standard deviation. All sequences are determined to be stationary by unit root test.

This may imply that the dynamic mechanism model of inflation extended in this chapter with richer dynamic mechanism characteristics still has scope for further expansion. In reality, due to the closer ties between China's economy and the world economy in recent years, the supply and demand in the international market is highly likely to affect the pricing strategies and pricing mechanisms made by domestic enterprises. It becomes an important influencing factor in the trend of domestic inflation, thereby weakening the driving effect of the traditional domestic supply and demand factors (namely, domestic output gap) on inflation. In this context, the elements of globalization may be transmitted from the international market to the domestic one through various channels, thereby exerting an impact on domestic prices and the inflation formation mechanism. Therefore, the impact of the elements of globalization on the trend of domestic inflation is an important direction worthy of attention for future studies. This issue will be further analyzed in Chapter 14.

10.5 Conclusions

This chapter studies the formation of inflation expectations as well as the influence mechanism between inflation expectations and real inflation from the perspective of media opinion. The authors first quantified the information on media opinion from the first quarter of 2001 to the first quarter of 2012 through the statistics on the number and tone of articles on inflation and other issues on the WiseNews and GENIUS FINANCE databases with the widest coverage as well as Reference News and People's Daily, the top two newspapers in China in terms of circulation and influence. Then, the authors obtained the data on the publicly expected inflation rate through the "future price expectation index" in the "table of urban savings income and price diffusion index" issued by the People's Bank of China and the macroeconomic forecast data released by Weekly on Stocks. On this basis, this chapter finds through rigorous measurement tests that media opinion in China has a significant positive driving effect on public expectations. The more the media reports on related content such as inflation, the stronger the public expectations about rising inflation rates in the future. This chapter further analyzes the impact of public expectations on the real inflation rate by establishing a micro-based dynamic mechanism model of inflation. The results show that public expectations have a significant positive impact on the real inflation rate.

The research findings in this chapter provide new ideas and perspectives for China's inflation expectations and inflation management issues in a new era. For the monetary authorities, it is obviously necessary to attach high importance to the influence and guiding role of media opinion on public expectations. Especially at a time of subtle changes in macroeconomic policy regulation, the authors can consider making full communication and cooperation with the news media. Cooperation leads to richer and more transparent information in the media opinion, thus realizing effective management of inflation expectations and real inflation. The more open the media reports, the more channels of information the public have, and the more transparent the information. Further information transparency and openness may weaken the impact of reports with negative sentiments on public expectations. In the long term, open media reports may help to weaken the impact of media opinion on public expectations about inflation.

As far as the news media is concerned, relevant workers, especially journalists covering financial news, should gain rich professional knowledge, improve their professional competence, and boost their skills on news theory and news commentary. They should report on relevant issues in a more scientific and rational way, and attach importance to the possible impact of media opinion on public expectations. At the same time, the relevant publicity departments can actively hold events for media workers to "gain practical experience, change the style of work, and improve the style of writing," and respond to the call of the central government by exploring more positive news at the grassroots level. They should fundamentally improve the code of ethics for journalists, guard against extreme and exaggerated reports on issues such as prices for the sake of high click rates or high circulation, and avoid reports with negative sentiments that may provoke public panic. At the same time, media opinion should give consideration to the state macro-control direction and ensure implementation according to relevant policies as far as possible. This is not to advocate for one-sided media reports. It is hoped that the media reports objectively and rationally on issues, and avoids negative emotions and distorted values that impact the public's positive expectations and prejudice market confidence through the amplification of media opinion.

In summary, the news media and relevant decision-makers should work together, especially on major issues and hot issues that affect stable national economic development such as inflation. Exaggerated reports and exaggerated and negative reports without foundation should be avoided. From the extended significance of the research in this chapter, media opinion may exert an impact at the level of inflation expectations, and also has an important impact on other aspects related to macroeconomic policies. Future research can provide more in-depth analysis of the ties between media opinion and macroeconomic policies. Obviously, these analyses will provide more supplements and updates for the findings of the research in this chapter, and provide more reference for the scientific preparation and effective implementation of macroeconomic policies in China.

Notes

1   In reality, the authors also examined the "CCER China Economic Watch" (aka the "Long Run forecast") compiled by the China Center for Economic Research of Peking University (current National School of Development of Peking University). The China Center for Economic Research of Peking University invites other economic research institutions to forecast ten indicators such as GDP, industrial added value, CPI, investment, interest rate, and exchange rate on a quarterly basis. The "Long Run forecast" adopts the weighted average in compilation (weighted average is based on the calculation results of historical forecast error adjustment by forecast institutions; the smaller the average absolute prediction error, the larger the weight coefficient), and the forecast results of various institutions are calculated comprehensively. The authors selected the

CPI (year-on-year) Long Run forecast index as the expected inflation rate. According to the availability of raw data, the sample interval for Long Run forecast is from the fourth quarter of 2005 to the first quarter of 2012. Judging from the time sequence performance of the data, the "Long Run forecast" is very close to the trend of forecast data released by the Weekly on Stocks, and the corresponding empirical analysis results are similar. Therefore, the results of the "Long Run forecast" are omitted in this chapter.

2 Participating forecast institutions include Essence Securities, China Center for Economic Research of Peking University, Beihang University Competitiveness and Risk Research Center, Beijing Tianze Economic Research Institute, Financial Products and Investment Research Center of University of International Business and Economics, Everbright Securities, State Information Center, Guotai Junan Securities, Haitong Securities, Hongyuan Securities, Bank of Communications, Nankai Institute of Economics, Shenyin Wanguo, China Merchants Securities, China International Capital Corporation Limited, Agricultural Bank of China Financial Market Department, Institute of Quantitative and Technical Economics of Chinese Academy of Social Sciences, Bank of China Global Financial Markets Department, China Securities, CITIC Securities, BOC International, JP Morgan Chase, BNP Paribas Securities (Asia) Limited, Merrill Lynch, UBS Securities, Nomura international Hong Kong, Standard Chartered Bank.

3 According to the statistics from the Chinese newspaper media network.

4 Specifically including Financial Accounting, International Financial News, Financial Times, Economic Information Daily, Economic Daily, People's Daily, China Economic Times, China Business Journal, China Business Times, Beijing Youth Daily, Shenzhen Special Zone Daily, Shenzhen Economic Daily, Southern Metropolis Daily, 21st Century Business Herald, Caijing.

5 Specifically including Beijing Evening News, Beijing Morning News, Beijing Youth Daily, Chengdu Economic Daily, Tonight News Paper, Jiefang Daily, Nanfang Daily, Qilu Evening News, Southern Metropolis Daily, Yangcheng Evening News, Chongqing Morning News, Jiangnan City Daily, Shanghai Morning Post.

6 Specifically including People's Daily, Guangming Daily, Science and Technology Daily, Southern Weekend, and Qianjiang Evening News.

7 Specifically including Economic Daily and Shanghai Securities News.

11 External shocks, monetary policy, and the structural change of inflation dynamics

11.1 The structural change of inflation dynamics

Since the reform and opening-up, the evolution of China's inflation dynamics has attracted attention and to some extent reflected the historical trajectory of China's economic development, macroeconomic policy adjustments, and changes in external shock factors. As has been mentioned before, the inflation rate experienced dramatic changes in the 1980s and 1990s, and then entered a period of stable progression in the late 1990s. Despite a significant increase in 2007, the inflation rate showed a downward trend in 2008 due to the global financial crisis triggered by the US subprime mortgage crisis. In general, the inflation rate has remained at a relatively low level in recent years and caused concerns among decision-makers about continued deflation, which also happened in the late 1990s.

These ups and downs in China's inflation rate have attracted economists to explore the driving factors of these changes and the interaction between inflation and other economic variables. Some important research has been conducted, including research on China's low inflation (deflation) and its solutions by Yu (1999) and Fan (2002); Hasan's (1999) research on the long-term relationship of equilibrium between China's monetary policy and inflation; Liu and Xie's (2003) study of the correlation between economic growth and inflation dynamics; Gerlach and Peng's (2006) research on the relationship between real GDP gap and inflation dynamics; and Gong and Lin's (2007) analysis of the micro-causal factors of the low inflation–high growth model. Although the analytical perspectives, research methods, and research aims of this literature are different, there is a common and important theme: Are China's inflation dynamics changing in a way that makes it easier for decision-makers to consolidate and stabilize the inflation rate? If there are real changes in the inflation dynamics, what are the causes?

The above questions come down to inflation persistence, one of the most important characteristics of the evolution of inflation dynamics. Inflation persistence measures the length of time that inflation deviates from its equilibrium level after being affected by a random shock. The longer the time, the stronger the inflation persistence. It can be inferred that if the inflation persistence is weakened, the influence of any factors that promote or suppress inflation on the future trend of inflation will be weakened. Therefore, changes in inflation persistence have important practical significance for judging the future trend of inflation dynamics.

If the inflation persistence changes, what are the driving factors? This is a matter of greater concern to academics and decision-makers. According to the relevant research in recent years (such as Williams, 2006; Stock and Watson, 2007), changes in inflation persistence may be caused by macroeconomic policies and systemic improvements in the economic system on the one hand, and changes in external shocks in different historical periods, which affected macroeconomic policies and economic development, on the other hand. The latter is also called "luck" because of its randomness.

In both cases, if systemic changes in macroeconomic policy have a significant impact on changes in inflation persistence, policy adjustments can be used to effectively guide the inflation persistence to change in a way that is expected by decision-makers, thus hedging against the adverse impact of random external shocks on the inflation dynamics. Otherwise, if the fundamental properties of random external shocks (for example, volatility) change, resulting in changes in the characteristics of inflation persistence, then the source of external shocks and the causes of the changes will be the focus of the research.

It can be argued that the in-depth study of changes in China's inflation persistence characteristics and their driving factors is particularly important in the context of the current unstable global financial situation and the large-scale consolidation of the world economy. The study involves not only the judgment of whether China's economic policy significantly affects the inflation persistence, but also the direction and intensity of policy adjustment, as well as how to formulate and implement appropriate macroeconomic policies, in order to prevent the emergence of high inflation similar to that of the 1980s and 1990s, and to avoid the problem of deflation and liquidity traps, thereby reducing the risk of rendering monetary policy ineffective.

However, it is not easy to clarify the essential drivers of changes in inflation persistence, and this is particularly true for China. On the one hand, with the deepening of market economy reform, the systematic economic structure and macroeconomic policy have undergone great changes in the recent decade. Since the late 1990s, with the continuous implementation of "prudent" monetary policy, multiple measures have been taken to replace the single channel of direct credit in the 1980s, such as control of total volume, window guidance, and interest rate adjustment, which improved the effectiveness of monetary policy. On the other hand, there seem to be significant changes in external shocks. Notably, the frequency of external shocks affecting real economic output, inflation, and monetary policy has increased. The 2008 global financial crisis has made us realize that global shocks may also have an impact on the domestic economy, adding to a more complicated mix of factors affecting the important domestic economic indicators. Currently, there is a lack of systematic quantitative analysis on whether these external shocks will lead to structural changes in the inflation persistence.

To this end, this study uses the median unbiased estimation and unknown structural break tests to investigate the characteristics of inflation persistence changes.

In order to explore the driving factors of inflation persistence changes, a multivariate dynamic model is established based on the interaction between China's real economic output, inflation, and monetary policy, and contrast simulation analysis is conducted by analyzing the intrinsic relationship between SVAR and VAR. The empirical results indicate that the persistence of China's CPI inflation rate underwent significant structural changes in 1997, and more than 80% of this transformation can be explained by the systematic improvement of macroeconomic policies, while there is a lack of evidence to show that the transformation results from "luck." The contrast simulation analysis shows that whether it is using real GDP growth rates or using traditional real GDP gaps to measure real economic output, similar conclusions can be drawn and therefore the results are reliable.

11.2 Tests and identifications of the structural change

11.2.1 The model

This chapter's estimate of inflation persistence is consistent with existing standard literature (e.g. Taylor, 2000). The inflation persistence is measured by the coefficient sum of the lagged variable in the autoregressive (AR) model, so the basic model is set to

$$\pi_t = c + \alpha(L)\pi_{t-1} + \varepsilon_t \tag{11.1}$$

Here π_t stands for inflation rate, c is a constant term, ε_t denotes a sequence-independent disturbance term, $\alpha(L) = \alpha_1 + \alpha_2 L + ... + \alpha_n L^{n+1}$ represents a lag operator polynomial, n is the optimal lag period selected according to certain criteria, and $\alpha(L) = \alpha_1 + \alpha_2 L + ... + \alpha_n L$ is defined as a measurement indicator of inflation persistence. It should be noted that due to the possible collinearity between the lagged variables, regression analysis of Equation 11.1 might result in inaccurate standard deviations of the coefficients of some lagged variables, which might have further influence on statistical inference. To this end, we will rewrite Equation 11.1

$$\pi_t = c + \rho\pi_{t-1} + \sum_{i=1}^{n-1} \varphi_i \Delta\pi_{t-i} + \varepsilon_t \tag{11.2}$$

$\Delta\pi_{t-i} = \pi_{t-i} - \pi_{t-i-1}$ represents lagged differences. Unfolding and sorting Equation 11.2 gives the same equation as Equation 11.1. In addition, the coefficient ρ in Equation 11.2 is equal to the coefficient sum of each lagged variable in Equation 11.1, that is, the coefficient of inflation persistence. In this way, even if there is a collinearity problem in Equation 11.1, the estimated value of the inflation persistence coefficient and the corresponding standard deviation obtained from Equation 11.2 can still be reliable.

At the same time, since the independent variable of the AR model contains the lagged term of the dependent variable, the selection of the lag period must ensure that ε_t is not sequentially correlated. Therefore, we followed the principle of "from general to special" in the process of setting up the AR model. The maximum lag order is set to 8, and the optimal lag order is determined according to AIC. The Breusch–Godfrey LM is used in order to test serial correlation, so that the AR model does not have serial correlation at the traditional level of significance.

During the test and estimation, the inflation rate is measured by the year-on-year growth rate of the consumer price index (CPI), which is closely related to macroeconomic development and macroeconomic policy adjustment. The raw data for the inflation rate come from the National Bureau of Statistics. Because the officially released inflation data are in the form of year-on-year growth rates, the inflation rate variable is no longer seasonally adjusted during the empirical analysis. The raw data of the inflation rate are released on a monthly basis. Hence, the corresponding quarterly data are determined by the rate of the last month of each quarter. The sample is dated from the first quarter of 1983 to the fourth quarter of 2008, based on the research objectives and the availability of the data.

11.2.2 The unknown structural break test

The test of structural change in econometrics can be traced back to the Chow Test put forward in the 1960s. The Chow Test assumes a known structural break, while the development of an unknown structural break test in recent years has provided a more suitable design for us to analyze the structural changes in the inflation persistence. The theory of the unknown structural break test proposed by Andrews and Ploberger (1994) is a perfect match for the current study. Based on this theoretical development, Hansen (1997) proposed the *p*-value to calculate the corresponding test statistics. Therefore, we use Andrews and Ploberger's method to test the unknown structural break of the inflation dynamic model, and then use Hansen's (1997) method to calculate the *p*-value.

According to Andrews and Ploberger's theory, it is assumed that Φ, the coefficient matrix of $m \times 1$, represents the parameter in the dynamic model, Equation 11.2. If $t < k$, then $\Phi = \Phi_1$; if $t \geq k$, then $\Phi = \Phi_2 (\Phi_1 \neq \Phi_2)$. In addition, $m \leq k \leq T - m$, and T represents the sample size. Assuming that the search domain of the unknown structure break parameter is τ, we firstly calculate a series of Wald test statistic $W_T(\tau_i)$ corresponding to all possible breaks $k = T\tau_i$ in the search domain. The hypothesis of the test is that there will not be any structural changes in the parameters of the model when the structural break is k. It is not difficult to find that this unknown break parameter k did not appear in our original hypothesis, but in the alternative hypothesis. Such a parameter is called the interference parameter in the statistical hypothesis test. After obtaining $W_T(\tau_i)$, the maximum Wald statistic can be further calculated, i.e.

$$SupW = SupW_T(\tau_i) | \tau_i \in [\tau_{\min}, \tau_{\max}]$$ (11.3)

If the *SupW* statistic is statistically significant, its corresponding breakpoint is the point at which the structural change occurs.

Andrews and Ploberger further proposed another two test statistics with optimal characteristics for the detection of structural changes in the presence of interference parameters, namely the exponential-Wald (*ExpW*) statistic and the mean-Wald (*AveW*) statistic, respectively defined as

$$ExpW = \ln\left\{ \int_{\tau_{\min}}^{\tau_{\max}} \exp[0.5W_T(\tau)]d\tau \right\} \tag{11.4}$$

$$AveW = \int_{\tau_{\min}}^{\tau_{\max}} W_T(\tau)d\tau \tag{11.5}$$

Andrews and Ploberger's (1994) research shows that even under asymptotic conditions, the above three test statistics present non-standard statistical distributions. Therefore, in the process of calculating the test statistics of the unknown structural break, it is necessary to construct a function for calculating the *p*-value, in order to capture the non-standard distribution features. We use the non-standard distribution function proposed by Hansen (1997) to calculate the *p*-values corresponding to the *SupW*, *ExpW*, and *AveW* statistics, which are denoted as p-sup, p-exp, and p-ave, respectively. Recording the unknown structural break test statistic as *z*, the calculation function of the asymptotic *p*-value under this non-standard distribution can be written as

$$p\left(z|\gamma\right) = 1 - \chi^2\left(\gamma_0 + \gamma_1 z + \ldots + \gamma_m z^m \big| \eta\right) \tag{11.6}$$

$\chi^2\left(z|\eta\right)$ represents the cumulative chi-square distribution with a degree of freedom η. γ is the parameter to be estimated. In the actual calculation process, we use the quantile estimation to determine the polynomial $\gamma_0 + \gamma_1 x + \ldots + \gamma_m x^m$, and use the heteroscedasticity-consistent covariance matrix under unconstrained conditions to calculate the corresponding *p*-value.

Using the methods described above, we have carried out a structural break test on the overall coefficient, constant term, persistence coefficient, and other lag coefficient of the AR model of Equation 11.2, with the time period starting from the first quarter of 1983 to the fourth quarter of 2008, in order to judge whether there are structural breaks in China's inflation persistence and, if so, the specific time of the structural break. This will provide a basis for further segmentation of samples in order to study the characteristics of inflation persistence in different periods. Table 11.1 shows the results of the structural break test.

It can be seen from Table 11.1 that the *p*-value corresponding to the overall coefficient of the AR model is much smaller than 0.01, indicating that the AR model has undergone significant structural change at the level of 1% significance. The test results show that the structural change occurred in the second quarter of 1996. In addition, from the test results of other coefficients, the constant term and the persistence coefficient show significant changes at the traditional level of significance. Although the structural change of the persistence coefficient and

Table 11.1 AR model unknown structural break test results

	p-sup	*p-exp*	*p-ave*	*Breakpoints*
Overall coefficient	0.000	0.000	0.001	1996Q2
c	0.006	0.002	0.010	1996Q4
ρ	0.095	0.052	0.049	1996Q2
φ	0.118	0.094	0.118	1999Q2

Note: 1996 Q2 represents the second quarter of 1996.

the overall coefficient in the AR model occurred during the same time period, the change of the constant term occurred later, in the fourth quarter of 1996.

11.2.3 Estimate of the inflation persistence

In order to investigate the persistence coefficient of the AR model in the sample interval which contains the breakpoint, we made estimations on the AR model of CPI inflation rate in different sample intervals, based on the estimated value of time breaking point of the total coefficient in Table 11.1. It is notable that since the constant term also showed structural changes in the fourth quarter of 1996, the next sample interval starts from the first quarter of 1997, so as to avoid the impact of the change on the estimation. For the purpose of comparison, we also made estimations on the inflation persistence coefficient in the overall sample.

Theoretically, when making estimations on the AR model of Equation 11.2, as long as there is no serial correlation in the random error term, we will be able to obtain statistically consistent coefficient estimates using the ordinary least squares (OLS). However, Phillips (1977) shows that even if the model settings are correct, OLS estimations of ρ in Equation 11.2 are still statistically biased. This is particularly the case when the true value of ρ is close to 1. Moreover, the traditional asymptotic confidence interval corresponding to the estimated value of ρ is also not accurate enough.

To fix this problem, we use the grid-bootstrap estimation proposed by Hansen (1999). Essentially, this method uses the bootstrap technique to simulate a finite sample distribution of OLS estimates for a range of possible ρ values. In the predetermined grid system, the bootstrap is used to define the quantile function, and then the grid-bootstrap confidence interval corresponding to the given confidence level (e.g. 90%). Compared with the traditional estimation method, the grid-bootstrap method provides not only unbiased estimates, but also correct confidence intervals for both stationary models and unit root models. In the test process, we firstly construct a 90% confidence interval for the persistence coefficient ρ, using the quantile function which is consistent with the bootstrap distribution, and then use the 50% percentile of the grid-bootstrap estimate to calculate the median unbiased estimate of ρ (recorded as "MU"). In the simulation calculation of grid-bootstrap estimates, we set the grid number to 200 and the bootstrap simulation number to 1999, and then use the standard deviation corrected by White heter-oskedasticity to reduce the sensitivity of statistical inference.

Based on the above estimation methods, Table 11.2 summarizes the estimates of inflation persistence in different sample intervals. Firstly, we compared the estimates of the inflation persistence coefficient before and after the breakpoint. The results in Table 11.2 show that the least squares estimate is 0.841 before the structural change and then decreases to 0.748 after the change; the median unbiased estimate decreases from 0.865 before the structural change to 0.782 after the change. Both the traditional estimation and the grid-bootstrap median unbiased estimation show that the persistence of the CPI inflation rate has obviously weakened after 1997, and the extent of weakening is about 10%. If the structural change is not considered, the inflation persistence coefficient estimated based on the overall sample interval will reach 0.9 or higher.

In addition, since the autoregressive model is used here and the lag term of the dependent variable appears at the right side of the regression equation, the test of serial correlation is crucial for the validity of the conclusions drawn from the statistical results. It can be seen from the *p*-value (p-auto) corresponding to the serial correlation test reported in Table 11.2 that the optimal lag order determined by AIC can ensure that there is no serial correlation in Equation 11.2. Therefore, the validity of the results is ensured.

On the whole, the persistence of China's CPI inflation rate has significantly weakened after 1997. This result has important implications for the formulation and implementation of macroeconomic policies. Inflation persistence indicates the duration of inflation or deflation that deviates from the long-term equilibrium level after a random shock. The weakening of the persistence means that the continual impact of a random shock on the future trend of inflation will decrease. Therefore, it creates favorable conditions for the central bank to respond to inflation or deflation, and the cost of adjusting inflation or deflation is reduced.

What are the factors that have led to structural changes in the inflation persistence? The introduction of this chapter tells us that the structural changes in the inflation persistence may be triggered by systemic policy adjustments or changes in the attributes of random external interference factors (i.e. luck). Research

Table 11.2 Estimated inflation persistence results in different sample intervals

Sample interval	ρ-MU	ρ-OLS	$\bar{R}^2$	p-auto	lag
Overall sample	0.941	0.923	0.94	0.44	6
Before the structural change	0.865	0.841	0.92	0.91	6
After the structural change	0.782	0.748	0.74	0.90	4

Note: p-auto refers to the *p*-value of the serial correlation test; lag refers to the optimal lag order of the AR model determined by AIC.

conducted in recent years on the inflation persistence in developed countries such as the United States (e.g. Stock and Watson, 2007) shows that structural changes in the inflation persistence are mainly caused by changes in the attributes of random interference factors, which means that "luck" is the main driving force contributing to the changes in the inflation persistence. This being the case, it implies that there is less room for the macroeconomic policy to take effect, and decision-makers may need to pay more attention to random shock factors rather than systematic policy adjustments. We will analyze this problem in the next chapter, focusing on the specific situation in China.

11.3 Inflation persistence change: Contrast simulation analysis

11.3.1 Theoretical discussion on the driving force of the change

The first section of this chapter mentions that there are two main theoretical explanations for changes in the inflation persistence: One is the change in the attributes of random external interference factors, and the other is the systematic improvement of monetary policy. In terms of the random shock, Stock and Watson (2007) pointed out that if the scale of random shock factors changes, the data generation process of the inflation rate will be affected, and therefore the inflation persistence may also be weakened. However, it should be noted that essentially the shock factor occurs randomly, so the change in inflation persistence might be only temporary. This kind of shock factor may change again at any time, causing the inflation persistence to change again. Hence, some of the literature has interpreted these factors as "luck."

In contrast, the impact of systematic changes in monetary policy on the inflation persistence does not occur randomly. In fact, there is a mechanism for the policy to take effect. For example, as decision-makers continuously learn lessons from past experiences of formulating, implementing, and adjusting policies, and actively promote the development and improvement of monetary policy, the operational mechanism of monetary policy will be significantly improved. When the monetary policy adjustment mechanism develops from a relatively inefficient stage to a new efficient stage, the authorities can respond more promptly and effectively to changes in core economic indicators (such as the inflation rate and economic growth rate), thereby boosting market players' confidence in the central bank's ability to stabilize inflation (and promote economic growth). In this way, policy intentions are more easily transmitted through the market, the transparency of policy objectives is increased, and the credibility of the central bank will also increase. Stable market expectations will permeate economic behaviors such as pricing, investment, and consumption.

According to standard inflation dynamics theory (such as Zhang et al., 2008), the forward-looking degree (i.e. expectations) and the persistence level constitute a convex combination in the inflation dynamics equation (that is, the sum of the two coefficients is 1). Therefore, when stable market expectations dominate inflation dynamics, the inflation persistence which reflects the hysteresis effect will be correspondingly weakened. This is consistent with the inflation dynamics theory proposed by Zhang et al. (2008), who put forward the idea that "sluggish" inflation will transform into price stickiness. In essence, the systematic improvement of monetary policy enhances the effectiveness of policies promulgated by the central bank and increases the transparency and credibility of policies, thereby affecting the macro mechanism of inflation dynamics through micro-market behaviors, and ultimately leading to the structure change in the persistence of inflation.

It is not difficult to conclude from the above analysis that whether it is to examine the impact of random external shocks on inflation persistence, or to examine the impact of monetary policy on inflation persistence, it is necessary to put the inflation rate in a multivariate dynamic system which portrays monetary policy, inflation, and real economic development, so that we can make interpretations on the degree of impact of different factors on changes in inflation persistence through contrast simulation analysis. Next, we will discuss the basis, form, and estimation results of the multivariate dynamic model.

11.3.2　The multivariate dynamic model

In order to analyze the driving force of changes in inflation persistence, we need to construct a multivariate model that captures the dynamic relationship between inflation and related economic variables, and then estimate the parameters of the multivariate model in different sample intervals (including the variance–covariance matrix of random shock factors). Using the estimation results as the basis of the data generation process, we then compare and simulate the inter-matched parameters in different sample intervals to obtain simulation data on the inflation rate under different combinations, and further estimate the inflation persistence coefficient. In this way, we can determine the driving factors of changes in inflation persistence by comparing the different persistence coefficients corresponding to the different simulation data in the case of different parameter matching.[1]

In the contrast simulation analysis, the construction of a multivariate dynamic model is the key. Such a model should not only reflect the impact of changes in real economic output on inflation, but also capture the dynamic interaction between macroeconomic policy adjustments and real economic output on the one hand, and inflation on the other hand. Because the dynamic transmission mechanism of the short-term inflation rate is mainly reflected through the macroeconomic policy, especially monetary policy, we consulted the main intermediary target of monetary policy released in the *Monetary Policy Implementation Report* by the People's Bank of China over the years, and decided that the M2 growth rate (M2GR) would be used as an indicator of monetary policy. The raw data come from the International Financial Statistics database.[2]

In addition, in order to increase the reliability of the empirical results, not only the real GDP growth rate, but also the real GDP gap variable calculated through IIP filtering is used in the analysis. However, since China has only released nominal GDP data, and the quarterly nominal GDP can be only dated back to 1992, it is necessary to obtain the quarterly data of real GDP from 1983 to 2008 before calculating the GDP growth rate and CDP gap. To this end, we firstly select 2000 as the base year, and then according to the officially released nominal GDP data for 1992–2008 and the corresponding growth rate of constant prices, we convert the nominal GDP into real GDP. Finally, we use Abeysinghe and Gulasekaran's (2004) method to convert the real GDP annual data released by the National Bureau of Statistics from 1983 to 1992 into quarterly data, thereby obtaining the complete real GDP time series data. Based on the data, we calculate the real GDP growth rate (RGDPGR) and real GDP gap (HPGAP).

Thus, we set up the following structural vector autoregressive model (SVAR):

$$\begin{cases} A(L)Y_t = \varepsilon_t, \varepsilon_t \sim (0, \Omega_\varepsilon) \\ Y_t = (\text{RGDPGR} \quad \text{CPI} \quad \text{M2GR})', \\ A(L) = A_0 - \sum_{i=1}^{p} A_i L^i \end{cases} \tag{11.7}$$

Here, the matrix A_0 is used to capture the instantaneous relationship among different variables, L is the lag operator, p is the optimal lag order determined by AIC, and ε_t is the vector white gaussian noise. Equation 11.7 is called SVAR because the individual disturbance terms contained in ε_t are independent of each other and each sub-disturbance term is structurally meaningful. For example, the disturbance term in the third line of Equation 11.7 is the random shock that influences monetary policy. The disturbance terms in the other two equations are random shocks influencing real economic output (demand shock) and inflation (supply shock).

According to the standard time series analysis theory (Zhang, 2008b), when making estimations with the SVAR model, the coefficient matrix A_0 can be set (for example, to the lower triangular matrix) to meet the identification requirements of the SVAR, and then the estimation results can be obtained. Since the SVAR model in this study is mainly used for simulation analysis, the simulation data can be obtained through the conversion between the structural and the reduced form of the VAR model. Specifically, we can rewrite Equation 11.7 as

$$Y_t = \Phi(L)e_t, e_t \sim (0, \Omega_e) \tag{11.8}$$

Here, $\Phi(L) = A_0^{-1} A_i$, $e_t = A_0^{-1} \varepsilon_t$. Comparing Equations 11.7 and 11.8, it is not difficult to obtain the variance–covariance matrix of the disturbance term in the reduced VAR $\Omega_e = A_0^{-1} \Omega_\varepsilon (A_0^{-1})'$. Based on the relationship between the structural and reduced VAR, we use Equation 11.8 as the data generation process for simulation analysis, and investigate the persistence characteristics of inflation data generated by the intermatching of Φ and Ω_ε in different sample intervals. In the simulation process, the coefficients of the reduced VAR model are worked out by least squares estimation. The identification and estimation of A_0 and the variance of the disturbance term in SVAR are obtained by the constraint conditions of the Wood Causal Chain. The initial value of the simulation process is decided by the actual observation value of the VAR model. The generated sample size is consistent with the sample intervals considered before. The first 100 simulation values in the generated data are eliminated, in order to reduce the sensitivity resulting from the initial value.

For the purpose of clarification, we use $\left(\hat{\Phi}_1, \hat{\Omega}_1\right)$ and $\left(\hat{\Phi}_2, \hat{\Omega}_2\right)$ to represent the combination of the model coefficient matrix and the structural disturbance vector variance–covariance matrix before and after the structural change respectively, and $\left(\hat{\Phi}_1, \hat{\Omega}_2\right)$ to represent the combination of the model coefficient matrix before the structural change and the structural disturbance vector variance–covariance matrix after the structural change. The meaning of $\left(\hat{\Phi}_2, \hat{\Omega}_1\right)$ and $\left(\hat{\Phi}_1, \hat{\Omega}_2\right)$ is similar. In this way, we can generate inflation sequence corresponding to the respective sample sizes through these four different combinations and simulations, and then use the generated simulation data to estimate the inflation persistence coefficient. Be it Equation 11.8 or 11.7, the change of its coefficients represents the systematic change caused by policy adjustment (Williams, 2006). The changes in the variance–covariance matrix of the disturbance term before and after the structural change represent the change due to "luck." In this way, we determine the cause of the structural change in inflation persistence. For example, the estimation results from $\left(\hat{\Phi}_1, \hat{\Omega}_2\right)$ reflect the inflation persistence under the condition that there is no systematic change in the policy but a change in the attributes of the random shock. Conversely, the estimation results from $\left(\hat{\Phi}_2, \hat{\Omega}_1\right)$ reflect the inflation persistence under the condition that there is no change in the attributes of the random shock but a systematic change in the policy.

11.3.3 The contrast simulation results

On the basis of the above constructed model and contrast simulation design, we have worked out the results and presented them in Table 11.3. The table summarizes the simulation results of the aforementioned four cases. For each case, we report the estimate of the inflation persistence coefficient corresponding to both the OLS and grid-bootstrap median unbiased estimation (MU). The results for the two different

Table 11.3 Estimation of inflation persistence through contrast simulation with VAR model

Real economic variable	Estimation method	$\rho\left(\hat{\Phi}_1, \hat{\Omega}_1\right)$	$\rho\left(\hat{\Phi}_2, \hat{\Omega}_2\right)$	$\rho\left(\hat{\Phi}_1, \hat{\Omega}_2\right)$	$\rho\left(\hat{\Phi}_2, \hat{\Omega}_1\right)$
HPGAP	OLS	0.840	0.613	0.833	0.669
	MU	0.872	0.621	0.864	0.681
RGDPGR	OLS	0.832	0.385	0.857	0.457
	MU	0.863	0.399	0.886	0.466

measures of real economic variables (HPGAP and RGDPGR) are summarized in Table 11.3. We will analyze the results of the contrast simulation below.

Firstly, in the simulation analysis results shown in Table 11.3, $\rho\left(\hat{\Phi}_1,\hat{\Omega}_1\right)$ and $\rho\left(\hat{\Phi}_2,\hat{\Omega}_2\right)$ represent the inflation persistence coefficient estimated from the VAR model before and after the structural change (i.e. the first quarter of 1997). Without exchanging the sample information, the estimated results of respective samples in the VAR model before and after the structural change are worked out and simulated, thereby obtaining the inflation rate sequence and the estimated inflation persistence coefficient. Taking the HPGAP as an example, the OLS and MU estimates for the inflation persistence coefficient before 1997 are 0.840 and 0.872, respectively, which are basically consistent with the estimates of the corresponding samples in the AR model we reported earlier in Table 11.2 (OLS and MU estimates are 0.841 and 0.865 respectively); in the sample interval after 1997, the OLS and MU estimates obtained from the VAR model simulation analysis have decreased, at 0.613 and 0.621, respectively. The falling range is greater than the corresponding results obtained from the AR model shown in Table 11 (0.748 and 0.782, respectively). In terms of the estimated results of RGDPGR (the last two rows of Table 11.3), the inflation persistence also decreases in the second sample interval, and the ratio is even greater. It can be seen that after considering the interaction between inflation, real economic output, and monetary policy, the inflation persistence still shows a significant weakening after the structural change, and the scale of the weakening in the multivariate system is greater than in the univariate model. This shows that the inflation persistence is not only affected by changes in the inflation rate itself, but also by other factors such as policies.

Secondly, the last two columns of Table 11.3 show the experimental results after the exchange of sample information. Firstly let's look at the HPGAP results. If in the VAR model the coefficient matrix before the structural change is kept unchanged, and the disturbance term matrix after the structural change is used (i.e. $\rho\left(\hat{\Phi}_1,\hat{\Omega}_2\right)$), then the MU estimate is 0.864 and the OLS estimate is 0.833. This estimation result has only a slight difference from the corresponding result of the column of $\rho\left(\hat{\Phi}_1,\hat{\Omega}_1\right)$ (MU = 0.872, OLS = 0.840). That is to say, if the coefficient matrix of the VAR model remains unchanged and only the disturbance term variance–covariance matrix is changed, the inflation persistence basically does not change. Conversely, if the disturbance term matrix before the structural change is kept unchanged, and the coefficient matrix of the VAR model after the structural change is used (i.e. $\rho\left(\hat{\Phi}_2,\hat{\Omega}_1\right)$), then the MU estimate becomes 0.681 and the OLS estimate becomes 0.669. The results show that if the disturbance term matrix is unchanged and the coefficient matrix of the VAR model changes, the inflation persistence will be significantly weakened. In addition, comparing the results of $\rho\left(\hat{\Phi}_2,\hat{\Omega}_1\right)$ and $\rho\left(\hat{\Phi}_1,\hat{\Omega}_1\right)$, $\rho\left(\hat{\Phi}_2,\hat{\Omega}_2\right)$, and $\rho\left(\hat{\Phi}_1,\hat{\Omega}_2\right)$ respectively, we can reach the degree of interpretation of changes in the VAR model coefficient on the weakening of inflation persistence. For example, the result calculated based on the MU estimate is $(0.872 - 0.681)/(0.872 - 0.621) = 76\%$ (the result calculated based on the OLS estimate is 75%). If RGDPGR represents the real economic output, it can be concluded from a similar calculation that the VAR model coefficient change has a higher degree of interpretation of the inflation persistence change, and the result calculated based on the MU estimate is 87% (the result calculated based on the OLS estimate is 84%).

Overall, through the contrast simulation analysis of the multivariate dynamic model, we find that the main cause of the structural change of inflation persistence is the change of the VAR model coefficient, and there is no evidence that the variance–covariance matrix of random shocks has led to changes in the inflation persistence. That is to say, the change in China's inflation persistence dynamics after 1997 is mainly driven by systematic policy changes rather than by changes in "luck."

11.4 The impact of monetary policy improvements on the structural change of inflation dynamics

Contrast simulation analysis has provided clear quantitative results for us to understand the drivers of changes in the inflation persistence. Here we further analyze the implications of the quantitative results. On the one hand, we will discuss the fact that China's monetary policy has been continuously developed and improved since the reform and opening-up; on the other hand, we will analyze how the systematic improvement in monetary policy has contributed to changes in China's inflation persistence. The discussion here is closely related to the theoretical discussion on the causes of changes in inflation persistence in Chapter 9.

First of all, in the past decade or so, China's monetary policy has made considerable progress in all aspects; the adjustment mechanism especially has been systematically improved. It is known that before the reform and opening-up, there was actually no such adjustment mechanism in China's monetary policy. In the mid-1980s, with the establishment of the central bank system, the adjustment mechanism began to come into being. From the 1980s to the mid-1990s, the government was learning from its own experiences and exploring the operational rules of monetary policy. Since then, a series of policies aimed at improving the central bank's policy adjustment mechanism have been introduced. For example, in March 1995, the National People's Congress passed the *Law of the People's Republic of China on the People's Bank of China*, which established the status of the People's Bank of China as a central bank in the state legislation. Subsequently, the interbank lending market was established in 1996, and the functions of the central bank were further strengthened. In April 1997, the State Council promulgated the *Regulations on the Monetary Policy Commission of the People's Bank of China*, which clarified the responsibilities of the Monetary Policy Commission and laid the foundations for the further improvement of the monetary policy adjustment mechanism. In addition, since May 1998, the RMB open market operation has resumed and its scale has gradually expanded, thus further enhancing the functions of the central bank in regulating the money supply and the liquidity level of commercial banks, as well as guiding the trend of market interest rates. After 1998, the People's Bank of China further diversified its means in macroeconomic control, transitioning from a direct regulation mode that relied on directive plans on loan size to an indirect regulation mode that applied various monetary policy tools together with proportional management methods (Qian, 2000).

In the process of improving monetary policy, the macro-price control policy implemented by the state since May 1998 has played the role of a quasi-"inflation target system," making the adjustment mechanism of the macroeconomic policy on overall price changes more flexible, complete, and orderly than ever. In fact, the *Pricing Law of the People's Republic of China* passed by the National People's Congress in December 1997 clearly stated that "Stabilizing the overall market price is an important macroeconomic policy goal of the country." Therefore, based on the actual development of the national economy, the country determined that stabilizing the overall market price level was a regulatory target, and included it in the national economic and social development plan. Moreover, a comprehensive mix of policies and measures in the areas of monetary, fiscal, investment, import, and export were used in order to alleviate inflation or deflation pressures.

The specific content of the systematic improvement of China's monetary policy mentioned above reflects the fact that the transparency and credibility of China's monetary policy are gradually increasing. Since the beginning of the 21st century, the transparency and credibility of monetary policy have been greatly improved. For example, since 2001, the People's Bank of China has released the *China Monetary Policy Report* to the public on a quarterly basis, analyzing in-depth the macroeconomic and financial situation, interpreting operational rules of the monetary policy, and disclosing the monetary policy orientation, including credit profiles, policy operations, market analysis, and economic trend predictions. These have provided an important basis for the market to interpret the policy intentions of decision-makers and to judge policy trends in the future. Thanks to these systematic measures, the central bank has also enhanced its transparency and credibility.

In addition, the expectation survey system used by the central bank to assist monetary policy formulation has also been improved, which provides a guarantee for the credibility of policy making. For example, the central bank conducts quarterly surveys on urban depositors nationwide through the household savings questionnaire system. It uses standardized questionnaires and interviews to review urban residents' expectations for future income and price changes. Based on the responses to the questionnaire, four diffusion indices are constructed. After 2000, the design of this survey system was made more scientific. Previously, the question about residents' judgment and expectations of price was "What is your opinion on the recent market price trend", but after 2000, the questions was changed into "How do you expect the price to change in the next month, compared with the price now?" The information obtained from the survey can be coded into

Table 11.4 Changes in transparency indicators of the monetary policy of the People's Bank of China

	Administration	Economic	Procedure	Policy	Operation	Overall
Before 1997	1	0.5	0	0.5	0.5	2.5
After 1997	3	2.5	2	3	2	12.5

quantitative data on inflation expectations through some statistical methods. The expectation survey system developed by the central bank is similar to the Federal Reserve's "Greenbook Survey" and the "Survey of Professional Forecasts." The system provides important information for the central bank to accurately grasp market information and to formulate targeted policies.

As can be seen from the above, the transparency of China's monetary policy has improved rapidly in the past decade. In order to clarify the changes in transparency and credibility brought about by the systematic improvement of monetary policy, and according to Eijffinger and Geraats' (2006) central bank transparency quantitative indicators, we worked out the corresponding scores of the People's Bank of China before and after 1997. The overall transparency index consists of "administration," "economy," and another three indicators. Each indicator has a minimum score of 0, and a maximum score of 1, based on a 0.5 increment.[3] According to the score criteria of each indicator, Table 11.4 presents the results of the calculation. It can be seen that the transparency of China's monetary policy scored 12.5 points after 1997, compared with 2.5 points before 1997. This comparison confirms the fact that the systematic improvement of China's monetary policy has led to a significant increase in policy transparency.

Taken together, China's monetary policy adjustment mechanism has undergone an important transformation since 1997. The systematic improvement of monetary policy has made the transmission of the central bank's policy intentions to the market more timely and clearer. Taking into consideration the theoretical discussion of the reasons for changes in the inflation persistence, it can be seen that these systematic improvements in monetary policy will affect micro-market behaviors such as market expectations, pricing, and investment, and stabilize market expectations of future economic development and inflation trends. The changes in this micro-mechanism will further affect the macro-mechanism of inflation dynamics, and finally lead to structural changes in the inflation persistence. This theory is consistent with the historical development of China's monetary policy discussed above.

11.5 Conclusions

Inflation persistence has practical significance for judging the trend of inflation dynamics and analyzing the direction and scale of macroeconomic policy adjustment. This chapter analyzes the changes in the persistence characteristics of China's CPI inflation rate from 1983 to 2008, by using the structural break test and the median unbiased estimation. It is found that inflation persistence after 1997 is significantly weakened. This change suggests that in the last decade or so, the period in which China's CPI inflation rate deviates from the equilibrium level after being affected by random external shocks has been shortened. From the perspective of macroeconomic regulation and control, the weakening of inflation persistence is a positive change, because it means that the same scale of policy regulation adjustment can take effect in a shorter period of time, which will help the central bank to effectively control inflation or deflation.

In order to further explore the driving factors of this structural change of inflation persistence, this chapter constructs a multivariate dynamic model that captures the interaction between China's real economic output, inflation rate, and monetary policy, using contrast simulation analysis. According to the results of the analysis, systematic policy improvement is the main cause of the weakening of China's inflation persistence, and the change of "luck" has little effect on the change in the inflation persistence.

Judging from the trajectory of China's economic development and macroeconomic policy changes, the quantitative results of this chapter are consistent with the reality of a series of macroeconomic policy adjustments made in China since the mid-1990s. To some extent, this shows that the establishment of the central bank's functions, the continuous development and improvement of the monetary policy adjustment mechanism, and the appropriate intervention and guidance of the state on price changes have all promoted systematic policy changes and improved the transparency and credibility of monetary policies. Therefore, the persistence characteristics of inflation are transformed in a favorable way.

The results of this study also show that changes in China's inflation dynamics are quite different from those of developed countries. For example, Taylor (2000) finds that the inflation persistence in the United States has also significantly weakened in recent years, but Stock and Watson's (2007) quantitative research on the driving factors shows that the change has mainly been caused by changes in "luck." It is not convincing enough to attribute the changes to systematic policy adjustment. The difference between China and the US shows that there may be fundamental differences in the way that different economic development models and policy adjustment methods influence inflation dynamics. It is not sensible to copy other countries' experience and policies without considering their applicability. In particular, with the policy objectives of regulating inflation while avoiding deflation, systemic policy improvement is still the focus for China. It is not appropriate to focus too much on exploring random shocks, and it is even worse to regard "luck" as a given condition when determining the direction and scale of policy adjustment in order to control inflation or deflation.

It should be pointed out that the exploration of the driving factors of changes in the inflation persistence in this chapter is mainly based on the fact that monetary policy is closely related to short-term inflation dynamics. Therefore, the systematic change of macroeconomic policy is mainly reflected through the systematic improvement of monetary policy. It is possible that other factors may also affect the inflation persistence. In the past decade or so, China's economic structure and economic development model have been in a state of continuous development and change, and these factors may also affect the persistence characteristics of inflation dynamics. Therefore, future research can further expand the dynamic model constructed in this chapter and incorporate more influencing factors into the analysis. If the model can be expanded but the samples are not accessible, the simulation analysis can be considered, applying the algorithm of McCallum (1998) or Söderlind (1999) in the constructed theoretical model. Rudebusch (2005) made a useful attempt in this aspect, which provided a good reference for future research.

Notes

1   Contrast simulation analysis has great applicability in the macroeconomic field. For example, Stock and Watson (2002), and Ulrich and Kuzin (2005) used contrast simulation analysis to explore economic periodic changes in the United States and Germany.
2   Of course, in recent years, progress has been made in interest rate liberalization, and the importance of interest rates as a monetary policy tool is increasingly apparent. However, considering that control of total volume is still the main policy tool of the central bank, and taking into account the availability of the sample, the M2 growth rate is used here as the monetary policy indicator. In addition, since there is no substantial impact on the simulation results if other variables such as the effective exchange rate are added to the model, the analysis is based on the three-variable SVAR model.
3   Each quantitative indicator is scored according to several sub-items. For details, please refer to the appendix of Eijffinger and Geraats (2006).

12 Excess liquidity and inflation dynamics in an open environment

12.1 Excess liquidity in an open environment

After entering the 21st century, domestic and foreign economic and financial situations have been changing more quickly, and the worldwide financial storm that happened in 2007–2008 caused great impact to the global economic situation. Therefore, the year 2008 can be regarded as a watershed in the economic development of China and the world in the past dozen years since 2000. In this chapter, the author specially chooses the ten years before 2008 as the research sample, and by analyzing the excess liquidity and inflation dynamics of China in that period, will hopefully provide a theoretical and empirical basis for the excess liquidity and inflation dynamics seen in an open environment.

In examining the period around the year 2007, it can be seen that the domestic commodity prices had been increasing continuously, and the inflation measured in CPI had reached a ten-year peak. Although afterwards, against the background of the impact of the global financial tsunami and domestic economic structural adjustment, China's overall commodity price growth rate (inflation rate) showed a downward trend, this was due to the fact that almost all countries reduced their interest rates substantially and issued moneys in massive quantities, and the potential risk of inflation still cannot be neglected. Meanwhile, the reform on the RMB exchange rate mechanism has been deepening, and in 2007 the RMB even showed a trend of accelerated appreciation at some points. From the second half of 2008, with the change in the global financial crisis situation (Chen and Zhang, 2008), the appreciation of the RMB has slowed down. From the beginning of 2014 to the beginning of 2015, the value of the RMB in relation to the dollar even showed a trend of depreciation compared with previously. The exchange rate parity relation change will be discussed in detail in Chapter 13.

Although in recent years some change has occurred in the RMB exchange rate trend, the appreciation pressure faced by the RMB and the economic logic behind that pressure at the time still deserve our meditation. In particular, the appreciation pressure on the RMB exchange rate at the time and the appeal asking to curb inflation through the appreciation of the RMB urge us to reflect on the correlation between the RMB exchange rate fluctuation and the inflation dynamics before 2008. In or around the year 2007, a lot of economists advocated for the curbing of inflation through the appreciation of the RMB. Just to mention, Ha (2007) suggested that the accelerated appreciation of the RMB should be "the most effective" way for China to counteract inflation. In their research report, Liang and Qiao (2007) pointed out that the accelerated and sharp appreciation of the RMB was the "only" way of solving China's inflation problem, otherwise China had to accept high inflation rates. Zhang and Hu (2008) simulated the relationship between the appreciation of the RMB and China's inflation by using a theoretical model, and were inclined to support the strategy of accelerating the appreciation of the RMB. All these studies concluded that with the appreciation of the RMB China's export trade would maintain its high-speed growth, and the trade surplus and investment would further increase, which would consequently lead to the real economic output far exceeding the potential economic output, and then people's consumption demand would be kept high, which would be bound to cause more serious inflation.

However, even if we temporarily omit the impact of the 2007–2008 global financial crisis on the international balance of payments, the above conclusions regarding the relationship between the exchange rate and trade surplus are still controversial. For instance, the research carried out by MacKinnon (2007) suggests that the accelerated appreciation of the RMB cannot change the present condition of the Sino–US trade imbalance, and China's trade surplus is related to citizens' habits in consumption and saving. Also, Cooper (2008) thinks the trade surplus of the US is not caused by the disequilibrium in exchange rates, and he further points out that the trade surplus of the US is caused by the globalization of financial markets and the change in the geographical location of the population. Nonetheless, the key research points of MacKinnon (2007) and Cooper (2008) are not about the RMB exchange rate fluctuations or China's inflation.

The domestic researchers are more concerned about the relationship between the RMB exchange rate fluctuation and inflation dynamics. For instance, the research carried out by Bei and Zhu (2007) acknowledges rather profoundly the potential impact of RMB appreciation on inflation. However, they also suggest that external appreciation of the RMB may lead to the swelling of domestic asset prices, rather than causing CPI increases in the traditional sense. From this perspective, their viewpoints are consistent with the research results of Li and He (2007), i.e. they all think that RMB appreciation will cause excess liquidity and consequently increase asset prices, but will not have a noticeable effect on the CPI or inflation rate. Does this mean that RMB appreciation has nothing to do with the CPI increase? Or will further acceleration in appreciation transmit a contractionary effect to inflation? To answer these questions, we need to carry out a comprehensive and in-depth study on the dynamic transmission process of inflation and the dynamics behind it, and thus discover the scientific basis for the choices faced currently by China's macroscopic policy-makers. Despite the fact that the present trend of the RMB exchange rate against USD has changed, it is still of significance for understanding the past and predicting the future to reflect on and study the logical relation between inflation and the RMB exchange rate before 2008.

In view of the above, this chapter will begin with an analysis of the dynamic transmission process of China's inflation and the potential driving factors of inflation, establish a dynamic measuring model based on the quarterly data of 1998–2008, and, by taking into full consideration the possible influences on the indigenous structural changes brought by the 2005 RMB exchange rate mechanism reform, make an empirical analysis of the driving factors of inflation. As indicated by the research results in this chapter, during the ten years from 1998 to 2008, the RMB exchange rate fluctuation had no significant transmission effect on domestic inflation, while the traditional excess liquidity indices (such as the Marshall K Index, i.e. the ratio between M2 and nominal GDP) show a significant positive effect on the CPI inflation rate, and are always the leading indicators of inflation, which is a relationship that remained stable even after the 2005 RMB exchange rate mechanism reform.

Therefore, the dramatic one-way change of the RMB exchange rate cannot regulate materially the trend of domestic inflation, and will on the contrary activate speculation on the foreign exchange market and cause frequent flow-in and flow-out of capital in a short period, which is unfavorable to the stabilization of the domestic financial market. In 2007, the accelerated appreciation of the RMB intensified the excess domestic liquidity, and consequently influenced market confidence in commodity price stability and heightened the inflation expectations. In a word, the argument for curbing inflation through RMB appreciation should not be advocated, and the strategy of accelerated appreciation should be carried out with even more caution. On the other hand, facing the new global economic and financial situation, the continuous one-way depreciation of the RMB exchange rate is also unfavorable to the sound development of China's economy.

12.2 Excess liquidity and inflation dynamic change: The typical facts

The researchers advocating the curbing of inflation through RMB appreciation deem that the inflation during 2007–2008 was a reflection of the pressure faced by RMB appreciation, and thus appreciation can solve inflation problems. That is to say, RMB appreciation has some inhibiting effect on domestic inflation. This seems correct from a static perspective. However, viewed dynamically, such a viewpoint neglects the current factual mechanism of inflation dynamic transmission in China, i.e. the inflation effect caused by excess liquidity brought about by RMB appreciation far exceeds the inhibiting effect of RMB appreciation on inflation.

The loose monetary policies of countries around the world have not led to the prevalence of inflation, and global inflation has remained at a moderately low level. For example, Figure 12.1 shows the sequential variation of the quarterly CPI inflation rate (on a year-on-year basis) of China and the US during 1998–2008, and, to be specific, during these ten years, the average CPI inflation

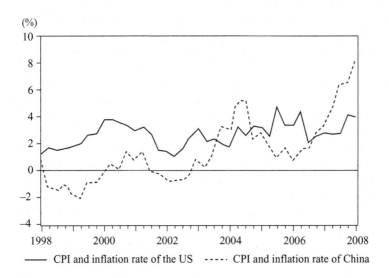

Figure 12.1 The CPI inflation rates of China and the US from the first quarter of 1998 to the first quarter of 2008. Source: National Bureau of Statistics, Federal Reserve Bank of St. Louis.

rate of China was only 1.3%, while that of the US was around 2.5%. According to the data reported by the International Financial Statistics, in the same period the average inflation level of the world's major countries has also remained below 3%.

On the surface, it seems that the connection between money supply and inflation has been broken, and Friedman's conclusion that "inflation is always and everywhere a monetary phenomenon" looks to have been challenged by the reality. However, we must note that the connection between money supply and inflation is not a simple one-to-one static causal relationship, and, viewed from the absolute level, the connection between money supply and inflation is often apt to cover up the dynamic transmission mechanism between them. In fact, the linkage relationship among the economic variables usually has some time lag, and thus a dynamic perspective should be able to reflect a more objective reality. In particular, there must be some time gap between money supply and inflation, and the change of money supply in relation to the economic aggregate (i.e. excess liquidity index) will probably be reflected dynamically in the fluctuation of inflation. For example, when the central bank begins to issue more money for certain reasons, the market may not understand immediately the effect on prices, and the workers may not ask to raise wages right away, but when more and more additional money is created and promotes the demands, the market will gradually become aware of the increase in prices, and the prices of durables and hard assets may also rise with people's enhanced financial awareness.

In the meantime, when the market expectations on the coming inflation gradually become popular with the excess money supply, both the producers and the sellers will consequently change their pricing strategies, and consumers' consumption patterns and investment activities will also change accordingly. A very typical example is that because of the worry about the appreciation of money in their hands due to accelerated inflation, some people who actually have no demand or urgent need for housing may choose to invest in real estate. After a certain period, real estate prices will naturally rise gradually, and such a trend of increase will be heightened by the tide of widespread speculations. Similarly, driven by expectations of inflation, the public will not only choose to invest in real estate, but also in equities and funds, which will then promote the accelerated swelling of asset prices as evidenced by similar characteristics shown in the quick prospering of China's capital market during 2006–2007.

During the process of rapid increases in real estate and stock prices, the asset appreciation will react on market expectations, and the increase in commodity prices will become more acceptable to the people. In particular, when the housing prices increase continuously, consumers' price sensitivity regarding ordinary consumer goods will decrease, and the enterprises will gradually be aware that the increase in price will not have negative effects on their sales. If at the same time energy prices (such as oil prices) also increase, the manufacturers will be more justified in increasing their prices. In that case, we will see that the degree of product price increase may far exceed that of raw material price increase, which keeps inflation at a high level. To illustrate, Figure 12.2 describes the dynamic flow from excess liquidity to inflation.

Till then, inflation caused by an excess money supply begins to arise. Fundamentally speaking, the subsequent phenomena have shown that the excess liquidity caused by an excess money supply or the deflation brought by tightened monetary supply will have a dynamic transmission effect on inflation. Here, we need to emphasize again the dynamic perspective of problem analysis, because even in periods of low inflation rates (such as the deflation in China during 1998–2003), the inflation rates were not constant, but often showed a dynamic path of either an increase or a decrease. Therefore, if the monetary supply changes in relation to the economic aggregate, then it may probably be transmitted dynamically to the inflation indicators.

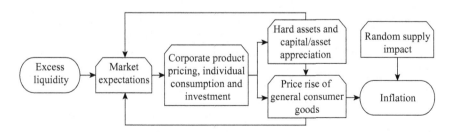

Figure 12.2 Dynamic flow from excess liquidity to inflation.

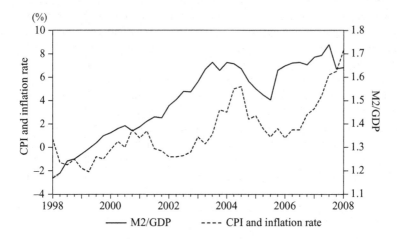

Figure 12.3 China's M2/GDP ratio and CPI inflation rate from the first quarter of 1998 to the first quarter of 2008. Source: National Bureau of Statistics, People's Bank of China.

To further exemplify that such a dynamic transmission mechanism of inflation is particularly applicable to China, Figure 12.3 is a time sequential chart of the M2 and nominal GDP ratio and the CPI inflation rate from the first quarter of 1998 to the first quarter of 2008.[1] As is seen from Figure 12.3, the dynamic trends of the M2/GDP ratio and CPI inflation rate show very similar characteristics in the sample range. If you look at the chart carefully, you will also find that the M2/GDP ratio will usually precede inflation by around a season. If the CPI inflation rate is moved ahead by a season, as in Figure 12.4, the two almost show the same correspondence of increase and decrease. That is to say, China's monetary aggregate (in relation to GDP) and inflation show a very close dynamic connection. In the following chapters, this relationship and other related connotations will be illustrated by using formal measuring models.

The inflation dynamic transmission mechanism discussed above expounds from a new dynamic perspective the quantity theory of money put forward by Friedman. Meanwhile, the inflation dynamic transmission process described in Figure 12.2 is also an update of the New Keynesian theory of the inflation dynamic transmission mechanism as put forward by Clarida et al. (1999) for a certain development period of China, and the system composed of the New Keynesian Phillips curve, the savings-investment model, and the monetary policy reaction equation with interest rate adjustment as the core as put forward by Clarida et al. (1999) has been widely recognized and used. In this system, the main transmission process of inflation is carried out by the interaction between interest rate, economic output, and inflation rate.

However, we have noticed that China and the foreign countries are quite different in economic development models and policy regulation methods, so that

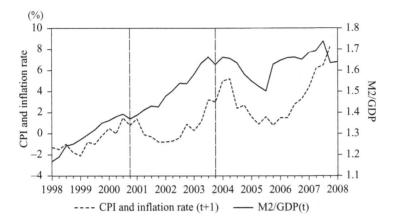

Figure 12.4 M2/GDP ratio and CPI inflation rate moved ahead by one season.

in view of the actual situation in China, the model and mechanism put forward by Clarida et al. (1999) may have two major problems. Firstly, the system fully weakens the role of the monetary aggregate, which deviates from the actual situation of China as discussed above. Taking the US as an example, its M2/GDP ratio has maintained a basically constant value (around 0.5) in a long period, without a noticeable relation with the inflation rate.

Secondly, because the import and export trade of China is very active, and the net export holds an unneglectable proportion in the GDP, the exchange rate factor may possibly affect the domestic inflation. As a matter of fact, in recent years the international academic community has, through the research on the exchange rate transmission effect of the domestic price fluctuation of a country (such as Choudhri and Hakura, 2006), deemed that the exchange rate fluctuation can in the end be substantially transmitted to the fluctuation in domestic prices. Obviously, if such thinking can be applied to China, we expect to see that the RMB exchange rate (such as the effective exchange rate or the Sino–US exchange rate) shall be a significant driving factor during the inflation dynamic transmission process. Moreover, if RMB appreciation can curb domestic inflation, we should at least see the statistical significance of the effect of the RMB–USD exchange rate on inflation after the 2005 exchange rate reform, which will be verified in the next section.

In a word, for China, it is of critical importance to take the factors of the monetary aggregate and exchange rate into consideration if the inflation dynamic transmission model. Therefore, the dynamic measuring model used in the next section of this chapter has been improved on the basis of the traditional model framework, and is an inflation dynamic model established by combining China's monetary policy tools and inflation transmission models (as indicated in Figure 12.2).

12.3 Excess liquidity and inflation dynamic change: An empirical analysis

12.3.1 Basic model and the results

Based on the information indicated in Figures 12.3 and 12.4, China's monetary aggregate shows a close dynamic connection with the economic output ratio (M2/GDP) and the CPI inflation rate, and the M2/GDP ratio usually precedes inflation. Therefore, we need to take this characteristic into full consideration during the measurement modeling. Meanwhile, according to the analysis in Figure 12.2, we can easily see that the transmission process from the excess money supply to inflation involves many other intermediate variables, yet here the core of the problem to be analyzed is to investigate whether the excess money supply (i.e. excess liquidity) has a dynamic transmission effect on inflation. Accordingly, if the intermediate variables are all included in the model system, it will not only neglect the essence of the problem, but may also lead to inaccurate measuring results because of multicollinearity.

Therefore, the basic model established in this chapter has taken into consideration the excess liquidity indices and whether the exchange rate has a significant dynamic driving effect on inflation. In view of the that, the basic model will be established as the following:

$$\pi_t = c + \alpha(L)\pi_{t-1} + \beta(\text{M2/GDP})_{t-1} + \gamma s_{t-1} + u_t \tag{12.1}$$

In which π_t refers to the inflation rate at the time t, s_{t-1} refers to the change rate of the RMB nominal effective exchange rate at the time, u_t represents the random impact factor at the time t (such as the supply shock indicated in Figure 12.2), while $\alpha(L) = \alpha_1 + \alpha_2 L + \alpha_3 L^2 + \ldots + \alpha_p L^{p-1}$ is a lagging operator polynomial, in which p refers to the optimum lag phases judged according to certain rules (such as SIC).

Please note that in Equation 12.1, in addition to the indicators of excess liquidity and exchange rate, the lag effect of inflation itself is also taken into consideration. Such a model design not only captures the inertial characteristics of inflation, but can also guarantee materially that Equation 12.1 can sufficiently depict the multi-period large effect of excess liquidity and exchange rate on the inflation rate, which may fit better with the actual situation in China. To illustrate this, we can use the basic property of lagging operators, and rewrite Equation 12.1 as:

$$\pi_t = c' + \beta\varphi(L)(\text{M2/GDP})_{t-1} + \gamma\varphi(L)s_{t-1} + \varphi(L)u_t \tag{12.2}$$

In which $\varphi(L) = [1 - \alpha(L)L]^{-1}$, $c' = c / \varphi(L)$.

After changing the format, we can see that Equation 12.2 actually depicts the effect of multi-period lag of excess liquidity and the exchange rate on inflation. Therefore, although Equation 12.1 only formally shows the single-period lag of those two variables, it guarantees that the possible multi-period lag effect will not be neglected.

During the process of analysis using Equation 12.1, the sample range covers the period from the first quarter of 1998 to the first quarter of 2008, the CPI inflation rate (on year-on-year basis) data come from the National Bureau of Statistics, the monetary aggregate data in M2/GDP indicators from the People's Bank of China, the nominal GDP data from the monthly reports of the National Bureau of Statistics on economic climate, and the nominal effective exchange rate data from the International Financial Statistics. Here it should be pointed out specifically again that because M2 is a stock indicator while GDP is a flow indicator, in the calculation of M2/GDP, M2 is the data corresponding to the current season, while GDP needs to use the mobile aggregates of four seasons. In consistence with the standard practices in study, this chapter hypothesizes the variable data as in a stationary time series. During the practice, the results given by the unit root test show that the hypothesis of stationary time series is relatively justified.

According to the aforesaid design, Table 12.1 summarizes the OLS estimates of the basic Equation 12.1. Firstly, the estimates show the coefficient β of the excess liquidity index has statistical significance under the traditional significance standard, which means the excess liquidity is really a significant driving factor of inflation. The point estimate value of the coefficient is 4.014, which means with other conditions remaining constant, for every percent of increase in M2/GDP, the CPI inflation rate will increase by about 4 percentage points. On the other hand, the coefficient of nominal effective exchange rate fluctuation has no significance, so that the effective exchange rate shows no significant dynamic driving effect on inflation, which suggests that the transmission effect of RMB exchange rate fluctuation on China's inflation is not obvious. This result is almost identical to the research conclusions of He (2008).

Besides, the optimum lag phases of lagging operator polynomial given by SIC are four phases. Based on standard theory of time series analysis, the total of inflation lag variable coefficients in all the phases (i.e. $\alpha(1) = \sum \alpha_i, i = 1, 2, 3, 4$) reflects the intensity of inflation inertia, so that Table 12.1 also reports the corresponding inertia coefficient estimate (0.673) of inflation. As the inflation inertia coefficient is closer to 1, the inflation inertia is higher, therefore the empirical results here indicate that China's inflation inertia during 1998–2008 was at a medium to high level.

Table 12.1 The dynamic model estimates of China's inflation during 1998–2008

$\hat{\alpha}(1)$	$\hat{\beta}$	$\hat{\gamma}$	p-auto	$\bar{R}^2$	Lag phase
0.673***	4.014**	0.222	0.595	0.86	4
(0.171)	(1.653)	(3.504)			

Note: *** and ** represent respectively the statistical significance of the statistics under the 1% and 5% percentage levels. The lag phase is the model optimum lag intervals chosen based on SIC. p-auto refers to the *p*-value of the correlation test of the Breusch–Godfrey LM series (lagging to the fourth phase).

Another point that should be explained is that, because here we are studying the dynamic model, the lag variable in the dependent variables is on the right of the regression equation. Therefore, whether the conclusions drawn by the serial correlation test based on the estimates will be critical. For that purpose, we carried out the Breusch–Godfrey LM serial correlation test. We can see from the *p*-value indicated in the table that, despite the four lag phases, the model shows no significant serial correlation, and thus the reliability of the measuring results is maintained as much as possible.

To sum up, the regression results of Equation 12.1 show that in the inflation fluctuation of China during 1998–2008, the ratio between the monetary aggregate and economic output is a significant dynamic driving factor, while the exchange rate fluctuation shows no significant dynamic transmission effect on domestic inflation. Of course, the analysis here has considered neither the possible effect of the factors of exchange rate mechanism reform on the estimation results of the measuring model, nor the possible dynamic interactions among the variables. Therefore, we will carry out a robust analysis on the basic conclusions in the following.

12.3.2 Robust analysis

The robust analysis will mainly consider two issues: One is to investigate the possible effect of the 2005 exchange rate mechanism reform on the results of the basic model; the other is to expand the one-dimensional basic model to the multi-dimensional vector autoregression model, and thus, on the basis of full consideration of the dynamic interactions among the various variables of the system, investigate whether the dynamic effect of random impact factors of excess liquidity on inflation is in agreement with the above results.

Firstly, important changes occurred to the RMB exchange rate mechanism in July 2005, which might bring the problem of structural change to the measuring model. For that purpose, we carried out a test on the structural change of the model in the sample range. As for the choice of testing method, in view of the ubiquitous time-lag effect during actual economic operation, we investigated the problem by using the unknown breakpoint structural change test given by Andrews and Ploberger (1994), rather than presuming a known change point as the sample breakpoint.

Secondly, according to the theory of Andrews and Ploberger, is it hypothesized that the coefficient matrix Φ of $m \times 1$ indicates the parameters in the basic model, $\Phi = \Phi_1$ when $t < k$, and $\Phi = \Phi_2$ ($\Phi_1 \neq \Phi_2$) when $t \geq k$, and they meet the condition $m \leq k \leq T - m$, in which T refers to the size of full sample. Besides, it is hypothesized that the search field of unknown breakpoint structural parameters is τ (usually the middle 70% of the area of the sample T is chosen), and the series of Wald test statistics $W_T(\tau_i)$ corresponding to all the possible breakpoints $k = T\tau_i$ in the field, while the original hypothesis of the statistical test was that the parameters in the model don't have structural change when the structural breakpoint is not k. It is easy to find that the unknown breakpoint parameter k here is present not in the original hypothesis, but only in the alternative hypothesis conditions, the parameters of which are called the interference parameters in the statistical test. After the value of $W_T(\tau_i)$ is obtained, it is possible to continue to calculate the statistics of maximum-Wald (*SupW*), i.e.:

$$SupW = SupW_T(\tau_i)\big|\tau_i \in [\tau_{min}, \tau_{max}] \tag{12.3}$$

If the statistic of *SupW* has statistical significance, the corresponding breakpoint will be the time point when structural change occurs.

Andrews and Ploberger further put forward the other two test statistics of optimum statistical property when the interference parameters exist, i.e. the statistics of the exponential-Wald (ExpW) and the mean value-Wald (AveW). The research of Andrews and Ploberger showed that because of the existence of interference parameters, even in progressive conditions, the above-mentioned test statistics correspond to the non-standard statistical distribution. Therefore, we used the non-standard distribution parameters of Hansen (1997) to calculate the *p*-values corresponding to the three statistics here, and obtained the correct adjoint probability. During the actual calculation, we used the heteroscedasticity of the model under unconstrained conditions to modify the corresponding *p*-values in the matrix.

According to the design above, we tested the structural stability of Equation 12.1 during 1998–2008, and judged relatively accurately whether structural change had occurred in China's inflation dynamic model at what time point, which provides the scientific basis for analyzing the robustness of basic model results. Table 12.2 reports the test results on the structural change of unknown breakpoints in the basic model. It is easy to see that although the maximum-Wald statistics occurred in the second quarter of 2005, the *p*-values corresponding to the three statistics in the structural change test are far beyond the conventional significance level, which indicates that the original hypothesis that there is no structural change in the basic model cannot be rejected. Therefore, we conclude that there is no structural change in the basic model.

Table 12.2 The test results of Andrews–Ploberger structural change of unknown breakpoints

	Statistical value	p-value	Breakpoint
Maximum – Wald	3.239	0.853	The second quarter of 2005
Exponential – Wald	0.992	0.531	
Mean – Wald	1.883	0.422	

Note: The original hypothesis was that no structural change occurs to the regression model, and the *p*-values corresponding to the test statistics were calculated based on the method given by Hansen (1997).

During the practice, we further tried to hypothesize the year 2005 as a structural breakpoint and used the dummy variables to re-estimate the basic model, and also tried replacing the effective exchange rate by the RMB–USD exchange rate during regression. However, under any of the conditions, the excess liquidity index constantly appears as a significant driving factor of inflation, and the exchange rate variable has no statistical significance without exception. The above analysis indicates that the basic model results have not changed along with the exchange

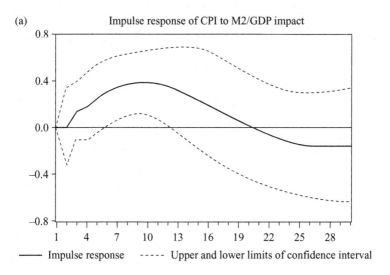

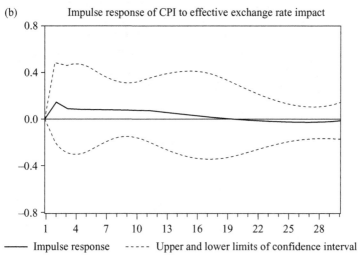

Figure 12.5 The impulse response function of inflation after the impact of the M2/GDP ratio and exchange rate fluctuation.

rate mechanism reform, and even after the accelerated appreciation of RMB, it showed no inhibiting effect on inflation.

The second issue considered in robustness analysis is the possible dynamic interactive effect among the various variables of the basic model. For that purpose, we established a ternary vector autoregression (VAR) model composed of the inflation rate, M2/GDP ratio, and exchange rate fluctuation, and the lag phases of the vector model are determined by SIC. In that case, the dynamic path of the CPI inflation rate after the random impact of the unit standard deviations corresponding respectively to excess liquidity and exchange rate will be obtained through a standard Cholesky decomposition, i.e. the impulse response function (see Figure 12.5). As the dynamic information covered by the VAR model is more varied, the impulse response function can further reflect the response modes and amplitude of inflation after different kinds of impact. Figure 12.5 depicts the time sequence of the impulse response function calculated on the basis of the VAR model (in which the dashed line indicates the upper and lower bounds of the 90% confidence interval).

Figure 12.5 shows that inflation has obviously different responses to different kinds of impact. After the impact of excess liquidity, a noticeable positive response occurs, which indicates that the aggravation of excess liquidity caused by random factors will bring a higher inflation rate, and such a driving effect will only begin to decrease after reaching its peak after around two years (i.e. eight lag phases). On the other hand, after the random impact of exchange rate fluctuation on inflation, the impulse response function just slightly deviated from the 0 point, which indicates that the response of inflation to the impact of exchange rate fluctuation is slight.

To sum up, China's inflation during 1998–2008 was significantly affected by the dynamics of the excess liquidity factor, while the exchange rate fluctuation lacked a transmission effect on inflation, and even when the exchange rate mechanism reform was taken into account and the vector model was adopted, the results still remained robust.

12.4 The transmission logic from excess liquidity to inflation

From the results of quantitative analysis above, we can see that excess liquidity has basically been driving China's inflation in recent years, while this excess liquidity emerged from and alongside the background of RMB appreciation expectations. Let us stretch the focal length of time slightly, and recall the process of RMB exchange rate appreciation. Actually, since 2003, the RMB has being facing the pressure of appreciation from various parties, particularly the USA. After several rounds of the game, the RMB exchange rate mechanism reform made a breakthrough from July 2005. Since then, the RMB exchange rate against USD began to increase, and from the end of 2006, the trend of appreciation became more apparent with an accelerating pace of appreciation. Meanwhile, we did not see any reversal in China's double surplus in the international payment balance, but rather the momentum of continuous increase. Figure 12.6 depicts the dynamic

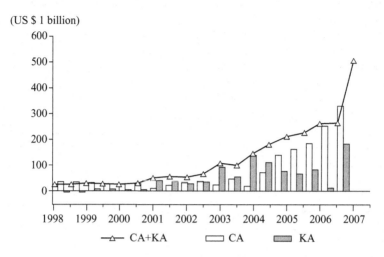

Figure 12.6 Double surplus of China's international payment balance during 1998–2007.
Source: State Administration of Foreign Exchange.

trend of surplus in the current account (CA) and capital and financial account (KA, hereafter referred to as capital account) of China since 1998. Obviously, since the exchange rate mechanism reform, the double surplus has increased substantially and continuously, represented especially by the almost vertical increase in 2007, and the increase in the surplus of the current account has been more noticeable.

Of course, the long-term surplus of China after the appreciation of the RMB is not in compliance with the judgment of international financial theories that the appreciation will lead to the shrinking of export and thus reduce the surplus. McKinnon (2007) deemed that this phenomenon is due to the different consumption and saving patterns of Chinese and US citizens. However, just in the aspect of import and export trade, many export-oriented enterprises of China faced increasing pressure after the RMB appreciation, and the export volume of the enterprises has decreased noticeably. According to the statistics in the first quarter of 2008, on a year-on-year basis, the growth rate of export decreased by 6 percentage points, while the growth rate of import increased by 10 percentage points, which thus reduced the commodity trade surplus in the first quarter by 4.9 billion USD, i.e. around 10%.

Although the scale of commodity trade surplus somewhat decreased, driven by the RMB appreciation, short-term profit-seeking capital of a considerable size rushed into China by all means through various legal channels in the international payment balance, causing the superficial on-going substantial increase in the surplus. In particular, according to the study carried out by He (2008), the compensation of employees and investment income under the current account as well as the current transfer account have been extremely active in recent years (e.g. investment income after 2005 changed from the previous net outflow for a long period (negative) to a net inflow (positive)), while the current transfer account also increased swiftly, which are all the typical characteristics of hot money flowing into China through the current account.

Because of the RMB appreciation expectations, the size of foreign exchange inflow under the capital account has also been increasing. For example, foreign direct investment (FDI) and the currency and deposit account both indicated the inflow of hot money. Especially since 2008, the increase in FDI has been exceptional. According to the statistics released by the Ministry of Commerce, in the first quarter of 2008, the FDI actually used by China amounted to 27.4 billion USD, increasing by more than 60% on a year-on-year basis. In fact, FDI has begun to show momentum of substantial increase since the end of 2007. Based on experience, as the foreign exchange earned by FDI can be retained in remittance accounts opened by the banks, or be sold through the banks, which facilitates the inflow of hot money in the name of FDI, it is thus probable that there may be a considerable amount of speculative capital in FDI. The currency and deposit account under the capital account also showed a trend of vertical increase in recent years, which is mostly due to the short-term capital, and such an exceptionally substantial increase suggests that driven by expectations of further RMB appreciation, the inflow of short-term speculative capital into China was gaining momentum, and the international hot money accelerated its speed of building positions in China.

Against such a background, China's foreign exchange reserve increased continuously, and to absorb the double surplus flowing in in great size, the central bank had to supply a large amount of money to the market, which caused a great increase in funds outstanding for foreign exchange. Figure 12.7 depicts the ratio between the funds outstanding for foreign exchange and the monetary aggregate (M1) during January 2000–April 2008, from which we can see clearly that after 2005 the funds outstanding for foreign exchange in China exceeded 50% of M1,

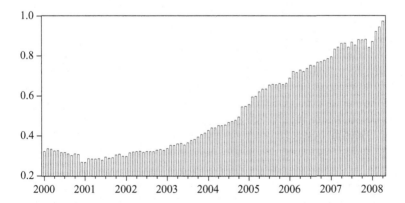

Figure 12.7 The ratio between the funds outstanding for foreign exchange and the M1 during January 2000–April 2008. Source: People's Bank of China.

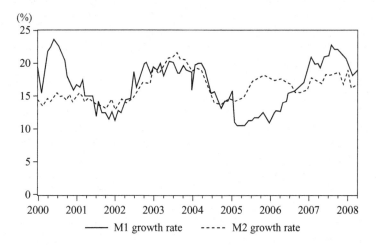

Figure 12.8 Year-on-year growth rate of China's monetary aggregates during January
2000–April 2008. Source: People's Bank of China.

and even reached almost 90% after 2007, which means that, driven by the RMB
appreciation expectations, increasing amounts of international money were flowing in, and thus China's money supply and excess money supply was rather a
passive action to a large extent.

Because of that, the narrow and broad money supply in China has maintained
a growth rate of more than 10% in recent years. Figure 12.8 gives the year-on-
year growth rate of the monetary aggregate M1 and M2 during January 2000–
April 2008. Apparently, since 2005, the growth rate of broad money aggregate
M2 has remained at around 16%, and obviously increased substantially during
2005–2006, while the growth rate of M1 began to grow from 2005, and reached
over 20% at the beginning of 2007, and then decreased slightly in 2008 but still
remained at a high level of more than 18%.

The rapid swelling of money supply will undoubtedly cause excess liquidity
in the whole economy, which will inevitably trigger speculation in the end, and
consequently the capital market and real estate market will become overheated,
and afterwards, the market will gradually acquire new expectations of future inflation. Once the market expects that commodity prices will continue to increase, the
consumers will be apt to accept such an increase, which will result in increases in
commodity prices far beyond those in raw material costs. In that case, the inflation
will prevail, and such a transmission route is the situation depicted in Figure 12.2.

Therefore, the root of the inflation that happened in China during 2007–2008
was that with the subtle influence of market expectations, the excess liquidity
driven by the RMB appreciation was finally transmitted to changes in consumer
prices. As we can see clearly from Figures 12.3 and 12.4, the excess liquidity
index and the CPI inflation rate showed almost exactly the same trend, with the

excess liquidity index usually preceding inflation, which means China's inflation in recent years is obviously characterized by excess liquidity, which is mainly caused by the RMB appreciation.

12.5 Conclusions

The chapter reviewed the excess liquidity and inflation of China during 1998–2008, and analyzed the dynamic connection between the two. Starting from the dynamics among exchange rate fluctuation, M2/GDP index, and inflation, we used a dynamic measuring model to make an empirical analysis of the effect of RMB exchange rate fluctuation on domestic inflation. The results of the analysis show that when the inflation is high, it is not sensible to try to inhibit it through the accelerated appreciation of the RMB. The results further suggest that although China's inflation problem has been mitigated as the slowdown in world and domestic economic growth eases, regulating China's commodity prices (inflation or deflation) through the RMB exchange rate fluctuation will have limited effects in the transitive period of the RMB exchange rate mechanism. Therefore, facing the new situation, it is urgent that the monetary authority further maintains the stability of the RMB exchange rate.

The analysis in this chapter also indicates that when analyzing the issues of RMB appreciation and inflation with existing economic theories, we must not neglect the actual situation faced currently by China's economy. During 2007–2008, the inflationary effect of the excess liquidity due to the RMB appreciation was far beyond the deflationary effect. Nevertheless, some people may deem that the serious inflation during 2007–2008 was due to insufficient RMB appreciation, but we must be objective and admit that the exchange rate fluctuation may have an "overshooting" effect, and if the RMB appreciation speeds up, after a certain period of time, a considerable number of export-oriented enterprises will inevitably be pushed to the edge of bankruptcy or exit from the industries, and the short-term capital will probably seek quick outflow after interest arbitrage. In such cases, the negative impact on China's economy cannot be under-estimated, and even if the inflation is curbed successfully, the price to pay will be an economic depression, which is something we would rather not see. For example, the so-called "syndrome of ever-higher yen" in 1990s finally led to the economic downturn of Japan for a period of ten years (1992–2002), which we should reflect on. Currently, when China's economy is facing the impact of a global financial crisis, neither substantial continuous appreciation nor substantial depreciation of the RMB will be feasible.

This chapter concludes that the strategy of exchange rate adjustment should adopt the basic principle of internal and external balancing and dynamic coordination. Externally, the unpredictability of RMB exchange rate fluctuation should be further enhanced, and control over the inflow and outflow of international capital should still not be eased in the near future. When it is difficult to control capital inflow and outflow, measures will be taken on mandatory supervision and control of the capital that has already flowed in. Meanwhile, efforts should be made to send information to the relevant countries continuously through various channels, so that they will be conscious that the increased fluctuation of the RMB exchange rate will lead to a greater negative impact of the current financial crisis on China's economy, which will be unfavorable to the overall world economic development. Internally, considering that the aftermath of the global financial crisis has not been wiped out, only by maintaining the relative stability of the RMB exchange rate, guiding the domestic market expectations appropriately, and gradually increasing the flexibility of the economic system can we maintain sustainable economic development.

To sum up, in such a period of significant change in the current world economic situation, we should not rely entirely on continuous RMB appreciation or depreciation to regulate commodity prices and promote economic growth. To mention specifically, under the situation of global economic downturn, the continuous depreciation of national currency cannot still be the magic pill for maintaining sustainable economic development. Only through the dynamic collaboration between the government, enterprises, and the market, can we be well-prepared to successfully realize the economic goals in the new stage, which will not only be favorable to China's economic development, but also be significant for the benign development cycle of the world economy.

Note

1   Note: Because M2 is a stock indicator and GDP a flow indicator, during the calculation of M2/GDP, the current-season data of M2 and the movement and total values of GDP in four seasons are used.

13 Exchange rate parity relation change and inflation dynamic mechanism

13.1 Exchange rate regime and economic and financial condition change

This chapter is a continuation of Chapter 12. In this chapter, we will further discuss the PPP and interest rate parity of the RMB exchange rate. In order to remain consistent with the analytical logic of the previous chapters, we will still analyze the period of the RMB to US dollar appreciation trend (before 2010 in this chapter). For the background and mechanism of the RMB to US dollar exchange rate change in recent years (after 2013), we will have more discussions in appendix to this chapter.

In the new environment of international capital flow, it seems to bring many problems to a country's financial stability to use a fixed exchange rate system or a fixed exchange rate system as the nominal anchor of monetary policy. In this context, more and more countries in the world have begun to reform the exchange rate system. In the process of exchange rate system change, some countries have adopted stricter fixed exchange rate systems, and more countries have tried to adopt more flexible exchange rate policies. Among them, China's exchange rate system transition in recent years has attracted the attention of the whole world.

As we all know, since the 21st century, after many rounds of games between China and major trading partners, especially the United States, from July 2005, the original single dollar-pegged exchange rate system was transformed into a managed floating exchange rate mechanism pegged to a basket of currencies. After the exchange rate reform, the value of RMB against the US dollar rose all the way up until around 2010. Figure 13.1 depicts the time sequence change of the RMB to US dollar exchange rate (direct pricing method) from 2005 to 2010. We can see that from the second half of 2005 to the first half of 2008, the rapid appreciation trend of RMB to US dollar is very obvious. From 2008 to the beginning of 2010, due to the impact of the international financial crisis, the rapid appreciation trend of RMB against the US dollar slowed down. By the end of 2013, RMB began to depreciate against the US dollar.

During the period of RMB's accelerated appreciation against the US dollar, great changes have taken place in the economic and financial situations of China and the US. Figure 13.2 depicts the dynamic trend of the federal funds rate and

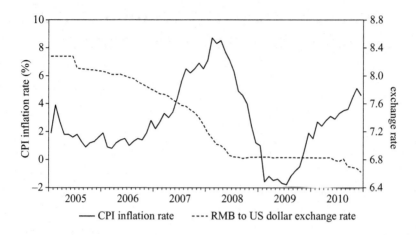

Figure 13.1 CPI inflation rate and RMB to US dollar exchange rate (direct pricing method): January 2005–December 2010. Source: National Bureau of Statistics, People's Bank of China.

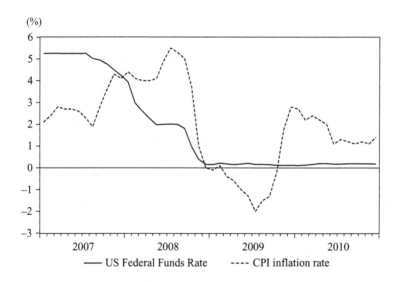

Figure 13.2 US federal funds rate and CPI inflation rate: January 2007–December 2010. Source: Federal Reserve St. Louis Branch.

CPI inflation rate from January 2007 to December 2010. We see that after the subprime crisis broke out in early 2007, the Federal Reserve began to cut the benchmark interest rate continuously in order to stimulate economic growth. Take the federal funds rate, a monetary policy tool of the United States, as an example. In September 2007, the interest rate dropped to 4.94%, and in January 2008, it dropped to 3.94%. In May 2008, the federal funds rate fell again to a low level of 1.94%. Since then, the Federal Reserve has been implementing a low interest rate policy close to zero. As the pace of economic recovery in the United States has been relatively slow after the crisis, the inflation rate in the United States has remained relatively low since 2008.

In the same period, China's economy has also experienced cyclical changes, but the relevant economic indicators show significantly different characteristics from the US economic trend. Especially since 2007, China's ten-year-long (1997–2006) low inflation situation has changed. The domestic CPI inflation rate reached new highs for 12 months in a row, and inflation showed a significant high trend (see Figure 13.1). At that time, in order to cope with the risk brought by high inflation, China changed its prudent monetary policy to a tight monetary policy at the end of 2007. In this process, China's interest rate level stepped into an upward channel.

Since the beginning of 2008, due to the impact of the global financial crisis caused by the US subprime mortgage crisis, real economic growth slowed down, and the overall inflation level began to decline. In response to the impact of the international financial crisis on the real economy, the Chinese government announced in November 2008 that it would gradually implement a 4-trillion-yuan economic stimulus plan, and in 2009, it would change the direction of monetary policy from tight to moderately loose. Against the background of loose macro policy, from 2009 to 2010, China's domestic inflation rate showed a gradual upward trend.

From the dynamic path of the CPI inflation rate depicted in Figure 13.1, it can be seen that from July 2009 to December 2010, the domestic inflation rate kept rising in most periods. It is worth noting that, in comparing the dynamic trend of the inflation rate and exchange rate in Figure 13.1 during this period, it is not difficult to find that RMB began to show an obvious appreciation trend against the US dollar again. In order to cope with the rapid rise of domestic prices and the superimposed effect of the possible impact on international liquidity caused by the appreciation of RMB, China's monetary policy began to shift from moderately easing to prudent at the end of 2010, which is in essence inclined to moderately tight, so the domestic interest rate began to rise accordingly.

Given the series of economic and financial changes in China and the United States, the one-way appreciation of RMB against the dollar in 2005–2010 is closely related to the dynamic changes of interest rates and inflation rates in China and the United States. This kind of connection has a significant impact on China's economic development, so the issue of RMB appreciation has attracted the general attention of scholars at home and abroad. However, there seems to be no consensus on the impact of RMB appreciation on domestic inflation and overall economic operations. For example, in the early stage of the exchange rate reform in 2005, Ding (2005) and Chen (2006) proposed through an analysis of international experience that the exchange rate reform of RMB needs to maintain basic stability through policy adjustment, and the rapid and substantial appreciation of the RMB will be contrary to the overall interests of China's economic development.

The above views have not been accepted by other scholars. Roubini (2007), for example, holds the opposite view. He believes that only by further increasing the pace of appreciation of the RMB can China stabilize its international trade surplus, effectively control inflation in China, and alleviate internal and external imbalances. Ha (2007) also put forward similar views, and point out that China should use the RMB appreciation strategy to alleviate the pressure of internal and external imbalances. Zhang and Hu (2008) simulated and analyzed the relationship between RMB appreciation and China's inflation by using theoretical models, and the results seemed to support the strategy of accelerating RMB appreciation. However, because the pure simulation is too idealized, it may ignore the dynamic interaction between economic variables in real economic life, so whether the simulation results are accurate remains to be further studied. Indeed, through analyzing the long-term equilibrium relationship between RMB and the world's major currencies the study of Qin (2010) found that RMB does not have a substantial economic basis for appreciation compared with other currencies.

Compared with the above studies, McKinnon (2007) considered the issue of RMB appreciation more holistically. He not only refuted Roubini's (2007) view that appreciation can reverse China's surplus situation by citing the differences of residents' consumption and saving habits between China and the United States, but also used data on interest rates, exchange rates, and inflation rates in China and the United States to show that the two countries are forming an international parity relationship (relative purchase). It is suggested that China should determine the appreciation range of RMB according to the inflation rate difference between China and the United States, so as to make exchange rate adjustment a new option for China's monetary policy. It is worth noting that although McKinnon (2007) disagrees that appreciation can change the trade imbalance between China and the United States, he believes that as long as the RMB exchange rate is adjusted according to the international parity relationship to maintain sustainable appreciation, China can effectively control imported inflation.

The intellectual collision between Chinese and foreign scholars on the mode of RMB exchange rate transition has made a positive contribution to our understanding and analysis of RMB exchange rate transition and thinking about the choice of monetary policy in the new situation. In particular, McKinnon's (2007) study on the relationship between international parities seems to have designed a new feasible path for China's monetary policy in an open economic environment. However, we have noticed that since the adjustment of the RMB exchange rate system in 2005, the dynamic path evolution of various nominal variables (especially the interest rate and inflation rate) in China and the United States has changed significantly. In such a context, McKinnon (2007) proposed the measure of adjusting the exchange rate of RMB against US dollar based on the international parity relationship, which is likely to be just a temporary measure. In particular, under the dynamic development pattern of international finance after the new global financial crisis, whether this kind of international parity relationship is still established is obviously facing a real test. Therefore, it is necessary to explore and analyze the possible new pattern of international parity relations between China and the United States, so as to provide new ideas and clues for RMB exchange rate adjustment strategies, and to re-examine and rethink the policy suggestions put forward by the existing studies.

13.2 New pattern of exchange rate parity between China and the US

We mentioned in Section 13.1 that McKinnon (2007) compared the dynamic trend of exchange rate appreciation, inflation rates, and interest rates between China and the United States between 2004 and 2006, and found that the movement path of the RMB exchange rate against the United States dollar was basically consistent with the movement path of the inflation rate difference and the interest rate difference between the two countries, that is, relative purchasing power parity and uncovered interest rate parity were established. According to this finding, McKinnon proposed that China's inflation rate could be effectively adjusted through exchange rate changes on the basis of relative purchasing power parity. However, in recent years, the international economic and financial situation has changed dramatically, and so have the economic situations of China and the United States. Therefore, whether the current international parity relationship is still established needs to be re-analyzed. We will test these two kinds of international parity relations.

13.2.1 Relative purchasing power parity

Before analyzing the relationship between China and the United States, in order to explain the problem conveniently, we use π to express the inflation rate and Δs to express the exchange rate (year-on-year) change rate calculated by the direct pricing method. In addition, we use superscript d to represent domestic (Chinese) variables and superscript f to represent foreign (US) variables. According to the theory of relative purchasing power parity, if the change rate of the exchange rate between China and the United States is roughly equal to the difference between the inflation rates of the two countries, then the relationship of relative purchasing power parity is established, namely

$$\Delta s_t = \pi_t^d - \pi_t^f \tag{13.1}$$

McKinnon (2007) believes that since the reform of the RMB exchange rate system in 2005, there has been a relative PPP relationship between China and the

United States. From Equation 13.1, it is easy to get the expression of China's inflation rate:

$$\pi_t^d = \pi_t^f + \Delta s_t \tag{13.2}$$

McKinnon (2007) proposed according to Equation 13.2 that as long as China pegged the inflation level π_t^f of the United States to regulate the change of Δs_t, the inflation rate π_t^d in China could be controlled at a relatively stable level. For example, if the current inflation rate in the United States is $\pi_t^f = 5\%$, and China expects to keep the inflation rate at 2%, then the goal of a 2% inflation rate can be achieved by adjusting the exchange rate of RMB against the US dollar to keep its appreciation range (corresponding to a negative value of Δs_t) at 3%.

In order to investigate this problem, we describe the changes in the time sequence of the CPI inflation rate, inflation rate gap, and RMB appreciation against the US dollar in 2004–2010 in Figure 13.3. Among them, the inflation rate is measured by the year-on-year growth rate of the CPI, and the appreciation rate of RMB is calculated by the year-on-year growth rate under the direct pricing method of RMB against the US dollar. It can be seen clearly from the figure that in the sample range studied by McKinnon (2007), that is, from July 2005 to September 2006, the inflation rate difference between China and the United States really coincides with the time path of RMB appreciation. In this period alone, McKinnon (2007) claims that the relative PPP relationship is tenable, and adjusting the exchange rate of RMB against the US dollar on this basis will help maintain a relatively balanced domestic inflation rate. However, after September

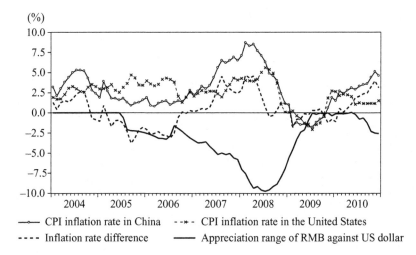

Figure 13.3 Inflation rate difference between China and the United States and RMB appreciation: January 2004–December 2010. Source: National Bureau of statistics, People's Bank of China.

2006, we can see that the dynamic trend of the inflation rate difference between China and the United States and the appreciation range of RMB completely deviated from the relationship of relative purchasing power parity. Moreover, with the increase of the appreciation range of RMB, the deviation degree of the two trends also increased significantly, which lasted until the beginning of 2009.

It is worth noting that when the appreciation of RMB against the US dollar fell briefly from the beginning of 2009 to the middle of 2010, the difference between the appreciation of the RMB against the US dollar and the inflation rate of China and the US returned to a basically equal position. At this time, the exchange rate change and inflation change between the two countries returned to a relatively balanced state. However, since July 2010, there has been a rapid appreciation of the RMB against the US dollar. At this time, the inflation rate gap between China and the United States again deviates from the equilibrium path of relative purchasing power parity.

The above analysis shows that the relative PPP relationship proposed by McKinnon (2007) has changed significantly in middle and late 2006. The fundamental reason for this change is that before the middle of 2006, due to the fact that the expectation of RMB appreciation in the international financial market has not shown a very strong trend, China's monetary authorities still had effective control over capital inflow. Under such circumstances, the central bank can still offset the excess foreign exchange accumulation to prevent the excessive growth of the currency, so as to effectively control the inflation below the level of 2–3 percentage points in the United States, that is to say, just keep the same level as the appreciation of the RMB against the dollar. However, from the second half of 2006, due to the stronger expectations of accelerated appreciation of RMB, the acceleration of capital inflow, and the continuous growth of money entering through the channels of foreign exchange, huge pressure of excessive growth of the domestic money supply has formed, which has promoted the inflation levels of China to catch up with those of the United States. In 2008–2009, in the short period after the impact of the global financial crisis, as the appreciation rate of RMB against the US dollar slowed down temporarily, the impulse of international short-term capital flowing into China was restrained to some extent, so the growth rate of China's money supply also slowed down. However, the pressure of RMB appreciation continued to increase, resulting in the dynamic trend of the nominal variables related to China and the United States continuing to deviate from the relationship of relative purchasing power parity.

The above process can also be confirmed by the dynamic trend of China's currency supply index M1 and M2 growth rate (year-on-year) depicted in Figure 13.4. It can be seen from Figure 13.4 that whether the narrow money M1 (cash in circulation + bank demand deposits) or the broad money M2 (M1 plus household savings deposits and enterprise time deposits), the growth rate has a significant upward turning point in the middle of 2006. The change of the M1 growth rate is particularly prominent. Before September 2006, the M1 growth rate remained at 10–15%. But after that, the growth rate of M1 surged all the way to a high of 20% in 2007. The growth rates of M1 and M2 slightly fell back in 2008, but jumped to the historical highs of nearly 40% and 30% respectively after 2009.

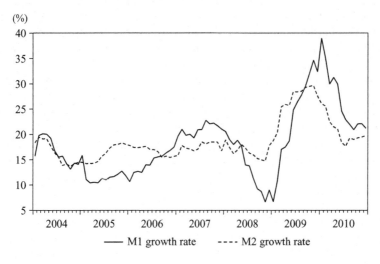

Figure 13.4 Growth rate of money supply in China: January 2004–December 2010.
Source: People's Bank of China.

13.2.2 Uncovered interest parity

McKinnon (2007) also pointed out that there is a parity relationship between China and the United States, that is, the interest rate difference between the two countries is basically equal to the corresponding exchange rate change rate. To illustrate this relationship, McKinnon compared the one-year London Interbank Offered Rate (LIBOR) of the US dollar with the one-year central bill rate issued by the People's Bank of China in 2004–2006, and found that this interest rate difference was consistent with the change rate basis of RMB against the US dollar, namely

$$\Delta s_t = i_t^d - i_t^f \tag{13.3}$$

Where i is the nominal interest rate and other symbols have the same meanings as above.

McKinnon pointed out that since China's exchange rate reform in 2005, the interest rate of China's central bank bill has been basically determined by the appreciation path of RMB against the US dollar through the interest rate parity relationship of Equation 13.3. In particular, the fact that the US dollar interest rate is higher than the corresponding RMB interest rate in this period shows that the holders of RMB assets are willing to accept a lower rate of return due to the appreciation trend of RMB against the US dollar, while the holders of US dollar assets are just the opposite. This kind of situation coincides with the content of the parity relation of the interest rate. According to McKinnon, there is downward pressure on the return on RMB assets as the RMB continues to appreciate.

However, it seems that the interest rate levels of China and the United States are not completely subject to the endogenous decision mechanism of exchange rate changes; especially after mid-2006, the above interest rate parity relationship has changed significantly. The key point is that McKinnon (2007) did not consider the inflationary pressure caused by the high growth of China's money supply after the appreciation of the RMB, and underestimated the huge impact of the US subprime mortgage crisis on the Fed's interest rate policy. To illustrate the problem, Figure 13.5 depicts the dynamic path of the one-year dollar LIBOR and central bank bill yield, interest rate difference, and RMB appreciation against the US dollar from January 2004 to May 2008. As can be seen from Figure 13.5, before September 2006, the trend of interest rate difference between China and the United States is indeed consistent with the path of RMB appreciation, and the two curves are relatively consistent. The interest rate difference seems to be determined by the appreciation range of RMB against the US dollar.

However, in fact, the development and change in the domestic economic situations of China and the United States are the leading factors that affect the change of interest rate. For China, since the pressure of domestic inflation has become increasingly prominent since 2007, the monetary authorities have responded strongly to domestic inflation, so the tight monetary policy of shrinking credit and tightening money was fixed at the end of 2007. In this context, China's interest rate began to rise gradually. For example, the one-year central bill rate was less than 3.0% in the first three months of 2007, and then it rose all the way up to 4.0% by the end of 2007. At the beginning of 2008, it still showed a slight upward trend. Obviously, in the process of adjusting interest rates, China has put

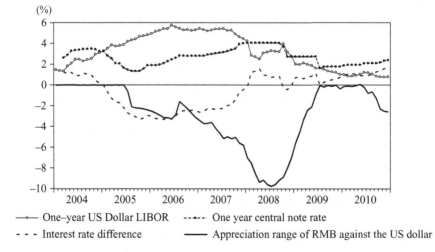

Figure 13.5 One-year interest rate difference between China and the US and the appreciation range of RMB against the US dollar: January 2004–December 2010. Source: CEIC database, People's Bank of China.

the domestic inflation factor in the first place. However, there is no realistic basis for the view of McKinnon (2007) that the exchange rate factor determines the interest rate level of China through interest rate parity, at least for the situation after the mid-2006.

Not only that, in the United States, the outbreak of the subprime mortgage crisis caused by the credit crisis in the housing market prompted the Federal Reserve to start to ease monetary policy at the end of 2007. In order to invigorate the domestic economy and avoid recession as much as possible, the United States began to cut interest rates. As we can see from Figure 13.5, the one-year US dollar LIBOR was inversely linked to the corresponding Chinese interest rate in January 2008. While the RMB continued to appreciate, the interest rate of RMB exceeded the yield of US dollar assets. Obviously, this situation is totally different from the interest rate parity proposed by McKinnon (2007), and the interest rate parity relationship between China and the United States has undergone a new transformation.

13.3 Inflation dynamic mechanism under exchange rate parity relation change

The emergence of a new pattern of international parity relations indicates that China is still facing severe challenges from internal and external imbalances. Domestically, the speed of price rising is accelerating, and the upward pressure of inflation is becoming increasingly prominent. In addition, in the open economic environment, restricted by the level of foreign interest rates, the role of interest rate instruments in the implementation of domestic monetary policy is limited, and monetary authorities have to rely on mandatory credit collection and release, adjustment of the deposit reserve ratio, and other instruments. However, the appreciation of RMB has not improved China's balance of payments surplus, which means China has to face the problem of accelerating the inflow of international speculative capital in the process of appreciation.

In fact, the most fundamental reason for the reversal of the international parity relationship between China and the United States in recent years and China's imbalance at home and abroad is the appreciation expectation formed by the continuous appreciation of the RMB. We will first analyze the dynamic transmission mechanism between the transformation of international parity relations and the emergence of internal and external imbalances, and then establish a dynamic econometric model to prove this logical relationship.

13.3.1 Conduction mechanism

With the change of the international parity relationship, the adjustment of the RMB exchange rate is facing severe challenges. Especially in the process of accelerating the appreciation of the RMB in the short term, the international financial market has high expectations for the forward rise of the RMB, having greater confidence in going long with the RMB at the spot. Driven by the expectation of further appreciation of RMB, international capital will naturally speed up the pace of opening positions in the Chinese market.

Theoretically speaking, the real rate of return of capital is the fundamental factor affecting its flow direction. Therefore, we can explain the trend of international capital against the background of RMB appreciation according to the relationship between the inflation rates, interest rate levels, and exchange rates of China and the United States. Suppose R is the real rate of return of monetary capital, and π and i are still the inflation rate and nominal interest rate respectively. In this way, the real rate of return of a dollar capital in the United States can be expressed as

$$R^f = i^f - \pi^f \tag{13.4}$$

According to standard international financial theory, if the conversion cost is not considered, then the real return rate of the asset after entering China should be expressed as

$$R^d = i^d - \pi^d - \Delta s \tag{13.5}$$

That is to say, after this asset is converted into an RMB asset in China, the exchange rate of RMB against the US dollar directly affects its real income.

Now, assuming the expected acceleration of RMB appreciation, the value of Δs under the direct pricing method should be negative. Therefore, if the capital holder thinks that the result given in Equation 13.5 is higher than the value given in Equation 13.4, he will inevitably choose to enter the Chinese market. Combined with this analysis, from the perspective of actual data, it is not difficult to understand why the expectations of RMB appreciation will lead to the influx of international capital into China. Figure 13.6 depicts the real rate of return between RMB and the US dollar from January 2004 to December 2010, in which the latter is calculated by the difference between the one-year LIBOR of the US dollar and the inflation rate of US CPI, and the latter is calculated by subtracting the inflation rate of Chinese CPI from the one-year RMB central note rate plus the appreciation rate of RMB against the US dollar.

As can be seen from Figure 13.6, before the appreciation of RMB, namely, before July 2005, the real rate of return of international capital in the form of the US dollar in the United States is generally slightly higher than the real rate of return of equivalent capital in China. From July 2005 to September 2007, the real rate of return of capital in China and the United States rose in parallel. The real rate of return in China was higher than that in the United States in most of the period, but the gap was not large, slightly lower than 2 percentage points on average. However, with the acceleration of RMB appreciation in the second half of 2007, the real interest rate gap between China and the United States continues to increase, especially since the beginning of 2008; the gap between the real return rate of capital in China and the United States has exceeded 4 percentage points. Since then, the real rate of return of international capital in China has shown a

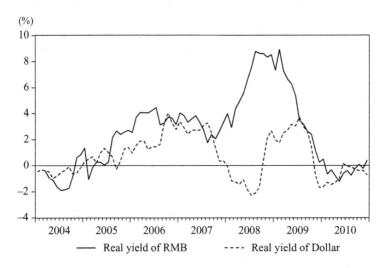

Figure 13.6 Comparison of real yield of RMB and USD from January 2004 to December 2010. Source: CEIC database, People's Bank of China.

significant upward trend, while the real rate of return in the United States has begun to decline, or even reach a negative value. Although the real yield gap between China and the United States narrowed from the end of 2009 to the first half of 2010, the real yield of capital in China was significantly higher than that in the United States in most periods.

It should be noted that when international investors compare the real rate of return of investment, it is likely that the weight given to China's inflation (π^dD) will be smaller than the actual value in Equation 13.2, or it will not be considered. This is because if the return of assets can finally flow back to the investor's country, the investor is only concerned about the size of $i^d - \Delta s$. At this time, the international capital inflow effect caused by the accelerated appreciation of RMB will be more obvious. If China's interest rate level continues to rise, the value of $i^d - \Delta s$ will further increase; in this case, the real rate of return for foreign investment to enter the Chinese market will be more considerable. A recent study further verified our judgment: According to a variety of different methods to calculate the inflow scale of "hot money," the short-term international capital inflows between 2005 and 2009 were 52.6 billion, 98.9 billion, 39.3 billion, 167.3 billion, and 69.1 billion US dollars respectively. However, in 2010, the scale of international capital inflow to China showed an extraordinary leapfrogging growth, with an increase of 195.6 billion US dollars.

Against the background of RMB appreciation, the fact that international speculative capital has accelerated its inflow can be seen from China's balance of payments surplus in recent years. Using the data released by the State Administration of Foreign Exchange, Figure 13.7 depicts the dynamic trend of China's current

(One million US dollars)

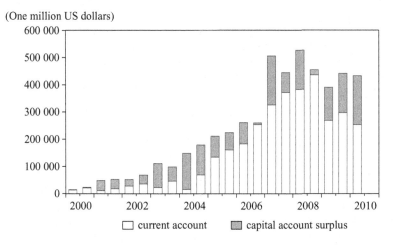

Figure 13.7 Current account and capital account surplus of China in 2000–2010.
Source: CEIC database.

account and capital and financial account surpluses in 2000–2010 (half-year frequency). It is not hard to see from Figure 13.7 that after the reform of the RMB
exchange rate in 2005, with the continuous appreciation of RMB, the sum of
China's double surpluses did not shrink, but continued to rise, especially in 2007.
From 2008 to 2010, China's total double surplus remained at a high level. It can
be seen that, while the RMB continues to appreciate, China's balance of payments
double surplus has not been improved, but shows a relatively obvious upward
trend.

Obviously, China's sustained surplus after RMB appreciation does not con-
form to the judgment of international financial theory that appreciation will
reduce the surplus. The main reason is that, driven by the expectation of RMB
appreciation, a considerable amount of short-term profit-seeking capital tries to
flow into China through various legal channels in the balance of payments, resulting in the situation that the balance of payments continues to grow substantially.
According to statistics released by the State Administration of Foreign Exchange,
employee compensation, investment income, and current transfer items under the
current account have been very active in recent years. For example, after 2005,
the investment income items changed from the previous long-term net outflow to
net inflow, and the balance of current transfer items has also increased rapidly in
recent years. These are the typical characteristics of speculative capital flowing
into China. The FDI under the capital account, as well as currency and deposit
items, also show signs of "hot money" influx: FDI began to show significant
growth momentum at the end of 2007, and its growth volume since 2008 is even
more amazing. In January 2008, for example, China's total FDI reached US $11.2
billion, an increase of more than 109% year-on-year. According to Zhang (2008),

FDI under capital account is becoming an important channel for "hot money" to flow into China.

All this suggests that speculative capital is accelerating its flow into China, driven by expectations of further appreciation of the RMB. In this context, China's total currency has maintained rapid growth in recent years. We have seen in Figure 13.4 that since 2005, the growth rate of the money supply has been accelerating, especially the growth rate of M1, which has been kept at a high level since 2005. Except for a short fall in 2009, it climbed to a high of nearly 40% by the beginning of 2010.

Therefore, with the continuous influx of international capital into the Chinese market, the growth of China's domestic money supply has accelerated, and the problem of excess liquidity has become increasingly prominent. However, the rise of capital asset prices driven by excess liquidity, even if not directly reflected in the prices of ordinary consumer goods, will also encourage the market to gradually form inflation expectations, leading to high inflation. For China's monetary authorities, since the main goal of monetary policy is to maintain price stability and economic growth, the policy response equation can be expressed as

$$I = f(\omega_\pi \pi, \omega_y y) \tag{13.6}$$

Where I is the policy tool, π and y are the inflation rate and economic growth rate (or output gap), ω_π and ω_y are the weights given by monetary authorities to inflation and economic growth respectively, and $f(\bullet)$ is the functional relationship. If the function here is linear and the monetary policy tool is the short-term interest rate, then Equation 13.6 corresponds to the famous Taylor rule in monetary policy analysis (Taylor, 1993). Although the main monetary policy tool in China is not interest rate, the research of Xie and Luo (2002) shows that Taylor rule can still be used as a reference standard to measure the tightness of China's monetary policy.

Furthermore, from the relation described in Equation 13.6, it is not difficult to see that when the inflation problem is prominent, the weight of inflation ω_π will rise. In other words, monetary authorities will adjust policy instrument I to cope with inflation. At this time, in addition to the control of the total amount of money, interest rates will naturally rise accordingly. In this way, with high domestic inflation, China and the United States have reversed their purchasing power parity. In addition, the rising interest rate in China (while the subprime mortgage crisis led to the US interest rate cut), which led to the change in the interest rate parity relationship between China and the United States, at the same time, encouraged foreign speculative capital to flow into China. Through such a dynamic transmission mechanism, China is currently facing the double pressure of inflation and RMB appreciation, and the risk of internal and external imbalances in economic development is very serious. In order to clearly demonstrate the process of transition from RMB appreciation expectations to the international parity relationship, the above dynamic transmission path is summarized in Figure 13.8.

From the above analysis, we can see that the appreciation of RMB does not solve the problem of economic imbalance at home and abroad. On the contrary, the appreciation expectations formed in the process of accelerating the appreciation

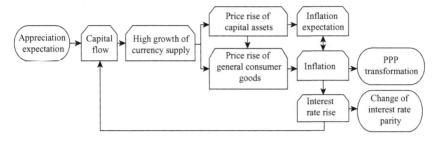

Figure 13.8 Dynamic conduction process of internal and external imbalance.

of RMB have resulted in changes in the international parity relationship and intensified the internal and external imbalance. This fact is further clarified by using econometric analysis.

13.3.2 Econometric analysis

The appreciation expectations formed in the process of RMB appreciation lead to the excessive growth of currency, which is then transmitted to domestic inflation, leading to the reversal of international parity relations and the aggravation of domestic and foreign economic imbalances. In order to further prove this transmission process, we test the dynamic relationship between RMB appreciation expectations and the currency growth rate, and between the currency growth rate and inflation. Because there is no data on RMB appreciation expectations in reality, one of the ways to obtain the time series data of appreciation expectations is to adopt the hypothesis of rational expectation, namely

$$E_t[\Delta s_{t+1}|\Omega_t] = \Delta s_{t+1} - e_{t+1} \qquad (13.7)$$

Where $E_t[\Delta s_{t+1}|\Omega_t]$ represents the appreciation expectation of the $t + 1$ period based on t time and previous information set Ω_t, and e represents the prediction error. In this way, we can obtain the actual observation sequence of RMB appreciation expectations by using the relationship of Equation 13.7, and then analyze the influence of appreciation expectations on the growth rate of total currency (the M1 or M2 growth rate is represented by Δm_t). For this purpose, regression estimates are made for the following equations:

$$\Delta m_t = c + \gamma E_t[\Delta s_{t+1}|I_t] + \varepsilon_t \qquad (13.8)$$

Where ε_t is a sequence-independent disturbance factor. To estimate Equation 13.8, we essentially estimate that

$$\Delta m_t = c + \gamma \Delta s_{t+1} + u_t \qquad (13.9)$$

Where $u_t = (\varepsilon_t - \gamma e_{t+1})$. Because Equation 13.9 may have endogenous problems (the compound disturbance terms u_t and Δs_{t+1} are not orthogonal), the generalized moment (GMM) regression method should be used, and the 1–2 lag series of Δm_t and Δs_t should be selected as the instrumental variables. In the regression process, we use the Newey–West correction matrix to eliminate the influence of noise information in the compound disturbance term on the estimation result of the variance–covariance matrix.

According to the above design, Table 13.1 reports the generalized moment estimation results of Equation 13.9. As can be seen from Table 13.1, the growth rate of M1 is significantly affected by the expected appreciation. If the coefficient $\tilde{\gamma}$ is negative, it means that the appreciation rate of RMB is expected to increase by 1% under the condition that other conditions remain unchanged, which will lead to an increase of 6.4% in the total amount of money M1. In addition, appreciation expectations and the M2 growth rate also show statistical significance, with the same impact direction as M1. We note that the estimated coefficient corresponding to M2 is slightly smaller than that corresponding to M1, which is consistent with the reality, because M2 contains long-term deposits, while this response to the expectation of RMB appreciation is weak.

According to the results of Table 13.1, we further set up a dynamic model between the growth rate of money supply and the inflation rate, namely

$$\pi_t = c + \phi(L)\pi_{t-1} + \theta\Delta m_{t-1} + v_t \tag{13.10}$$

Where $\phi(L) = \phi_1 + \phi_2 L + \phi_3 L^2 + \ldots + \phi_n L^{n-1}$ represents polynomial of delay operator of order n, and represents the disturbance term independent of sequence. Equation 13.10 considers the factors of the money growth rate based on the dynamic autoregressive model of inflation, in which the regression factor of the lag operator is used to capture the inertial characteristics of inflation, that

Table 13.1 Estimated results of the impact of RMB appreciation expectations on the currency growth rate

Δm_t	$\tilde{\gamma}$
M1 growth rate	−6.43***
	(1.63)
M2 growth rate	−2.77**
	(1.21)

Note: The sample interval is from January 2005 to December 2010; * * * and * * indicate that the statistics have statistical significance at the level of 1% and 5% respectively; the modified standard deviation of Newey–West is reported in brackets.

Table 13.2 M1 regression results of growth rate and inflation
dynamic model

Δm_t	$\hat{\phi}(2)$	$\hat{\theta}$	p-auto	Optimal lag period
M1 growth rate	0.936*** (0.038)	0.034** (0.015)	0.200	6
M2 growth rate	0.906*** (0.044)	0.009 (0.022)	0.253	6

Note: The sample range is from January 2005 to December 2010; the standard deviation of the white heteroscedasticity correction is reported in brackets; p-auto represents the *p*-value of the correlation test of the Breusch–Godfrey sequence (lag to sixth order).

is, $\phi(1) = \phi_1 + \phi_2 + \ldots + \phi_n$, which indicates the inertia level (Zhang, 2008). In the actual modeling and estimation process, the number of lag periods follows AIC (with six periods as the maximum value), ensuring that there is no sequence correlation in the residual term of the model.

The least squares estimation results of Equation 13.10 are summarized in Table 13.2. From the regression results, we can see that M1 growth rate is a significant driver of the CPI inflation rate. Assuming that other conditions remain unchanged, every 1% increase in M1 will significantly increase the CPI inflation rate by 0.34%. Although the driving effect of the M2 growth rate on the CPI inflation rate is not statistically significant, the driving direction is still positive. These results show that the positive pressure of the money supply growth rate on the inflation rate does exist. Of course, there is no absolute "other conditions unchanged" in reality, but only the change of money supply, such as stable public expectations or monetary policy hedging, may weaken the monetary driving effect of inflation. However, considering the reality of China in recent years, the pressure of monetary growth on inflation cannot be ignored.

The above analysis is carried out separately from a single equation. We can also consider the appreciation expectations, inflation, and money growth rate as a vector system, build a three-variable vector autoregressive model, and then obtain the dynamic change path of the core variables after different random shocks in the system through certain decomposition methods (such as the Cholesky decomposition), that is, the impulse response function. The results calculated by this method also verify the logic of the above analysis (no report due to the length).

13.4 Conclusions

This chapter analyzes the relationship between relative purchasing power parity and interest rate parity between China and the United States from the reform of the RMB exchange rate system in 2005 to 2010, and points out that the acceleration of RMB appreciation has resulted in the emergence of a new pattern of international parity relations, which has led to the aggravation of the imbalances at home and abroad in China's economic development. From the analysis of the transmission mechanism in this chapter, we can see that the appreciation expectations formed by the continuous appreciation of RMB will attract the rapid inflow of international speculative capital in the short term, which will lead to a passive and substantial increase in the total supply of domestic currency, and finally to domestic inflation, which will lead to a new pattern of international parity relations. The analysis logic and basic conclusion of this chapter are consistent with Chapter 12.

In the long run, if the RMB continues to appreciate rapidly and substantially, on the one hand, the impact of the exchange rate on export enterprises will accumulate to a certain extent, which will likely lead to a sharp decline in China's net exports, while the downturn in export trade will directly affect domestic employment and economic growth; on the other hand, speculative capital has the motivation and strategy to short China's capital market, especially after entering China's market and making gains, speculative capital will not stay for a long time, but will find outflow channels. Once capital begins to flow out, it is likely to dampen market confidence, lead to low investment, sluggish consumption, falling asset prices, and ultimately exacerbate economic volatility and increase the risk of economic recession. If there is such a bad cycle, the long-term consequences of RMB appreciation will be economic recession and deflation.

This conclusion may remind us of the great impact of the change of the yen exchange rate mechanism on Japan's economy during 1970–1995. Before the 1970s, the exchange rate of the Japanese yen against the US dollar was fixed at 360:1. After the famous Nixon shock in 1970, the Japanese yen began to appreciate driven by the Japanese exclusion trend. By 1995, the exchange rate of the Japanese yen against the US dollar reached 80:1, resulting in a large amount of international hot money flowing into Japan in a short period (1970–1974), which made the inflation rate of Japan at that time soar. However, from 1975, the deflation effect of appreciation began to emerge, and Japan began to experience deflation. After 1991, Japan experienced a decade-long economic recession, the so-called "lost decade." It is worth noting that McKinnon's (2007) study shows that the appreciation of the yen brought about by the "Japan exclusion trend" promoted by the United States politically is very similar to the appreciation of RMB caused by the current "China exclusion trend" faced by China.

All of this shows that in the process of RMB exchange rate mechanism transition, we must correctly distinguish the short-term results and long-term effects of accelerated RMB appreciation, and clearly recognize the main causes of current domestic inflation, not simply based on the theory that "appreciation can curb inflation," and not blindly advocate using RMB appreciation to solve the internal and external imbalances. We must also realize that at present, China's financial system and policy adjustment mechanism are still in a transition period of development and improvement, and export-oriented enterprises at the micro level also need some time to adjust their industrial structure and gain competitive advantage.

Therefore, what is urgently needed is not to accelerate the appreciation or sharp depreciation of the RMB, but to maintain the relative stability of the exchange rate, so as to reasonably guide the international market's expectations of the change of the RMB exchange rate. At the same time, with the increasing complexity of capital control, it is necessary to further increase the flexibility of capital control and actively introduce supporting policies and regulations to strengthen the supervision and control of monetary authorities over the inflow of capital, especially short-term capital. On this basis, we should strengthen the innovation of monetary policy tools, further use the asymmetric interest rate increase strategy and the differential deposit reserve system in credit regulation and deposit reserve ratio adjustment, so as to strive for sufficient buffer time for the interest rate marketization process, and provide sufficient time for export-oriented enterprises to adjust their structure and gain their advantages. In the process of gradual improvement of infrastructure at the micro and macro levels, it is the right choice to gradually realize the balance and transition of the exchange rate mechanism in order to meet the current challenges of imbalance at home and abroad and maintain long-term and stable economic development.

Appendix: Basic logic of RMB exchange rate fluctuation

From the beginning of 2014, the exchange rate of RMB against the US dollar seemed to suddenly drop sharply, and the continuous appreciation trend of the previous few years turns into an obvious depreciation trend. Therefore, the media began to report and explain all kinds of reasons for and backgrounds of RMB devaluation. For a while, "RMB devaluation" replaced the "appreciation" which seemed to be talked about the previous night and became the new focus of public opinion. In fact, both the appreciation and devaluation of RMB have inherent basic economic logic, but this basic logic is covered in various seemingly professional but too short-term analysis waves.

There may be different reasons for the "analysis" and "interpretation" of the recent devaluation of RMB, but at the same time, it implies a very interesting phenomenon, that is, the media's analysis of economic phenomena mostly stays on the basis of "short review," while the basic logic of economics is often ignored. For example, in January 2014, many economic commentators were still very boldly predicting, "in 2014, the RMB exchange rate (against the US dollar) reaching 5 has become a high-probability event." If we search for "RMB exchange rate is lower than 6" in Google or Baidu, we will find that the basis of this analysis and conclusion is intriguing, because at that time (at the end of 2013), the RMB exchange rate against the US dollar was about 6.10, and the figure of 6.10 was obviously close to 6.0, so it is not difficult to guess the chaotic logic behind these bold predictions.

At the same time, it is worth noting that in recent years, much of the media has interpreted the devaluation of RMB as a policy intervention of the People's Bank of China and the State Administration of Foreign Exchange, and even the US media have used this interpretation to warn about the decline of RMB (called " seriously concerned"). This is another funny thing. When the effect of China's macro policy adjustment is not shown in time, all kinds of media rush to criticize China's policy adjustment failure; China's policy adjustment is ineffective on the market, and suddenly the media enlarge the capacity of China's relevant decision-making organs infinitely. It seems that the People's Bank of China must be omnipotent and can manipulate the foreign exchange market at will overnight.

In fact, even the "omnipotent" US (Federal Reserve) can't be so omnipotent and manipulate the market. Therefore, the trend of the RMB exchange rate against the US dollar is not led by monetary authorities. In other words, even if the monetary authority intervenes in the foreign exchange market, it is also subject to the dynamic changes of various relevant economic indicators (variables), and even many so-called interventions are caused by dynamic changes of economic indicators, rather than the exogenous decisions of the monetary authority.

For the devaluation of RMB relative to the US dollar in 2014, we can explain the basic logic of the RMB devaluation trend in the near future by comparing the most basic long-term influencing factors of the China-US currency exchange rate, i.e. the asset yield rate and the price change rate (i.e. inflation rate) between China and the United States. Based on this logic, we have proposed in many training and research reports from October to December 2013 that the appreciation (pressure) of RMB against the US dollar in 2014 is not strong, and the RMB exchange rate tends to depreciate. But that view was unpopular at the time, even though it now appears to be a fait accompli.

As we all know, since the beginning of the 21st century, after many rounds of games with major trading partners, especially the United States, China has transformed the original single pegged exchange rate system into a managed floating exchange rate system pegged to a basket of currencies since July 2005. After the exchange rate reform, the value of RMB against the US dollar rose consistently, especially from the second half of 2005 to the first half of 2008; the rapid appreciation trend of RMB against the US dollar is very obvious. From 2008 to the beginning of 2010, due to the impact of the international financial crisis, the rapid appreciation trend of RMB against the US dollar slowed down. However, after May 2010, the RMB began to appreciate rapidly against the US dollar, and the appreciation continued until January 2014.

It should be noted that while the exchange rate of RMB against the US dollar has changed, the economic and financial situation of China and the US has also changed dramatically. Especially after the subprime crisis broke out in early 2007, the Federal Reserve began to cut the benchmark interest rate continuously in order to stimulate economic growth. Take the federal funds rate, a monetary policy tool of the United States, as an example. In September 2007, the rate dropped to 4.94%, and in January 2008, it fell to 3.94%. In May 2008, the federal funds rate was again brought to a low of 1.94%. Since then, until now, the Federal Reserve has been implementing a low interest rate policy. As the pace of economic recovery in the United States has been relatively slow after the crisis, the inflation rate in the United States has remained at a relatively low level since 2008.

In the same period, China's economy has also experienced cyclical changes, but the relevant economic indicators show significantly different characteristics from the US economic trend. Especially since 2007, China's low inflation situation of the previous ten years (1997–2006) has undergone subtle changes. The domestic CPI inflation rate has constantly reached new highs, and inflation has been significantly high. At that time, in order to cope with the risk of high inflation, China changed its prudent monetary policy into a tight one at the end of 2007. Although China's CPI inflation rate has not increased significantly in recent years, it has been higher than that of the United States. In this process, China's interest rate level also began to rise.

From the beginning of 2008, due to the impact of the global financial crisis caused by the US subprime mortgage crisis, the growth of China's real economy has slowed down, and the overall level of inflation has begun to decline. In response to the impact of the international financial crisis on the real economy, the Chinese government announced in November 2008 that it would gradually implement a 4-trillion-yuan economic stimulus plan, and then changed the direction of monetary policy from tight to moderately loose in 2009. Against the background of loose macro policy, from 2009 to 2010, China's domestic inflation rate rose gradually again. It is worth noting that comparing the dynamic trend of the inflation rate and exchange rate in Figure 13.9 during this period, it is not difficult to find that the RMB once again shows a significant appreciation trend against the US dollar. In order to cope with the rapid rise of domestic prices and the superimposed effect of the possible impact of international liquidity caused by the appreciation of RMB, China's monetary policy began to shift from moderately loose to stable at the end of 2010, which is in essence inclined to moderately tight, so the domestic interest rate began to rise accordingly.

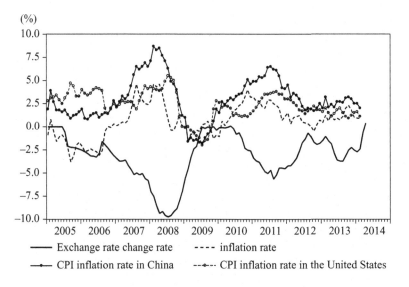

Figure 13.9 China–US inflation rate gap and RMB appreciation: January 2005–March 2014. Source: Federal Reserve St. Louis Branch.

The comparison of inflation rates and interest rate changes between China and the United States described above is actually the comparison of the two most basic indicators in the international parity relationship (PPP and interest rate parity) of the exchange rate. According to the PPP relationship, if the domestic inflation rate is higher than that of foreign countries for a long time, the local currency will depreciate; according to the interest rate parity relationship, if the domestic interest rate is higher than that of foreign countries for a long time, the local currency will also depreciate. Based on this, we first describe in Figure 13.9 the CPI inflation rates of China and the United States from January 2005 to March 2014, and the time series of the inflation rate difference and the rate of change of RMB against the dollar. The inflation rate is measured by the year-on-year growth rate of the CPI, and the appreciation rate of RMB is calculated by the year-on-year growth rate under the direct pricing method of RMB against the US dollar. It can be seen clearly from the figure that from July 2005 to September 2006, the inflation rate difference between China and the United States really coincides with the time series path of RMB appreciation. However, after September 2006, we can see that the dynamic trend of the inflation rate difference between China and the United States and the appreciation range of RMB completely deviated from the relationship of relative purchasing power parity. Moreover, with the increase of the appreciation range of RMB, the deviation degree of the two trends also increased significantly, which lasted until the beginning of 2009.

It's worth noting that when the appreciation of RMB against the US dollar fell briefly from the beginning of 2009 to mid-2010, the appreciation of RMB against the US dollar returned to a state basically equal to the inflation rate difference, and at this time, the exchange rate change and inflation of the two countries returned to a relatively balanced state. However, since July 2010, there has been a rapid appreciation of the RMB against the US dollar. At this time, the inflation rate gap between China and the United States again deviates from the equilibrium path of the relative PPP relationship.

The above analysis shows that the relationship between relative PPPs changed significantly in the second half of 2006. The fundamental reason for this change is that before the middle of 2006, the expectations of RMB appreciation in the international financial market had not shown a very strong trend, so the control of capital inflow by the Chinese monetary authorities was more effective. Under such circumstances, the central bank can still hedge the excess foreign exchange accumulation to prevent the excessive growth of the currency, so as to effectively control inflation at the level of 2 to 3 percentage points lower than the inflation rate of the United States, which is exactly the same as the appreciation of the RMB against the dollar. However, since the second half of 2006, the expectations of accelerated appreciation of RMB have become stronger, resulting in the acceleration of capital inflow, and the continuous growth of money put in through the channels of the foreign exchange account, which has put huge pressure on the rapid growth of the domestic money supply, thus encouraging China's inflation to catch up with the United States. In 2008–2009, in the short period after the impact of the global financial crisis, as the appreciation rate of RMB against the US dollar slowed down temporarily, the impulse of international short-term capital flowing into China was restrained to some extent, and the growth rate of China's money supply also slowed down. However, the pressure of RMB appreciation continued to increase, resulting in the dynamic trend of the nominal variables related to China and the United States continuing to deviate from the relationship of relative purchasing power parity.

It should be noted that after 2009, the situation that deviated greatly from the PPP relationship lasted for five years until 2014. Therefore, the pressure of the RMB exchange rate imbalance against the US dollar accumulated in the early stage must be released for a period of time. According to the basic content of the PPP, if the inflation rate of China's general goods is higher than that of the United States for a long time, then RMB will have devaluation pressure against the US dollar. Therefore, the premium (devaluation) of RMB in 2014 to the US dollar exchange rate was an inevitable manifestation of this pressure release.

In addition, from the perspective of interest rate parity, we can also judge the trend of the exchange rate of RMB against the US dollar. Figure 13.10 depicts the one-year LIBOR of the US dollar and Shanghai Interbank Offered Rate (Shibor) of the same period from January 2006 to March 2014, as well as the dynamic path of interest rate difference and the exchange rate of RMB against the US dollar. It can be seen from the figure that before September 2006, the trend of interest rate difference between China and the United States was basically consistent with the path of RMB appreciation, and the two curves were relatively consistent. The interest rate difference seemed to be determined by the appreciation

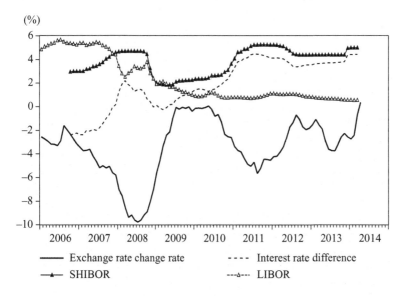

Figure 13.10 One-year interest rate difference between China and the United States and RMB appreciation: January 2006–March 2014. Source: Federal Reserve St. Louis Branch, CEIC database.

range of RMB. However, in fact, the development and change of the domestic economic situations of China and the United States are the leading factors that affect the change of interest rate. Since 2007, China's domestic inflation pressure has become increasingly prominent, and the monetary authorities have responded strongly to domestic inflation. Therefore, the tight monetary policy of shrinking credit and tightening money was fixed at the end of 2007. In this context, China's interest rate level began to rise gradually. Since 2008, the United States has been pursuing an ultra-low interest rate policy. From Figure 13.10, it can be clearly seen that the American interest rate has been significantly lower than that of China since 2009, bringing pressure to the appreciation trend of the US dollar exchange rate in the long run.

Of course, the evaluation of the RMB exchange rate trend based on purchasing power parity and interest rate parity is based on the long-term perspective. In the short term, the trend of the RMB exchange rate will also be affected by many factors such as the short-term economic outlook, investor sentiment, policy intention, and the international political climate of the two countries. But on the whole, the two-way fluctuation of the RMB exchange rate in 2014 will be significantly enhanced, and the fluctuation range will also be expanded. An overall trend of a slight depreciation of RMB relative to the US dollar in 2014 is a high-probability event. If the long-term prediction is made for the next two to five years, the RMB may face the pressure of depreciation in the long term. It is predicted that the RMB may depreciate by 5–10% in five years, that is to say, the exchange rate of RMB against the US dollar may be revised back from 6.2 to 6.5 or even 6.8.

Of course, from the perspective of the long-term development trend of the world economy, it is possible to form a four-pillar world monetary pattern of the US dollar, euro, RMB, and yen in the next five years or so (to 2020), and the value of the four currencies will reach a phased equilibrium state of 1:1:6.5:100. However, for the healthy development of China's economy and even the world economy, what is urgently needed is not the rapid appreciation or devaluation of RMB, but to maintain the relative stability of the exchange rate and realize two-way floating, so as to gradually improve the RMB exchange rate formation mechanism. At the same time, with the increasing complexity of capital control, China needs to further increase the flexibility of capital control, and actively introduce supporting policies and regulations to strengthen the supervision and control of the monetary authorities over the inflow of capital, especially short-term capital. On this basis, we should increase the innovation of monetary policy tools, strive for sufficient buffer time for the process of interest rate liberalization, and provide sufficient time for export-oriented enterprises to adjust their structure and gain their advantages. Therefore, in the process of gradual improvement of infrastructure at the micro and macro levels, it is still the right choice for China to deal with the challenges of domestic and foreign imbalances and maintain long-term and stable economic development by gradually realizing the balance and transition of the exchange rate mechanism.

14 Globalization and inflation dynamics

14.1 The Myth of High Growth and Low Inflation and Globalization

Since the mid-1990s, China's inflation has featured a low and stable performance. It can be seen from the previous chapters of this book that in the mid-1990s, China's CPI inflation reached its peak of more than 20%, but since then it has gradually declined. Although there was a significant increase in 2004, 2007, and 2010, the general trend has been relatively stable, with the peak level under 10%. China's low inflation and rapid economic growth in the same period formed a striking contrast, which was named in academic circles (such as Gong and Wei, 2007) as the Myth of High Growth and Low Inflation. The myth is not the focus of this chapter, but the phenomenon of high domestic economic growth that is not accompanied by long-term high inflation has inspired us to think about the international factors that influence domestic inflation.

For example, will the supply and demand of the international market also affect the pricing strategy and pricing mechanism of domestic enterprises, thus significantly impacting domestic inflation, and even exceeding the driving effect of the traditional domestic supply and demand factors (i.e. domestic output gap) on inflation? To this end, it can be especially noticed that since the middle and late 1990s, China's trade with other countries has become increasingly frequent. Cross-border economic activities have greatly promoted the economic ties between China and the rest of the world through direct and indirect channels, and China is more deeply involved in economic globalization. In this context, the factors of globalization may be transmitted from the international market to the domestic market through various channels, thus affecting the formation mechanism of domestic prices and inflation. Obviously, if the factors of globalization significantly affect the trend of domestic inflation, then the macro-policy adjustment related to inflation needs to expand from the domestic perspective to the international perspective.

However, in recent years, there has been a heated debate on whether the factors of globalization should be included in domestic inflation drivers, and there is no consensus in the existing research. For example, Tootell (1998) took the overseas output gap of the six major trading partners of the United States as an indicator variable of factors of globalization; estimating the traditional Phillips curve model in the United States with the data from 1973 to 1996, it turned out that no evidence has been found of the impact of globalization on domestic inflation in the United States. Gamber and Hung (2001) also studied the impact of globalization on inflation in the United States under the framework of the traditional Phillips Curve model, but with the number of major trading partners increased to 35 and the sample interval updated to 1999. Their results showed that the factors of globalization have a positive impact on inflation in the United States, but only at a level of 10% can the impact be statistically significant. If the trading partners are OECD countries, then the impact of globalization indicator variables (measured by the overseas output gap) on US inflation is no longer significant (Hooper et al., 2006). In view of the weak empirical evidence in the United States, Ball (2006) argued that factors of globalization could barely have a significant impact on domestic inflation because domestic firm pricing is mainly influenced by domestic excess demand on its marginal cost, with little relevance to the international market. But this conclusion seems to be more applicable to closed economies or small open countries. For large open countries like China, the situation may be different.

Recently, Borio and Filardo (2007) gave evidence supporting the impact of globalization on inflation in OECD countries. This paper observes the relationship between globalization and domestic inflation in 17 OECD countries from 1985 to 2005 based on the traditional Phillips Curve model. It is found that the weighted average foreign output gap has a significant positive impact on domestic inflation and shows an upward trend. However, the traditional Phillips Curve model of Borio and Filardo (2007) is too rigid, and the foreign output gap calculated by the specific trade proportion is a fixed weight, so the result is not robust. After re-using the time-varying trade share to update the weight of the foreign output gap, Ihrig and other researchers (2010) found that the globalization factor had no significant driving effect on inflation in OECD countries.

Compared with foreign countries, China has done fewer studies on globalization and inflation. However, we note that a recent article (Zhang and Li, 2010) has conducted a more in-depth study on globalization and inflation. But it analyzes the panel data based on emerging market countries as a whole, which may not fully reflect the characteristics of China's price formation mechanism. More importantly, the existing documents are similar to the most of the documents mentioned above in terms of the setup of models, which are based on the traditional Philips Curve model without taking into consideration the dynamic mechanism of inflation based on the microfoundation and structural characteristics. The theoretical basis of such models is relatively weak. Although it can be more convenient to directly introduce the elements of globalization into macro-analysis, the specific forms of introducing variables (dynamic or static) are arbitrary, resulting in a lack of strict constraints on the manifestations of macro-models. This is a common problem in existing literature.

In fact, for the micro-dynamic inflation mechanism model (especially the New Keynesian Phillips curve model), researchers represented by Roberts (1995), and Gali and Gertler (1999) have provided an epoch-making theoretical basis. Under such a theoretical framework, studies done by Wang et al. (2001), Ceng et al. (2006), Li and Wang (2011), and Yang (2011) have given important inspiration for further analysis of China's inflation problem. On the basis of this literature, this chapter introduces the factors of globalization into the pricing mechanism of micro firms based strictly on the micro theoretical foundation, and then constructs the inflation dynamic mechanism model with factors of globalization based on the microfoundation instead of subjectively adding the factors of globalization directly to the macro-inflation model, which is essentially different from the existing studies (such as Zhang and Li, 2010).

In the process of constructing the theoretical model, we should not only avoid deviating from the basic theoretical hypothesis, but also avoid sequence correlation caused by fossilized dynamic mechanism setting to the empirical model. In the empirical analysis, this chapter also creatively takes advantage of the projection technology of instrumental variable information set to avoid introducing additional random noise information caused by directly obtaining the inflation expectation sequence from a rational expectation hypothesis. This method further makes it possible to test the sequence correlation of econometric models. Although this expansion seems to be only a small step forward, it is crucial to improving the accuracy and scientific nature of the analysis results. Therefore, the main contribution of this chapter is the expansion of theoretical models based on a microfoundation and prudent innovation in the process of quantitative analysis.

14.2 Inflation dynamics with globalization

In the process of analyzing the influence mechanism of globalization on inflation, the key is to build a rigorous theoretical model. Such a model should not only reflect the impact of factors of globalization on the domestic inflation rate from the macro mechanism, but also cannot be separated from the micro basis of the modern inflation dynamic mechanism theory. Therefore, in the construction of the theoretical model, based on the New Keynesian sticky-price theory, we introduce the factors of globalization into the micro manufacturer pricing mechanism, and deduce the inflation dynamic mechanism model with factors of globalization from the micro mechanism, so that the obtained macro theoretical model has a solid micro basis. We will see later that this model is essentially a New Keynesian Phillips curve model widely used in modern macroeconomic analysis, but this chapter has carefully and reasonably expanded the specific forms of the dynamic mechanism and the introduction of globalization indicators. This expansion makes the empirical analysis described hereunder more consistent with China's inflation mechanism.

Specifically, we take the classic sticky-price theory as the basis, but there are two key differences in the specific pricing model of micro enterprises. Firstly, in the traditional sticky-price theory model (Taylor, 1980; Rotemberg, 1982; Calvo, 1983), it is generally assumed that micro enterprises only pay attention to future inflation and real economic performance in the process of pricing their products, an assumption which belongs to the so-called "forward-looking" pricing model.

Although Gali and Gertler (1999) creatively divide enterprise pricing into "forward-looking" and "backward-looking," the historical inflation rate considered in the model is only one period behind, which is quite different from the reality. This problem will lead to the rigidity of the final macro theoretical model, resulting in significant sequence correlation in the empirical model, which makes the follow-up econometric analysis invalid. Therefore, on the basis of the traditional sticky-price theory, we not only consider the "forward-looking" and "backward-looking" enterprise pricing models, but also allow "backward-looking" enterprises to consider the weighted average form of the multi-period historical inflation rate in pricing, so as to make the theoretical assumptions more close to the reality.

Secondly, the existing micro enterprise pricing theory does not consider the influence of factors of globalization. But as mentioned in the first section, with the deepening of globalization, the operation of foreign economies (especially the economic trend of major trading partner countries) influences the product-pricing mode of all kinds of enterprises imperceptibly. This kind of influence is not limited to trade products, because the operation of foreign economies will affect the international commodity market and factor market, and then transmit to all levels of the domestic market. Therefore, we introduce the factor of globalization (foreign output gap) into the pricing mechanism of micro enterprises, and assume that the "forward-looking" enterprises not only consider the domestic economic operation in the future, but also consider the foreign economic operation in the pricing process, so as to improve the micro pricing mechanism of enterprises.

According to the above description, we assume that in the economic environment of monopoly competition, enterprises at the micro level have the ability to price their products. At the same time, it is assumed that all enterprises maintain a fixed price level for a certain period of time, and they will not consider re-pricing until they are affected by some random signals. In this way, the price adjustment has "Stickiness." At the same time, when enterprises are pricing, they will consider the price level set by other relevant enterprises in the past, that is to say, a certain enterprise will consider the past price situation when setting the current price of products. Now it is assumed that the probability that an enterprise will change its price in any given period is $1-\theta(0<\theta<1)$, and p_t is the total price level of period t (natural logarithm form, the same below). This price is determined by the weighted sum of the total price level of the previous period and the newly established price level of all enterprises in period t $\left(p_t^*\right)$, that is

$$p_t = \theta p_{t-1} + (1-\theta)p_t^* \tag{14.1}$$

In the original model of Calvo (1983), it is assumed that all enterprises have "forward-looking" characteristics in the pricing process, that is, the price is completely determined by a company's rational expectation of the future domestic economic operation. However, since the end of the 20th century, the academic community has reached a basic consensus that there will always be a certain proportion of enterprises in the economic performance to adopt the "back-end" pricing method. In the process of setting prices, they will refer to the past industry pricing standards, and at the same time, they will revise the prices according to the historical inflation rate. Therefore, we assume that the enterprises with a ratio of ω adopt the "backward-looking" pricing model, and the price is p_t^B, while the enterprises with a ratio of $1 - \omega$ adopt the "forward-looking" pricing mechanism, and the level is p_t^F. In this way, the new price level (relative to the overall price level) determined by all enterprises in period t can be expressed as

$$p_t^* = (1-\omega)p_t^F + \omega p_t^B \tag{14.2}$$

The price level p_t^F set by "forward-looking" enterprises is generally in the traditional sticky-price theory as the discounted sum (such as Gali and Gertler, 1999) of the expected total output gap (namely, the natural logarithm difference between real GDP and potential GDP) and the inflation rate (e.g. Gali and Gertler, 1999). Considering that "forward-looking" enterprises pay special attention to future economic trends in the pricing process, and naturally pay attention to the global economic situation when pricing products in the context of globalization, we modify the traditional assumptions to allow "forward-looking" enterprises to consider the elements of globalization in pricing. From the perspective of the impact mechanism, in the case of a high degree of globalization, a foreign output gap can first affect foreign commodity prices, and then affect domestic manufacturers' pricing decisions through import prices. The output gap of foreign countries may also affect the pricing of enterprises through the factor market. In fact, globalization to some extent weakens the relationship between domestic output and demand, which may reduce the sensitivity of enterprise pricing to a domestic output gap, that is, the impact of a domestic output gap is partially transferred to the foreign output gap.

Therefore, the pricing model of "forward-looking" enterprises can be written as:

$$p_t^F = \theta\beta \sum_{s=0}^{\infty} (\theta\beta)^s E_t\pi_{t+s+1} + (1-\theta\beta) \sum_{s=0}^{\infty} (\theta\beta)^s E_t\zeta \left(k_y^d y_{t+s}^d + k_y^f y_{t+s}^f \right) \tag{14.3}$$

Where π_t represents inflation rate, $E_t\pi_{t+1}$ represents the predicted inflation rate of the $t + 1$ period based on time t and previous information set, β represents the subjective discount factor, and ζ is the structural parameter introduced in the process of logarithmic linearization (ζ has economic meaning, see Woodford, 2003 for details). In addition, y_t^d and y_t^f represent the domestic output gap and foreign output gap respectively, and k_y^d and k_y^f measure the corresponding weight of the domestic and foreign output gap respectively. It is not difficult to see that when the weight of the foreign output gap is 0, Equation 14.3 is completely consistent with the model in the traditional literature. Further iterations of Equation 14.3 can rewrite the pricing model of "forward-looking" enterprises in the following form:

$$p_t^F = \theta\beta E_t\pi_{t+1} + (1-\theta\beta)\zeta \left(k_y^d y_t^d + k_y^f y_t^f \right) + \theta\beta E_t p_{t+1}^F \tag{14.4}$$

For the pricing mechanism of "backward-looking" enterprises, we expand the inflation rate lag in the traditional literature, namely

$$p_t^B = p_{t-1}^* + \pi_{t-1} + \rho^*(L)\Delta\pi_{t-1} \tag{14.5}$$

Where $\rho^*(L) = \rho_1^* + \rho_2^* L + \rho_3^* L^2 + \ldots + \rho_q^* L^{q-1}$ denotes the polynomial of the lag operator, and q denotes the order of lag. In the empirical analysis, the value of q needs to be determined according to AIC and the sequence correlation test.

According to Equations 14.1–14.5, we can obtain the macro-inflation dynamic mechanism model based on the micro enterprise pricing mechanism

$$\pi_t = c + \gamma_e E_t \pi_{t+1} + \gamma_b \pi_{t-1} + \sum_{i=1}^{q-1} \alpha_i \Delta\pi_{t-i} + \delta_d y_t^d + \delta_f y_t^f + \eta_t \tag{14.6}$$

Where c is a constant term, η_t is a random disturbance term, and the other coefficients are intuitively explained in Equation 14.6. These coefficients are the combination of the underlying structural parameters in the micro model of Equations 14.1–14.5, namely

$$\begin{cases} \gamma_e = \theta\beta\psi^{-1} \\ \gamma_b = \left[(1-\omega) - \theta\beta(1-\omega)(1-\theta)\rho_1^*\right]\psi^{-1} \\ \alpha_i = (1-\omega)(1-\theta)\left[\rho^*(L) + \theta\beta\rho'(L)\right]\psi^{-1} \\ \delta_d = k_y^d \omega(1-\theta\beta)(1-\theta)\varsigma\psi^{-1} \\ \delta_f = k_y^f \omega(1-\theta\beta)(1-\theta)\varsigma\psi^{-1} \\ \psi = \theta + (1-\omega)(1-\theta) + \theta\beta(1-\omega) + \theta\beta(1-\omega)(1-\theta)\rho_1^* \\ \rho^*(L) = \rho_1^* + \rho_2^* L + \ldots + \rho_q^* L^{q-1} \end{cases} \tag{14.7}$$

Compared with the existing literature, the inflation dynamic model of Equation 14.6, based on the expansion of the micro basis, not only has the basic characteristics of the New Keynesian Phillips curve, but also adds a richer dynamic mechanism. At the same time, it introduces the key index variables of globalization, which can be used as the benchmark model for analyzing the inflation dynamic mechanism in the context of globalization.

It should be noted that the coefficients γ_e and γ_b in Equation 14.6 respectively measure the impact of inflation expectations and inflation inertia (or persistence) on the current inflation rate. From the perspective of New Keynesian economics, if γ_b is not zero, it shows that not only is the price level rigid, but also the inflation rate itself is sticky. For the comparison of the size of γ_e and γ_b, the mainstream research represented by Gali and Gertler (1999) assumes that rational expectation should be dominant in the New Keynesian Phillips curve theoretical model, that is, γ_e is much larger than γ_b. But whether this conclusion is suitable for China, there is no convincing research conclusion at present. Even for developed countries (such as the United States), recent studies (such as Zhang et al., 2008, 2009) have given conclusions opposite to Gali and Gertler. In addition, the corresponding coefficients δ_d and δ_f of the domestic output gap and foreign output gap respectively measure the pressure level of the domestic and foreign output gap on the current inflation rate. If δ_f is significantly greater than zero, it shows that the operation of foreign economies has a significant impact on the level of domestic inflation. Of course, the specific values of the above parameters need to be determined through empirical analysis.

14.3 Domestic and foreign output gaps and dynamic mechanism of inflation

The basic variables involved in this chapter include the inflation rate, domestic output gap, and foreign output gap. According to the availability of relevant variables of China and its major trading partners, the sample interval is between the first quarter of 1995 and the fourth quarter of 2010. The inflation rate is measured by the year-on-year growth rate of CPI, and the original data are from the National Bureau of Statistics. The gap in domestic output is calculated on the basis of GDP (i.e. real GDP) calculated at constant prices. At present, China has not directly published the quarterly real GDP data, so we take 1997 as the base period, and calculate the real GDP quarterly data according to the nominal GDP quarterly data published by the National Bureau of statistics since 1992 and the constant price growth rate in the corresponding period. Then, we adjust the real GDP series on a quarterly basis, and then get the real GDP gap through the standard HP filter, as a measure of the domestic output gap.

For the foreign output gap, we consider the 17 most important trading partners of China's mainland (Hong Kong, Indonesia, Japan, Malaysia, Singapore, South Korea, Thailand, Taiwan, UK, Germany, France, Italy, Netherlands, Russia, Canada, the United States, and Australia), and a weighted average the real GDP gap calculation of the major trading partners (based on HP filtering). The GDP data of countries and regions are from the CEIC database. The weight of each country and region in the gap calculation is determined according to its trade proportion to the mainland of China (changing year by year), that is, the ratio of the total import and export between each trading partner and the mainland of China to the total trade between the mainland of China and 17 countries and regions. For a clearer explanation, Table 14.1 reports the trade share of 17 major trading partners of China's mainland between 1995 and 2010.

According to the average situation between 1995 and 2010, Japan, the United States, Hong Kong, South Korea, Taiwan, Germany, Singapore, Russia, Australia, and the United Kingdom are the top ten trading partners of China. However, from the specific data of each year, the trade proportion of each trading partner changes year by year (for example, after 2004, the United States replaced Japan as China's largest trading partner). As the proportion of trade between countries and regions and the mainland of China is changing every year, in the process of calculating the foreign output gap, we calculate it year by year according to the specific value of the proportion of trade between countries and the corresponding real GDP gap in

Table 14.1 Proportion of trade of mainland China's 17 main trade partners with mainland China (%)

Year	Australia	Canada	France	Germany	Hong Kong, China	Indonesia	Italy	Japan	South Korea	Malaysia	The Netherlands	Russia	Singapore	Thailand	Taiwan, China	UK	US
1995	1.8	1.8	1.9	5.7	18.5	1.5	2.2	23.9	7.1	1.4	1.7	2.3	2.9	1.4	7.4	2.0	17.0
1996	2.1	1.7	1.7	5.3	16.4	1.5	2.1	24.2	8.0	1.5	1.8	2.8	3.0	1.3	7.6	2.1	17.2
1997	1.9	1.4	2.0	4.6	18.4	1.6	1.7	22.1	8.7	1.6	2.0	2.2	3.2	1.3	7.2	2.1	17.8
1998	1.9	1.6	2.2	5.3	16.7	1.3	1.8	21.3	7.8	1.6	2.2	2.0	3.0	1.4	7.5	2.4	20.1
1999	2.1	1.6	2.2	5.3	14.5	1.6	1.9	21.9	8.3	1.8	2.1	1.9	2.8	1.4	7.8	2.6	20.3
2000	2.2	1.8	2.0	5.1	14.0	1.9	1.8	21.6	9.0	2.1	2.1	2.1	2.8	1.7	7.9	2.6	19.3
2001	2.2	1.8	1.9	5.7	13.6	1.6	1.9	21.3	8.7	2.3	2.1	2.6	2.7	1.7	7.9	2.5	19.6
2002	2.1	1.6	1.7	5.6	13.9	1.6	1.8	20.4	8.8	2.9	2.1	2.4	2.8	1.7	8.9	2.3	19.5
2003	2.0	1.5	2.0	6.3	13.1	1.5	1.8	20.0	9.5	3.0	2.3	2.4	2.9	1.9	8.8	2.2	18.9
2004	2.3	1.8	2.0	6.1	12.7	1.5	1.8	18.9	10.1	3.0	2.4	2.4	3.0	2.0	8.8	2.2	19.1
2005	2.6	1.8	1.9	5.9	12.8	1.6	1.7	17.2	10.5	2.9	2.7	2.7	3.1	2.0	8.5	2.3	19.8
2006	2.6	1.8	2.0	6.1	12.9	1.5	1.9	16.1	10.4	2.9	2.7	2.6	3.2	2.2	8.4	2.4	20.4
2007	2.9	2.0	2.2	6.1	12.8	1.6	2.0	15.3	10.4	3.0	3.0	3.1	3.1	2.3	8.1	2.6	19.6
2008	3.4	2.0	2.2	6.6	11.7	1.8	2.2	15.3	10.7	3.1	3.0	3.3	3.0	2.4	7.4	2.6	19.2
2009	4.0	2.0	2.3	7.0	11.6	1.9	2.1	15.1	10.3	3.4	2.8	2.6	3.2	2.5	7.0	2.6	19.7
2010	4.4	1.8	2.2	7.1	11.5	2.1	2.2	14.8	10.3	3.7	2.8	2.8	2.8	2.6	7.2	2.5	19.2

Notes: Data herein are the total trade volume of a certain country or region with mainland China/total trade volume between China and the aforesaid 17 countries or regions; the raw data are obtained from the CEIC database. The trade partners are selected based on the availability of trade data on mainland China and main economies of the world as furnished by the CEIC database.

that year, and finally obtain the series of foreign output gap in the sample interval. Of course, before calculating the output gap, all real GDP figures are seasonally adjusted.

According to the above description, Figure 14.1 depicts the dynamic timing path of the CPI inflation rate and output gap at home and abroad from the first quarter of 1995 to the fourth quarter of 2010. It can be seen from the figure that the domestic output gap and the foreign output gap have a certain periodicity in the overall change trend, but there are obvious differences in the specific change dynamic potential at each time point, especially the location and time of the peak and trough. At the same time, Figure 14.1 shows that China's inflation rate has gradually fallen from a high of nearly 20% in 1995. Although it has maintained a relatively stable trend in general, it also has relatively obvious ups and downs in different years. For example, in 1998, 2002, and 2009, China's inflation rate was negative (i.e. deflation); in 2004, 2007, and 2010, the inflation rate once again rose to a cyclical high.

It is worth noting that, although the fluctuation of domestic inflation level is generally consistent with the trend of the domestic output gap, the phenomenon of the domestic output gap rising but the inflation rate falling (such as 1998, 2002, 2005) also appears in some periods. Compared with the domestic output gap, the foreign output gap is smoother, and the cyclical change seems to be more consistent with the trend of the domestic inflation rate. It can also be seen from the figure that the trough of the foreign output gap in 1998, 2003, 2005, and 2009 is completely consistent with the lowest point of the domestic inflation rate in the

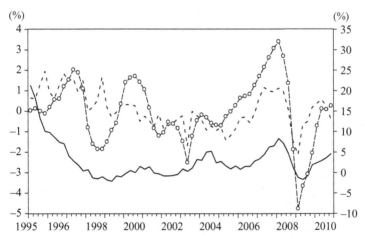

Figure 14.1 CPI inflation rate and output gap at home and abroad: Q1 1995–Q4 2010.
Source: The original data are from the CEIC database and calculated by the author.

same period, and the peak of the foreign output gap in 2001, 2004, 2007, and 2010 is also highly consistent with the peak of the domestic inflation rate. The information provided in Figure 14.1 suggests that globalization may be an important factor in the study of domestic inflation dynamics.

In addition, there are several explanations for the data in the empirical analysis. First of all, for the monthly frequency data (CPI inflation rate and M2), we use the observation value of the last month of each quarter as the corresponding quarterly data to avoid the introduction of additional sequence correlation in the frequency conversion process, which affects the accuracy of measurement estimation (especially the standard deviation estimation of relevant parameters) in empirical analysis. Secondly, from the following analysis, we will see that the year-on-year growth rate of China's broad money M2 should also be used as a instrumental variable in the empirical estimation. In order to ensure the reliability of measurement and statistical inference, we test the stationarity of all time series data including the M2 growth rate. According to the standard unit root test results (ADF and PP unit root test), for all variables studied in this chapter, the original hypothesis that the variable contains the unit root can be rejected at a 5% significance level, so all variables are stationary series. Because the unit root test is a routine standardized test, it is not reported here.

14.4   Does globalization affect inflation dynamics: An empirical analysis

Based on the relevant data introduced above, this part estimates Equation 14.6, in the hope of obtaining relatively reliable parameter estimation results through a scientific and rigorous econometric analysis process so as to judge whether the globalization factors represented by the foreign output gap are the significant driving factors of domestic inflation and to obtain the influence degree of inflation expectations and inflation inertia on the spot inflation rate. Although Equation 14.6 is not complex in form, it is not easy to make a regression estimation and obtain scientific and stable results. In particular, it should be noted that Equation 14.6 is a dynamic model, and contains rational expectation variables and output gap variables of the current period (rather than the lag period). This requires that we should carefully deal with three key problems in the measurement and estimation, namely, the endogenous problem, the measurement of inflation expectations, and the sequential correlation problem. As can be seen from the following discussion, regardless of which problem is ignored, the measurement results will be distorted or even wrong.

14.4.1 Endogenous problems

Because the independent variables in Equation 14.6 include inflation expectations and immediate output gap variables, the endogeneity of the model must be considered. Specifically, because inflation expectations are based on all the relevant information before period t, the stochastic factors (such as a supply shock caused by the change of international oil prices) that affect the spot inflation rate are likely to also affect inflation expectations. At the same time, according to the standard macroeconomic analysis framework (such as Stock and Watson, 2002), the random factors affecting the spot inflation rate are likely to affect the spot output gap (both at home and abroad). Therefore, there may be a non-orthogonal relationship between the disturbance term and the independent variable in Equation 14.6, that is, there is an endogenous problem.

In practice, we use Durbin–Wu–Hausman test to confirm that the original hypothesis of "statistical consistency of least squares estimation" is rejected at the traditional significance level. For this reason, the regression estimation of Equation 14.6 needs to use the instrumental variable estimation method to obtain the point estimation value and the corresponding standard deviation of the parameters. It should be noted that the basic idea of the Durbin–Wu–Hausman test is to compare the parameter estimation vectors of least square estimation and instrumental variable estimation, and construct statistics subject to chi-square distribution for test. Of course, in practice, based on the combination of projection matrix of independent variable and instrumental variable, we test the hypothesis through the standard Frisch Waugh Lovell principle in econometric analysis. See Durbin (1954), Wu (1973), Hausman (1978), Davidson and MacKinnon (1989) for the specific process.

For the selection of instrumental variables, we should not only consider the economic relationship between instrumental variables and their respective variables in the model, but also consider the rationality of the number of instrumental variables relative to the sample size, and ensure that the instrumental variables are independent of the disturbance term. Therefore, we choose the output gap at home and abroad and the 1–2 lag term of China's M2 growth rate as instrumental variables. In addition, the constant term and the lag term of all inflation rates on the right side of the model (in practice, AIC and the sequence correlation test introduced below jointly determine the lag term of five periods) are also included in the instrumental variable set. The rationality of instrumental variable selection is further determined according to Hansen's (1982) J test. The original hypothesis of this test is that all instrumental variables are exogenous. If the original hypothesis is not rejected, it indicates that the selection of instrumental variables is relatively reasonable.

14.4.2 The measurement of inflation expectations

For the measurement of inflation expectations, it is a standard practice to obtain inflation expectation data through the rational expectation hypothesis. In essence, this method uses the real inflation rate of the $t + 1$ period to represent the expected value of the inflation rate, i.e.

$$E_t \pi_{t+1} = \pi_{t+1} - e_{t+1} \tag{14.8}$$

Where e_{t+1} indicates rational expectation error. This method of obtaining inflation expectation series can be traced back to the early literature of McCallum (1976),

Cumby et al. (1983), and Hayashi and SIMS (1983), and is also used in important literature of Roberts (1995) and Gali and Gertler (1999).

Although inflation expectation data can be easily obtained by the rational expectation hypothesis directly, we can see from Equation 14.8 that this kind of rational expectation processing method will inevitably introduce additional noise information, that is, a rational expectation error e_{t+1}. At this time, a disturbance term η_t is no longer used to estimate Equation 14.6, but a compound disturbance term $u_t = \eta_t - \gamma_e e_{t+1}$. In this case, the standard deviation of the disturbance term estimated by the model actually becomes $\sqrt{\sigma_\eta^2 + \sigma_e^2 - 2\sigma_{\eta e}}$ (σ^2 represents variance, $\sigma_{\eta e}$ represents covariance). Even if the error term η_t of the original model is orthogonal to the rational expected error, the accuracy of the final estimated standard deviation will be affected.

In addition, because we use the rational expectation hypothesis to obtain the inflation expectation series directly, and actually deal with the compound disturbance term, it will bring another very critical problem, that is, we can't test whether the original disturbance term η_t in Equation 14.6 has sequence correlation. Since Equation 14.6 is a dynamic model, if η_t has sequence correlation, then strictly speaking, using any lag term as a instrumental variable cannot give effective estimation results. Of course, even if η_t can be stripped out, the traditional sequence correlation test is not suitable for dynamic models such as Equation 14.6 under the estimation of instrumental variables. This issue will be discussed more clearly below.

Therefore, in order to avoid the above problems caused by the direct use of the rational expectation hypothesis to obtain inflation expectation series, we use Pagan (1984) for reference, and use the projection technology of the instrumental variable information set to obtain the inflation expectation series. Specifically, we do not deviate from the hypothesis of rational expectation, but we do differ from the traditional way in technical treatment, that is, instead of directly substituting π_{t+1} into the econometric model, we use the projection of π_{t+1} on the given instrumental variable information set matrix Z to obtain the inflation expectation sequence, namely

$$E_t \pi_{t+1} = P_Z \pi_{t+1} \tag{14.9}$$

Where P_Z is the standard projection matrix $\left(P_Z = Z(Z'Z)^{-1}Z'\right)$. It can be proved that this projection technology has no effect on the point estimation of 2SLS, and the standard deviation obtained by regression is more accurate in theory (because it avoids the interference of additional noise information on the estimation of the variance–covariance matrix), and solves the problem that the sequence correlation of disturbance items in the original model cannot be tested.

14.4.3 Sequence correlation

As mentioned above, whether Equation 14.6) can obtain reliable estimation results depends on another key problem, namely sequence correlation. For the dynamic model of Equation 14.6, if the disturbance term has sequence correlation, it means that the inflation lag term is not orthogonal to the disturbance term, which will lead to the correlation between the lag term of other relevant time series variables and the disturbance term. At this time, even if we use instrumental variable regression, the results do not have statistical consistency and are biased. Therefore, when estimating Equation 14.6, it is necessary to test whether the model has sequence correlation. However, the traditional sequential correlation test (such as the Breusch–Godfrey test) is invalid in instrumental variable estimation mode. In fact, since the 1980s, the field of econometrics has been paying attention to the serial correlation test under the estimation of instrumental variables, especially after a series of studies by Godfrey et al. (1988), Davidson and MacKinnon (1993), Cumby and Huizinga (1992), and Godfrey (1994), which has developed quite well, but has not received enough attention and application in the study of the inflation dynamic mechanism.

For this reason, we test Equation 14.6 according to the sequence correlation test method proposed by Godfrey (1994) under the estimation of instrumental variables. Because the introduction of this test in the existing literature mostly stays at the theoretical level, which is not convenient for researchers to practice (such as writing programs), we briefly explain the core content of this test here. Its basic idea is based on the following auxiliary regression equation:

$$\tilde{\eta}_t = Xb + \rho(L)\tilde{\eta}_{t-1} + \varepsilon_t \tag{14.10}$$

Where $\rho(L)$ is the polynomial of the lag operator, $\tilde{\eta}$ is the residual sequence obtained after the estimation of the instrumental variable (2SLS) in the original model, X is the independent matrix in the original Equation 14.6, and ε is the disturbance term of the auxiliary equation (heteroscedasticity is allowed, but sequence correlation is not allowed). For convenience of explanation, we need to rewrite Equation 14.10 into the following vector form:

$$\tilde{\eta} = X_1 b + X_2 \rho + \varepsilon \tag{14.11}$$

Where X_1 represents the independent variable matrix of the original model, and X_2 represents the lag term of $\tilde{\eta}$ in Equation 14.10. Now suppose that the original set of instrumental variables is Z, then the instrumental variables used to estimate the auxiliary Equation 14.10 or 14.11 must include the lag term $\tilde{\eta}$ on the basis of Z, and the expanded set of instrumental variables is represented by W. In addition, the projection matrix $P_W = W(W'W)^{-1}W$ (other projection matrices) is defined, and $\tilde{\varepsilon}_r$ is the residual sequence corresponding to Equation 14.11 when $\tilde{X}_i = P_W X_i\,(i=1,2)$, $M_1 = I - P_{\tilde{X}_1}$ (I is the unit matrix), $S_r^2 = \tilde{\varepsilon}_r'\tilde{\varepsilon}_r\,/\,(T-r)$ (T represents the sample size, r represents the dimension of matrix X_2).

In this way, we can test whether $\tilde{\eta}$ has sequence correlation by calculating the following LM statistics (the original assumption is $\rho = 0$):

$$LM = \tilde{\eta}' P_{M_1 \tilde{X}_2} \tilde{\eta}\,/\,rS_r^2 \tag{14.12}$$

Where r is the number of constraints, and the test statistics are asymptotically distributed near $F_{(r,T-r)}$. We calculate and report the p-value corresponding to the statistic in the empirical analysis. Note that according to Kiviet (1986), the missing value of $\tilde{\eta}$ caused by the lag operation needs to be interpolated with 0 in order to make the test result more accurate.

14.4.4 Estimation results

According to the above description, Table 14.2 reports the instrumental variable estimation (2SLS) results of Equation 14.6, in which columns (1) to (4) are the estimated values and standard deviations of the core parameters in the model, column (5) shows the p-values of the joint significance test for all the lag terms of inflation rate in Equation 14.6, and columns (6) and (7) report the Godfrey (1994) instrumental variable sequence correlation test. In the last column, the goodness of fit statistic correction R^2 is reported. In addition, in the process of estimating Equation 14.6, we also investigated the situation when the coefficients of inflation expectations and inflation inertia meet the convex combination constraint (i.e. $\gamma_e + \gamma_f = 1$). The results are reported in the last row of Table 14.2. Because there is a high degree of correlation between inflation expectation series and inflation lag term, the convex combination constraint can effectively alleviate the possible collinearity problem.

Based on the results reported in Table 14.2, we get the following important findings. Firstly, the coefficient δ_f of the foreign output gap is statistically significant at the level of 5% whether there is a convex combination constraint or not, and the point estimates are 0.10 and 0.09 respectively. This result shows that, with

Table 14.2 NKPC model estimation (2SLS) results with factors of globalization

	γ_e	γ_b	δ_d	δ_f	$p(\alpha_i)$	p-auto	p-J	$\bar{R}^2$
	(1)	(2)	(3)	(4)	(5)	(6)	(7)	(8)
	0.490***	0.495***	−0.015	0.102**	0.000	0.117	0.657	0.88
	(0.036)	(0.030)	(0.148)	(0.040)				
$\gamma_e+\gamma_f=1$	0.512***	0.488***	−0.005	0.091**	0.000	0.192	0.795	0.89
	(0.034)	(0.034)	(0.159)	(0.042)				

Note: The sample range is between the first quarter of 1995 and the fourth quarter of 2010; the optimal lag order of the model is determined as five according to AIC and the sequence correlation test (the maximum alternative order is eight); the instrumental variables are all lag terms of the inflation rate in the regression model, one to two lag terms of the domestic and foreign output gap, and one to two lag terms of China's M2 year-on-year growth rate; $p(\alpha_i)$ represents two to five lag terms of the inflation rate; p-auto refers to the p-value of Godfrey's (1994) instrumental variable sequence correlation test (the original assumption is no sequence correlation); p-J refers to the p-value of Hansen's (1982) J test (the original assumption is that all instrumental variables are exogenous); in parentheses, the Newey–West robustness standard deviation (HAC, fixed bandwidth) is reported; and *** and ** indicate the significance of the corresponding statistics at 1% and 5%, respectively. All the sequences were determined to be stationary by the unit root test.

other conditions unchanged, for every 1 percentage-point increase in the output gap of foreign countries, the domestic inflation rate will rise by 0.1 percentage point, that is to say, in the context of globalization, the development of foreign real economies will significantly affect the trend of the domestic price change rate. However, there is a sharp contrast between the estimated results of the domestic output gap coefficient and the corresponding results of the foreign output gap: The estimated value of the domestic output gap coefficient δ_d is not only very small in absolute value, but also not statistically significant.

Therefore, in the past 15 years or so, the impact of the economic operation of China's major trading partners on the inflation rate of domestic CPI has significantly exceeded the impact of the domestic output gap. This result provides an explanation for the phenomenon of a "low inflation rate and high growth rate" experienced by China in the past ten years (the puzzle of "Deflationary Expansion" in academic circles): Since the mid- and late 1990s, although the domestic economic growth has continued to run at a high level, the global economy (especially China's major trading partners) has generally grown slowly, and the period of excess supply (the gap is negative) has been significantly longer than that in China, thus significantly reducing domestic inflation pressure.

Secondly, the results of Table 14.2 show that the inflation inertia coefficient is slightly higher than the inflation expectation coefficient without constraints. Under the constraint of convex combination, the inflation expectation coefficient is slightly higher than the inflation inertia coefficient. That is to say, in 1995–2010, the driving effect of inflation expectations and inflation inertia on China's spot inflation rate is basically the same. At this point, the characteristics of China's inflation dynamic mechanism are obviously different from those of developed countries, especially the conclusion that rational expectations dominate the New Keynesian Phillips curve put forward by Gali and Gertler (1999). Because the contribution of expectations and inertia to inflation accounts for 50%, neither of them can be ignored in the analysis of the inflation-driving mechanism. This also implies that decision-makers should pay attention to the market expectations of future inflation and the historical performance of inflation in the process of inflation management.

Thirdly, from the *p*-value of the joint significance test of inflation rate lag, the test results are statistically significant (*p*-value is 0) with or without constraints. This shows that in reality, the pricing decisions of micro enterprises do take into account the inflation performance of previous periods, not limited to the lag information of the inflation rate in the first period. This result also shows that the inflation model described by the New Keynesian Phillips curve is more consistent with the reality after adding a more dynamic mechanism. At the same time, we note that the *p*-value of the Godfrey (1994) instrumental variable sequence correlation test is greater than 10% in all cases, which indicates that Equation 14.6 has no sequence correlation. This also ensures the validity of instrumental variable estimation in this chapter.

In practice, we also compare the estimation results of the model without increasing the multi-stage lag term of inflation rate (that is, Equation 14.6 only retains the one-stage lag term of inflation rate). The results show that the p-value of the correlation test of instrumental variables is less than 5%, which indicates that the disturbance term has significant sequence correlation due to the rigidity of the model. At the same time, the p-value of Hansen's (1982) J test and the result of modified R^2 reported in Table 14.2 show that the original hypothesis that the set of instrumental variables is exogenous cannot be rejected at the traditional significance level (that is, the selection of instrumental variables is reasonable), and the goodness of fit of the model is reasonable. All the above results show that the augmented model is more reasonable than the traditional model of Gali and Gertler (1999). In practice, we also use the inflation expectation series estimated by the unobservable component stochastic volatility model and the inflation expectation series transformed from the "future price expectation index" in the "table of income and price diffusion index of urban depositors" issued by the People's Bank of China to estimate the model, so as to avoid the possible impact of the rational expectation hypothesis on the conclusion, and then make the conclusion more convincing. The corresponding results are basically consistent with the conclusions in Table 14.2. To save space, these results are not reported here.

In addition, as a comparison, we estimate the model only considering domestic output gap (i.e. excluding foreign output gap variables in Equation 14.6) and report the corresponding results in Table 14.3. We note that if the model is set up to deliberately omit the foreign output gap, the point estimates of the domestic output gap will increase significantly (from –0.005 in Table 14.2 to 0.089), and the driving direction of the inflation rate is consistent with the traditional theory, although it is not statistically significant. The results in Table 14.3 suggest that in the process of modeling China's inflation dynamic mechanism, if the variables of the foreign output gap are ignored, the inflation-driving effect of the domestic output gap will become larger, because the impact of the foreign output gap is artificially transferred to the domestic output gap at this time, which may lead to misleading conclusions.

Of course, the estimation of the benchmark model of Equation 14.6 is based on the fixed sample interval from 1995 to 2010. In practice, it may be necessary to consider whether the driving effect of the foreign output gap on the domestic

Table 14.3 Estimation results of the NKPC model without factors of globalization (2SLS)

	γ_e	γ_b	δ_d	$p(\alpha)$	p-auto	p-over	$\bar{R}^2$
	0.477***	0.520***	0.089	0.000	0.097	0.436	0.87
	(0.110)	(0.066)	(0.111)				
$\gamma_e + \gamma_f = 1$	0.482***	0.518***	0.089	0.000	0.151	0.600	0.89
	(0.068)	(0.068)	(0.101)				

Note: The instrument variable does not include the lag term of the foreign output gap, and the rest are the same as in Table 14.2.

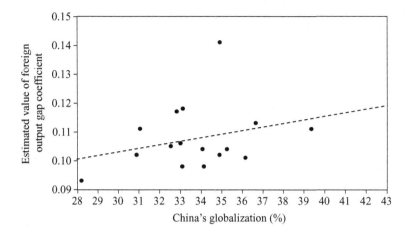

Figure 14.2 Scatter diagram of estimated output gap coefficient and globalization degree (dotted line in the figure is the regression fitting line).

inflation rate changes with the change of sample time, especially whether the impact of the foreign output gap on the domestic inflation rate (i.e. the coefficient) increases with the increasing degree of globalization. Therefore, we take the fourth quarter of 2010 as the end point of the sample, 1995 as the starting time, and gradually move forward from the starting time to the first quarter of 2000 (to ensure that the sample is not too small). In this way, we estimate the moving sample of Equation 14.6, so as to obtain a series of estimates of the foreign output gap coefficient corresponding to the variable sample interval. After obtaining the estimation results, we take the degree of globalization (trade openness) as the abscissa, and the estimated value of the foreign output gap coefficient as the ordinate, and draw the scatter diagram of the two in Figure 14.2. From the graph results, the estimated value of the output gap coefficient varies slightly with the sample starting point, but most of them are between 0.10 and 0.14, which is basically consistent with the results in Table 14.2. From the perspective of the overall change trend (i.e. the regression fitting line in Figure 14.2), the influence of the foreign output gap on the domestic inflation rate shows a trend of increasing with the increasing degree of globalization.

14.5 Conclusions

Based on the typical fact that the degree of economic globalization is increasing day by day, this chapter introduces the real GDP gap variables of 17 of China's major trading partners into the micro manufacturer pricing mechanism, and deduces the theoretical model of China's inflation dynamic mechanism from the micro basis. The theoretical model derived in this chapter not only has the basic characteristics of the New Keynesian Phillips curve model, but also adds the elements of globalization and a richer dynamic mechanism. This chapter uses the quarterly data from 1995 to 2010 to test the theoretical model. In the empirical analysis, we carefully consider the endogeneity, sequence correlation, and inflation expectation measurement of the model, and design new projection technology of instrumental variable information set to solve the impact of additional random noise information introduced by the rational expectation hypothesis on the estimation results. At the same time, we apply the sequence correlation test under instrumental variable estimation (unconventional sequence correlation test). It ensures the validity of measurement and estimation results.

Through rigorous theoretical derivation and econometric design, this chapter draws three main conclusions: Firstly, since 1995, the impact of the foreign output gap on inflation has significantly exceeded that of the domestic output gap. This means that the dynamic trend of domestic inflation in recent decades is closely related to the trend of the global economy, and the factors of foreign supply and demand have a systematic driving effect on domestic inflation through the international market. This result also suggests that the rapid growth of the domestic economy but relatively low inflation levels in the last decade may (at least to some extent) benefit from economic globalization. Secondly, both inflation expectations and inflation inertia have a significant impact on the domestic inflation rate, and the degree of impact is basically the same, there is no question of which is the dominant. Thirdly, to use the New Keynesian Phillips curve model to analyze China's inflation, more dynamic mechanisms must be added in order to effectively eliminate the sequence correlation and obtain scientific and reliable empirical results. If the problem of sequence correlation is ignored, the empirical analysis of the New Keynesian Phillips curve will collapse, to which the academic world should pay attention.

In short, under the increasingly open economic conditions, factors of globalization will affect the domestic price formation mechanism through the product market and the factor market. In the product market, the output gap affects the price of foreign products, and then affects the domestic price through the import price. In the factor market, foreign excess demand reflects the impact of labor and capital on domestic supply and demand, and then affects the domestic price formation mechanism. Insufficient domestic demand (or supply) can be offset by strong foreign demand (or supply exceeds demand). Therefore, globalization can adjust the imbalance of domestic supply and demand through the supply and demand of the external product market or factor market, and stabilize the domestic price level. This may explain the mystery of "deflationary expansion" of China's experience from one side.

From the perspective of development, with the progress of science and technology (including communication and transportation), the frequent trade cooperation, and the opening of international markets, the world economy will be more closely linked. Therefore, various factors of globalization that affect domestic inflation will play an increasingly important role with the deepening of this trend. The formulation of macro policy should not only pay attention to the operation of the domestic economy, but also integrate the operation of foreign economies into the decision-making response information set of inflation management. Of course, because the domestic monetary authorities do not have direct control over the elements of globalization, the central bank's work of controlling inflation in the context of globalization will become more complex and challenging. Only by paying close attention to the changes of the world market and constantly improving the financial system, monetary system, and economic structure can China's resistance to external shocks be continuously improved.

Appendix: Global NKPC model based on the open economy DSGE model

The NKPC model in the main part of this chapter is based on Calvo's "supplier" model. Based on the classic studies of Obstfeld Rogoff (1995, 1996, 2000), Clarida et al. (2002), Smets and Wouters (2002), and Gali and Monacelli (2005) on the DSGE model of an open economy, we deduce the inflation dynamic mechanism model with factors of globalization. In the establishment of the DSGE model of an open economy, the price stickiness of Calvo (1983) is still the core mechanism of model establishment. Consistent with the standard literature, our model deduction process is based on the interaction between a country (or home country) and the world economy (or major trading partners). In order to facilitate the explanation and try to remain consistent with the definition of the variable in the main body of this book, we use the subscript i to represent the specific country i, the subscript D to represent "domestic," the subscript F to represent "foreign," the superscript $*$ to represent "world," and the lower case variable is the natural logarithm form of the upper case variable. Based on the above description, we start from the typical activities of the family sector and the enterprise sector, and then get the analytical expression of the general equilibrium inflation dynamic mechanism model.

Firstly, from the perspective of the demand side, the objective utility function of the family sector can be written as

$$E_0 \sum_{t=0}^{\infty} \beta^t U(C_t, N_t) \tag{14.13}$$

Where N_t represents labor time, and C_t represents the comprehensive consumption index. In an open environment, the consumption index C_t consists of two parts, namely

$$C_t \equiv \left[(1-a)^{\frac{1}{\eta}} (C_{D,t})^{\frac{\eta-1}{\eta}} + \alpha^{\frac{1}{\eta}} (C_{F,t})^{\frac{\eta-1}{\eta}} \right]^{\frac{\eta}{\eta-1}} \tag{14.14}$$

Where $C_{D,t}$ and $C_{F,t}$ represent the domestic products consumed by the household sector and the products imported from abroad, both of which are given by the standard invariant substitution elasticity function; parameter α reflects the degree of domestic preference, and η measures the degree of substitution of domestic and foreign goods.

For the family sector, the budget constraint for maximizing the utility is

$$\int_0^1 P_{D,t}(j)C_{D,t}(j)dj + \int_0^1\int_0^1 P_{i,t}(j)C_{i,t}(j)djdi + E_t(Q_{t,t+1}Z_{t+1}) \tag{14.15}$$

$$\le Z_t + W_t N_t + T_t$$

Where j represents the commodity category, $P_{D,t}$ represents the domestic sales price of products produced in China (hereinafter referred to as "domestic product price"), $P_{i,t}$ represents the price of goods imported from country i (denominated in domestic currency, the same below), Z_{t+1} represents the nominal income of the portfolios held by households in the period $t+1$, W_t represents the nominal wage, T_t represents the total tax, $Q_{t,t+1}$ represents the stochastic discount factors related to nominal income of portfolio.

In the open environment, the demand function of the household sector for goods is also divided into two parts, namely

$$C_{D,t}(j) = \left(\frac{P_{D,t}(j)}{P_{D,t}}\right)^{-\varepsilon} C_{D,t}, C_{i,t}(j) = \left(\frac{P_{i,t}(j)}{P_{i,t}}\right)^{-\varepsilon} C_{i,t} \tag{14.16}$$

Where the domestic price $P_{D,t}(j) \equiv \left(\int_0^1 P_{D,t}(j)^{1-\varepsilon} dj\right)^{\frac{1}{1-\varepsilon}}$, the import price from country i $P_{i,t}(j) \equiv \left(\int_0^1 P_{i,t}(j)^{1-\varepsilon} dj\right)^{\frac{1}{1-\varepsilon}}$, and ε is the representative elasticity of substitution.

In addition, suppose that $P_{F,t} \equiv \left(\int_0^1 P_{i,t}^{1-\gamma} di\right)^{\frac{1}{1-\gamma}}$ represents the total import price index based on the sum of foreign countries (where γ represents the degree of substitution of products from different countries), then the optimal consumption plan for the domestic household sector when consuming products imported from country i is:

$$C_{i,t} = \left(\frac{P_{i,t}}{P_{F,t}}\right)^{-\gamma} C_{F,t} \tag{14.17}$$

Because domestic consumption consists of domestic products and foreign products consumed by the household sector, the domestic consumption price can be expressed as $P_t \equiv [(1-\alpha)(P_{D,t})^{1-\eta} + \alpha(P_{F,t})^{1-\eta}]^{\frac{1}{1-\eta}}$. In this way, the optimal consumption plan for the household sector when consuming domestic and imported products is

$$C_{D,t} = (1-\alpha)\left(\frac{P_{D,t}}{P_t}\right)^{-\eta} C_t, C_{F,t} = \alpha\left(\frac{P_{F,t}}{P_t}\right)^{-\eta} C_t \tag{14.18}$$

Based on the above assumption, domestic household consumption expenditure is $P_{D,t}C_{D,t} + P_{F,t}C_{F,t} = P_t C_t$. Therefore, the budget constraint formula (Equation 14.15) can be rewritten as

$$P_t C_t + E_t(Q_{t,t+1}Z_{t+1}) \leq Z_t + W_t N_t + T_t \tag{14.19}$$

If the given utility function is $U(C,N) \equiv (1-\sigma)^{-1}C^{1-\sigma} - (1+\varphi)^{-1}N^{1+\varphi}$, then the optimal conditions of the family sector are

$$C_t^\sigma N_t^\varphi = W_t / P_t \tag{14.20}$$

And

$$\beta \left(\frac{C_t}{C_{t+1}}\right)^\sigma \left(\frac{P_t}{P_{t+1}}\right) = Q_{t,t+1} \tag{14.21}$$

The traditional stochastic Euler equation can be obtained by taking the expectation of Equation 14.21 and sorting it out, which gives

$$\beta R_t E_t \left[\left(\frac{C_{t+1}}{C_t}\right)^{-\sigma} \left(\frac{P_t}{P_{t+1}}\right)\right] = 1 \tag{14.22}$$

Where $R_t = (E_t Q_{t,t+1})^{-1}$ represents the total return on risk-free discounted bonds.

According to Equation 14.20 and Equation 14.22, corresponding logarithmic linearization forms can also be obtained

$$\begin{cases} w_t - p_t = \sigma c_t + \varphi n_t \\ c_t = E_t\{c_{t+1}\} - \dfrac{1}{\sigma}(r_t - E_t\{\pi_{t+1}\} - \rho) \end{cases} \tag{14.23}$$

Where $\rho \equiv \beta^{-1} - 1$ represents the time discount rate and $\pi_t \equiv p_t - p_{t-1}$ is the inflation rate of CPI.

In addition, according to the standard bilateral trade term $S_{i,t} = P_{i,t} / P_{D,t}$, the general terms of trade at home and abroad after logarithmic linearization can be written as $s_t = \int_0^1 s_{i,t} di$. In this way, according to the basic definition of P_t in Equation 14.18 and the theory of absolute purchasing power parity, the relationship between the CPI price index and domestic product price and foreign product price can be obtained, and then, according to the basic calculation formula of the CPI inflation rate (natural logarithmic difference of price), the relationship between the CPI inflation rate and the domestic product price can be obtained, that is

$$\pi_t = \pi_{D,t} + \alpha \Delta s_t \tag{14.24}$$

Suppose e represents the nominal effective exchange rate in the form of natural logarithm and $p_t^* \equiv \int_0^1 P_{i,t}^i di$ represents the world price index (in the form of natural logarithm). Then according to the law of one price and the definition of $P_{F,t}$ in Equation 14.17, we can obtain the linear relationship of terms of trade, the nominal effective exchange rate, domestic price, and world price, that is

$$s_t = e_t + p_t^* - p_{D,t} \tag{14.25}$$

Of course, according to the basic definition of the real exchange rate q and the nominal exchange rate, the relationship between the real exchange rate and terms of trade can also be obtained:

$$q_t = s_t + p_{D,t} - p_t = (1 - \alpha)s_t \tag{14.26}$$

Let's consider the relationship between domestic consumption and world consumption. We can set the first-order conditional expression of the family sector of any country i in a similar way to the setting of Equation 14.21, namely

$$\beta \left(\frac{C_{t+1}^i}{C_t^i} \right)^{-\sigma} \left(\frac{P_t^i}{P_{t+1}^i} \right) \left(\frac{\varpi_t^i}{\varpi_{t+1}^i} \right) = Q_{t,t+1} \tag{14.27}$$

Where ϖ represents the bilateral nominal exchange rate. By combining Equation 14.21 and Equation 14.27 and using the basic definition of the real exchange rate, and then taking the integral on both sides of the obtained expression, we can get the relationship between domestic consumption and world consumption as follows

$$c_t = c_t^* + \frac{1}{\sigma} q_t = c_t^* + \left(\frac{1 - \alpha}{\sigma} \right) s_t \tag{14.28}$$

Where $c_t^* \equiv \int_0^1 c_t^i di$ is the world consumption index (natural logarithm).

Secondly, for the enterprise department of the supplier, according to the standards set by Clarida et al. (2002) and Gali and Monacelli (2005), we write the enterprise production function with different products and linear technical input form as $Y_t(j) = A_t N_t(j)$, where A_t represents the exogenous technical parameters. In this way, according to Gali and Monacelli (2005), the real marginal cost of domestic enterprises can be written as

$$mc_t = -v + w_t - p_{D,t} - a_t \tag{14.29}$$

Where $v \equiv -\log(1 - \tau)$, τ represents employment subsidy, and $a_t \equiv \ln(A_t)$. Then, according to the relation between the real total output (expressed by y_t as its natural logarithm) and employment in China, and through linear first-order expansion, we can get the following relation:

$$y_t = a_t + n_t \tag{14.30}$$

As for the enterprise pricing mechanism, it is consistent with the second section of this chapter (but $k_y^f = 0$ in the provisional Equation 14.3. The corresponding results are given in the following Equation 14.35. We will analyze the general equilibrium based on the above basic models of the demand side and supply side. By clearing the conditions of the commodity market and using the basic definition of gross domestic output, we can obtain the expression of the relationship between gross domestic output and consumption, terms of trade, and exchange rate, namely

$$y_t = c_t + \alpha \gamma s_t + \alpha(\eta - \sigma^{-1})q_t = c_t + \frac{\alpha\omega}{\sigma} s_t \tag{14.31}$$

Where $\omega \equiv \sigma\gamma + (1-\alpha)(\sigma\eta - 1)$. According to the clearing conditions of the world market and combining Equation 14.21, Equation 14.27, and Equation 14.28, we can get the relationship between the total domestic output and the total world output (we make $\sigma_\alpha \equiv [(1-\alpha) + \alpha\omega]^{-1}\sigma$):

$$y_t = y_t^* + \frac{1}{\sigma_\alpha} s_t \tag{14.32}$$

Next, we rewrite Equation 14.29 according to Equation 14.23, Equation 14.28, Equation 14.30, and Equation 14.31:

$$mc_t = -v + \xi_d y_t + \xi^* y_t^* + u_t \tag{14.33}$$

Where $\xi_d \equiv (\sigma_\alpha + \varphi), \xi^* \equiv (\sigma - \sigma_\alpha), u_t \equiv -(1+\varphi)a_t$. We further use the definition of the total output gap (i.e. the difference between the static values of y_t and y_t^* and their respective static values), Equation 14.33 can be rewritten as

$$mc_t = c^* + \xi_d \hat{y}_t + \xi^* \hat{y}_t^* + u_t \tag{14.34}$$

Where $c^* \equiv -v + \mu(\xi_d + \xi^*)$, and $\hat{y}_t$ and $\hat{y}_t^*$ represent the domestic and world output gaps respectively.

Finally, according to Woodford (2003) and referring to the derivation process similar to that in the second section of this chapter, we can first obtain the NKPC model in the a closed economy, namely

$$\pi_t = \gamma_e E_t \pi_{t+1} + \gamma_b \pi_{t-1} + \sum_{i=1}^{q-1} \alpha_i \Delta\pi_{t-i} + \lambda mc_t \tag{14.35}$$

The definition of each coefficient is similar to those in the second section of this chapter and Woodford (2003). Then, we substitute Equation 14.34 into Equation 14.35 to obtain the NKPC model that includes the globalization factor (i.e. the output gap of foreign countries) in the open economy

$$\pi_t = c + \gamma_e E_t \pi_{t+1} + \gamma_b \pi_{t-1} + \sum_{i=1}^{q-1} \alpha_i \Delta \pi_{t-i} + \delta_d \hat{y}_t + \delta^* \hat{y}_t^* + \bar{\lambda}_t \tag{14.36}$$

Where $c \equiv \lambda c^*, \delta_d \equiv \lambda \xi_d, \delta^* \equiv \lambda \xi^*, \bar{\lambda}_t \equiv \lambda u_t.$

At this point, we prove that the inflation dynamic mechanism model with factors of globalization derived from the "supplier" in the second section of this chapter can also be derived from the open economy DSGE model system, and the final macro expression of the model is completely consistent. However, from the perspective of the transmission path of the operation of the world economy (factors of globalization) to domestic inflation, the derivation process based on the DSGE model system reflects the micro links more carefully and fully; of course, the whole derivation process is relatively cumbersome. In addition, if we consider the relationship between Equation 14.24, Equation 14.25, Equation 14.26, and Equation 14.32 above, it is not difficult to see that Equation 14.36 can also be rewritten to include exchange rate variables. Of course, whether the exchange rate variables should be explicitly expressed in the inflation dynamic mechanism model should be decided according to the attribute of the research problem. As far as this chapter is concerned, we have investigated the possible influence of exchange rate factors (including the nominal effective exchange rate, the real effective exchange rate, and the RMB–dollar exchange rate) on the inflation rate in practice, but the corresponding estimation results show that exchange rate variables are not statistically significant without exception.

15 Disparities and consistencies

The study of the dynamic formulation mechanism of inflation is of great significance to the scientific formulation and implementation of macroeconomic policies, especially monetary policies. The dynamic evolution of inflation is related to predictions about future inflation as well as the governance and regulation of inflation or deflation. The research on this topic is of particular importance especially under the current circumstances of an ever-changing global financial situation and rapid consolidation of the world economic structure. In recent years, with the intertwining of the promising prospects of China's economic development and the turbulent waves of the global financial tsunami, the study of the dynamic formation mechanism of inflation has been pushed to a climax.

It is worth noting that as for the research on how inflation is formed, the existing literature mostly distinguishes different types of inflation from the perspective of its driving factors, such as "cost-driven," "demand-driven," and "mixed" inflation formation mechanisms. Although these theories are very important for the understanding of the causes of a country's price changes in a specific period, leading-edge studies in recent years have shown that it is more in line with the practical laws of economic development to carry out an analysis by incorporating the various economic variables which affect inflation into a dynamic linkage system, and to study the factors driving price changes from a dynamic perspective. Although dynamic systems may intersect or overlap with traditional theoretical systems in terms of the formulation in different situations, for example, the names of independent variables and dependent variables of different model systems may be the same, while due to the existence of dynamic mechanisms, the economic implications of the dynamic mechanism of inflation are more abundant than those of the static theory of inflation.

In view of this fact, this book, with the dynamic analysis as a basic line, studies the dynamic formation mechanism of inflation in China from 13 different perspectives. To sum up, these perspectives include the perspective of the inflation cycle, the internal transmission of price index, the upstream and downstream transmission of price chain, industry tide, goods financialization, asset market equilibrium, the compromise between monetarism and New Keynesianism, the target mismatch of inflation as well as the expectation-driven perspective, the perspective of structural change in external shocks and dynamic features, excess liquidity in an open environment, the exchange rate parity relationship change, and the globalization perspective. Based on these different perspectives, this book conducts an in-depth study on the dynamic formation mechanism of inflation, which greatly enriches the application of the inflation dynamics theory, and at the same time broadens the macro-decision-making approach of regulating and controlling inflation.

From the different perspectives mentioned above, this book has formed multiple logics of the dynamic formation mechanism of inflation: Not only the internal circular driving logic of price indicators, but also the logic of dynamic interaction between different price indicators; not only the logic industry tide and goods financialization focused on the capital rotation model in reality, but also the logic of monetary driving based on traditional theory, and not only the logic of inflation target mismatch in the closed environment, but also the logic of excess liquidity and globalization driving in the open environment.

Making further comparisons among the multiple logics of the dynamic formation mechanism of inflation, we can find that there are both disparities and consistencies among the different logics. The first disparity of the multiple logics (or, to be more precise, the difference between different logics) is the logical divergence of one-way driving and vector interaction. As for the one-way driving logic, it means that the analytical framework and analysis thinking focus on how related factors affect inflation unilaterally, without considering the reverse effect of inflation on various driving factors. With such a logical assumption, the corresponding analytical framework is a one-dimensional model, such as in Chapters 2, 5, 6, 7, 10, 12, 13, and 14 in this book. The analytical framework of these chapters uses inflation as a dependent variable and other indicators (whether physical or monetary) as independent variables. The dynamic formation mechanism of inflation is analyzed by the one-dimensional model. Unlike the one-way driving logic, the analysis logic of vector interaction takes the possible two-way interaction mechanism between inflation and other related variables into consideration. Therefore, Chapters 3, 4, 8, 9, and 11 of this book analyze the dynamic formation mechanism of inflation based on multi-dimensional vector systems, which not only observe the impact of related factors on inflation, but also consider the reverse effect of inflation.

The second disparity in the multiple logics is that there are differences in the macro-environment setting of the analytical framework in each chapter, that is, the disparity between closed and open environments. From this point of view, Chapters 1–11 of this book belong to the analysis logic in the closed environment, while Chapters 12–14 belong to analysis thinking in the open environment. Under the circumstances of a closed economic environment, the influence of international or global factors can be neglected temporarily. At this time, the analytical framework does not take into account the impact of international capital flows, exchange rate changes, and globalization on the dynamic formation mechanism of domestic inflation. Conversely, when the closed environment is changed into an open environment, the above elements will obviously show up in the analytical framework or model settings. Then of the corresponding analytical frameworks of the two logics, which is more reasonable? In fact, both of the two analytic logics are reasonable, but with different focus. Or it can be interpreted in the way that the weighting of domestic and foreign factors is set differently in the two environments, and the respective analysis results provide us with different understandings of the dynamic formation mechanism of inflation. Moreover, even if the open environment is not clearly defined, the analytical framework partly based on the closed environment takes into account the sensitive influence of the exchange rate and other factors on the results in the analysis process.

Although there are two disparities or differences in the multiple logics of the dynamic formation mechanism of inflation, they are only different in the setting angle of the analytical framework, and are not exclusive to each other. As a matter of fact, the consistency of multiple logics is the main thread of this book. The consistency of multiple logics lies in the dynamic nature of the analytical framework, the endogeneity of inflation, and the uniformity of basic theories.

The first consistency of the multiple logic is that the analytical frameworks of different logics show dynamic features, that is, all model settings contain inflation lags. By incorporating the lagged term of inflation, the persistence feature of inflation is recognized in all analysis logic. The so-called inflation persistence, also known as inflation viscosity or inflation inertia, refers to the trend duration of inflation deviating from its equilibrium state after being shocked by random disturbance factors. The longer it lasts, the more persistent the inflation and the more obvious the lagging effect of monetary policy will be. Therefore, the persistence of inflation objectively determines the response speed of inflation to policy changes. Previous studies (such as Fuhrer, 1995) have also shown that it generally takes several quarters or even years for inflation to return to its expected level after it is hit and deviates from the central bank's expected target in a period of strong inflation persistence. In this case, the effect of monetary policy will inevitably be strongly lagged. On the other hand, if inflation is less persistent, the lagging effect of monetary policy will be relatively weakened. Therefore, in the process of analyzing the effect of monetary policy, if it fails to accurately reflect the real characteristics of inflation persistence, there are is a chance of inappropriate or even wrong policy recommendations.

The main reason why we recognize the dynamic nature of the inflation model in different logical analytical frameworks is that inflation is considered to have strong persistence in reality. According to the definition, the level of inflation persistence can be reflected by the autocorrelation function (ACF) of the time series variables of the inflation rate. Figure 15.1 shows the autocorrelation function diagrams of China's main inflation indicators (CPI inflation rate, GDP deflation index inflation rate, and commodity retail price index inflation rate, namely CPI, GDPD, and RPI respectively; these are quarterly data on the year-on-year growth rate, ranging from the first quarter of 1980 to date). At the same time, according to the definition of the autocorrelation function, its value range is [0,1]. In order to compare with a time series data stream with a medium persistence level and to make sure it presents a general result, we use a simple first-order autoregressive model based on the persistence coefficient of 0.5 to

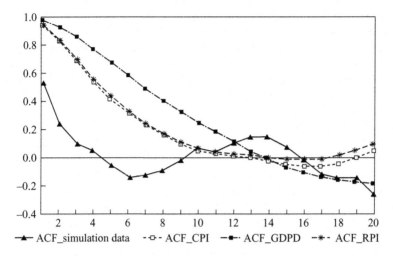

Figure 15.1 The time sequence trajectory of China's inflation rate and autocorrelation function of simulation data.

simulate and generate the observation sequence equivalent to the sample (the initial term in the simulation process is set to be 0, and the white Gaussian noise with the average random error term being 0 and the variance being 1). Then the sample autocorrelation function of the simulation data is calculated and depicted in Figure 15.1. It can be clearly seen from the figure that the autocorrelation function of China's three inflation indicators is gradually approaching zero with no exception, and generally takes more than one year (over four lag durations) to attenuate to zero slowly, especially the autocorrelation functions of the GDP deflator inflation rate. Compared with the autocorrelation function of simulation data with a moderate persistence index, the attenuation of the autocorrelation function of the inflation rate in China is obviously slower than that of the simulation data with a persistence coefficient of 0.5.

The above facts show that it takes more than a year for China's inflation index to return to its expected value after it deviates from its expected level and is hit by a random shock, such as a deflationary monetary policy shock to curb inflation. In this case, the analytical framework of any inflation formation mechanism should be based on a dynamic model.

The second consistency of the multiple logics is the endogenous nature of inflation. Whether it is a single-variable model or a multi-variable vector model, whether in a closed or open environment, the endogenous nature of inflation is considered as the premise. For a one-way model system, since the variables of inflation are usually dependent variables, the endogenous nature is quite obvious. For the vector model system, the endogenous nature of inflation can be easily noticed as well, because in the process of studying the dynamic interaction of variables, it has been established that the mechanism of inflation is affected by other factors. Therefore, all the analytical logics in this book are consistent in understanding the endogenous nature of inflation.

The third consistency of the multiple logics is the consistency of basic theory, which means that the analytical framework is mainly based on the theoretical framework of New Keynesian economics, especially the macro-dynamic model with a microfoundation of recent years. Even a realistic analysis based on the monetarist theoretical framework should figure out its internal logical relationship with the New Keynesian theory in the first place, after which further empirical analysis should be carried out. Therefore, the macro-theoretical framework based on a microfoundation is a main clue throughout the multiple logics in this book. However, it should be pointed out that instead of carrying out in-depth analysis at the micro level, this book focuses on the macro-analysis. In the future, more efforts should be made in carrying out analysis at the micro level. Especially in recent years, with China's economy gradually moving towards a "new normal," some typical facts can be seen clearly. Firstly, the "excess liquidity" at both the monetary and financial levels. In the monetary sector, it seems that the persistent high level of M2/GDP is no longer of the analytical interest that it was in the past; in the banking sector, the relatively high margin reserve ratio undoubtedly means that the financial system does not lack liquidity. Secondly, the relationship between finance and the real economy is becoming more and more complex, speeding up the formation of economic financialization. Whether it is a price tool or a quantity tool, the resource allocation decisions made by the monetary authorities in the financial sector based on their own risk return trade-offs only have an "indirect" influence. Even if the long-term interest rates achieved through QE in developed economies are reduced, the resulting R&D boom is still based on the previous round of asset price collapse; otherwise it is hard to say whether the situation that financial resources pursue assets while breaking away from real economies will show up again. This might be a realistic reflection of Schumpeter's theory of creative destruction, but it is more likely to be the inevitable feature of economic financialization discussed in Chapter 6 of this book. Thirdly, the monetary policy framework and tool reform is not as orderly as the textbooks say. At least what we have observed is not the "law of one price": With the loosening up of RMB trade settlement, Chinese currency gradually outflows to foreign countries, forming two types of interest rates at home and abroad. The prospect of appreciation and higher risk-free rates are driving the domestic currency to become international; on the other hand, China's foreign exchange reserves and the resulting foreign exchange share may no longer be the main form of base currency in the future. At the same time, it is clear that the "interest rate corridor" which is widely implemented in various countries is still a policy with the nature of a price buffer.

The above typical facts show that all theoretical hypotheses based on small open economies cannot constitute a theoretical foundation to explain China's problems. Similarly, the traditional macro-analytical framework based on equilibrium theory may be too rigid to capture the behavior logic of micro-individuals in reality. Therefore, we may need to pay more attention to such a basic question in future research: What is the target of China's macro decisions ? The resulting basic analysis paradigm is the macro decision at the micro level.

In a word, this book studies the dynamic formation mechanism of inflation from different logical perspectives, and puts forward some new ideas and explanations. Of course, this book cannot cover all the problems in this field, but with the continuous development of research in this area, there will be more and more profound understanding of the dynamic formation mechanism of inflation in China among academia and decision-makers. From this point of view, the basic research work in this book may be of some value in promoting the development of related research. With this in mind, I am more confident and enthusiastic about the basic research work. It is also such confidence and enthusiasm that inspire the young economists of our generation to do their scientific research work with unremitting efforts, and to explore and innovate continuously in the relevant fields of national economic development.

References

Aalbers, M. (2008). The financialization of home and the mortgage market crisis. *Competition and Change, 12*, 148–166.

Abeysinghe, T., & Gulasekaran, R. (2004). Quarterly real GDP estimates for China and ASEAN4 with a forecast evaluation. *Journal of Forecasting, 23*(6), 431–447.

Akerlof, G.A., Dickens, W.T., & Perry, G.L. (2000). Near-rational wage and price setting and the long-run Phillips curve. *Brookings Papers on Economic Activity, 1*(1), 1–60.

Albanesi, Stefania, Chari, Varadarajan V., & Christiano, Lawrence J. (2003). Expectation traps and monetary policy. *The Review of Economic Studies, 70*(4), 715–741.

Andrew, L., & Piger, J. (2004). *Is inflation persistence intrinsic in industrial economies* (European Central Bank Working Paper, No. 334).

Andrews, D.W.K. (1993). Tests for parametric instability and structural change with unknown change point. *Econometrica, 61*(4), 821–856.

Andrews, D.W.K., & Chen, H. (1994). Approximately median-unbiased estimation of autoregressive models. *Journal of Business and Economic Statistics, 12*(2), 187–204.

Andrews, D.W.K., & Ploberger, W. (1994). Optimal tests when a nuisance parameter is present only under the alternative. *Econometrica, 62*(6), 1383–1414.

Arrighi, G. (1994). *The long twentieth century: Money, power, and the origins of our times*. London: Verso.

Artis, M.J., Bladen-Hovell, R.C., Osborn, D.R., Graham, S.W., & Zhang, W. (1995). Predicting turning points in the UK inflation cycle. *The Economic Journal, 105*(432), 1145–1164.

Balke, N., & Mark, W. (2007). The relative Price effects of monetary shocks. *Journal of Macroeconomics, 29*(1), 19–36.

Ball, L. (1993, November/December). How costly is disinflation? The Historical Evidence. *Federal Reserve Bank of Philadelphia Business Review, 19*, 17–28.

Ball, L. (1994). Credible disinflation with staggered Price-setting. *American Economic Review, 84*, 282–289.

Ball, L. (1995). Disinflation with imperfect credibility. *Journal of Monetary Economics, 35*(1), 5–23.

Ball, L. (1999). Efficient rules for monetary policy. *International Finance, 2*(1), 63–83.

Ball, L. (2000). *Near-rationality and inflation in two monetary regimes* (NBER Working Papers, No. 7988).

Ball, L. (2006). "Has globalization changed inflation?" (NBER Working Papers, No. 12687).

Ball, L., Mankiw, N.G., & Romer, D. (1988). The new Keynesian economics and the output-inflation trade-off: Comments and discussion. *Brooking Papers on Economic Activity, 1*, 1–82.

Bei, Duoguang, & Zhu, Xiaoli. (2007). An analysis of the coexistence of external devaluation and internal appreciation of RMB. *Economic Research Journal (in Chinese)*, *42*(9), 32–48.

Bernanke, B.S., Boivin, J., & Eliasz, P. (2005). Measuring the effects of monetary policy: A factor-augmented vector autoregressive (FAVAR) approach. *The Quarterly Journal of Economics*, *120*, 387–422.

Blanchard, Olivier. (2009). The State of Macro. *Annual Review of Economics, Annual Reviews*, *1*(1), 209–228.

Boivin, J., & Giannoni, M. (2002). Assessing changes in the monetary transmission mechanism: A VAR approach. *Economic Policy Review*, *8*, 97–111.

Borio, C., & Filardo, A. (2007). *Globalization and Inflation: New Cross-country Evidence on the Global Determinants of Domestic Inflation* (BIS Working Papers, No. 227).

Burns, A.F., & Wesley, M. (1946). *Measuring business cycles, NBER book series studies in business cycles*. New York, NY: National Bureau of Economic Research Inc.

Carroll, Christopher D. (2003). Macroeconomic expectations of households and professional forecasters. *The Quarterly Journal of Economics*, *118*(1), 269–298.

Calvo, A. (1983). Staggered prices in a utility-maximizing framework. *Journal of Monetary Economics*, *12*(3), 383–398.

Cecchetti, S., & Guy, D. (2006). Has the inflation process changed? *Economic Policy*, *21*(46), 313–352.

Chari, Varadarajan V., Christiano, Lawrence J., & Eichenbaum, Martin. (1998). Expectation traps and discretion. *Journal of Economic Theory*, *81*(2), 462–492.

Chen, Yanbin, Tang, Shilei, & Li, Du. (2009). Can money supply predict China's inflation? *Economic Theory and Business Management*, *29*(2), 24–30.

Chen, Yucai. (2011). International commodity price volatility and domestic inflation: An empirical analysis based on Chinese data. *Chinese Review of Financial Studies*, *3*(5), 22–43.

Chen, Yulu. (2006). It is time to deal with the reserve currency crisis. *Financial View (in Chinese)*, *5*, 34–35.

Chen, Yulu, & Zhang, Chengsi. (2008). New global financial crisis and strategic adjustment of China's foreign exchange reserve management. *Studies of International Finance*, *29*(11), 4–11.

Choudhri, E., & Dalia, H. (2006). Exchange rate pass-through to domestic prices: Does the inflationary environment matter. *Journal of International Money and Finance*, *25*(4), 614–639.

Christiano, L.J., Eichenbaum, M., & Evans, C.L. (2005). Nominal rigidities and the dynamic effects of a shock to monetary policy. *The Journal of Political Economy*, *113*(1), 1–45.

Clarida, R., Gali, J., & Gertler, M. (1999). The Science of Monetary Policy: A new Keynesian Perspective. *Journal of Economic Literature*, *37*(4), 1661–1707.

Clarida, R., Gali, J., & Gertler, M. (2000). Monetary policy rules and macroeconomic stability: Evidence and some theory. *The Quarterly Journal of Economics*, *115*(1), 147–180.

Clarida, R., Gali, J., & Gertler, M. (2002). A simple framework for international monetary policy analysis. *Journal of Monetary Economics*, *49*(5), 879–904.

Clark, Todd (2006). Disaggregate evidence on the persistence of consumer price inflation. *Journal of Applied Econometrics*, *21*(5), 536–587.

Cogley, T., & Sargent, T.J. (2001). *Evolving post-world war II US Inflation dynamics, NBER macroeconomics Annual 2001* (pp. 331–373). Cambridge, MA: MIT Press.

Cogley, T., & Sbordone, A. (2005). *A search for Structural Phillips Curve* (The Federal Reserve Bank of New York staff report, 203).

Cooper, R. (2008). Global imbalances: Globalization, demography, and sustainability. *Journal of Economic Perspectives*, *22*(3), 93–112.

Corvoisier, S., & Mojon, B. (2005). *Breaks in the mean of inflation-how they happen and what to do with them* (European Central Bank Working Papers, No. 451).

Cumby, R.E., & Huizinga, J. (1992). Testing the auto correlation structure of disturbances in ordinary least squares and instrumental variables regressions. *Econometrica, 60*(1), 185–195.

Cumby, R.E., Huizinga, J., & Obstfeld, M. (1983). Two-step two-stage least squares estimation in models with rational expectations. *Journal of Econometrics, 21*(3), 333–355.

Davidson, R., & MacKinnon, J. (1989). Testing for consistency using artificial regressions. *Econometric Theory, 5*(3), 363–384.

Davidson, R., & Mackinnon, J. (1993). *Estimation and inference in econometrics.* Oxford: Oxford University Press.

Ding, Zhijie. (2005). The vulnerability of capital flow in China. *Modern Commercial Bank (in Chinese), 11*, 15–18.

Durbin, J. (1954). Errors in variables. *Review of the International Statistical Institute, 22*(1/3), 23–32.

Eijffinger, S., & Geraats, P. (2006). How transparent are central banks? *European Journal of Political Economy, 22*(1), 1–21.

Engelen, E. (2002). Corporate governance, property, and democracy: A conceptual critique of shareholder ideology. *Economy and Society, 31*(3), 391–413.

Estrella, A., & Fuhrer, J.C. (2002). Dynamic inconsistencies: Counterfactual implications of a class of rational-expectations models. *American Economic Review, 92*(4), 1013–1028.

Estrella, A., & Fuhrer, J.C. (2003). Monetary policy shifts and the stability of monetary policy models. *The Review of Economics and Statistics, 85*(1), 94–104.

Fan, Conglai. (2002). Supply shock, total Price decline and monetary contraction. *Financial Research, 25*(4), 32–39.

Fan, Gang. (1999). Overcoming credit contraction and banking system reform: Analysis of macro-economic situation in 1998 and prospects for 1999. *Economic Research Journal (in Chinese), 34*(1), 5–10.

Fan, Zhiyong. (2008). Is China's inflation driven by wage cost? *Economic Research Journal (in Chinese), 43*(8), 102–112.

Fischer, S. (1977). Long-term contracts, rational expectations, and the optimal money supply rule. *The Journal of Political Economy, 85*(1), 191–205.

Frey, G., & Matteo, M. (2007). Econometric models of asymmetric Price transmission. *Journal of Economic Surveys, 21*(2), 349–415.

Friedman, M. (1956). *Studies in the quantity theory of money.* Chicago, IL: University of Chicago Press.

Friedman, M. (1963). *Inflation: Causes and consequences.* Asia Publishing House.

Friedman, M. (1968). The role of monetary policy. *American Economic Review, 58*(1), 1–17.

Froud, J., Haslam, C., Johal, S., & Williams, K. (2000). Shareholder value and financialization: Consultancy promises, management moves. *Economy and Society, 29*(1), 80–110.

Fuhrer, J.C. (1995). The persistence of inflation and the cost of disinflation. *New England Economic Review, 12*(1), 3–16.

Fuhrer, J.C. (1997). The (un) importance of forward-looking behavior in price specifications. *Journal of Money, Credit, and Banking, 29*(3), 338–350.

Fuhrer, J.C. (2006). Intrinsic and inherited inflation persistence. *International Journal of Central Banking, 2*, 49–86.

Fuhrer, J.C., & Moore, G.R. (1995). Inflation persistence. *The Quarterly Journal of Economics, 110*(1), 127–159.

Gadzinski, G., & Orlandi, F. (2004). *Inflation persistence in the European Union, the Eura area and the United States* (European Central Bank Working Papers, No. 414).

Gali, J., & Gertler, M. (1999). Inflation dynamics: A structural econometric analysis. *Journal of Monetary Economics, 44*(2), 195–222.

Gali, J., Gertler, M., & López-Salido, J.D. (2005). Robustness of the estimates of the hybrid new Keynesian Phillips curve. *Journal of Monetary Economics, 52*(6), 1107–1118.

Gali, J., & Monacelli, T. (2005). Monetary policy and exchange rate volatility in a small open economy. *Review of Economic Studies, 72*(3), 707–734.

Gamber, E.N., & Hung, J.H. (2001). Has the rise in globalization reduced US inflation in the 1990s? *Economic Inquiry, 39*(1), 58–73.

Gao, Tiemei, Liu, Hongyu, & Wang, Jinming. (2003). Empirical analysis of price fluctuation in China's transition period. *Social Sciences in China, 24*(6), 73–83.

Gao, Yanyun. (2009). International comparison of CPI compilation and publication. *Statistical Research, 27*(9), 15–20.

Gerlach, S., & Peng, W. (2006). Output gaps and inflation in China's mainland. *China Economic Review, 17*(2), 210–225.

Godfrey, L. (1994). Testing for serial correlation by variable addition in dynamic models estimated by instrumental variables. *The Review of Economics and Statistics, 76*(3), 550–559.

Godfrey, L., McAleer, M., & McKenzie, C. (1988). Variable addition and Lagrange multiplier tests for linear and logarithmic regression models. *Review of Economics and Statistics, 70*(3), 492–503.

Goodfriend, M. (1993). Interest rate policy and the inflation scare problem: 1979–1992. *Economic Quarterly, 79*(1), 1–23.

Goodfriend, M., & King, R.G. (1997). The new neoclassical synthesis and the role of monetary policy. In *NBER macroeconomics Annual 1997* (pp. 231–283). Cambridge, MA: MIT Press.

Goodfriend, M., & Prasad, E. (2006). *A framework for independent monetary policy in China* (IMF Working Papers, No. 06/111).

Gong, Gang, & Lin, Yifu. (2007). Overreaction, the Explanation of China's economy Deflationary Expansion. *Economic Research Journal (in Chinese), 42*(4), 53–66.

Gordon, R. (1982). Price inertia and policy ineffectiveness in the United States, 1890–1980. *The Journal of Political Economy, 90*(6), 1087–1117.

Ha, Jiming. (2007, December 7). Monetary tightening and RMB appreciation are the most effective way to fight against inflation. *Shanghai Securities News*.

Hamilton, J. (1989). A new approach to the economic analysis of nonstationary time series and the business cycle. *Econometrica, 57*(2), 357–384.

Hamilton, J. (1996). This is what happened to the oil price-macroeconomy relationship. *Journal of Monetary Economics, 38*(2), 215–220.

Hansen, B. (1997). Approximate asymptotic P values for structural change tests. *Journal of Business and Economic Statistics, 15*(1), 60–80.

Hansen, B. (1999). The grid bootstrap and the autoregressive model. *The Review of Economics and Statistics, 81*(4), 594–607.

Hansen, L. (1982). Large sample properties of generalized method of moments estimators. *Econometrica, 50*(4), 1029–1054.

Harding, D., & Adrian, P. (2002). Dissecting the cycle: A methodological investigation. *Journal of Monetary Economics, 19*(2), 365–381.

Harvey, A.C., Thomas, T., & Herman, V.D. (2007). Trends and cycles in economic time series: A bayesian approach. *Journal of Econometrics, 140*(2), 618–649.

Hasan, M. (1999). Monetary growth and inflation in China: A re-examination. *Journal of Comparative Economics, 27*(4), 669–685.

Hausman, J. (1978). Specification tests in econometrics. *Econometrica, 46*(6), 1251–1272.

Hayashi, F., & Sims, C.A. (1983). Nearly efficient estimation of time series models with predetermined, but not exogenous, instruments. *Econometrica, 51*(3), 783–798.

He, Liping. (2008). RMB exchange Rate and China's current account surplus in recent years. *Journal of Financial Research, 31*(3), 13–27.

He, Liping, Fan, Gang, & Hu, Jiani. (2008). Consumer price index and producer Price index, which is the driver? *Economic Research Journal (in Chinese), 43*(11), 16–26.

He, Qiang. (2003). Economic growth, inflation and policy expectation. *Price: Theory and Practice, 23*(7), 21–23.

Hooper, P., Slok, T., & Dobridge, C. (2006, July). *Understanding US Inflation, Global markets research*. Frankfurt: Deutsche Bank.

Hu, Angang. (1999). Characteristics, causes and countermeasures of deflation in China. *Management World, 15*(3), 10–23.

Huo, Teh-Ming. (2008). Understanding the current inflation in China. *International Economic Review, 31*(5), 29–30.

Ihrig, J., Kamin, S., Lindner, D., & Marquez, J. (2010). Some simple tests of the globalization and inflation hypothesis. *International Finance, 13*(3), 343–375.

Ireland, P.N. (2004). Technology shocks in the new Keynesian model. *The Review of Economics and Statistics, 86*(4), 923–936.

Jensen, H. (2002). Targeting nominal income growth or inflation. *The American Economic Review, 92*, 928–956. New York, 1963.

Jondeau, E., & Bihan, H.L. (2005). Testing for the new Keynesian Phillips curve. *Additional International Evidence, Economic Modelling, 22*(3), 521–550.

Jones, C. (2002). *Introduction to economic growth* (2nd ed.). New York, NY: W.W. Norton & Company.

Judd, P., & Rudebusch, G.D. (1998). Taylor's rule and the fed: 1970–1997. *Federal Reserve Bank of San Francisco Economic Review, 3*, 3–16.

Karpetis, C., & Varelas, E. (2012). Fiscal and monetary policy interaction in a simple accelerator model. *International Advances in Economic Research, 18*(2), 199–214.

Kim, C.J., Nelson, C.R., & Piger, J. (2004). The less volatile US economy: A bayesian investigation of timing, breadth, and potential explanations. *Journal of Business and Economic Statistics, 22*(1), 80–93.

King, R.G., & Watson, M. (1994). The postwar US Phillips curve: A revisionist econometric history. *Carnegie-Rochester Conference Series on Public Policy, 41*, 157–219.

King, R.G., & Wolman, A.L. (1999). What should the monetary authority do when prices are sticky? In *Monetary policy rules* (pp. 349–398). Chicago, IL: University of Chicago Press.

Kiviet, J. (1986). On the rigour of some misspecification tests for modelling dynamic relations. *The Review of Economic Studies, 53*(2), 241–261.

Krippner, G. (2005). The financialization of the American economy. *Socio-Economic Review, 3*(2), 173–208.

Kydland, F.E., & Prescott, E.C. (1977). Rules rather than discretion: The inconsistency of optimal plans. *The Journal of Political Economy, 85*(3), 473–491.

Lazonick, W., & Sullivan, O. (2000). Maximizing shareholder value: A new ideology for corporate governance. *Economy and Society, 29*(1), 13–35.

Levin, A.T., & Piger, J.M. (2004). *Is inflation persistence intrinsic in Industrial Economies* (European Central Bank Working Papers, No. 334).

Li, H. (2005). *Testing alternative models of price adjustment, Mimeo.* Boston, MA: Brandeis University.

Li, Hao, & Wang, Shaoping. (2011). China's inflation expectation and inflation stickiness. *Statistical Research, 29*(1), 43–48.

Li, Laya. (1994). The relationship between expectation and uncertainty. *Economic Review (in Chinese), 9*, 12–19.

Li, Shaolin, & Chen, Yingying. (2010, October 25). Who will take over apple White sugar when there is a high tide of agricultural product speculation. *China Securities News.*

Li, X., & Jinyu, H. (2007). Excess liquidity control requires multi-pronged approach. *China Economist, 5*, 19–29.

Liang, H., & Hong, Q. (2007). *China: How significant is the exchange rate pass-through effect on CPI inflation* (Goldman Sachs Global Economic Research Report).

Lin, Yifu. (2007). The tide phenomenon and the reconstruction of macroeconomic theory in developing countries. *Economic Research Journal (in Chinese), 42*(1), 126–131.

Lin, Yifu, Wu, Hemao, & Xing, Yiqing. (2010). The formation mechanism of wave phenomenon and overcapacity. *Economic Research Journal (in Chinese), 45*(10), 4–19.

Linde, J. (2005). Estimating new-Keynesian Phillips curves: A full information maximum likelihood approach. *Journal of Monetary Economics, 52*(6), 1135–1149.

Liu, Haolan. (2007). An empirical analysis of the Price transmission mechanism: Taking national and provincial data as an example. *China Price, 19*(7), 3–6.

Liu, Jinquan, & Xie, Weidong. (2003). An empirical analysis of the dynamic Correlation between China's Economic Growth Rate and Inflation Rate. *The Journal of World Economy, 26*(6), 48–57.

Liu, Lin. (2010). The real estate industry has become an important pillar industry in China. *China Investment, 25*(1), 102–103.

Liu, Shucheng. (1997a). Deflation can neither be overestimated nor underestimated. *Economic Research Journal (in Chinese), 34*(10), 23–30.

Liu, Shucheng. (1997b). On the Phillips curve in China. *Management World, 13*(6), 21–33.

Lucas, R. (1976). Econometric policy evaluation: A critique. *Carnegie-Rochester Conference Series on Public Policy, 1*, 19–46.

Lv, Jianglin. (2001). The causes of China's deflation policy. *Economic Research Journal (in Chinese)*, (3).

Ma, Dan, & Tu, Yue. (2006). Inflation, output gap and inflation uncertainty – A test of the Phillips curve of China's additional expectations. *Statistics & Decision, 22*(16), 72–74.

MacKinnon, J.G. (1996). Numerical Distribution Functions for Unit Root and Cointegration Tests. *Journal of Applied Econometrics, 11*(6), 601–618.

MacKinnon, J.G., Alfred, H., & Leo, M. (1999). Numerical distribution functions of likelihood ratio tests for cointegration. *Journal of Applied Econometrics, 14*(5), 563–577.

Mankiw, N.G., & Reis, R. (2002). Sticky information versus sticky prices: A proposal to replace the new Keynesian Phillips curve. *The Quarterly Journal of Economics, 117*(4), 1295–1328.

Mavroeidis, S. (2005). Identification issues in forward-looking models estimated by GMM, with an application to the Phillips curve. *Journal of Money, Credit, and Banking, 37*(3), 421–448.

McCallum, B. (1976). Rational expectations and the natural rate: Some consistent estimates. *Econometrica, 44*(1), 43–52.

McCallum, B.T. (1998). Solutions to linear rational expectations models: A compact exposition. *Economics Letters, 61*(2), 143–147.

McCallum, B.T. (2001). Monetary policy analysis in models without money. *Federal Reserve Bank of St Louis Review, 83*(4), 145–164.

McCallum, B.T., & Nelson, E. (1999). An optimizing IS-LM specification for monetary policy and business cycle analysis. *Journal of Money, Credit, and Banking, 31*(3), 296–316.

McCallum, B.T., & Nelson, E. (2004). Timeless perspective vs. discretionary monetary policy in forward-looking models. *Federal Reserve Bank of St Louis Review, 86*(2), 43–56.

McCallum, B.T., & Nelson, E. (2005). Targeting versus instrument rules for monetary policy. *Federal Reserve Bank of St Louis Review, 87*(5), 597–611.

McKinnon, R. (2007). Why China should keep its dollar peg. *International Finance, 10*(1), 43–70.

Meltzer, A.H. (1995). Monetary, credit and (other) transmission processes: A monetarist perspective. *The Journal of Economic Perspective, 9*(4), 49–72.

Mishkin, F. (2007a). Inflation dynamics. *International Finance, 10*(3), 317–334.

Mishkin, F. (2007b). *The economics of money, banking and financial markets* (8th ed.). Boston, MA: Pearson Education, Inc.

Mitchell, W.C. (1927). *Business cycles: The problem and its setting.* New York, NY: National Bureau of Economic Research Inc.

Mitchell, W.C., & Arthur, B. (1938). Statistical indicators of cyclical revivals. *NBER Bulletin, 69*, 1–12.

Neiss, K., & Nelson, E. (2005). Inflation dynamics, marginal cost, and the output gap: Evidence from three countries. *Journal of Money, Credit, and Banking, 37*(6), 1019–1045.

Obstfeld, M., & Kenneth, R. (1995). Exchange rate dynamics redux. *Journal of Political Economy, 103*(3), 624–660.

Obstfeld, M., & Kenneth, R. (1996). *Foundations of international macroeconomics.* Cambridge, MA: MIT Press.

Obstfeld, M., & Kenneth, R. (2000). New directions for stochastic open economy models. *Journal of International Economics, 50*(1), 117–153.

O'Reilly, G., & Whelan, K. (2005). Has euro-area inflation persistence changed over time. *The Review of Economics and Statistics, 87*(4), 709–720.

Orphanides, A., & Noren, S.V. (2005). The reliability of inflation forecast based on output gap estimates in real time. *Journal of Money, Credit and Banking, 37*(3), 583–600.

Pagan, A. (1984). Econometric issues in the analysis of regressions with generated regressors. *International Economic Review, 25*(1), 221–247.

Palley, T. (2008). *Financialization: What it is and why it matters* (IMK Working Papers, No. 04-2008).

Phelps, E. (1967). Phillips curves, expectations of inflation and optimal employment over time. *Economica, 34*(135), 254–281.

Phillips, K. (1996). *Arrogant capital: Washington, wall street, and the frustration of American politics.* New York, NY: Little, Brown & Company.

Phillips, K. (2002). *Wealth and democracy: Apolitical history of the American rich.* New York, NY: Broadway Books.

Phillips, P. (1977). Approximations to some finite sample distributions associated with a first-order stochastic difference equation. *Econometrica, 45*, 463–485.

Pivetta, F., & Reis, R. (2007). The persistence of inflation in the United States. *Journal of Economic Dynamics and Control, 31*(4), 1326–1358.

Qian, Xiaoan. (2000). *The formation and development of China's monetary policy.* Shanghai: Shanghai People's Publishing House.

Qin, Duo, Xinhua, He. (2010). Is the Chinese Currency Substantially Misaligned to Warrant Further Appreciation? (Working Papers, No. 660) Queen Mary University of London, School of Economics and Finance.

Reis, Ricardo. (2006). Inattentive producers. *The Review of Economic Studies, 73*(3), 793–821.

Restuccia, D., Yang, D., & Zhu, X. (2008). Agriculture and aggregate productivity: A quantitative cross-country analysis. *Journal of Monetary Economics, 55*(2), 234–250.

Roberts, J.M. (1995). New Keynesian economics and the Phillips curve. *Journal of Money, Credit and Banking, 27*(4), 975–984.

Roberts, J.M. (1997). Is inflation sticky? *Journal of Monetary Economics, 39*(2), 173–196.

Roberts, J.M. (1998). *Inflation expectations and the transmission of monetary policy* (Finance and Economics Discussion Paper, No.43). Board of Governors of the Federal Reserve System.

Roberts, J.M. (2005). How well does new Keynesian sticky-price model fit the data. *Contributions to Macroeconomics, 5*, 1–37.

Roberts, J.M. (2006). Monetary policy and inflation dynamics. *International Journal of Central Banking, 2*, 193–230.

Romer, D. (2006). *Advanced macroeconomics* (3rd ed.). New York, NY: McGraw-Hill.

Rosser, J. (2000). *From catastrophe to chaos: A general theory of economic discontinuities* (2nd ed.). Boston, MA: Kluwer Academic Publishers.

Rotemberg, J.J. (1982). Sticky prices in the United States. *The Journal of Political Economy, 90*(6), 1187–1211.

Roubini, Nouriel. (2007). Why China should abandon its dollar peg. *International Finance, 10*(1), 71–89.

Rudd, J., & Whelan, K. (2005). New tests of the new Keynesian Phillips curve. *Journal of Monetary Economics, 52*(6), 1167–1181.

Rudd, J., & Whelan, K. (2006). Can rational expectations sticky-Price models explain inflation dynamics. *American Economic Review, 96*(1), 303–320.

Rudd, J., & Whelan, K. (2007). Modelling inflation dynamics: A critical survey of recent research. *Journal of Money, Credit and Banking, 39*, 155–170.

Rudebusch, G.D. (2002a). Assessing nominal income rules for monetary policy with model and data uncertainty. *The Economic Journal, 112*(479), 402–432.

Rudebusch, G.D. (2002b). Term structure evidence on interest rate smoothing and monetary policy inertia. *Journal of Monetary Economics, 49*(6), 1161–1187.

Rudebusch, G.D. (2005). Assessing the Lucas critique in monetary policy models. *Journal of Money, Credit and Banking, 37*(2), 245–272.

Rudebusch, G.D., & Svensson, L.E.O. (1999). Policy rules for inflation targeting. In *Monetary policy rules*. Chicago, IL: University of Chicago Press.

Samuelson, P. (1939). A synthesis of the principle of acceleration and the multiplier. *Journal of Political Economy, 47*(6), 786–797.

Sbordone, A.M. (2005). Do expected future marginal costs drive inflation dynamics. *Journal of Monetary Economics, 52*(6), 1183–1197.

Sensier, M., & Osborn, D. (2004). Modelling UK inflation: Persistence, seasonality and monetary policy (Discussion paper series, No.46). Manchester: Centre for Growth and Business Cycle Research, Economic Studies of the University of Manchester.

Shenyin & Wanguo Research Institute. (2008, 22 August). Analysis on the internal mechanism of PPI affecting CPI. *Shanghai Financial News*.

Shi, Chenyu. (2011). "The Financialization of Bulk Commodity". *China Finance, 46(7), 96*.

Shi, J.H., Fu, X., & Xu, W. (2008). The transmission of RMB exchange rate change to China's price level. *Economic Research, 43*(7), 52–64.

Shi, Wenqing. (2000). *Research on China's Inflation*. China Finance and Economics Press.

Sichel, D.E. (1994). Inventories and the three phases of the business cycle. *Journal of Business and Economic Statistics, 12*(3), 269–277.

Smets, F., & Wouters, R. (2002). Openness, imperfect exchange rate pass-through and monetary policy. *Journal of Monetary Economics, 49*(5), 947–981.

Söderlind, P. (1999). Solution and Estimation of RE Macro models with Optimal Policy. *European Economic Review, 43*(4–6), 813–823.

Staiger, D., Stock, J.H., & Watson, M.W. (1997). *How precise are estimates of the natural Rate of unemployment, reducing inflation: Motivation and strategy*. Chicago, IL: University of Chicago Press.

Stock, J.H., & Watson, M.W. (1999a). Business cycle fluctuations in US macroeconomic time series. In *Handbook of macroeconomics*. New York, NY: Elsevier.

Stock, J.H., & Watson, M.W. (1999b). Forecasting inflation. *Journal of Monetary Economics, 44*(2), 293–335.

Stock, J.H., & Watson, M.W. (2002). *Has the business cycle changed and why?* (NBER macroeconomics annual). Cambridge, MA: MIT Press.

Stock, J.H., & Watson, M.W. (2003). Forecasting output and inflation: The role of asset prices. *Journal of Economic Literature, 41*(3), 788–829.

Stock, J.H., & Watson, M.W. (2007). Why has US Inflation become harder to forecast? *Journal of Money, Credit, and Banking, 39*, 3–34.

Svensson, L.E.O. (1999). Inflation targeting: Some extensions. *Scandinavian, Journal of Economics, 101*(3), 337–361.

Svensson, L.E.O. (2005). Targeting rules vs. instrument rules for monetary policy: What is wrong with McCallum and Nelson. *Federal Reserve Bank of St Louis Review, 87*, 613–625.

Svensson, L.E.O., & Woodford, M. (2003). Indicator variables for optimal policy. *Journal of Monetary Economics, 50*(3), 691–720.

Svensson, L.E.O., & Woodford, M. (2004). Implementing optimal policy through inflation-forecast targeting. In *Inflation targeting*. Chicago, IL: University of Chicago Press.

Tang, K., & Wei, X. (2010). *Index investment and financialization of commodities* (NBER Working Papers, No. 16385).

Taylor, J.B. (1979). Staggered wage setting in a macro model. *The American Economic Reviewvol, 69*, 108–113.

Taylor, J.B. (1980). Aggregate dynamics and staggered contracts. *The Journal of Political Economy, 88*(1), 1–23.

Taylor, J.B. (1993). Discretion versus policy rules in practice. *Carnegie-Rochester Conference Series on Public Policy, 1*, 195.

Taylor, J.B. (1995). The monetary transmission mechanism: An empirical framework. *The Journal of Economic Perspectives, 9*(4), 11–26.

Taylor, J.B. (1999a). Staggered price and wage setting in macroeconomics. In *Handbook of macroeconomics*. New York, NY: Elsevier.

Taylor, J.B. (1999b). The robustness and efficiency of monetary policy rules as guidelines for interest rate setting by the European Central Bank. *Journal of Monetary Economics, 43*(3), 655–679.

Taylor, J.B. (2000). Low inflation, pass-through, and the pricing power of firms. *European Economic Review, 44*(7), 1389–1408.

Thomas, L.B. (1999). Survey measures of expected US Inflation. *Journal of Economic Perspective, 13*(4), 125–144.

Thomas, L.B. (2006). *Money banking and financial markets*. Mason, OH: Thomson South-Western.

Tommaso, P. (2008). *Structural time series models for business cycle analysis* (CEIS research paper).

Tootell, Geoffrey M.B. (1998). Globalization and US inflation. *New England Economic Review, 36*(Jul), 21–33.

Ulrich, F., & Vladimir, K. (2005). Declining output volatility in Germany: Impulses, propagation, and the role of monetary policy. *Applied Economics, 37*(21), 2445–2457.

UNCTAD. (2011). *Price formation in financialized commodity markets*. New York, NY and Geneva: The Role of Information, United Nations.

Walsh, C.E. (2003a). *Monetary theory and policy* (2nd ed.). Cambridge, MA: MIT Press.

Walsh, C.E. (2003b). Speed limit policies: The output gap and optimal monetary policy. *American Economic Review, 93*(1), 265–278.

Wan, Guangcai, Chen, Zhang, & Liu, Li. (2009). Structural imbalance, wave phenomenon and inflation-deflation reversal. *The Journal of Quantitative & Technical Economics, 26*(12), 3–18.

Wang, Chengyong, & Ai, Chunrong. (2010). Nonlinear smooth transformation of China's economic cycle. *Economic Research Journal (in Chinese), 45*(3), 78–90.

Wang, Guogang. (2008). The weight of food in CPI should be reduced. *China Economic and Trade Herald, 25*(5)7–8.

Wang, Shaoping, Tu, Zhengge, & Li, Zinai. (2001). Phillips curve and its applicability to China. *Social Sciences in China, 22*(4), 64–75.

Wang, Xuesong. (2007). Empirical analysis of Price transmission mechanism in China. *Price: Theory and Practice, 27*(9), 29–30.

Wang, Yiming, & Zhao, Liuyan. (2006). Inflation expectation and money demand: A test of the mechanism of actual and nominal adjustment. *Finance & Trade Economy, 27*(8), 3–9.

Wei, Jianing. (2007, December 7). Repentance in the 1980s. *Modern Bankers*.

Wei, Jianing, Zhu, Mingchun, Wang, Yueping, & Shen, Haiyu. (1991). The current interest rate is suitable for no adjustment. *Selected Essentials of Development Research Center of the State Council* (18).

Weinhagen, J. (2005). Price transmission within the PPI for intermediate goods. *Monthly Labor Review, 128*, 41–49.

Westerhoff, F. (2006). Samuelson's multiplier – Accelerator model revisited. *Applied Economic Letters, 13*(2), 89–92.

White, H. (1980). A heteroskedasticity-consistent covariance matrix estimator and a direct test for heteroskedasticity. *Econometrica, 48*(4), 817–838.

Williams, J.C. (2006). *Inflation persistence in an era of well-anchored inflation expectations*. Federal Reserve Bank of San Francisco Economic Letter.

Williams, K. (2000). From shareholder value to present-day capitalism. *Economy and Society, 29*(1), 1–12.

Willis, J.L. (2003). Implications of structural changes in the US Economy for pricing behavior and inflation dynamics. *Economic Review, 88*, 5–27. Federal Reserve Bank of Kansas City.

Woodford, M. (2003). *Interest and prices: Foundations of a theory of monetary policy*. Princeton, NJ: Princeton University Press

Wu, D. (1973). Alternative tests of independence between stochastic regressions and disturbances. *Econometrica, 41*(4), 733–750.

Wu, Jinglian. (1992). Go all out to build the infrastructure of market economy. *Reform, 8*(2), 4–11.

Wu, Jun, & Tian, Juan. (2008). Analysis of structural inflation: Based on the current inflation in China. *Journal of Financial Research, 31*(9), 91–100.

Xie, Ping, & Luo, Xiong. (2002). *Taylor rule in transition economies: A case of China's monetary policy*. Working paper.

Xie, Ping, & Shen, Bingxi. (1999). Deflation and monetary policy. *Economic Research Journal (in Chinese), 34*(8), 14–17.

Xu, Yaping. (2009). Public learning, expectation guidance and effectiveness of monetary policy. *Journal of Financial Research, 32*(1), 50–65.

Yang, Fan. (2006, August 15). *The price magic wand, China's two inflations in the 1980s* (21st Century Business Herald).

Yang, Jisheng. (2009). Expectation of currency, excess liquidity and the dynamic nature of inflation in China. *Economic Research Journal (in Chinese), 44*(1), 106–117.

Yang, Xiaojun. (2011). Empirical research on China's new Keynesian Phillips curve. *Statistical Research, 29*(2), 13–18.

Yin, Jianfeng. (2008). Financial market and oil price bubble. *China Money, 8*(11), 36–41.

Yu, Yongding. (1999). Breaking the vicious circle of deflation. *Economic Research Journal (in Chinese), 34*(7), 3–9.

Yuan, Jiang. (2009). Mandatory technological change, binary differentiation and China's inflation model. *Management World, 25*(3), 9–20.

Yuan, Jiang, & Zhang, Chengsi. (2009). Mandatory technology change, unbalanced growth and China's economic cycle model. *Economic Research Journal (in Chinese), 44*(12), 17–29.

Yun, T. (1996). Nominal Price rigidity, money supply endogeneity, and business cycles. *Journal of Monetary Economics, 37*, 345–370.

Zalewski, D.A., & Charles, J.W. (2010). Financialization and income inequality: A post Keynesian institutionalist analysis. *Journal of Economic Issues, 44*(3), 757–777.

Zarnowitz, V. (1992). *Business cycles: Theory, history, indicators, and forecasting*. Chicago, IL: University of Chicago Press.

Zeng, Lifei, Xu, Jiangang, & Tang, Guoxing. (2006). China's new Keynesian hybrid Phillips curve under the open economy. *The Journal of Quantitative & Technical Economics, 23*(3), 76–84.

Zhang, Baojun, & Hu, Zongyi. (2008). CGE research on the impact of RMB appreciation on inflation. *Statistics and Decision, 24*(5), 134–138.

Zhang, Chengsi. (2007a). Low inflation, pass-through, and a discrete monetary policy for monetary policy in China. *China and World Economy, 15*(2), 59–73.

Zhang, Chengsi. (2007b). Review on the theory of dynamic mechanism of short-term inflation rate. *Management World, 23*(5), 133–145.

Zhang, Chengsi. (2008a). China's inflation inertia and its monetary policy implications. *Economic Research Journal (in Chinese), 43*(2), 33–43.

Zhang, Chengsi. (2008b). *Financial metrology – time series analysis perspective*. Dalian: Northeast University of Finance and Economics Press.

Zhang, Chengsi. (2008c). The dynamic path change of inflation and its enlightenment. *Journal of Financial Research, 31*(3), 1–12.

Zhang, Chengsi. (2008d). Structural instability of US Inflation persistence. *Applied Economics Letters*, *15*(14), 1147–1151.

Zhang, Chengsi. (2009a). Dynamic trend of RMB exchange rate change and inflation. *Studies of International Finance*, *30*(5), 87–96.

Zhang, Chengsi. (2009b). Review of China's inflation cycle and macro policy implications. *Asia Pacific Economic Review*, *27*(2), 66–70.

Zhang, Chengsi. (2010). Long-term equilibrium, price and monetary drive. *Economic Research Journal (in Chinese)*, *45*(6), 42–52.

Zhang, Chengsi. (2011). RMB appreciation and the new pattern of China US international parity relations. *Finance & Trade Economy*, *32*(6), 44–50.

Zhang, Chengsi. (2012). *Financial metrology – time series analysis perspective*. Beijing: Renmin University Press.

Zhang, Chengsi. (2012). Globalization and China's inflation dynamic mechanism model. *Economic Research Journal (in Chinese)*, *47*(6), 33–45.

Zhang, Chengsi, & Clovis, J. (2010). The new Keynesian Phillips curve of rational expectations: A serial correlation extension. *Journal of Applied Economics*, *13*(1), 159–179.

Zhang, Chengsi, & Hong, P. (2008). Excess liquidity and inflation dynamics in China: 1997–2007. *China and World Economy*, *16*(4), 1–15.

Zhang, Chengsi, & Li, Ying. (2010). Research on the dynamic mechanism of globalization and inflation: Based on the experience analysis and enlightenment of emerging market countries. *The Journal of World Economy*, *33*(11), 24–36.

Zhang, Chengsi, & Liu, Zhigang. (2007). Research on the persistent change of inflation Rate and analysis of policy implications in China. *The Journal of Quantitative & Technical Economics*, *25*(3), 3–12.

Zhang, Chengsi, & Lu, Zhe. (2014). Media public opinion, public expectation and inflation. *Journal of Financial Research*, *37*(1), 29–43.

Zhang, Chengsi, Osborn, D., & Kim, D. (2008). The new Keynesian Phillips curve: From sticky inflation to sticky prices. *Journal of Money, Credit, and Banking*, *40*(4), 667–699.

Zhang, Chengsi, Osborn, D., & Kim, D. (2009). Observed inflation forecasts and the new Keynesian Phillips curve. *Oxford Bulletin of Economics and Statistics*, *71*(3), 375398.

Zhang, Huiqing, & Wang, Jian. (2012). Research on determinants and transmission mechanism of inflation evolution in China. *Finance & Trade Economy*, *33*(2), 98–105.

Zhang, Lingxiang, & Zhang, Xiaodong. (2011). Periodic fluctuation and nonlinear dynamic adjustment of inflation Rate. *Economic Research Journal (in Chinese)*, *46*(5), 17–31.

Zhang, Ming. (2008). The scale and channel of hot money flowing into China. *International Finance (in Chinese)*, *7*, 59–64.

Zhang, Xiaohui, Ji, Zhihong, & Li, Bin. (2010). Changes in inflation mechanism and policy response. *The Journal of World Economy*, *33*(3), 56–70.

Zhao, Liuyan, & Wang, Yiming. (2005). Money stock and price level: Empirical evidence of China. *Economic Science*, *29*(2), 26–38.

Index

Page numbers in **bold** denote tables, in *italic* denote figures

Printed in the United States
by Baker & Taylor Publisher Services